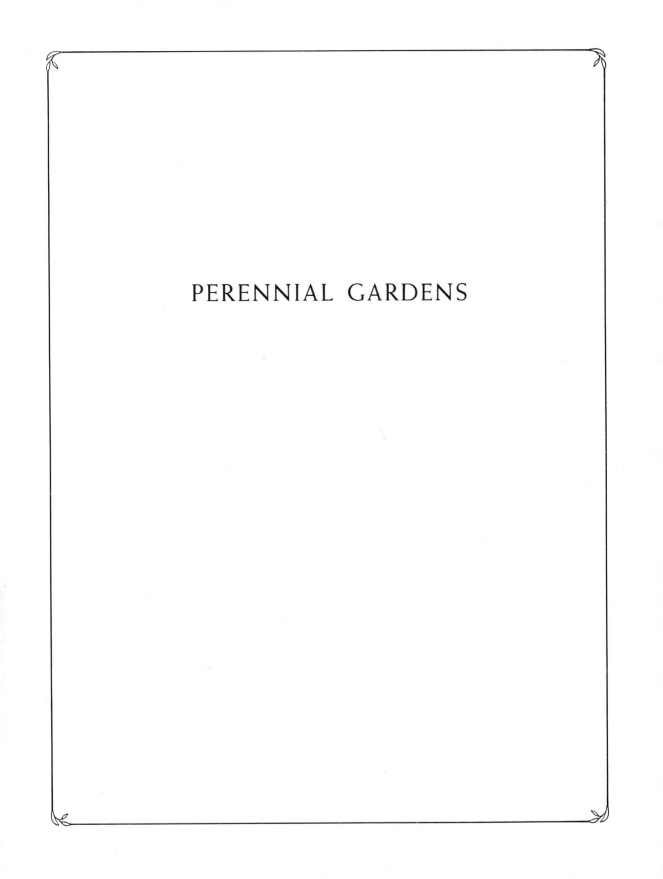

PERENNIAL GARDENS

Also by John Williamson

THE OAK KING, THE HOLLY KING, AND THE UNICORN

JOHN WILLIAMSON

PERENNIAL GARDENS

a practical guide to home landscaping

illustrated by Ippy Patterson

HARPER & ROW, PUBLISHERS

New York, Cambridge, Philadelphia, San Francisco, Washington

London, Mexico City, São Paulo, Singapore, Sydney

FIRST EDITION

DESIGNED BY RUTH BORNSCHLEGEL

COPYEDITED BY KATHERINE G. NESS

INDEX BY AURALIE LOGAN

Library of Congress Cataloging-in-Publication Data

Williamson, John, 1948–
Perennial gardens.

Bibliography: p.
Includes index.
1. Landscape gardening.   2. Gardens—Designs   and
plans.   3. Herb gardening.   4. Wild flower gardening.
5. Herbs—Dictionaries.   6. Perennials—Dictionaries.
7. Wild flowers—Dictionaries.   I. Title.
SB473.W53   1988   635'.04   87-12094
ISBN 0-06-015858-1

88 89 90 91 92 MPC 10 9 8 7 6 5 4 3 2 1

For Jamake Highwater

CONTENTS

A section of color plates follows page 88

CAUTION — *These plants are poisonous*

Aconitum	Conium	Hyoscyamus
Atrope	Datura	Mandragora
Caulophyllum	Digitalis	Taxus
Colchicum	Helleborous	Veratrum

INTRODUCTION

WHAT DOES THE NURSERY RHYME "Jack and Jill" have to do with gardening? Well, for me, a great deal. I come from Somerset, part of England's West Country, an area where many nursery rhymes originated. For ten years I lived in Kilmersdon, at the base of Jack and Jill Hill. For centuries my ancient stone cottage there has been called Tumblers Bottom, and local folklore holds that this peculiar name was a reference to a "Jack and Jill incident." The legend is supported by the existence of an old stone well at the top of the hill. Furthermore, the Jillsons, a family of ancient lineage, are still living in Kilmersdon. And this surname, which derives from "son of Jill," removes the legend of Jack and Jill from fable and places it in a historical context.

During my residence in this corner of Somerset, I established a herb farm—and, of course, what better name for a nursery than "Tumblers Bottom Farm"? The unique nature of the enterprise was the range of plants we offered. The three hundred or so listed items included culinary, aromatic, old-fashioned, and medicinal plants.

The practical knowledge I have acquired through many years' experience cultivating herbs and perennials has been enriched by the invaluable information I have gained from chin-wagging with countless customers, herbalists, folklorists, gypsies, homeopaths, a few witches, and lots of country people.

In my early years, I lived in a wild part of North Wales. This enabled me to study the rich native flora—plants used by local people in their everyday lives. One of the first plants I was told about was comfrey. For centuries comfrey has been used to heal fractures, bruises, and sprains of all kinds. Indeed, one of the vernacular names of comfrey, "knitbone," records for posterity this herb's ability. An old gypsy lady once told me that if a saucepan of bones was cooked overnight with comfrey root and water, by morning all the bones would set in a continuous string. Having neither the time nor the inclination to try this experiment, I can't vouch for its success.

One day when there was a knock on the door of Tumblers Bottom, I was greeted by the sight of a middle-aged woman with her right leg encased in plaster. This anxious customer ignored my salutations and with a heavy German accent announced, "I voot like to buying six comfrey plants. You can please to let me having a few leaves immediately to use." As the world of herbs has more than its fair share of eccentrics, I was prepared for occasions such as this. So I complied with her requests and gave her the comfrey, whereupon she withdrew a fierce-looking knitting needle from her handbag. And as I did not want to be a human pincushion, my instincts told me to step back. But very soon my trepidation turned to curiosity as I watched the woman push comfrey leaves into her plaster cast with the aid of the knitting needle. When the task was done she shook my hands with Teutonic vigor, paid me, and departed. And what a strange sight she presented! In one arm she carried her precious comfrey plants, under the other arm was wedged her crutch, and below her right knee a frill of greenery adorned her cast. Was this how wounded Knights of the Garter once looked? In any event, I had renewed respect for comfrey.

It was experiences such as these that prompted me to start writing about my marvelous life among plants, which started at Tumblers Bottom.

Unquestionably my fascination with perennials grew from my love of England's splendid door gardens, whose color and variety dress the land from early spring to the last fragile days of fall. It was the generosity and beauty of these gardens that intrigued me—the faithful reawakening of lovely plants that seemed to fade and die in the winter only to return each spring. Perennials bloom every year, increasing in luxuriance and beauty as they mature. For almost all the months of the calendar, their blossoms provide a stunning succession of color. Even in the depths of winter, faded clumps of dormant plants provide a picturesque landscape of dried leaves, stems, and seeds. Once planted, a perennial garden renews itself automatically, almost magically. During the first few days of spring, these plants reappear like a gift from the earth, more luminous and lush than they were the prior year. I have come

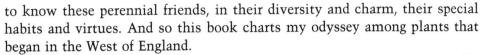

to know these perennial friends, in their diversity and charm, their special habits and virtues. And so this book charts my odyssey among plants that began in the West of England.

In time the reputation of Tumblers Bottom increased, and it eventually led to commissions to design some very special gardens, such as the one at the Cloister of Beaulieu Abbey, in Hampshire, for Lord Montagu of Beaulieu. This particular planting was indirectly responsible for my first American commission—designing the medieval garden at The Cloisters of The Metropolitan Museum of Art in New York City.

For the past twelve years I have lived in America and have gardened in such diverse states as Colorado, Alabama, Connecticut, and California. In Tuscaloosa, Alabama, I created three gardens for Jim Boone, a newspaper mogul. Encounters with poisonous snakes, kudzu vines, extreme summer heat, and a work crew that couldn't understand a word of my strong English accent provided a horticultural initiation I will never forget. On the first day that we were constructing a native wild-flower garden on the shores of Lake Tuscaloosa, as I stepped back to admire some newly planted dogwoods, the foreman—a witty guy called W.M.—charged at me with a fierce-looking machete. Even before I could utter a cry of anguish he had rushed past me and speared a timber rattlesnake I was about to step on! It was a rather dramatic event, but it certainly broke the ice between the crew and me. Working for all these years in America has made me realize how different gardening conditions are on each side of the Atlantic. Yet I am always amazed when I ignore textbook warnings and succeed in growing an English plant of treasured memory in my Connecticut garden.

Years ago, long before I came to the United States, I started to write down some of my garden experiences. I would look up from my desk and gaze through the ancient windows of Tumblers Bottom. There I saw Jack and Jill Hill, and I would reflect on the fate of those fabled twins, often wishing that the herb gardens that surrounded my stone house had existed centuries before, for the plants I grew would certainly have been better for Jack's broken crown than Jill's simple physic of "vinegar and brown paper."

Chapter One

PRACTICAL GARDENING

THIS BOOK CONTAINS DESIGNS for a wide variety of perennial gardens. Wild-flower enthusiasts, herb gardeners, and lovers of flowers in general will find plans that will enhance any garden, large or small. You will find flower beds for sun and shade, even ideas for creating gardens for permanently arid or damp parts of the landscape. The plans are not inflexible, and if a particular shape or size does not fit into your scheme, you can make the necessary changes when laying out the design. If you want to economize, cut down on the number of plants used in each plan. You may have to wait a little longer for the mature garden, but economizing will not affect the final design. If some plants are difficult to obtain, don't be timid about making substitutions—especially if you can get a closely related alternative. Garden centers and mail-order companies can be very helpful in making appropriate substitutions. All the material used in these designs is described in Chapter Five, the "Encyclopedia of Plants."

Before rushing out and preparing a flower bed, take some time to look at your property. Assess where a garden would have the most impact on the overall landscape. Better still, prepare a *base plan* and set long-term goals for a completed garden. A base plan is a bird's-eye-view drawing of the property. It will help you to see both the possibilities and the problems in your landscape. Planning on paper helps to crystallize your thoughts. If you start with a plan, your garden will be much more effective, and in the early stages, mistakes can be removed with an eraser rather than with a spade and hours of backbreaking work.

You do not have to be an artist to make a base plan. All that is required is a 50- to 100-foot tape measure, some tracing paper, and graph paper in a convenient scale—say, 1/16 inch. If you have a survey of your property (this usually accompanies the deed), you can take a shortcut and transfer these specifications to your drawing.

Measure your house and mark the dimensions on a note pad. Also note the position of the doors, windows, and various rooms. Locate property lines and the placement of any outbuildings, utility lines, sewer lines, septic tanks, paving, walls, fences, and major established trees and shrubs. All these elements will affect the design of your garden.

Measure the distance from the house to various landmarks and note them on the pad. Be sure to indicate the branch spread of trees and shrubs (if they are not full grown, estimate their spread at maturity). Large canopies will shade much of the garden, affecting the types of plants you can grow.

With arrows, mark the major lines of view—especially the sight lines from large windows in the house. These will help you to create interesting views by placing major trees and flower borders to full advantage. Record any problem areas, such as hot spots or damp parts of the yard. A dry, sunbaked place could become a desert garden. A sodden area could be transformed into a beautiful garden of water-loving plants.

Find north and mark it on your paper. This will enable you to locate sheltered areas in the east and the south. Taking note of protected areas is very important, for they can allow you to grow some late-flowering shrubs and perennials. If you have lived on your property a number of years, you are probably aware of such micro-climates there. Very cold and windy spots are at the other extreme. Here it might be wise to plant a windbreak, which would greatly expand the gardening potential.

Record all your observations on the pad and then transfer them , measuring carefully, to the graph paper. The result is your base plan (pictured opposite). Once you have it, you can start analyzing your property. Look at the good and bad vantages. A neighbor's untidy yard can be screened off with evergreens. A good view might be made even better with the addition of an island flower bed. By laying a sheet of tracing paper over the base plan, you can sketch various ideas and experiment with new designs. Pathways are vital, so give them plenty of thought. Try not to design walkways in a straight line; gentle curves are much more pleasing to the eye.

The sunny and shady areas marked on your base plan will help you decide what sort of garden you can realistically install. Take the time to view potential garden sites from inside the house. There is nothing nicer than being

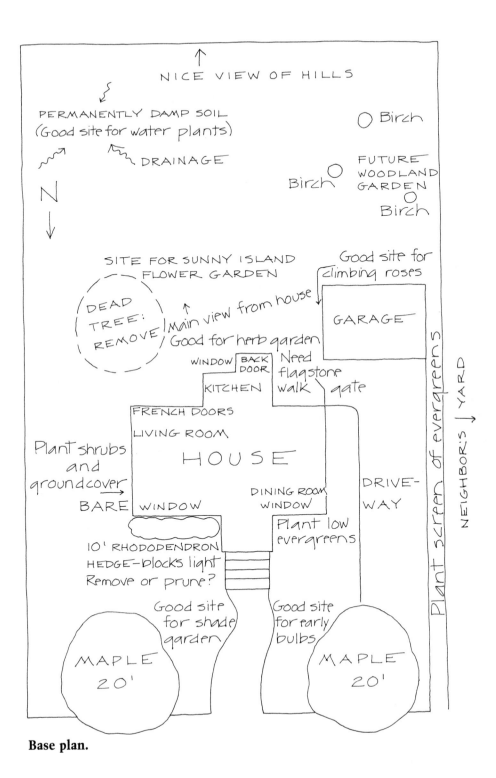

Base plan.

able to see a garden through a window. I discovered the secret of one friend who professed to enjoy washing dishes: from her kitchen window she can see her island flower beds, so when her arms are awash with suds she is enjoying her perennial borders!

The shape of the flower garden is strictly a matter of personal taste and available space. Rectangular flower borders are suitable for formal and geometric gardens. Perennials can also be very attractive when planted in front of a formal evergreen hedge, or a stone or brick wall.

Island beds allow freer and more informal designs and allow the plants to be viewed from all sides. In my opinion, these are the most exciting flower beds, and they permit a great latitude in design. Laid upon the ground, a flexible garden hose can be twisted and turned until an ideal shape is outlined. When you have created a shape you like, stand back and imagine what the flower bed will look like from different parts of the landscape. Islands will be the focal point in summer, and if a landscape has evergreens bordering the premises, when the perennials die down in winter, the focus of the garden will shift to the longer vista of these peripheral evergreens. Such a seasonal change of view can be very satisfying. It is important to site the bed in a pleasing location. If a flower bed is to be the focal point from a window or patio, do not place it in the middle of the line of sight. It will look much better if it is positioned slightly off the central axis.

If you are planning a more formal border in front of a hedge, do not plant the perennials right up against this shrubby enclosure. Both the hedge and the flowers will suffer. The less invasive roots of the perennials will have to compete for water and nutrients with the deep roots of the hedge, and the hedge will win! A 3-foot margin between hedging material and the flower border will allow the plants to develop good root systems and will also enable you to trim the hedge and keep it in shape. A background consisting of a stone or brick wall is another matter, yet even in this situation, you should leave about a foot or so between wall and plants. Rain runoff can wash away perennial plantings.

How about upkeep? A curvilinear border that is between 6 and 8 feet deep can easily be weeded from either side. So can a rectangular bed backed by a wall or hedge, if it is no more than 4 feet deep. In constructing deeper island borders and rectangular beds, it is helpful to place stepping-stones toward the middle of the flower garden. They will be a great help in weeding and maintaining these plantings.

You should also consider the months that you will be around to enjoy your garden the most. Many people take their vacations in the summer. With your schedule in mind, you might want to plant a garden that emphasizes spring- and fall-blooming flowers. Plans for two such seasonal gardens are presented in Chapter Three.

THE BASICS OF PLANTS

PERENNIALS, BIENNIALS, AND ANNUALS

A *perennial* is a plant that lives for a number of seasons. Their longevity is variable. Some perennials, like the peony, may survive for decades while others, like anchusa, may last only a few seasons. Most of the flowers and grasses mentioned in this book are *herbaceous perennials*—plants that die back to ground level in late fall and early winter and emerge again in the spring. (Many perennials, especially in milder areas, remain evergreen or do not die back until late winter.) Botanically, the word *herbaceous* refers to plants with non-woody stems. A garden of these perennials is often called a *herbaceous border*. The term *woody perennial* is applied to trees and shrubs—plants that do not die back in the fall and winter.

Many English gardening books use the terms *hardy perennial* and *tender perennial*. These terms indicate if the perennial under discussion is hardy in the United Kingdom. Since climatic conditions in the British Isles are very different from those of North America, this terminology is confusing to the American reader—especially since wet English winters (rather than really frigid weather) can determine if a perennial is hardy. Fortunately the majority of perennials are hardy, and I have attempted to clarify the degree of hardiness of plants when they are grown in the United States.

Biennials are plants that require two years to complete their life cycle. For the first season, they produce only foliage. In the second year blooms appear. After flowering, these plants set seed and die. By removing the flower heads during the second year, you can trick some biennials, like angelica, into becoming short-lived perennials.

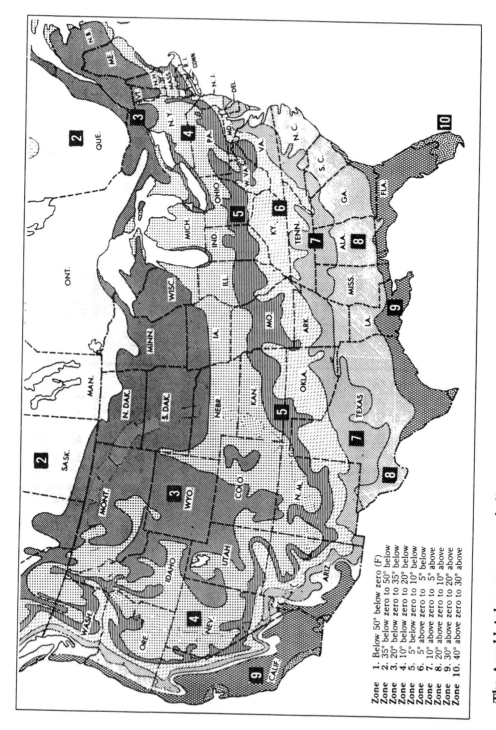

Zone 1. Below 50° below zero (F)
Zone 2. 35° below zero to 50° below
Zone 3. 20° below zero to 35° below
Zone 4. 10° below zero to 20° below
Zone 5. 5° below zero to 10° below
Zone 6. 5° above zero to 5° below
Zone 7. 10° above zero to 5° above
Zone 8. 20° above zero to 10° above
Zone 9. 30° above zero to 20° above
Zone 10. 40° above zero to 30° above

The Arnold Arboretum map of climate zones.

Annuals are plants that complete a full life cycle in one season. Seed germinates in spring (even later in some instances), and plants flower and set seed before the end of the year. Most annuals will self-sow, producing seed that germinates the same season or the following spring.

HARDINESS

How plants adapt to low temperatures is the most important consideration for gardeners. Climatically, the North American continent is extremely varied. To translate this variability into practical terms, the U.S. Department of Agriculture and the Arnold Arboretum at Harvard University have independently divided North America into ten separate climate regions called zones. The Arnold Arboretum map (opposite page) is the zone plan used in this book. Use this map to determine your climate zone. A zone is determined by the lowest winter temperatures and the annual average of frost-free days. For example, if you live in Zone 4, you can expect plants that grow in your climate to be able to survive temperatures of −20°F. Information on zone hardiness is not hard and fast—many plants will survive lower temperatures, especially if given winter protection and if grown in well-drained soil. If you live on the West Coast, the *Sunset New Western Garden Book* provides detailed maps of this region's complex climates. Similarly, gardeners in the Midwest and colder regions of the United States should consult John Subuco's excellent book, *The Best of the Hardiest.*

Recent interest in perennials has brought an influx of foreign plants— especially new varieties of flowers from England and ornamental grasses from Germany. Many of these plants are probably hardier than originally anticipated. The interest in grasses is a case in point, since many of these foliage plants are proving to be hardier than expected. The other good news is that climate, even in a small garden, can vary greatly. A south-facing bank or wall or an area close to the house will be considerably warmer than a windy north-facing hillside. Experience will enable you to find these most favorable areas, and one of the greatest joys for a gardener is successfully growing plants that, according to the book, are not supposed to be hardy. Do not be afraid to grow plants that are listed as hardy up to one zone warmer than your area. For instance, if you live in Zone 4, in favorable parts of your garden many Zone 5 plants might be hardy. This is especially true in areas that have continuous snow cover for the whole winter. Alternating freezing and thawing does more damage to plants than a constant low temperature. Many perennials need a cold spell during the year—winter dormancy of these plants is an intrinsic part of their growing cycle. This is especially true of plants like peony and border phlox—flowers that do not do well in areas of warm winters.

You also need to keep this zone range information in mind if you live in warmer climates. Many plants that thrive in Zones 7 and 8 will not grow well in Zone 9 areas. They either need the winter dormancy or cannot tolerate the persistent high summer temperatures associated with Zones 9 and 10.

One final caution—not in regard to weather, but in regard to English gardening books! As an Englishman who gardened in the West Country of the British Isles for more than ten years and who has been a gardener in North America for the past twelve years, I can say from personal experience that growing conditions are very different in our two countries. The climate of the British Isles is similar to that of the northwest coast of America—mild winters and mild summers with lots of moisture. Bear this in mind if you are reading English gardening books, for many of the plants described there will not take the extreme cold or heat typical of many areas of the United States.

BOTANICAL NAMES OF PLANTS (LATIN WITHOUT TEARS)

The vernacular names of plants vary from country to country, even from state to state. For instance, "geranium" can refer to the frost-sensitive red-flowering geranium in the window box or can be used to describe the hardy perennial geraniums grown in the flower garden. Many gardeners of German origin call hosta "funkia lily," while English gardeners might call these flowers "plantain lily." Without belaboring the point, it soon becomes clear that some agreed-upon international nomenclature is important for describing plants. The famous eighteenth-century Swedish scientist Carl Linnaeus provided the answer by devising a system using Latin (and sometimes Greek). The names may seem a bit complex at first, but at least they designate exactly the plant you have in mind.

Family Members of a botanical family all have a number of similar characteristics but are still individually very distinct. For instance, such diverse plants as rudbeckia, aster, and chrysanthemum all belong to the Compositae family. The distinguishing feature of these various flowers is their daisy-like blooms—and all members of the Compositae family have such blossoms.

Plants that belong to the pea family (Leguminosae) all have nitrogen-fixing nodules on their roots—structures that help them survive in very poor soil. Peanut and garden lupine are members of the Leguminosae family. Family names, such as Leguminosae, are printed in roman type with a capital initial.

Genus *(plural Genera)* Each botanical family is made up of a number of genera. Members of each genus have much closer ties than members of a family, and the close ties are what makes them a genus. Members of a genus are visibly recognizable as such. *Iris* is such a genus: all the members have distinctive flowers by which we can readily identify them. Sometimes a genus may contain only one member. This is known as a *monotypic* genus. The generic name is printed in italics and begins with a capital letter.

Species The genus is made up of a number of individual species. Species are naturally occurring plants that reproduce from seed; they are unimproved by man. The name of a species is always written in italics and begins with a lower-case letter. One name is used for both the singular and the plural. The species name is always used in conjunction with the genus. For example, *Magnolia* is a familiar genus. A popular species of *Magnolia* is commonly called star magnolia and botanically called *Magnolia stellata. Magnolia* is the genus, *stellata* is the species. Grammatically, you can speak of one *Magnolia stellata* or you can speak of ten *Magnolia stellata.*

Sometimes the name of the species tells us a lot about the plant. For instance, in Latin *stellata* means "star-shaped." *Rubra* means that some part of the plant, usually the flower, is red. *Alba* means "white," *aquaticus* means "water," and so on.

Members of the same species are very closely related. This is the level upon which plant breeders work and through hybridization create new varieties of garden flowers. For instance, *Rudbeckia fulgida* is the common black-eyed Susan; *Rudbeckia fulgida* Goldstrum is a hybridized plant which is a compact form of black-eyed Susan.

Variety When a species changes in the wild, its distinct forms are given an extra Latin name. This varietal name, like the species name, is always written in italics. For example, the mugo pine *(Pinus mugo)* is a conifer that matures at around 30 feet. A naturally occurring variety, however, is *Pinus mugo mughus,* which is much smaller and matures at around 6 feet. There are many other examples: The native American blue star, *Amsonia tabernae-*

montana, is a species with spearlike leaves. A naturally occurring variety of blue star, *Amsonia tabernaemontana salicifolia*, has narrower willow-like leaves (*salicifolia* means "willow-like leaves"). To indicate that a plant is a variety, the abbreviation *var.* may be incorporated into the Latin name. For example, *Amsonia tabernaemontana salicifolia* is sometimes written *Amsonia tabernaemontana* var. *salicifolia*. Likewise the variety of mugo pine, *Pinus mugo mughus*, is often written *Pinus mugo* var. *mughus*. A variety, like a species, always reproduces from seed.

Cultivar   *Cultivar* means "cultivated variety." These are man-made or natural variations within a species that do not normally reproduce from seed. Some are even sterile, and most cultivars have to be propagated vegetatively. Names of the cultivars are always printed in roman type, and they are usually fanciful. These varietal names are put into single quotes. *Iris sibirica* 'Caesar's Brother' is a cultivar of the Siberian iris. *Iris sibirica* 'Super Ego' is another.

Hybrids   Hybrids are crosses between different species. When an "x" appears with the Latin name of a plant you know you are dealing with a hybrid. In the Encyclopedia (Chapter Five), a number of hybrids are included. For instance, *Gaillardia* x *grandiflora*, commonly known as blanketflower, is a hybrid between two or more close species of gaillardia. In this instance the "x" always appears between the genus and species names.

Rarer hybrids exist. When they occur between members of different genera, they are called *bigeneric hybrids*. For instance, a cross between an aster and a solidago (goldenrod) is called a solidaster, and to indicate that this is a cross between two genera, it is written x *Solidaster*, with the "x" appearing before the hybrid genera name. Thus x *Solidaster*, strictly speaking, is written x *Solidaster hybridus*—it is a lovely late-flowering garden perennial.

BASICS OF GARDENING

SOIL

Before planting any garden, it is important to know something about your soil: what it is made of, how fast water drains through, and the pH level. The best way to find exactly what type of soil you have is to have it tested by a laboratory. This will not only determine the type of soil on your property, but the report will indicate what you need to do to make improvements. Soil testing is not very expensive. Details can be obtained by calling the Agriculture Department Extension Service in your area (this is usually found under United States Government listings).

There are three basic types of soil. To find yours, dig holes in a number of parts of the garden and examine the earth closely.

Sandy earth is well drained and crumbly. A ball made by squeezing this earth in the hand will easily break apart. Sandy soil warms up early in the spring, but water can all too easily pass through it. To make sandy soil more water retentive and fertile, add plenty of organic matter. Peat moss and rotted compost are ideal.

Clay soils are heavy and are difficult to work with a garden spade. Crushed in a closed fist, this type of earth retains its shape and does not easily fall apart. Heavy clay soil is slow to warm up in the spring and can badly impede drainage. Sand and organic matter worked into clay soils greatly improve them. If the clay is very dense, you might consider installing an underground drainage system — or, cheaper, you might grow perennials and shrubs in raised beds. These elevated garden areas can be made with cross-ties, brick, or stone. Once the walls are constructed, they can be filled with good-quality soil. Another alternative is to plant perennials that like to have "damp feet." A number of these plans are presented in Chapter Three.

Loam is soil that has the ideal proportions of clay, sand, and organic matter. Since it is moist, drains well, and is rich in nutrients, this is the perfect garden-growing medium. Loam is usually rich and dark and contains an abundance of earthworms.

DRAINAGE

I think that drainage is one of the most important factors that determine a plant's survival. I have learned this lesson from practical experience, having lost many perennials because I planted them in soil that did not drain well. Such water-bound soils are not too bad in the summer, but in winter, poorly draining soil can be lethal to plants. Standing water that will not drain away will more quickly kill a plant than plunging temperatures. Many perennials that are marginally hardy in my area have survived, and in some instances have remained evergreen, because I grow them on a very well drained embankment. If your garden is one mass of clay and you don't want to go to the expense of putting in drains or making raised beds, at least dig planting holes a couple of feet deep and replace the excavated earth with good loam.

SOIL PH

The pH scale is a measure of how acid or alkaline your soil is. This is important to determine, since plants need specific pH conditions for healthy growth. The scale runs from 1 to 14. Levels 1 to 6 indicate high acidity. The more acid a soil, the lower the reading. A pH of 7 indicates a neutral soil, and anything between 8 and 14 is alkaline. As the number increases, so does the alkalinity. Most perennials prefer a neutral to slightly acid soil, although there are lots of exceptions. If your soil happens to be very alkaline, then you can improve it by adding powdered sulfur. Conversely, if the earth is very acid, then adding garden lime will bring up the pH to a more neutral level. In areas of heavy rainfall (much of the Northeast), soils are generally alkaline. I have neutral soil in my garden, so when growing plants that like a slightly more alkaline soil—such as peony and gypsophila—I usually add some lime to the soil in which I plant them. For my rhododendrons, a sprinkling of sulfur keeps the earth on the acid side, which they prefer.

LIGHT

Light is one of the most important factors for the healthy growth of plants. All perennials need some daily sunlight, but most prefer some shade, at least for a few hours every day—even those plants that are said to require full sun. This is especially true in more southern areas of the United States, where perennials will need some protection from strong midday sun. Keep these considerations in mind when deciding where to establish flower beds. Very few perennials like to be grown in a totally open site that is exposed to sunlight from dawn to dusk. In general, when growing perennials that like a sunny site, try to locate these gardens in areas that will be shady for a few hours at midday. In other words, situate these flower borders so that they have morning and afternoon sun, but get shade at noontime. For instance, if you are planning one of the designs for a sunny border, site the garden in the middle of the lawn, but try to notice where and when shade from buildings and large trees is cast and locate the garden accordingly.

SHADE

There are various types of shade, which vary from very light shade to dense shade.

Light Shade During the summer months a lightly shaded part of the garden will receive full shade for a couple of hours each day. Another example of light shade is an area under a tree with lacy leaves, such as birch or mountain ash, or a woodland area under thin-leaved saplings. This dappled sunlight is considered light shade. Many of the plants that are listed as liking full sun will grow well in these conditions, or at worst will produce fewer blossoms.

Medium Shade These are areas of the garden that alternate between full sun and full shade, but get about five hours of full shade on the average summer day.

Full Shade Full shade occurs under a mature oak, evergreen, or other large-canopied tree. Even though these areas sound inhospitable, many perennials thrive under such conditions. A shade garden planted under an oak tree works very well. The roots of the oak go far down into the soil and do not compete for water with surface-rooted perennials. Other areas of full shade include north-facing borders that are surrounded by walls, and even dense woodland.

Deep Shade Deep shade is found under dense evergreens or in areas covered by decking. These areas are usually easy to identify, since moss and ferns will probably be the only plants that will survive there. I have a wooden deck on the north-facing side of my house; in the soil below the deck, year round, a fine colony of evergreen Christmas fern provides attractive foliage. If you have such a location, you might want to experiment with other ferns.

WATER

All plants need water. This is especially true for newly planted gardens. It is vital to the survival of borders to make sure that for the first few months they receive at least two good soakings per week, unless nature obliges with a good rain. Thoroughly wet the ground with a sprinkler. A light watering will do more damage than good: just moistening the soil makes the roots grow too close to the surface, and when this happens the slightest drought can kill the plants. A thorough soaking means leaving a sprinkler on in one section of the garden for an hour or more. If you are watering by hand, make sure that you do not aim fierce jets of water at the plants; this will more than likely wash the plants right out of the soil! In times of drought, make sure that your plants receive adequate water. Home owners who may have time for the garden only on weekends, or who are restricted in watering for one reason or another, might consider planting one of the Desert Gardens, Harriet's Garden, or even the Silver Garden described in Chapter Three. The plants in these designs are drought resistant. Many of them have special structures adapted to conserve water. Fine hairs on leaves, for instance, help retain moisture. This silky covering, which prevents water loss, creates the "silver" plants. The important thing to remember with flowers that are drought resistant is to plant them in deeply dug soil. Many of these plants have roots that, in order to search for water, go far down into the earth.

CONSTRUCTING A GARDEN

After you have chosen one of the gardens in this book, photocopy the design. A single piece of paper will be easier to work with, and this will also prevent the book's becoming dog-eared. Next, mark out the shape of the border by laying a garden hose on the ground to indicate the outline.

CLEARING

If the area is covered with brambles, undesirable shrubs, and trees, these must be removed with a chain saw, machete, or axe. (Preparation of a wild-flower meadow and other naturalistic gardens is discussed in detail in Chapter Four.) Before any flower garden is installed, weeds and unwanted lawn grass will also have to be removed. A number of methods are available, and depending on your preference, you can use either chemical or nonchemical methods.

Nonchemical Methods   If the garden is to be planted in an area of lawn, mark the outline with the hose. Then remove all the turf with a flat spade. This is not difficult, as most of the grass roots are within the top few inches of earth. By sliding a spade horizontally underneath the turf, the sod can be pried loose. (Use these chunks of sod to make compost. Invert the turf, pile the pieces atop each other, water well, and in about a year they will be converted into valuable compost.)

An alternative method is to cover the ground with black plastic, thereby smothering the grass. If this is done in June or July, the heat generated under the plastic will kill all grass and weeds within a few weeks.

The least successful nonchemical method is to chop up the weeds with a rototiller. This looks wonderful initially—you may ask yourself where the weeds have gone. But in a few weeks you will discover the answer. Docks, dandelions, and a host of other nasties will return in force from each fragment of chopped-up root.

Chemical Method   "Roundup" is one of the best chemical products for removing weeds from the soil. This spray efficiently kills unwanted grass or weeds. Roundup is slow-acting and is best applied when no rain is predicted for at least twenty-four hours, although the manufacturers say six hours is all that is necessary. This chemical does not harm the soil and is not residual—it simply breaks down into phosphates and nitrates. But when absorbed by weed foliage (both broad- and narrow-leaved plants), it affects their photosynthesis of food, and so the plants literally starve to death. Sprayed ground is usually ready for planting after about three weeks. In some states Roundup is not available; in these areas just look for any weed killer that contains glyphosate, the active ingredient in Roundup. (Ortho makes a 1 percent solution of glyphosate called Kleenup.) Obviously, considerable care must be used when handling any chemicals to avoid pollution or harm to wildlife or desirable plants. Always read product labels carefully.

SOIL PREPARATION

When the turf has been removed, or the plastic has smothered the grass, or the weed killers have gotten rid of unwanted plants, you will want to cultivate the ground to the deepest possible depth.

There are a number of ways to prepare the soil for a new flower bed. Considered the best by many gardeners, the following method is called *double digging.* Soil is removed from the entire planting site to the depth of one spade. This earth is temporarily stored on a sheet of polyethylene. The next layer of soil is then loosened with a spade or fork. If this subsoil contains a lot of clay, work in some peat moss, compost, or other organic matter. When this task is completed, shovel back the topsoil. This is not a task for the fainthearted! But when I tackle double digging, I always tell myself that the exercise is equivalent to at least two full workouts! If your soil is sandy or if you are fortunate enough to have earth that is very loamy, you probably only need to dig over the site to a spade's depth.

Another method, which is almost as good as double digging, is to use a mechanical rototiller. These gas-powered machines have blades that chop and churn up the soil. I find going over the same ground a number of times with the rototiller the best way to cultivate a new patch of garden. These valuable machines can be rented (see machine rental services in the Yellow Pages).

After loosening the soil with a spade or rototiller, spread a 3-inch layer of peat moss or a 2-inch layer of compost over the entire site. Then sprinkle half a pound of 5-10-5 fertilizer for every 10 square feet of new garden. (This level of fertilizer is for the earth in the average garden; a soil analysis will help determine the proper amount for your landscape.) Work all the ingredients into the soil with a fork or rototiller, then rake the site flat. The soil is now ready for planting. Don't be alarmed at the earth being loose—this is fine for flowers.

Fertilizers Many people prefer to rely upon organic fertilizers like fish emulsion, dried blood, or bone meal. But many chemical fertilizers are also available. These contain nitrogen, phosphorus, and potassium, three elements vital for the healthy growth of plants. Commercial fertilizers contain various proportions of these elements. A code printed on the bag expresses the percentage of elements in each mix. It is always written in alphabetical order:

nitrogen, phosphorus, potassium. Sometimes these elements are abbreviated by their respective chemical symbols: N, P, K. A mnemonic I use to remember this order is "niphpo." These chemical mixes are sold in proportions such as 10-10-10 or 5-10-5. Obviously the higher the number the stronger the fertilizer. A bag of 5-10-5 contains 5 percent nitrogen, 10 percent phosphorus, and 5 percent potassium. A soil analysis will help you determine how much of each fertilizer to add to your earth. Check the fertilizer label to determine which proportions are appropriate for particular plants.

PLANTING

To facilitate the placement of plants in their final positions, divide the outline of the garden you've selected into a number of convenient sections by sprinkling flour upon the ground. Say you are following a "sausage shape" design of one of the island borders. By splitting the outline on the ground into three segments, correct positioning of plants will be made much easier. Some people use garden lime as a visual aid, but if your soil is already alkaline the addition of extra lime could affect the pH and ultimately make the growing medium unsuitable for some plants.

PERENNIALS

Perennials can be purchased at a garden center in containers or can be obtained bare-root from mail-order companies. Plants purchased from nurseries are usually grown in the containers. Before planting, remove the perennials from the pots by tapping the bottom of the container. Many of these plants will have roots that totally fill the pot. Before planting these, to encourage new root growth slice into the bottom of the root ball with a knife. Cut upwards for a couple of inches and then spread out the severed root ball. Bare-root plants from mail-order companies should be given a soaking before they are set in the ground. When planting perennials be generous, and make the hole larger than the root ball. Plenty of loose soil around newly planted roots will encourage vigorous growth. If you are planting bare-root perennials, make sure that you spread the roots out fully.

Most garden plants need to have their crowns level with the surface of the soil. (The crown is the place where roots and stems join.) There are some important exceptions: Oriental poppies need to be planted with their crowns 2 inches below the soil surface, and peonies need to have their buds ("eyes") 1 to 2 inches below the surface. The Encyclopedia in Chapter Five describes any special planting requirements for plants mentioned in this book. After digging in perennials, firm the soil around each plant by carefully treading around the crown of the plant. Then water well and surround the plant with an appropriate mulch.

TREES AND SHRUBS

Trees and shrubs come either bare-root, containerized, or "balled-and-bagged." Many trees and shrubs will probably survive if simply placed in a hole in the ground wide enough for the root ball. But the old gardening cliché "Don't dig a $5 hole for a $20 tree" is very sound advice. To encourage maximum growth, some extra care is needed when planting trees and shrubs. Dig a bigger hole than needed, and cover the bottom of the hole with good topsoil—a little extra well-rotted compost added to this is beneficial. (But don't use unrotted organic matter like green grass cuttings, for these will rot the roots.) If the tree or shrub is bare-root, carefully spread the roots out and cover them with a few inches of soil. Firm this earth down by treading lightly on the soil. Then fill in with the rest of the dirt. Tread down once more. Make a small ridge in the earth around the newly planted tree with some of the excavated soil, forming a saucer around it, which will help to retain water. Finally, give the shrub or tree a good soaking.

If trees or large shrubs are balled-and-bagged, dig a hole bigger than needed, replace some loose earth, and place the tree in position. Then roll back the burlap from the top of the root ball, cutting any strings as necessary. Fill in with topsoil, packing it down well. Make sure that the folded burlap is well buried. If it is exposed to air, this cloth can act like a wick and draw vital water away from the root ball. If you purchase a containerized tree or shrub and the roots are tightly bound in the pot, you might have to cut away the container with a knife. If the plant is root-bound, slice into the middle of the bottom of the root ball. Cut into the fibrous roots—do not cut major roots— a couple of inches, fold back the two halves so that they look like butterfly wings, and then set the plant onto the earth in the hole.

MULCH

Mulch serves many purposes. By covering the soil, a mulch helps it to retain moisture, suppresses weeds, and in winter, protects plants from some of the rigors of alternating thawing and freezing. Many mulches are available—wood chips, buckwheat hulls, pine bark—and it is a matter of personal taste which variety you select.

In cold areas of the country, an additional layer of mulch is very helpful in the winter. Salt hay is an ideal mulch since it is culled from salt marshes and it is improbable that weed seed in this straw will germinate away from briny soil. Some gardeners use evergreen branches. These are fine, but sometimes the needles can be a nuisance—especially in the following spring when you are digging around them with bare hands! In colder areas, if you are going to protect perennials with mulch, wait until the ground freezes, around Thanksgiving, and cover each plant with at least 2 inches of mulch. When mulching perennials, leave the crown of the plant uncovered. Remove this protection in the spring (but not too early), or leave it in place and let nature turn the straw into valuable compost.

PROPAGATION

A simple indoor greenhouse can be made very easily by placing a plastic storage box under a fluorescent light on a kitchen counter or basement workbench. Ordinary workshop fluorescent lights are ideal. It makes very little difference (except in expense) to use the so-called grow-lights. Space the plastic containers about 1 foot from the fluorescent tubes, and if convenient, install a timer on the light. Five to eight hours of light per day is ideal for growing seedlings. The electricity will cost only pennies. Most department stores sell clear plastic containers with removable lids; they are usually sold for storing sweaters and other clothes. Seeds can be sown in small pots and then placed in these containers. If you sow seeds in January or February, by early spring you will have many seedlings. This is how I grew the plants for my first "English wild-flower meadow." These seedlings can then be thinned and planted in individual pots and placed back in the plastic container. If you

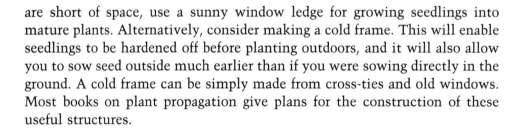

are short of space, use a sunny window ledge for growing seedlings into mature plants. Alternatively, consider making a cold frame. This will enable seedlings to be hardened off before planting outdoors, and it will also allow you to sow seed outside much earlier than if you were sowing directly in the ground. A cold frame can be simply made from cross-ties and old windows. Most books on plant propagation give plans for the construction of these useful structures.

PESTS

Bugs in the garden can be a nuisance, but indiscriminate spraying can kill beneficial insects as well as pests. Keep an eye open for insect and fungal infestations and remove badly infected leaves or stems. Don't throw these cuttings on the compost heap. Instead, discard them in a trash bag or burn the diseased material.

Common pests like Japanese beetle are now controllable with traps that attract the insect with sex hormones. Aphids, also called greenfly, can be very damaging to plants and shrubs. To eradicate aphids use a spray of malathion or a pyrethrum-based mix, carefully following the manufacturer's directions. If you don't want to use a chemical, spray plants with slightly soapy water. This will wash the aphids away from the infected plants. If I get any infestations of spider mite or greenfly in the greenhouse, I spray seedlings with very dilute malathion. A teaspoon per gallon of water is a sufficient concentration for killing these insects and does not harm the sensitive seedlings. A plastic hand sprayer — the type used for misting the leaves of house plants — makes the perfect container for this chemical.

Slugs are one of the most damaging pests in the garden. Poison pellets are available, but birds and chipmunks can also be poisoned by these pesticides. I have a cold frame, and for one reason or another, slugs seem to congregate in this area more than any other part of the garden. I solved this problem by collecting some of the toads on my property (they come out on warm evenings) and transferring them to the cold frame area. Soon all the slugs were gone and the toads were very fat and contented—especially one I named "Mr. T." This fine fellow has taken up permanent residence in the cold frame. Toads are fine creatures, not in the least sinister animals. Mr. T is so friendly that on summer evenings, he enjoys having his back scratched! Another method for eradicating slugs, and one not for the squeamish, is to go out at night with a flashlight and pick the slugs off the plants by hand. I pop them in a jam jar and throw this out with the garbage. Beer placed in shallow containers attracts slugs. The creatures, once in the beer pools, soon drown.

If you have serious fungal or insect pests in your garden, look for a copy of the *Ortho Problem Solver*, a book on garden pests; most garden centers have it. This handy volume gives "mug shots" of all harmful critters so you can identify the creature doing the damage to your plants. It also illustrates infected foliage and makes it easy to track down garden pests through the evidence of their destruction. Under each diagnosis, the *Ortho Problem Solver* gives a list of the appropriate chemicals for treating that disease or pest.

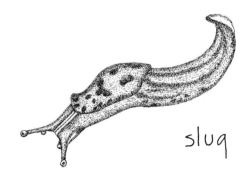

slug

Chapter Two

THE HERB GARDEN

HERB GARDENS TODAY are as popular as they were in the Middle Ages— though now we plant them for pleasure rather than as our only means of securing medication for ailments. Herb teas such as those blended by Celestial Seasonings and dried culinary herbs like those sold by Spice Islands occupy an enviable portion of supermarket shelves, and every mail-order catalogue worth its salt sells herbal candles and potpourri mixes.

In the United States, this renaissance of interest in herbs started about ten years ago. At that time I was designing the medieval garden for The Metropolitan Museum of Art, at The Cloisters. Many of the plants incorporated in the plan were unusual herbs—plants grown in gardens centuries ago, and therefore hard to locate in the few herb nurseries widely scattered across the United States and Canada. In fact, they were so difficult to locate that many had to be imported from Europe. I was able to collect other specimens from the wild in Connecticut and upper New York State—plants that were descendants of annuals and perennials that had survived the hazardous Atlantic crossing centuries ago, thanks to the diligence of the early settlers. The new botanical arrivals, like the early pioneers, took advantage of their new home-land and soon proliferated in alien soil. As a result, we now mistakenly believe many of these foreign plants are native American herbs.

Ten years later, the situation for the herb gardener is very different. For instance, when I peruse the Horticultural Society of New York's plant catalogues, I am always amazed, not only at the number of herb farms, but also at the incredible variety of plants these enterprises now offer to a discerning and interested public.

Why this renewed interest in herbs? The reasons are many. One is the greater familiarity with cuisines of other countries, and of course herbs are essential to gourmet cooking. More Americans are taking vacations abroad, and foreign travel has helped to arouse an interest in the domestic customs of other lands. The exotic markets, rich in herbs and spices, provide too tempting a treasure to remain only vacation memories.

Besides their culinary usage, herbs have also been made into an assortment of natural cosmetics, herbal teas, potpourri, and medicinal preparations. And all these herbal products have had a healthy commerce, producing a lucrative business that reflects a greater public interest in herbs.

Although the herbal renaissance is an American phenomenon, herb gardening is an ancient horticulture, one that goes back many centuries. Indeed, herbalism played a vital part in the development of civilization. To understand how a great reservoir of herbal knowledge was amassed, we need only look at the curiosity of children. Like infants today, ancient people probably put many plants, roots, and berries into their mouths. As William Thompson describes it: "Many were innocuous, a few nourished him, and some made him ill or even killed him. Some, however, relieved symptoms of discomfort or sickness and a very few, through hallucinations, took him from his mundane existence to realms of ethereal wonder. The plants in the latter two categories became his medicines." Being more attuned to their environment than modern man is, primal people would have been aware of how dogs hunt the meadows for special grass, and would have known that bears used selected plants to dress the wounds of their cubs. It seems highly probable that early man was not only directed by his own curiosity but followed the example of the other creatures he observed, and began to experiment with plants. For instance, far back in human history, somebody discovered that a tea made from poppy heads would stop the crying of children, and that the oil extracted from the fruit of the castor tree, taken in small doses, made a useful laxative. And that this same oil, used externally, provided a healing balm for burns and festering wounds. Such knowledge must have been acquired at a high price, however. For instance, just two or three castor beans, eaten by themselves, are deadly.

In the daily life of early man the plants of the field nourished body and mind, were vital adjuncts to rituals that celebrated the seasons, and were central to ceremonies of magic and medicine. With these plants our ancestors maintained that they could prevent evil forces and the demons of disease from entering their bodies—or if they were already infected, could expel them. Herbs also protected the home, barn, cattle, and all dairy products and farm crops. As Geoffrey Grigson points out, "It was necessary to have a knowledge of the kinds [of herbs], of when it was right or wrong to collect them, and of the ways and blends in which they were to be employed. So the physic garden was no fancy, no idle fun, but a need of life." Magic mixed with "botanical knowledge and medical knowledge was not surprising. After all, how remarkable that if you eat a plant, it keeps you alive! How remarkable some plants do the opposite, and do it with dispatch; that others affect the mind narcotically and strangely; that others have local effect on your body inside and out!"

In the myths of many lands there are accounts of the discoveries of useful plants, which provide an insight into how medicinal and culinary plants became known to man. For instance, Islamic teachers tell the story of how the stimulating effect of coffee was discovered. One day, according to William Ukers, "an Arabian goatherd noticed that his flock was unusually frisky, and believing that their mood was due to the effect of some fruits of a plant that they had been eating, tried the effect on himself. He became refreshed and gay and joined his goats in their saltatorial [leaping] revels. A monk, passing that way and learning the situation, believed that the spirit of Mohammed had guided him there, because here was something that would keep him awake during the long prayers and vigils. He conceived the idea of drying and boiling the fruits and thus gave coffee to the world." This myth, which tells the story of the discovery of caffeine as a stimulant to the nervous system, probably contains more than a grain of truth.

Our ancestors believed that herbs operate by some inherent force, a magic that must be controlled. They believed that this power came from supernatural beings, forces that resided in the plant or that held it under protection. In mythology it is usually the gods who discover magical plants and pass on this knowledge to worthy mortals. In fact, the first herbalists were the gods themselves. Geoffrey Grigson has given some examples:

> The Welsh have the story of the Doctors of Myddvai, descended from the fairy woman Nelferch—she came out of a lake in the Black Mountains and returned into the lake—who had the fairy woman's power, no doubt, to hurt as well as heal. The first of the Doctors of Myddvai was her son by an earthly father. She instructed him in the virtues of all plants and in the art of healing. The Irish have a tale that fairies were flung out of Heaven: then god threw plants down after the fairies, instructing them to be good and

useful (though matters were confused by the devil, who duplicated many herbs to make them more difficult to recognize). Names of plants and surviving scraps of belief show how many English kinds were associated with elf or fairy, or devil, or with that ultimate being of superstition, the poor witch.

There is an interesting collection of these herbs in the design for the Witch's Garden.

There were ancient ceremonies for the collection of plants. To obtain full benefit from healing plants they could be culled only on certain nights and only under the influence of an auspicious phase of the moon. Many pre-Christian writings advocate gathering herbs before sunrise while they are still moist with the magic moon dew. Iron digging tools had to be avoided, and the gatherer would be most likely to get herbs with the strongest therapeutic powers if he conducted these operations while naked. These "pagan" rites were Christianized during the Middle Ages. The vernacular names of plants record this heritage. Many European herbs still bear a name that associates them with the devil, elf, serpent, or death, while other names identify the flower with the Virgin, Christ, or one of the saints.

These plant remedies and their supernatural embellishments have been recorded by various civilizations for thousands of years. Sumerian tablets from 3000 B.C. list a short pharmacopoeia of domestic ingredients: acacia, figs, milk, salt, and saltpeter. An Egyptian manuscript, known as the Ebers Papyrus and dated 1550 B.C., gives a similar collection of recipes based upon animal and plant products.

From examining these ancient accounts, it soon becomes clear that defining a herb is no simple matter. In my opinion, one of the best definitions was put forward by the emperor Charlemagne over one thousand years ago: "The friend of physicians and the praise of cooks." This panoramic interpretation perfectly suits ancient herbal pharmacopoeias in which fruits, berries, tree barks, and plants all play an important role.

What about the first herb gardens? The oldest surviving illustrations of gardens are from Egyptian tomb paintings. These invariably depict a somewhat formal garden with a central pool surrounded by a generous assortment of fruit trees, including date palms and pomegranates, and vines. These gardens were not only ornamental orchards but herb gardens as well. Poppy, coriander, parsley, and mint were included in the list of common herbs used for food and medicine by the Egyptians.

With the progress of civilization came a greater understanding of the uses of plants. And by the first century B.C., we have excellent accounts by poets like Virgil of the types of herbs grown in Roman times. In the *Georgics*, Virgil describes a beekeeper's garden. In this cultivated plot the gardener grew "a few potherbs among the bushes, and white lilies around about, vervain, and poppies." Besides being decorative, lilies were used by the Romans as a medicinal herb. Vervain was a headache cure, and poppy was a well-known narcotic sedative. About one hundred years later, in the first century A.D., another Roman scholar, Columella, wrote a popular treatise on agriculture. Columella's book, *De re rustica*, contains a large section on horticulture, in which the author describes the garden of a man of modest means: Enclosed with walls or hedges made of sharp thorns, this "mixed garden" contains spring flowers — hyacinths, roses, and marigolds — grown for chaplets and garlands. (These floral wreaths were popular adornments for festive occasions both in the classical world and in the Middle Ages.) The major crops are vegetables and herbs, amongst them celery and parsley, beets, leeks, parsnips, cabbage, chicory, lettuce, onions, mustard, garlic, and mint.

Many of the herbs popular today, and in ancient times, originated in the Mediterranean regions. These plants became essential to the classical world, as medicine as well as for culinary seasoning. As the boundaries of the Roman empire expanded, horticultural expertise was carried to the farthest reaches of the domain. When the empire finally collapsed in the fourth century A.D., all cultural activities, including the classical garden legacy, were taken over by monks. For the next half millennium, in the turmoil of political strife that was the beginning of modern Europe, monasteries were the main custodians of Western civilization.

peppermint   spearmint

When choosing a site for the foundation of a monastery, aside from the desired isolation and seclusion, prime considerations were arable land and a good supply of water. Separation from the outside world gave the religious orders protection from the marauding hordes that swept the whole of Europe during these unsettled times. By laboriously copying countless manuscripts salvaged from the ancient world, the Christian monks rescued a wealth of classical knowledge, including herbal literature from all the ancient civilizations. Behind the stout monastery walls the monks became the main horticulturists of the Middle Ages.

Early in the history of the medieval church, monasteries followed dictates from religious leaders like the sixth-century theologian St. Benedict. Benedict's rule advocated work in the garden for everyone. He advised his followers to cultivate their own vegetables and herbs so that they might be self-sufficient. The Benedictine order dictated that the flesh of four-footed animals could not be eaten, although the meat of fish and birds was permissible. A great quantity of vegetables was consumed as a supplement to the allowed animal food. Sheep, goats, and cows provided dairy products and wool, and swine were raised mainly as a form of largesse to guests or as an exchange commodity for grains and vegetables. In order for the monastery to be self-sustaining, a large area of land was given over to the cultivation of plants. These gardens produced more than was needed for the immediate community, so excess crops and herbs were sold in neighboring towns. The monks not only provided botanical medicine for themselves but dispensed these drugs to any visiting pilgrims who were ailing. Sick people from surrounding villages also relied upon help from the monastic community.

From the earliest years monasteries were in contact with one another. Intercourse with foreign warriors and visiting ecclesiastics lessened the isolation of these holy orders. Scribes continuously copied books for their own communities and made duplicate manuscripts as gifts for other monastic libraries. By the late part of the Middle Ages, after centuries of copying and exchanging ancient writing and the works of contemporary authors, many monasteries could boast extensive libraries. This reciprocation of books helped to disseminate knowledge all over Europe. The constant journey of pilgrims from one religious shrine to another ensured that new ideas were widely circulated from town to town and from distant lands. Plants and seeds, as well as information about herbs and horticultural techniques, followed these same routes. Each monastery had the main herbal and medicinal texts from the ancient world. Prominent amongst these were the works of Dioscorides, Pliny, and Galen. And as new books were written by medieval authors, these, like the manuscripts from Latin and Hellenic writers, were slowly dispersed as copies were circulated throughout the Christian world.

The Crusaders later blazed a great highway on which the knowledge of the age traveled. From the beginning of the Holy Wars in the eleventh century, a stream of new plants was introduced to Europe from the East. This increased the variety of culinary and medicinal herbs as well as fruits and vegetables available in the monastery gardens. When plants were taken from their native environment and grown in an alien soil, their failure—through frost or heat prostration—was a cause for puzzlement. The medieval monks thought that herbs had been given by God and should therefore benefit mankind throughout the world. The realization that certain plants grew only under specific climatic conditions was startling to the gardeners of these early centuries. This led to persistent horticultural experimentation until at last monks began to realize that some native plants from specific regions of the globe could not be grown in other parts of the world.

From examining the literature, artwork, and architectural drawings of the Middle Ages, we can get a fairly complete picture of what these cultivated plots looked like. When interpreting depictions of medieval gardens or the horticultural literature of the period, we must remember, as Eileen Powers has explained, that "just as their fish commonly range from minnows to mermaidens, just as their lord will shoot the phoenix among his wild ducks and wood pigeons, so their gardens are apt to contain not only plants proper to all climates blooming happily in the same bed, but even such horticultural rarities as the mandrake." In the Benedictine monastery of St. Gall in Switzerland, there exists a ninth-century plan for a large monastic complex. The architect seems to have given much thought to the plan, attempting in his design to produce the utopian ideal of a religious community. Although it was never executed, the St. Gall plan is similar in layout to some monasteries that were constructed. The church forms the main building, and close by is the cloister. This structure is an open space, usually square or rectangular, surrounded on all sides by covered galleries that are arched on the open side. (This architectural concept goes back to the peristyle, the garden court of the Roman house.) The cloister formed the heart of the monastery, surrounded as it was by the important centers of life: the refectory, or dining hall, the dormitory, and the chapter house (a rectangular structure used for the ad-

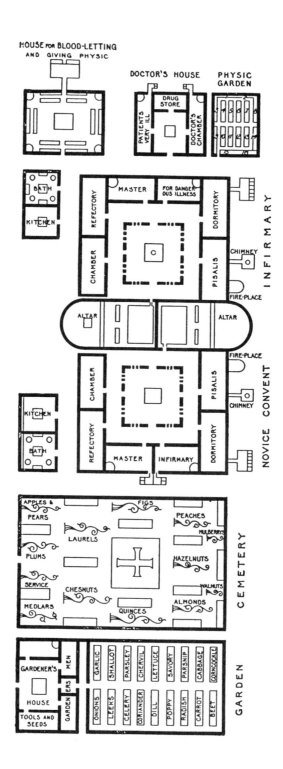

**Section of ninth-century plan of St. Gall.
(Redrawn by the Rev. R. Willis, *Archaeological Journal*, 1848)**

ministration of the monastery). The cloister was used by the monks for strolling, meditation, and conversation—if allowed by their particular order. In the Middle Ages, the open space in the center of a cloister was called the "garth," or yard. It was divided into quarters by walks leading from the openings in the four sides of the cloister. In the center, where the paths met, there would be a specimen tree, fountain, or tub for watering plants. The garden quadrants would be covered with turf. And amongst the grass, flower beds were dug.

What is valuable about the St. Gall plan is its clear identification of specific garden areas. Most of the cultivated areas depicted in these drawings are situated to the east of the church (see drawing). Adjacent to the doctor's house, the physic garden is illustrated. This plot consists of sixteen rectangular beds, each one labeled by the architect with the name of a medicinal herb. The list contains many of the plants that were used by physicians of the Middle Ages for alleviating and curing ailments. One room in the doctor's house is identified as an area to be set aside for bloodletting and the administration of herbal preparations. A library is close by, which would have made it easy for the physician to consult the monastery's collection of herbals and medical books.

In the St. Gall plan, the cemetery was to have served a dual purpose: burial ground and orchard. Below the cemetery the gardener's house is depicted, as well as quarters for the gardener's assistants, a room for tools and seeds, and a large vegetable garden. In the latter, the rectangular beds are labeled with the names of the most popular medieval vegetables: onions, garlic, leeks, shallots, parsley, coriander, chervil, dill, lettuce, poppy, radish, parsnip, carrot, cabbage, beet, and corncockle. Although today most of these plants are considered strictly culinary in use, in the Middle Ages they were believed to have medicinal properties as well. For instance, cabbage leaves were used as a dressing for wounds. We read in *Tacuinum Sanitatis* that leeks were prescribed to excite sexual desire and that an onion not only cures the bite of a mad dog but "when rubbed on bald patches restores hair growth."

Although the monasteries were the main horticultural centers of the Middle Ages, they did not have a complete monopoly on gardening. The plans of castles, although primarily designed for defense until the later centuries of the Middle Ages, did provide a small area for the cultivation of herbs and flowers. Space in these early citadels was limited, and so when gardens were created they were always modest in size.

The diet of the castle inhabitants consisted mainly of fish, fowl, and game, all heavily supplemented by vegetable produce. The culinary and medicinal herbs were obtained from neighboring villages under the feudal domination of the lord of the castle. This was a symbiosis of sorts: the men-at-arms and knights provided protection for the inhabitants who lived in proximity to the castle, and they in turn provided part of the animal and most of the plant produce for the table of the overlord. The medieval farmers had limited winter feed for their animals, so by December when the weather became bitterly cold, most of their livestock was slaughtered. The preservation of perishable foods was crude, and even when salted or cured the meat was often rancid by the return of warm weather in spring. Herbs were added not only to make animal flesh more appetizing but also to mask the unpleasant taste of spoilt meat.

Lucien Febvre has described the importance of herbs and spices in the medieval household:

> When there was red meat it was game or fowl. [The medieval period] did not know the stimulation provoked by . . . flesh food accompanied by alcohol and wine; it did not know the illusion of strength and power which modern man obtains from his usual food, nor the instant stimulation of the nervous system which, thanks to coffee, even the most humble know today. The closest equivalent . . . was spices, whose use was limited only by their enormous cost. People who used neither alcohol nor tobacco, nor coffee nor tea, and who only rarely ate red meat, got their stimulation from spices, setting themselves aflame with ginger and pepper and nutmeg and carefully concocted mustards.

If spices were not available, the medieval kitchens selected seasonings from strong herbs, such as rue, fennel, thyme, and garlic. Looking into a typical kitchen is an easy matter, for many detailed recipe books have survived from the Middle Ages. And although these menus can be easily reproduced in the modern home, in all truth they would not be too tempting to twentieth-century palates. A typical medieval salad—"salat" in Middle English—would contain any or all of the following: violet flowers, parsley, red mints, sage, purslain, ramsons (wild onion), daisies, primrose buds, dandelion, red nettle, borage flowers, and fennel! Ingredients that are fine individually, but together in one salad would be anything but a gourmet meal. In her book on medieval cookery, *Fabulous Feasts*, Madeleine Cosman states, "How piquant might stewed and stuffed capons taste whose recipe begins: 'Take parsley, sage, hyssop, rosemary, and thyme' and adds saffron, 'good herbs,' a pottel (2 quarts) of wine, raisins, sugar, and Ginger." Without belaboring the point, medieval seasoning would make the hottest East Indian curry seem bland!

Castles gradually changed from being little more than fortresses, and by the twelfth century some form of garden was generally situated on the terraces of the ramparts or outside the fortifications of the citadel. The plots outside the castle walls were enclosed and protected with high walls of wattle—structures made by interweaving osier, a species of willow—and were accessible to the castle, usually by a secret door built into the wall. The terraces of the ramparts provided space for miniature gardens where the chatelaine of the castle could seek distraction from the tedium of living in a fortress. These gardens must have provided a much-needed retreat from the tight community life of the citadel. Enthusiasts of the Middle Ages who might enjoy planting a medieval garden will find a plan for this type of garden at the end of this chapter.

In later centuries, these verdant plots became more sophisticated and acquired more embellishments. These were the castle gardens frequently mentioned in the romances of the troubadours. By the thirteenth century, Europe was becoming much more politically stabilized, and so the secular lords could, like the monks, provide themselves with pleasure gardens. From these humble beginnings the small gardens attached to the outer fortifications, and the tiny gardens of the terraces, developed into the sophisticated "plausances" (tree gardens) of the fourteenth century. These arbors were situated away from the main buildings of the castle. Fruit trees were an important component, and some broad-leafed trees were selected to provide shelter not only from the hot summer sun but also from the occasional heavy rainstorm.

parsley

The plausance was essentially an orchard, and depending on the magnificence of the castle, enclosed either by a simple wattle fence or by a more elaborate structure of stone. A major plausance would contain raised seats, arbors, and perhaps a fountain. In the later, more stable centuries of the Middle Ages, when a greater amount of time could be given to recreation, this garden became a popular place for receiving guests and staging tournaments, and provided a pleasant setting for courtly dancing and singing. In the summer months the plausance also provided a much-needed alternative to the poorly ventilated and dark living quarters of the keep. During these months of settled weather the inhabitants of the castle could enjoy dining in the open air, away from the smoky confines of the banqueting hall.

By the fourteenth century, for the first time since the days of the Roman empire, actual instructions for constructing gardens were given. In *Opus Ruralium Commodorum* [*The Advantages of Country Living*], a medieval Italian lawyer, Pietro Crescenzi, gave directions for the construction of a number of different gardens. For a king or rich lord he suggests making an elaborate garden of over twelve acres, and for a burgher, a smaller plot of one or two acres. Another garden, suitable for the limited space inside a small castle or manor house, was to be a modest plot of herbs. Concerning this small garden, Crescenzi writes: "Certain gardens may be made of herbs, some with trees yet others of both. When constructing only of herbs, they require poor solid soil, so they may produce fine plants which greatly please the sight. . . . The whole plot should be filled with fine turf. . . . Let the site of the garden be of such a measure as may sit the plants to be permanently grown in it, and it should be planted with fragrant herbs of all kinds, such as rue, sage, basil, marjoram, mint and the like, and similarly all kinds of flowers, such as violets, lily, rose, gladiolus and the like. Between the turf and the herbs, let there be a higher piece of turf made in the fashion of a seat, suitable for flowers and amenities; the grass in the sun's path should be planted with trees or vines, whose branches will protect the turf with shade, and cast a pleasant refreshing shadow. . . . Behind the turf plot let there be a great diversity of medicinal and aromatic herbs, which not only please by the odor of their scents, but by their variety of flowers, refresh the sight, among which rue should be mingled in many places for its beauty and greenness, and its bitterness will drive away poisonous animals from the garden. . . . If possible, a clear fountain should issue in the middle, because its purity produces much pleasantness."

This description, quoted by Sir Frank Crisp in *Medieval Gardens*, represents a typical garden of the late medieval period, containing the four elements considered essential: grass, trees, a raised garden seat, and, if possible, a fountain. The central area of the garden is lawn. Seating is provided by making a raised turf area bounded by boards or bricks. And if these elevated grass seats were large enough, then plants would either grow directly from the sod or be placed in pots upon the turf. Flowers and aromatic herbs were usually planted around the perimeter of the garden. Behind the turf seats, trees and vines trained on arbors provided shade during the heat of summer. Medieval gardens were lovely, lulling the senses with an earthy harmony. The aromatic turf seats released a heady perfume when gently bruised, birds sang in the shade trees, and the splash from the fountain brought tranquility to all who watched the silvery reflections in the pool.

During the Middle Ages gardens were not the sole prerogative of the nobility and clergy but were also enjoyed by people of less social distinction. Even before the rise of the merchant class in the fourteenth century, most houses of any dimension had some sort of garden consisting of a cultivated plot near the kitchen, used primarily for growing vegetables, potherbs for seasoning, and medicinal plants for healing. As early as the twelfth century, town gardens seem to have been quite numerous. William Fitzstephen, a biographer and contemporary of Thomas à Becket, wrote a description of London gardens of his era: "On all sides outside the houses of the citizens, who dwell in the suburbs, there are adjoining gardens planted with trees, both spacious and pleasing to the eye."

In the thirteenth century, Jon Gardener gave one of the first descriptions of what was actually grown in medieval town gardens. His Parisian garden contained a large area that was used for the cultivation of herbs. Gardener describes these plants as "good for men's bodies." His list includes mallow—a favorite medieval remedy for gout. Agrimony, another herb grown in his garden, was believed to be indispensable for healing wounds made with iron weapons as well as helping the mental condition of insomniacs and those who are absentminded. In this herb garden bugloss was also grown. For the medieval household this plant was a sure remedy for chest complaints. Gardener's marigold flowers were employed to heal scabs on the head. And this same plant, when properly prepared according to the medieval physician's recipe, even cured the pestilence! Other medicinal herbs grown in the garden were nightshade, pimpernel, self-heal, and adder's tongue. Near the medicinal herbs was the garden for potherbs: borage, leeks, garlic, mustard, onions, shallots, and scallions.

Marilyn Stokstad and Gerry Stannard have described the importance of therapeutic herbs: "The medicinal garden, or herb garden in the loosest sense, played a practical role throughout the Middle Ages second only to the kitchen garden. Medieval medicine, almost synonymous with drug therapy, depended heavily on medicaments of plant origin, a tradition that continues to the present day in folk medicine. . . . The health of its members depended upon ready access to medicaments composed of locally available plants. . . . The importance of medicinal plants can be gauged by the fact that the services of a professionally trained physician, as opposed to the local village herbalist, were available only to the wealthy." Peasants would more likely collect healing plants from the wild or purchase drug plants from an apothecary's shop. Whether grown in a garden or collected in the wild, for rich and poor alike, herbs provided relief from maladies, eased childbirth, protected the home and farm from supernatural agencies, provided stimulating beverages and added seasoning to an all too often bland diet. In the Middle Ages, from the cradle to the grave, human life was centered around these important plants.

In the Renaissance, gardens changed rapidly. An end to political strife meant that houses no longer had to be gloomy citadels but could be gracious dwellings, planned for pleasure and recreation. In the calmer centuries of the Renaissance the garden took on a new importance, and elaborate landscaping became the new vehicle by which power and wealth could be measured. Monarchs all over Europe vied with one another in the magnificence of their gardens.

The sixteenth century was an exciting time for plantsmen. New species of flowers were arriving almost daily from Turkey, the Indies, Mexico, and the Americas. Like the cultivated plots of the Middle Ages, the Renaissance garden was rectangular, defined by walls or hedges. But instead of being an adjunct to a building, the garden became a central element in the architecture of the house. Located in front of the dwelling, these formal gardens mirrored the grandeur of the building and at the same time reflected the elevated status of the owner.

As in the cloister yard of the Middle Ages, two main walkways intersected in the center of the garden. At the intersection a suitable statue or fountain provided a pleasing focal point. The whole garden was an exercise in geometry—walkways paralleled one another, and when they intersected, they crossed at right angles. To create leafy tunnels the designers of these gardens lined some of the walkways with trees. Others gardens were bordered with espaliered fruit trees. Various materials were used to cover the paths — some were lined with turf, others with sand. But perhaps the most popular walkways were those covered with a natural carpet of low-growing scented herbs, which emitted a delightful fragrance when walked upon. Orderly flower beds were planted between the paths and were generally edged with evergreens clipped into formal patterns — lavender, box, hyssop, cotton lavender, or rosemary. During the sixteenth century these geometric "knot" gardens came to dominate garden design. (As Rosemary Verey points out, Oriental carpets may have been the inspiration for these gardens. By the mid-fifteenth century these rugs were being imported into the Italian provinces, and a little later by the Dutch into Holland.)

John Parkinson, the seventeenth-century English herbalist and horticulturist, gave some explicit advice on the correct procedure for making a knot garden. He recommended "marjoram, savory and thyme" because "in the like manner being sweet herbs . . . will be used to boarder up beds and knots, and will be kept for a little while, with cutting, into some conformity." Parkinson mentioned that in the gardens of "great persons," cotton lavender was used for edging the knots because of "the rarity and novelty of this herb." To create designs inside these rectangles Parkinson recommended using "living herbs" or "dead materials" such as ground brick or colored gravel. Whatever material was chosen, inside the rectangular garden beds the selected

rosemary

plants, colored stones, or crushed bricks were arranged in formal designs such as interlocking patterns, heraldic devices, and coats of arms. (There is a plan for one of these knot gardens at the end of this chapter.)

Early in the seventeenth century, the English writer Gervase Markham suggested small herbs such as "penny royal, marjoram, chamomile, daisies, violets, basil and rue" for planting inside the knots outlined by the evergreens. These, the author stated, "will give grace unto the little squares."

Raised turf seats still were part of these Renaissance gardens, and trellises, arches, and arbors added to the formalism of the landscape. "Arbors," wrote John Parkinson in the seventeenth century, "also being both graceful and necessary, may be appointed in such convenient places, as the corners, or elsewhere, as may be most fit, to serve both for shadow and rest after walking." Parkinson stressed that "the fairer and larger your allies and walks be, the more grace your garden shall have, and the less harm the herbs and flowers shall receive, by passing by them that grow next unto the allies sides, and the better shall to your weeders cleanse both the beds and the aisles." Important advice for gardeners of all periods! Parkinson mentions that when planting the knots, herbs could be planted inside the patterns, or "outlandish flowers, that for their pride, beauty, and earliness, are to be planted in gardens of pleasure for delight."

During the sixteenth and seventeenth centuries, increasing skill in horticulture helped to greatly enrich the variety of plants available for flower borders. An Elizabethan parson, William Harrison (quoted in Scott-James and Lancaster's *The Pleasure Garden*), noted that the "art" of the gardener helped "nature in the daily coloring, doubling, and enlarging the proportion of our flowers. . . . So curious are our gardeners now in these days that they presume to do what they like with nature, and moderate her course in things as if they were her superiors. It is a world also to see how many strange herbs, plants and annual fruits are daily brought unto us from the Indies, America, Ceylon, Canary Isles, and all parts of the world."

As the mania for growing new plants became widespread, the design of gardens changed very quickly. When gardeners' eyes feasted on the vivid and enticing blossoms of the more exotic plants, the subtle colors of aromatic herbs paled by comparison. The death knell of the herb as an intrinsic part of the garden was finally sounded when Jacobean writers like William Lawson wrote, "It is meet that we have two gardens, a garden for flowers and a kitchen garden."

Another change took place in the landscapes of seventeenth-century Europe: the knot started to become less fashionable. Instead, gardens were landscaped in the French fashion and the parterre became the main vehicle of design. These differed from the Elizabethan knot in that their outline was nearly always made from clipped box. Parterres were also much more formal; their designs looked more like a "living embroidery" than a landscape. Fewer plants were used in the design, and in some instances no plants were used at all! As English garden writer Anne Scott-James states, parterres "looked best from above, and were rather like a decorated ceiling upside down." With this strict formality of design, flowers and herbs seemed unnecessary. According to the following account by Jacobean garden writer Sir Thomas Hanmer, by the middle of the seventeenth century flowers were suffering the same fate as herbs and were being removed from many of these gardens.

> In these days the borders are not hedged about with privet, rosemary or other such herbs which hide the view and prospect, and nourish hurtful worms and insects . . . but all is now commonly near the house laid open and exposed to the sight of the rooms and chambers, and the knots and borders are upheld only with very low colored boards or stone or tile. . . . Parterres as the French call them, are often of fine turf, but as low as any green to bowl on . . . with but few flowers in such knots, and those such as grow very low, least they spoil the beauty of the embroidery.

Although herbs were neglected in European pleasure gardens, these useful plants were still appreciated in the American gardens of the seventeenth century. The colonial settlers of North America had only recently established themselves in the New World, and therefore were concerned with creating cultivated plots that would provide food and medicinal herbs rather than with planting a purely aesthetic landscape. The early American pioneers did not have the time (or perhaps the inclination) to follow the whims of European garden fashion. Knots and parterres were not seen in America until the eighteenth century. For the first two centuries after the establishment of the New England colonies, the cultivated plots of American settlers were based upon the English cottage and farmhouse garden. This was a horticulture that centered upon the growing of vegetables, herbs, and a few flowers. Before the American Revolution the gardens of city merchants and country gentlemen were very similar to those of farmers. Like their earlier English counterparts, they consisted of enclosed plots usually situated at the front of the house. This garden (in America often called the parlor garden) was often enclosed by a whitewashed wooden fence made from pickets or stakes. The principal feature of the cultivated landscape was the main-axis walk. On either side of the main walkway the flower beds were planted as mirror images of each other. An architectural or ornamental feature such as an arbor, seat, summerhouse, or well provided a focal point for the whole garden. According to Edward Hyams, "The flowers grown were small selections of those chiefly grown in England . . . including lilies, peonies, a few bulbs, gillyflowers and hollyhocks. Marigold, poppy and saffron crocus were grown more for medicinal or culinary reasons than for ornament."

Easter lily

There seem to have been no great gardens in America until after the mid-eighteenth century. And when there were cultivated landscapes, they were often two or three decades behind gardens in the fashionable European styles. Most of the more ornate American gardens were planted by wealthy landowners. For many years after the Revolutionary War, the English Stuart gardens of the seventeenth century, with their knots and parterres, became the popular ideal for American country gentlemen and prosperous city merchants.

Herbs were grown in America from the earliest times. For example, George Fox, the seventeenth-century founder of the Quakers, willed some land that he had in the American colonies to the Pennsylvania Quakers. Part of his estate (described by Hyams) was to be used for planting "a Physic [medicinal herb] Garden, 'for the lads and lasses to know simples.'" In the American garden, herbs were cultivated not in a separate area but either in the vegetable plot or among the plants growing in the flower border. According to garden historian Rudy Favretti: "The concept of 'herb gardens,' such as those we often find associated with restored houses, bears little support in the [historic] literature [of the period]. It seems that herbs for medicine, cooking, or perfume, were rarely set apart in a separate garden, but rather grown as part of the larger garden, often in the border . . . or in small plots within the central garden itself."

The great exception to this general practice was the gardens of the Shakers. Because of their religious beliefs, Shakers did not accept the services of physicians and did not use patent medicines. Instead, they relied upon herbs for curing and preventing illness. Initially the Shakers collected their plants from the wild; later they planted seeds and raised herbs on their own land. By the nineteenth century, these self-sufficient gardens had grown into vast farms — commercial enterprises where the herbs were grown, dried, mechanically packaged, and labeled. The Shakers had an enterprising merchandising system that made nationwide distribution possible. They sold their dried herbs not only to an eager public but also to numerous hospital dispensaries and to the newly emerging American pharmaceutical companies.

In the nineteenth century, the industrialization of Europe caused a great migration of workers away from rural areas into urban centers. In the new technological society the individual was no longer self-sufficient, but came to rely upon a wide range of specialists. Personal independence gave way to specialization. Large markets provided this new urban population not only with vegetable produce but with herbs as well. Gardens in the new towns and cities were small. Freed from dependence on the land for sustenance and medicine, the new city householders no longer grew the wide range of herbs and vegetables they had when living in their rural homes. Instead, they cultivated a much greater variety of flowers. The age of the suburban garden had finally arrived. Although herbs were not widely grown in these gardens, employment of medicinal plants had not diminished. Indeed, before the advent of socialized medicine in England (with the National Health Service Act of 1948), every urban neighborhood had its own herbalist. Consulting a doctor, if one was available, was too expensive for many people. Medical advice, and the appropriate herbs to alleviate the ailment, were obtained by visiting a herbalist. Even as late as the 1960s many herbalists were still practicing in industrial towns. Cities like Manchester and Bolton boasted numerous shops where dozens of herbs were arranged in glass jars, and whole walls were lined with polished mahogany cabinets full of gold-lettered drawers, each one containing some dried herb or spice. I have in my library a copy of *Botanologia: the English Herbal* by Dr. William Salmon. Printed in 1710, this enormous book was the last of the great English herbals to be published. What is fascinating about my particular copy is that it belonged to George Stevens, a herbalist who practiced his profession in Bristol—and who was consulting the herbal until his retirement in the 1930s! If you are interested in medical herbalism, you might try planting a garden of healing herbs. A plan for a physic garden is given in this chapter.

In England, growing herbs as a commercial crop did have a brief revival during World War I. Blockades and military maneuvers interrupted shipments of herbs from the continent, and so for the first time in centuries, the English began to cultivate their own medicinal plants on a large scale. When European suppliers of botanical drugs resumed business after World War I, the effort to raise herbs in the British Isles was mainly abandoned. Today the only farmers who raise large amounts of herbs on English soil are the lavender growers in Norfolk.

As plants to be enjoyed and grown in the garden for their beauty and usefulness, herbs were not popular in England until they were rediscovered by Gertrude Jekyll and other nineteenth-century pioneer landscapers and horticulturists. Gardeners like Miss Jekyll observed that many of the medieval herbs were still being grown in cottage gardens. Free from the vacillations of fashion, these simple rural English gardens could be said to be direct survivals of the gardens of the Middle Ages. In these rustic plots, herbs like lavender grew alongside the more stately perennials. (The Dooryard Garden design in this chapter combines herbs with cottage flowers.) And in our own century, Vita Sackville-West in the 1930s created that gem of English gardens, Sissinghurst. One of the most exciting gardens in that rare landscape is devoted to herbs. Another modern English popularizer of herb gardens was Marjory Fish, a personal favorite among gardeners and horticultural writers. At East Lambrook Manor, Somerset, Mrs. Fish created an outstanding landscape of perennials, including a herb garden. Marjory Fish was a prolific writer and her popular books did much to promote the return of herbs to the English garden.

As the authors of *Garden Design* have stated, the social changes of the

1960s and 1970s "made a direct change in the profession of landscape architecture, with indirect influences on garden design. Environmental awareness, growing from nineteenth-century Romantic appreciation for the land, focused attention on the pernicious effects of a consumer-oriented society on natural systems, the sprawl of unlimited development, and the environmental dangers of industrial pollution. It propelled the profession into a position of political importance. The movement to 'return to nature' has given a renewed interest in preserving and even creating gardens and landscapes with native plants, and an interest in self-sufficiency has increased general interest in growing fruits and vegetables." As a vital adjunct to edible garden produce and native plants, herbs have also moved to the forefront of modern horticultural interest.

These are some of the reasons why today these plants have such a strong appeal. There are others. For instance, herbs are unique; no other group of plants can satisfy so many of our senses. Many are beautiful to look at. The green and silver shades, typical of herb foliage, are now being appreciated as we refine our sensibility to pastel colors. The smell of herbs is legendary. Aromatic leaves and flowers create a heady perfume that evokes a sense of purity and timelessness—intangible and intrinsic elements in all plants, but most apparent in herbs.

In many people's opinion, the herb is the soul of good food. And the genius of master chefs perhaps lies in being able to understand the delicate marriage between seasoning and food. The diversity of flavors inherent in many of these plants is amazing, from the pungency of rosemary to the subtle and permeating flavor of tarragon. The wonderful aspect of cooking with herbs is the range of creativity allowed. With the aid of these prolific plants simple fare can be transformed into gastronomic delights. Aspiring chefs might try planting a gourmet's garden—a plan for one is given in this chapter.

The fascinating lore of herbs, preserved for us in the pages of ancient herbals, is as scintillating to read today as it must have been centuries ago, when the wonders attributed to these plants were taken as a matter of fact. The herbs used and grown today are the same as those collected from the wild by early man in some remote time in prehistory. And in some instances these herbs are descendants of the medicinal and culinary plants cultivated by the ancient Egyptians thousands of years ago. Herbs are one of the few groups of widely grown plants that so far have not been genetically altered by man.

They remain as they always were—wild plants, easily grown by cultivation. These plants represent an unbroken heritage that takes us to the farthest reaches of human civilization. And yet today, people enjoy this fascinating and rewarding group of plants in ever greater numbers. In this dangerous and uncertain world, I often think of the words of the great Elizabethan herbalist John Gerard: "Who would therefore looke dangerously up at planets, that might safely look down at plants."

basil

garlic

HERB GARDEN DESIGNS

ELIZABETHAN KNOT GARDEN *An embroidery of herbs*

In addition to selecting a sunny part of the garden, take full advantage of this plan by using a site that will allow you to view the knot garden from above. Begin by marking a 10- by 10-foot square with stakes and string (diagram 1). Next, find the middle of the square by stretching cord across the diagonals. (The middle of the square is where the strings intersect.) Hammer a wooden stake into the center of the square and tie a length of cord to it. Then tie a funnel to the cord (diagram 2). Fill the funnel with dry sand (or flour), and use this to mark the circle on the ground (diagram 2). To make the outline of the arcs, place pegs at the center point of each side of the square. Using the string, funnel, and dry sand, delineate the arcs inside the square (diagram 3). To complete the knot design, run a cord from peg to peg (diagram 4) and mark the final diamond shape.

Plant the appropriate herbs as indicated along the lines of the circle, diamond, arcs, and square. Soon individual plants will form a solid mass. You now have an Elizabethan knot garden!

CIRCLE: **28 *Santolina chamaecyparissus*** — COTTON LAVENDER

DIAMOND: **16 *Santolina virens*** — GREEN SANTOLINA

ARCS: **40 *Hyssopus officinalis*** — HYSSOP

SQUARE: **36 *Thymus x citriodorus*** — LEMON THYME

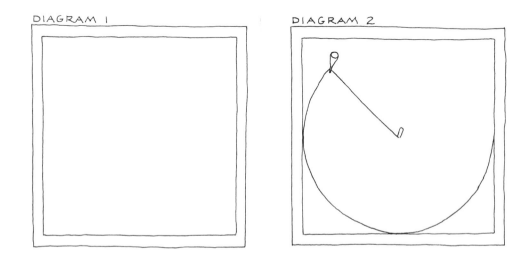

DIAGRAM 1

DIAGRAM 2

ELIZABETHAN KNOT GARDEN

10'

10'

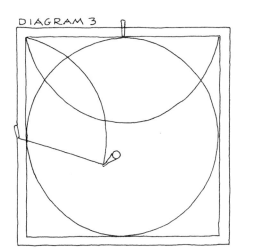

DIAGRAM 3

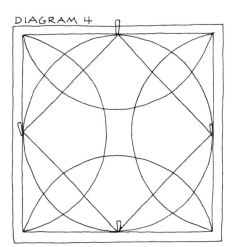

DIAGRAM 4

A FORMAL HERB GARDEN *Useful herbs in a formal setting*

Cotoneaster surrounds this garden. This attractive shrub has almost horizontal branches, and the bright red berries which appear in early fall stay on the plant until the following spring. Accenting the corner of each of the L-shaped beds is *Yucca filamentosa* 'Bright Edge.' This lovely perennial is evergreen, with white stripes on the margins of the pointed leaves. In the center of the garden is an apple—a tree that for centuries has been considered to have healing properties. Choose your favorite type of apple for this garden. A planting of tall green fennel surrounds the fruit tree, and roses add to the charm of the center garden. A selection of sweet-smelling herbs fills the five beds. This is a garden for full sun.

*25 **Alchemilla mollis** — LADY'S MANTLE
2 **Aloysia triphylla** — LEMON VERBENA
3 **Artemisia abrotanum** — SOUTHERNWOOD
24 **Cotoneaster horizontalis** — ROCKSPRAY COTONEASTER
13 **Dianthus caryophyllus** — CLOVE CARNATION
5 **Foeniculum vulgare purpureum** — BRONZE FENNEL
6 **Helichrysum angustifolium** — CURRY PLANT
6 **Heliotropium arborescens** — HELIOTROPE
12 **Lavandula angustifolia** — ENGLISH LAVENDER
1 **Malus** (any fruiting variety) — APPLE
9 **Melissa officinalis** — LEMON BALM
3 **Mentha x piperita** — PEPPERMINT
6 **Monarda didyma** 'Cambridge Scarlet' — RED BERGAMOT

12 **Nepeta x faassenii** — CATMINT
8 **Ocimum basilicum** 'Dark Opal' — PURPLE BASIL
3 **Pelargonium crispum** — LEMON PELARGONIUM
3 **Pelargonium crispum** 'Mable Grey'
3 **Pelargonium graveolens** 'Attar of Roses' — ROSE PELARGONIUM
3 **Pelargonium tomentosum** — PEPPERMINT GERANIUM
5 **Rosa** 'Crimson Glory' — ROSE
12 **Salvia officinalis** — SAGE
12 **Santolina chamaecyparissus** — COTTON LAVENDER
3 **Tanacetum vulgare** — TANSY
8 **Thymus vulgaris** — COMMON THYME
36 **Viola odorata** — SWEET VIOLET
4 **Yucca filamentosa** 'Bright Edge'

*Numbers in list are total quantities needed.
Numbers in the diagram indicate the quantity to be planted in each individual space.

A FORMAL HERB GARDEN

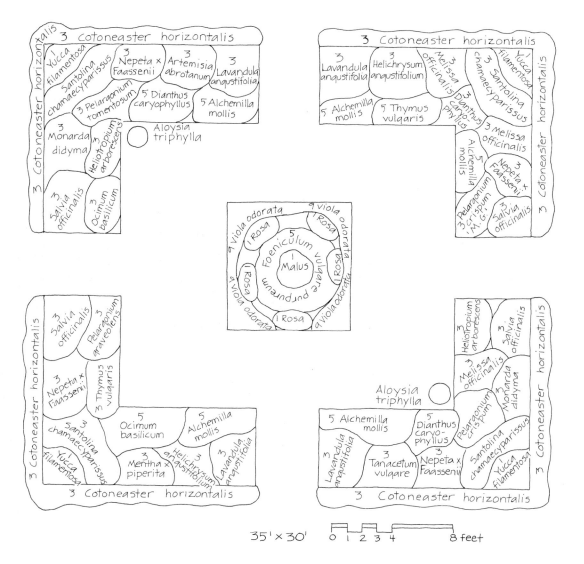

35' × 30'   0 1 2 3 4   8 feet

GOURMET'S GARDEN *All the herbs for the best food in the world*

This plan provides a comprehensive collection of the most useful herbs for the kitchen. A flagstone path meanders through the garden, enabling gourmet chefs to sniff and collect herbs to their heart's content. Tall plants like angelica and sweet cicely are placed in the center of the borders—these large herbs will be easy to reach from the pathway. Smaller plants like basil and balm will creep onto the flagstones. Stepping on and brushing against these aromatic herbs will fill the garden with a variety of scents. This plan is best for a sunny site.

*5 *Alchemilla mollis*—LADY'S MANTLE
5 *Allium sativum*—GARLIC
3 *Allium schoenoprasum*—CHIVES
1 *Aloysia triphylla*—LEMON VERBENA
5 *Anethum graveolens*—DILL
1 *Angelica archangelica*—ANGELICA
5 *Anthriscus cerefolium*—CHERVIL
3 *Artemisia dracunculus*—FRENCH TARRAGON
5 *Atriplex hortensis* 'Rubra'—RED ORACH
3 *Borago officinalis*—BORAGE
3 *Chenopodium bonus-henricus*—GOOD KING HENRY
3 *Chrysanthemum balsamita*—COSTMARY
5 *Coriandrum sativum*—CORIANDER
3 *Foeniculum vulgare*—FENNEL
6 *Helichrysum angustifolium*—CURRY PLANT
1 *Laurus nobilis*—SWEET BAY
3 *Levisticum officinale*—LOVAGE
6 *Melissa officinalis*—LEMON BALM
3 *Mentha x rotundifolia*—APPLE MINT
5 *Mentha spicata*—SPEARMINT

3 *Monarda didyma* 'Cambridge Scarlet'—RED BERGAMOT
3 *Myrrhis odorata*—SWEET CICELY
5 *Ocimum basilicum*—BASIL
5 *Ocimum basilicum* 'Dark Opal'—PURPLE BASIL
5 *Origanum majorana*—SWEET MARJORAM
3 *Origanum vulgare*—WILD MARJORAM, OREGANO
3 *Pelargonium graveolens* 'Attar of Roses'—ROSE PELARGONIUM
3 *Pelargonium tomentosum*—PEPPERMINT GERANIUM
5 *Petroselinum crispum*—PARSLEY
3 *Poterium sanguisorba*—BURNET
1 *Rosmarinus officinalis*—ROSEMARY
3 *Rumex scutatus*—FRENCH SORREL
6 *Salvia officinalis*—SAGE
6 *Satureja hortensis*—SUMMER SAVORY
6 *Satureja montana*—WINTER SAVORY
3 *Thymus x citriodorus*—LEMON THYME
3 *Thymus herba-barona*—CARAWAY THYME
3 *Thymus vulgaris*—COMMON THYME

*Numbers in list are total quantities needed.
Numbers in the diagram indicate the quantity to be planted in each individual space.

GOURMET'S GARDEN

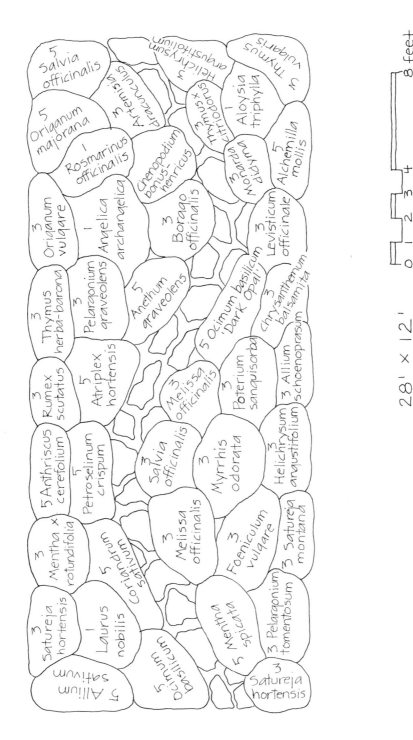

5 Salvia officinalis

5 Origanum majorana

1 Rosmarinus officinalis

3 Artemisia dracunculus

3 Helichrysum angustifolium

3 Thymus × citriodorus

5 Aloysia triphylla

5 Thymus vulgaris

Chenopodium bonus-henricus

3 Monarda didyma

5 Alchemilla mollis

3 Origanum vulgare

1 Angelica archangelica

3 Borago officinalis

3 Levisticum officinale

3 Thymus herba-barona

3 Pelargonium graveolens

5 Anethum graveolens

5 Ocimum basilicum 'Dark Opal'

3 Chrysanthemum balsamita

3 Rumex scutatus

5 Atriplex hortensis

3 Melissa officinalis

3 Poterium sanguisorba

3 Allium schoenoprasum

5 Anthriscus cerefolium

5 Petroselinum crispum

3 Salvia officinalis

3 Myrrhis odorata

3 Helichrysum angustifolium

3 Mentha × rotundifolia

5 Coriandrum sativum

3 Melissa officinalis

3 Foeniculum vulgare

3 Satureja montana

3 Satureja hortensis

1 Laurus nobilis

5 Ocimum basilicum

5 Mentha spicata

3 Pelargonium tomentosum

5 Allium sativum

3 Satureja hortensis

28' × 12'

0 1 2 3 4   8 feet

GOURMET'S GARDEN

MEDICINAL HERB GARDEN *Plants for making healing brews*

This is the perfect garden plan for people interested in medicinal herbs. A path curves through the collection, enabling all the plants to be picked or just enjoyed at close range. A garden such as this is the ideal place to bring a book on herbs, and in this delightful setting time could be spent studying important healing plants. This design is for a sunny site.

*6 **Achillea millefolium** — YARROW
6 **Aconitum napellus** — ACONITE
5 **Ajuga reptans** — CARPET BUGLE
6 **Alchemilla mollis** — LADY'S MANTLE
3 **Althaea officinalis** — MARSHMALLOW
3 **Artemisia absinthium** — WORMWOOD
6 **Asclepias tuberosa** — BUTTERFLY MILKWEED
3 **Calendula officinalis** — MARIGOLD, POT MARIGOLD
1 **Cytisus praecox** 'Moonlight' — MOONLIGHT BROOM
3 **Digitalis purpurea** — PURPLE FOXGLOVE
3 **Eryngium planum** — ERYNGO
3 **Foeniculum vulgare** — FENNEL
3 **Geranium maculatum** — WILD GERANIUM
3 **Hypericum perforatum** — ST.-JOHN'S-WORT
3 **Hyssopus officinalis** — HYSSOP

6 **Marrubium vulgare** — HOREHOUND
6 **Melissa officinalis** — LEMON BALM
3 **Mentha x piperita** — PEPPERMINT
3 **Mentha pulegium** — PENNYROYAL
6 **Monarda didyma** 'Cambridge Scarlet' — RED BERGAMOT
1 **Myrrhis odorata** — SWEET CICELY
3 **Polygonum bistorta** — BISTORT
6 **Pulmonaria officinalis** — LUNGWORT
1 **Rosmarinus officinalis** — ROSEMARY
3 **Ruta graveolens** — RUE
6 **Saponaria officinalis** 'Roseo-Plena' — SOAPWORT
1 **Sassafras albidum** — SASSAFRAS
9 **Symphytum officinale** — COMFREY
3 **Tanacetum vulgare** — TANSY
3 **Valeriana officinalis** — VALERIAN
3 **Verbena officinalis** — VERVAIN

*Numbers in list are total quantities needed.
Numbers in the diagram indicate the quantity to be planted in each individual space.

MEDICINAL HERB GARDEN

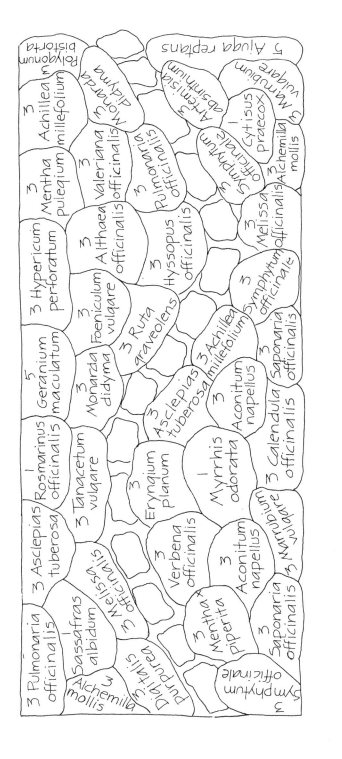

3 Pulmonaria officinalis

3 Asclepias tuberosa

1 Rosmarinus officinalis

5 Geranium maculatum

5 Achillea millefolium

Mentha pulegium

Monarda didyma

Polygonum bistorta

3 Hypericum perforatum

3 Althaea officinalis

Valeriana officinalis

5 Pulmonaria officinalis

Artemisia absinthium

5 Ajuga reptans

3 Tanacetum vulgare

3 Monarda didyma

Foeniculum vulgare

3 Ruta graveolens

3 Hyssopus officinalis

1 Symphytum officinale

1 Cytisus praecox

3 Marrubium vulgare

3 Melissa officinalis

3 Alchemilla mollis

3 Pulmonaria officinalis

3 Asclepias tuberosa

3 Achillea millefolium

3 Aconitum napellus

3 Symphytum officinale

3 Saponaria officinalis

3 Sassafras albidum

3 Melissa officinalis

3 Eryngium planum

1 Myrrhis odorata

3 Calendula officinalis

Alchemilla mollis

3 Digitalis purpurea

3 Verbena officinalis

3 Mentha piperita

3 Aconitum napellus

3 Saponaria officinalis

3 Marrubium vulgare

3 Symphytum officinale

28' × 12'

0 1 2 3 4 8 feet+

MEDICINAL HERB GARDEN

DOORYARD GARDEN *Step out of the house and be welcomed by cottage flowers and sweet-scented herbs*

This design makes use of aromatic herbs and old-fashioned perennials to enhance the entrance to a house. 'Climbing Cecile Brunner,' a fast-growing rose placed against the front wall of the house, will be covered with small pink blossoms from spring until the end of summer. Single hollyhocks give cottage-style charm to this dooryard garden. The pathways meander, enabling strollers to enjoy the perfume of the flowers and herbs. A birch provides light shade and gives an accent to the garden. Underneath this tree, a delightful carpet of purple ajuga merges into an evergreen ground cover of periwinkle *(Vinca minor)*. A mugo pine, surrounded by round stones, provides a delightful highlight to the corner of the garden. This evergreen pine is low growing, and when encircled by fist-sized stones, as in this design, will provide sculptural interest in both winter and summer. The evanescent flowers of a smoke tree at the corner of the house will add beauty to this garden for most of the summer.

*5 *Achillea filipendulina* 'Coronation Gold'— YARROW
 5 *Achillea taygetea* 'Moonshine'— YARROW
36 *Ajuga reptans* 'Burgundy Glow'— CARPET BUGLE
 6 *Alcea rosea* (single red variety)— HOLLYHOCK
 6 *Alchemilla mollis*— LADY'S MANTLE
 3 *Allium schoenoprasum*— CHIVES
 1 *Angelica archangelica*— ANGELICA
 3 *Artemisia abrotanum*— SOUTHERNWOOD
 6 *Artemisia absinthium* 'Lambrook Silver'— WORMWOOD
 1 *Betula papyrifera*— CANOE BIRCH
 3 *Borago officinalis*— BORAGE
 5 *Calendula officinalis*— MARIGOLD, POT MARIGOLD
 1 *Cotinus coggygria* 'Royal Purple'— SMOKE TREE
 5 *Dianthus caryophyllus*— CLOVE CARNATION
 3 *Digitalis purpurea* 'Excelsior Hybrids'— FOXGLOVE
 3 *Foeniculum vulgare purpureum*— BRONZE FENNEL
 6 *Iberis sempervirens* 'Autumn Snow'— CANDYTUFT

 3 *Lavandula angustifolia*— ENGLISH LAVENDER
 6 *Lavandula angustifolia* 'Hidcote'— HIDCOTE LAVENDER
 3 *Levisticum officinale*— LOVAGE
 3 *Melissa officinalis* 'Aurus'— GOLDEN LEMON BALM
 3 *Myrrhis odorata*— SWEET CICELY
 3 *Nepeta x faassenii*— CATMINT
 8 *Ocimum basilicum* 'Dark Opal'— PURPLE BASIL
 3 *Origanum vulgare*— WILD MARJORAM
 5 *Petroselinum crispum*— PARSLEY
 1 *Pinus mugo var. mughus*— MUGO PINE
 5 *Polygonum bistorta*— BISTORT
 1 *Rosa* 'Climbing Cecile Brunner'— ROSE
 1 *Rosmarinus officinalis*— ROSEMARY
 5 *Rudbeckia fulgida*— BLACK-EYED SUSAN
 3 *Salvia officinalis*— SAGE
 3 *Sedum spectabile* 'Autumn Joy'— STONECROP
 8 *Stachys byzantina*— LAMB'S EARS
 5 *Thymus serpyllum*— WILD THYME
 3 *Thymus vulgaris*— COMMON THYME
48 *Vinca minor*— PERIWINKLE

*Numbers in list are total quantities needed.
Numbers in the diagram indicate the quantity to be planted in each individual space.

DOORYARD GARDEN

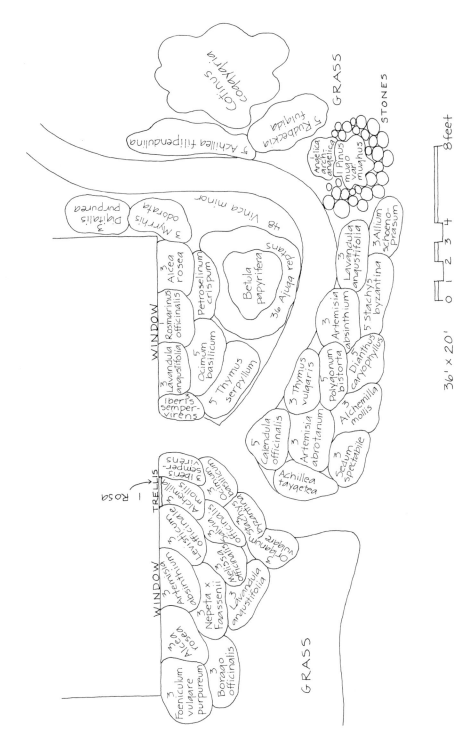

36' x 20'

0 1 2 3 4   8 feet

PATIO GARDEN *A formal garden of stone, cottage flowers, and herbs*

Added to an existing stone terrace, this garden will provide a wonderful area where people can mingle among flowers and aromatic herbs. In this plan a low stone wall, less than 3 feet tall, forms a rectangular enclosure. Flagstones laid on sand or gravel form pathways through a garden of herbs and cottage flowers. The outside of the wall provides a perfect background for more flowers and herbs. A birch tree accents one corner, adding beauty not only in the summer, but with its silver bark, in the winter as well. An evergreen, a mugo pine, is set into the stone terrace and surrounded by scented pelargoniums. (All this requires is the removal of some of the stones in the existing terrace and the preparation of well-tilled holes for the pine and the pelargoniums.) A wax myrtle hedge adjoins the stone terrace. Wax myrtle, or bayberry, is a fast-growing shrub that has a lovely scent. In front of the hedge Scotch thistle is featured. This is a very dramatic plant with huge silver leaves. The dark green foliage of the bayberry makes a wonderful background for the silver leaves of the Scotch thistle.

*6 *Achillea filipendulina* 'Coronation Gold' — YARROW

3 *Achillea millefolium* 'Fire King' — YARROW

6 *Achillea taygetea* 'Moonshine' — YARROW

8 *Alchemilla mollis* — LADY'S MANTLE

6 *Artemisia abrotanum* — SOUTHERNWOOD

6 *Artemisia absinthium* — WORMWOOD

3 *Atriplex hortensis* 'Rubra' — RED ORACH

1 *Betula papyrifera* — CANOE BIRCH

5 *Calendula officinalis* — MARIGOLD, POT MARIGOLD

3 *Dianthus x allwoodii* 'Doris' — CARNATION

3 *Eryngium amethystinum* — ERYNGO

6 *Foeniculum vulgare purpureum* — BRONZE FENNEL

3 *Hemerocallis* 'Lamplighter' — DAYLILY

3 *Hyssopus officinalis* — HYSSOP

3 *Iris sibirica* 'Caesar's Brother' — SIBERIAN IRIS

3 *Lavandula angustifolia* — ENGLISH LAVENDER

3 *Melissa officinalis* — LEMON BALM

5 *Myrica pensylvanica* — WAX MYRTLE, BAYBERRY

6 *Myrrhis odorata* — SWEET CICELY

3 *Nepeta x faassenii* — CATMINT

3 *Ocimum basilicum* 'Dark Opal' — PURPLE BASIL

3 *Onopordum acanthium* — SCOTCH THISTLE

1 *Papaver orientale* 'Big Jim' — ORIENTAL POPPY

6 *Pelargonium* species (Choose favorite type) — SCENTED GERANIUM

1 *Pinus mugo var. mughus* — MUGO PINE

1 *Rosa* species (Choose favorite climber) — ROSE

3 *Salvia officinalis* — SAGE

3 *Salvia sclarea* — CLARY SAGE

10 *Santolina chamaecyparissus* — COTTON LAVENDER

3 *Sedum spectabile* 'Autumn Joy' — STONECROP

11 *Stachys byzantina* — LAMB'S EARS

3 *Thymus x citriodorus* 'Argenteus' — SILVER LEMON THYME

6 *Thymus x citriodorus* 'Aureus' — GOLDEN LEMON THYME

3 *Thymus vulgaris* — COMMON THYME

3 *Verbascum chaixii* 'Album'

1 *Yucca filamentosa* 'Bright Edge'

*Numbers in list are total quantities needed.
Numbers in the diagram indicate the quantity to be planted in each individual space.

PATIO GARDEN

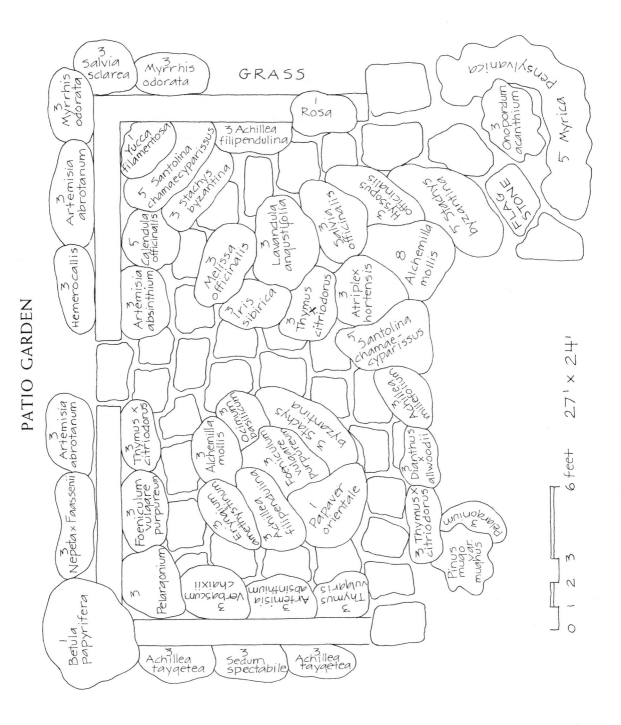

GRASS

3 Salvia sclarea

3 Myrrhis odorata

3 Myrrhis odorata

3 Artemisia abrotanum

3 Hemerocallis

1 Rosa

3 Onopordum acanthium

5 Myrica pensylvanica

1 Yucca filamentosa

5 Santolina chamaecyparissus

3 Achillea filipendula

3 Stachys byzantina

5 Calendula officinalis

3 Melissa officinalis

3 Lavandula angustifolia

3 Salvia officinalis

3 Hyssopus officinalis

5 Stachys byzantina

FLAG STONE

3 Artemisia absinthium

3 Iris sibirica

3 Thymus × citriodorus

3 Atriplex hortensis

8 Alchemilla mollis

5 Santolina chamae-cyparissus

3 Artemisia abrotanum

3 Thymus × citriodorus

3 Alchemilla mollis

3 Ocimum basilicum

5 Stachys byzantina

3 Achillea millefolium

3 Nepeta × Faassenii

3 Foeniculum vulgare purpureum

3 Erynthium amethystinum

3 Achillea filipendula

3 Foeniculum vulgare purpureum

1 Papaver orientale

3 Thymus × citriodorus

3 Dianthus × allwoodii

Betula papyrifera

3 Pelargonium

3 Verbascum chaixii

3 Artemisia absinthium

3 Thymus vulgaris

Pinus mugo var. mughus

3 Pelargonium

Achillea taygetea

3 Sedum spectabile

3 Achillea taygetea

27' × 24'

6 feet

0 1 2 3

0 1 2 3

HERB GARDEN FOR SHADE *Spicy blooms for shady gardens*

This plan is for people who want a herb garden, but because of a shady site, have not had success with traditional herb garden designs. Although herbs do best in sun, there are many culinary, aromatic, and medicinal plants that are quite happy when grown in light shade. This garden plan is fairly elaborate. A hedge of Hatfield yew surrounds the four triangular plots. This evergreen hedging is kept fairly low, just a couple of feet high. The garden contains culinary plants like parsley and lovage, along with medicinal herbs like valerian and tansy. The wide selection of perennials creates a multipurpose herb garden. In order to economize, the yew hedge (which is a bit pricy) could be eliminated. Grass would then surround the borders.

*21 **Ajuga reptans** 'Burgundy Glow' — CARPET BUGLE
12 **Alchemilla mollis** — LADY'S MANTLE
 3 **Allium schoenoprasum** — CHIVES
 4 **Angelica archangelica** — ANGELICA
 5 **Anthriscus cerefolium** — CHERVIL
 5 **Chamaemelum nobile** — ROMAN CHAMOMILE
 6 **Digitalis purpurea** — PURPLE FOXGLOVE
 6 **Levisticum officinale** — LOVAGE
12 **Melissa officinalis** — LEMON BALM
 3 **Mentha x piperita** — PEPPERMINT
 3 **Mentha x piperita** 'Citrata' — EAU-DE-COLOGNE MINT
 3 **Mentha spicata** — SPEARMINT

 6 **Monarda didyma** 'Cambridge Scarlet' — RED BERGAMOT
 6 **Monarda didyma** 'Croftway Pink' — PINK BERGAMOT
 3 **Myrrhis odorata** — SWEET CICELY
10 **Petroselinum crispum** — PARSLEY
 6 **Pulmonaria officinalis** — LUNGWORT
 3 **Rumex scutatus** — FRENCH SORREL
 3 **Ruta graveolens** — RUE
 6 **Symphytum officinale** — COMFREY
 9 **Tanacetum vulgare** — TANSY
48 **Taxus x media** 'Hatfieldii' — HATFIELD YEW
 9 **Valeriana officinalis** — VALERIAN

*Numbers in list are total quantities needed.
Numbers in the diagram indicate the quantity to be planted in each individual space.

HERB GARDEN FOR SHADE

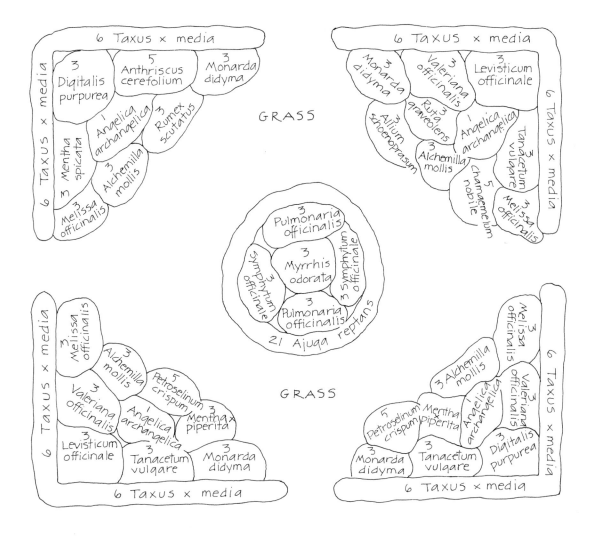

6 Taxus × media

3 Digitalis purpurea
5 Anthriscus cerefolium
3 Monarda didyma

6 Taxus × media

1 Angelica archangelica
3 Rumex scutatus

3 Mentha spicata
3 Alchemilla mollis

3 Melissa officinalis

GRASS

6 Taxus × media

3 Monarda didyma
3 Valeriana officinalis
3 Levisticum officinale

6 Taxus × media

Allium schoenoprasum
3 Ruta graveolens
1 Angelica archangelica
3 Tanacetum vulgare

3 Alchemilla mollis
5 Chamaemelum nobile
3 Melissa officinalis

3 Pulmonaria officinalis

3 Symphytum officinale
3 Myrrhis odorata
3 Symphytum officinale

3 Pulmonaria officinalis

21 Ajuga reptans

6 Taxus × media

3 Melissa officinalis
3 Alchemilla mollis
5 Petroselinum crispum

3 Valeriana officinalis
1 Angelica archangelica
3 Mentha piperita

3 Levisticum officinale
3 Tanacetum vulgare
3 Monarda didyma

6 Taxus × media

GRASS

3 Melissa officinalis

3 Alchemilla mollis
1 Angelica archangelica
3 Valeriana officinalis

5 Petroselinum crispum
Mentha piperita
3 Digitalis purpurea

6 Taxus × media

3 Monarda didyma
3 Tanacetum vulgare

6 Taxus × media

30' × 26'

0 1 2 3 4 8 feet

HERB GARDEN FOR SHADE

WITCH'S GARDEN   *An enchanter's garden of magical plants and trees*

Here is a garden plan for the apprentice witch or the student of the occult arts. In the center, a hawthorn dominates the design. Of all northern trees this one was considered the most magical. For centuries sorcerers weaved their spells under the boughs of the hawthorn. In spring, the tree is covered with the most heavenly blossoms, which by fall have ripened into scarlet berries. Magical mandrake is included in this garden, and so are all the flowers needed to make witches' "flying ointment." Such a collection of "powerfull" plants should not be planted by the fainthearted!

*6 **Achillea millefolium** – YARROW
 3 **Aconitum napellus** – ACONITE, WOLF'S BANE
 6 **Agrimonia eupatoria** – AGRIMONY
13 **Alchemilla mollis** – LADY'S MANTLE
 9 **Artemisia absinthium** – WORMWOOD
 6 **Artemisia vulgaris** – MUGWORT
 3 **Atropa belladonna** – DEADLY NIGHTSHADE
 8 **Calendula officinalis** – POT MARIGOLD
 5 **Campanula rotundifolia** – HAREBELLL
 6 **Chrysanthemum leucanthemum** – OXEYE DAISY
 3 **Conium maculatum** – POISON HEMLOCK
 1 **Crataegus monogyna** – HAWTHORN, MAY
 1 **Cytisus praecox** 'Moonlight' – MOONLIGHT
      BROOM
 3 **Datura stramonium** – THORN APPLE
 6 **Digitalis purpurea** – PURPLE FOXGLOVE
 3 **Filipendula ulmaria** – MEADOWSWEET
 6 **Foeniculum vulgare** – FENNEL
 3 **Helleborus niger** – CHRISTMAS ROSE, BLACK
      HELLEBORE
 3 **Hyoscyamus niger** – HENBANE
 8 **Hypericum perforatum** – ST.-JOHN'S-WORT

 3 **Hyssopus officinalis** – HYSSOP
 1 **Inula helenium** – ELECAMPANE
 3 **Leonurus cardiaca** – MOTHERWORT
 3 **Malva sylvestris** – MALLOW
 3 **Mandragora officinarum** – MANDRAKE
 5 **Mentha pulegium** – PENNYROYAL
 2 **Paeonia** 'Prince of Darkness' – PEONY
 1 **Paeonia** 'Sarah Bernhardt' – PEONY
 3 **Papaver orientale** 'May Sadler' – ORIENTAL
      POPPY
 5 **Petroselinum crispum** – PARSLEY
 3 **Pulmonaria officinalis** – LUNGWORT
 3 **Ruta graveolens** – RUE
 3 **Salvia officinalis** – SAGE
 5 **Sempervivum tectorum** – HOUSELEEK, HEN-AND-
      CHICKENS
 6 **Symphytum officinale** – COMFREY
 3 **Valeriana officinalis** – VALERIAN
 3 **Verbascum thapsus** – MULLEIN
36 **Vinca minor** – PERIWINKLE, SORCERER'S VIOLET,
      MYRTLE
 8 **Viola tricolor** – JOHNNY-JUMP-UP

*Numbers in list are total quantities needed.
 Numbers in the diagram indicate the quantity to be planted in each individual space.

WITCH'S GARDEN

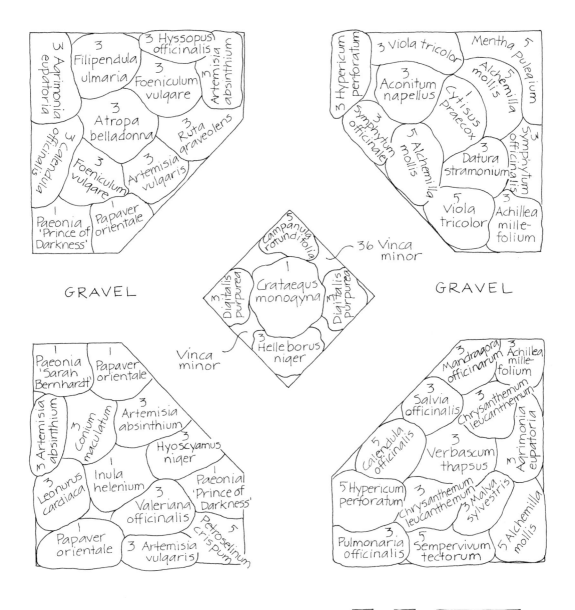

3 Agrimonia eupatoria

3 Filipendula ulmaria

3 Hyssopus officinalis

3 Artemisia absinthium

3 Foeniculum vulgare

3 Calendula officinalis

3 Atropa belladonna

3 Ruta graveolens

3 Foeniculum vulgare

3 Artemisia vulgaris

1 Paeonia 'Prince of Darkness'

1 Papaver orientale

3 Hypericum perforatum

3 Viola tricolor

5 Mentha pulegium

3 Aconitum napellus

5 Alchemilla mollis

1 Cytisus praecox

3 Symphytum officinale

5 Alchemilla mollis

3 Symphytum officinalis

3 Datura stramonium

5 Viola tricolor

3 Achillea millefolium

5 Campanula rotundifolia

36 Vinca minor

3 Digitalis purpurea

1 Crataegus monogyna

3 Digitalis purpurea

Vinca minor

5 Helleborus niger

GRAVEL

GRAVEL

1 Paeonia 'Sarah Bernhardt'

1 Papaver orientale

3 Artemisia absinthium

3 Conium maculatum

3 Artemisia absinthium

3 Hyoscyamus niger

3 Leonurus cardiaca

1 Inula helenium

1 Paeonia 'Prince of Darkness'

3 Valeriana officinalis

1 Papaver orientale

3 Artemisia vulgaris

5 Petroselinum crispum

3 Mandragora officinarum

3 Achillea millefolium

3 Salvia officinalis

3 Chrysanthemum leucanthemum

3 Arrimonia eupatoria

5 Calendula officinalis

3 Verbascum thapsus

5 Hypericum perforatum

3 Chrysanthemum leucanthemum

3 Malva sylvestris

5 Alchemilla mollis

3 Pulmonaria officinalis

5 Sempervivum tectorum

24' × 24'

0 1 2 3 4   8 feet

WITCH'S GARDEN

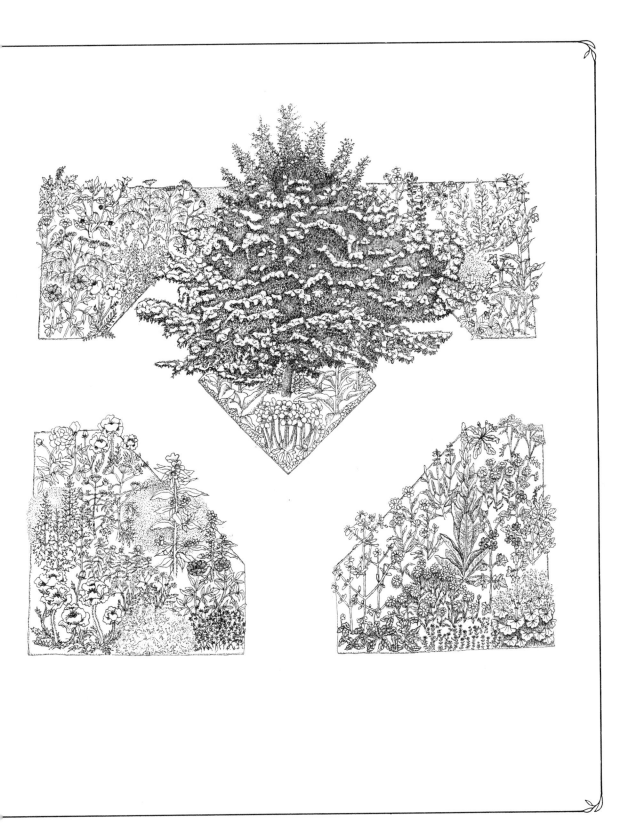

MEDIEVAL GARDEN *A delightful garden of ancient flowers*

This plan has many of the elements that I used in my design for the medieval garden at The Cloisters of The Metropolitan Museum of Art. Many of the plants are chosen because they appear in the Unicorn Tapestries—famous textiles on permanent display at The Cloisters. The central feature of the garden is an apple tree—select any favorite type. The flowers are selected from those actually used in medieval households, plants that decorated castles and monasteries and that were used as seasonings. This is a garden for full sun.

The 3-foot-high wattle fence that borders the outside of the garden is made of willow or alder. You will need stakes 1 inch thick and 4 feet long. Place them 1 foot apart and hammer them into the ground to a depth of 1 foot. (A straight crowbar is helpful for making the hole.) When the uprights are in place, take supple 4- to 6-foot lengths of willow or alder branches and simply weave them between the stakes.

*3 **Achillea millefolium**—YARROW
6 **Aconitum napellus**—ACONITE
3 **Agrimonia eupatoria**—AGRIMONY
10 **Ajuga reptans**—CARPET BUGLE
3 **Alchemilla mollis**—LADY'S MANTLE
3 **Althaea officinalis**—MARSHMALLOW
1 **Angelica archangelica**—ANGELICA
6 **Anthemis tinctoria**—GOLDEN MARGUERITE
3 **Artemisia abrotanum**—SOUTHERNWOOD
6 **Artemisia absinthium**—WORMWOOD
6 **Borago officinalis**—BORAGE
15 **Calendula officinalis**—MARIGOLD, POT
        MARIGOLD
9 **Campanula medium**—CANTERBURY BELLS
6 **Chrysanthemum balsamita**—ALECOST
3 **Chrysanthemum leucanthemum**—OXEYE DAISY
3 **Chrysanthemum parthenium**—FEVERFEW
3 **Digitalis purpurea**—PURPLE FOXGLOVE
18 **Endymion nonscriptus**—ENGLISH BLUEBELL
3 **Foeniculum vulgare**—FENNEL
6 **Fragaria vesca**—WILD STRAWBERRY
10 **Galium odoratum**—SWEET WOODRUFF

6 **Helleborus niger**—CHRISTMAS ROSE
6 **Hyssopus officinalis**—HYSSOP
1 **Inula helenium**—ELECAMPANE
6 **Lavandula augustifolia**—ENGLISH LAVENDER
3 **Lychnis flos-cuculi**—RAGGED ROBIN
1 **Malus** species—APPLE
3 **Marrubium vulgare**—HOREHOUND
9 **Melissa officinalis**—LEMON BALM
3 **Mentha x piperita**—PEPPERMINT
3 **Mentha spicata**—SPEARMINT
6 **Origanum vulgare**—WILD MARJORAM, OREGANO
3 **Physalis alkekengi**—CHINESE LANTERN
3 **Polygonum bistorta**—BISTORT
6 **Pulmonaria officinalis**—LUNGWORT
6 **Ruta graveolens**—RUE
6 **Salvia officinalis**—SAGE
3 **Saponaria officinalis**—SOAPWORT
3 **Satureja montana**—WINTER SAVORY
3 **Symphytum officinale**—COMFREY
9 **Tanacetum vulgare**—TANSY
3 **Verbascum thapsus**—MULLEIN
18 **Vinca minor**—PERIWINKLE

*Numbers in list are total quantities needed.
Numbers in the diagram indicate the quantity to be planted in each individual space.

MEDIEVAL GARDEN

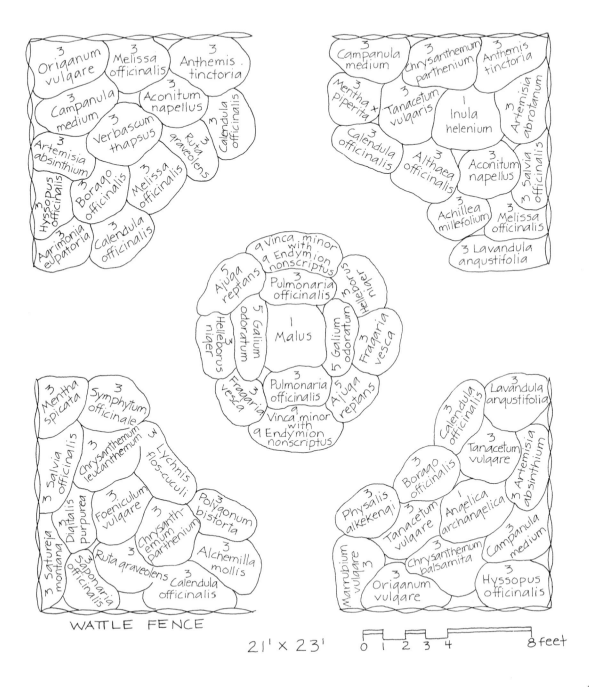

WATTLE FENCE

21' × 23'

0 1 2 3 4 8 feet

Chapter Three

THE PERENNIAL GARDEN

WHEN MOST OF US THINK ABOUT PERENNIAL GARDENS we conjure up picturesque images of English cottages circled by an exuberance of lush flowers—floral tapestries surrounded by rose-strewn walls. Visitors are irresistibly beckoned to the sturdy doorways of these rustic dwellings by narrow pathways partly overgrown with lush plantings of hollyhocks and poppies. The English cottage garden has been a horticultural heritage for centuries and continues to exert a strong influence upon gardeners today. The people who first built these picturesque cottages cultivated a wide range of hardy perennials—plants that survive the English winters and reappear year after year. At first these were wild flowers culled from the fields and hedgerows. Later they were exotic plants brought from the Continent during the Middle Ages by pilgrims, crusaders, and merchants. These foreign botanical specimens did not immediately get into the hands of the cottagers. Eventually, however, they made their way to the humblest village gardens as laborers took cuttings or seeds from the monastery or castle gardens where they worked. The gardens of the middle and upper classes followed the fashion of the day—sometimes almost flowerless, at other times filled with only exotic annuals. It was the cottage gardens that were the bastion of perennial plantings. But cottage gardens are not sterile repositories of familiar plants. As we shall see, these rustic landscapes provided a wellhead of inspiration for many of the great gardeners of the past, and still today affect the way we plan our flower borders. In fact these humble dwellings provided the only refuge for many perennials that were discarded by affluent gardeners.

It is from the English cottage garden tradition that we can trace the history of perennial flower beds. For as horticultural historian Anne Scott-James notes, the cottage garden "has been in its time a bastion of tradition, a sanctuary for plants trembling on the verge of extinction, and an inspiration for gardens larger and finer than itself." It is worth observing that the cottage garden has inspired some of the most important landscape innovators of the past one hundred years, including William Robinson, Gertrude Jekyll, Vita Sackville-West, and Margery Fish.

When did the English cottage garden begin? It is one of the oldest gardening traditions, so we have to look far back into history to find its origins. The Middle Ages provide some of the answers. In Europe, where serfs had worked the land under a rigid feudal system for centuries, the Black Death of 1349 decimated the population and brought about many social and economic changes, including the breakdown of servile labor. In England over one third of the population was killed by the plague, and only a tiny proportion of the rural labor force survived. This imbalance in supply and demand for a manual work force allowed the serfs to put a premium on their services. The barons, not wanting their lands to fall into decay, had to accept the new terms of employment demanded by the depleted labor force. Many serfs took over vacant land, and in essence they became tenant farmers, paying a yearly tribute to the overlords.

As laborers became more affluent, they grew more independent from the lord of the manor. New wealth enabled farmers to build permanent homes; so instead of the primitive hovels of previous centuries, the laborers were able to build cottages of stone and wood. With these permanent dwellings arose the cottage garden. These cultivated strips were used at first for growing vegetables and herbs. Peasants had a diet that seldom included meat, so these plants provided basic nourishment and, in many instances, the only seasoning available. Herbs were also the only source of medicine at this time. As feudal wars became less common, the political climates stabilized and the cottagers' social situation improved. Roy Genders has described this evolution: "Gradually a few flowering plants came to be grown not entirely for their beauty but more for their value in flavoring. All were plants growing naturally in hedgerows or woodland or there were those which may have been introduced at an early date in our history, possibly with the Romans or with the Norman invasion, like the clove-scented pink, *Dianthus caryophyllus*, which has become naturalized on old buildings and whose flowers were used to impart their fragrance to drinks."

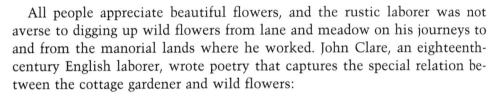

All people appreciate beautiful flowers, and the rustic laborer was not averse to digging up wild flowers from lane and meadow on his journeys to and from the manorial lands where he worked. John Clare, an eighteenth-century English laborer, wrote poetry that captures the special relation between the cottage gardener and wild flowers:

> The cottager when coming home from plough
> Brings home a cowslip root in flower to set
> Thus ere the Christmas goes the spring is met.

Chance hybrids—perhaps a double primrose tucked into the ferns in an embankment or a speckled violet growing in a forest clearing—would almost certainly catch the eye of an observant countryman. These botanical treasures were pried loose by hand, tucked into a pocket, and carried home to be set among the vegetables and herbs of the cottager's garden. Roy Genders describes the result:

> Thus the cottage garden became a place of delightful disorder, green cabbages grew with cabbage roses, daffodils with onions and with them grew marigolds, for the leaves were greatly in demand for use in stews with onions. With them too, grew the Madonna Lily and *Lychnis chalcedonica* [Maltese Cross], both of which are believed to have been introduced by those returning from the crusades.

madonna lily

Since village people are by nature conservative, the design of these cottage gardens did not vary much. For centuries rustic gardens followed a simple layout. An enclosed yard with a stone wall or wooden fence separated the cottage garden from the village road. A straight pathway led from this lane to the front door of the cottage. This walkway was edged with herbs, and behind them vegetables were planted. A few fruit trees and perhaps a beehive completed the basic plan. Ann Scott-James conjectures:

> How far the cottager picked up high-class notions as his prosperity increased is guesswork, but it is tempting to imagine an arbor or rustic arch in a medieval cottage garden, a knot or piece of topiary in an Elizabethan garden, and "improved" and double flowers from the same period. A number of foreign flowers such as hollyhocks, madonna lilies, tulips, sunflowers and dahlias certainly found their way into cottage gardens as and when they spread through Britain.

As the cottage gardens became more sophisticated, vegetables and fruits were restricted to a separate part of the garden. In many instances, tall hollyhocks and delphiniums backed the garden borders and shielded the vegetable plots from view from the sitting-room windows. In the sixteenth century, increased commerce overseas introduced many new flowers to English soil, including the Oriental hyacinth and the Star of Bethlehem, two plants from the Near East. At about the same time, Protestant Huguenot weavers, fleeing their Catholic persecutors in France, not only brought their weaving skills to the English shore but also supplied English gardeners with many new continental flowers, such as auriculas and erythronium. From the early seventeenth century on, many plants arrived from America. John Tradescant, a gardener who enjoyed royal patronage, introduced to English gardens the spiderwort and many blue asters. The wilds of Canada were the source of several goldenrods, rudbeckia, and helenium. These valuable introductions from North America greatly extended the growing season of the English flower garden. The seventeenth-century writer John Worlidge declared in 1677 that there was "scarce a cottage in most parts of the southern parts of England but hath its proportionable garden, so great a delight do most of men take in it." . . . In the late eighteenth century it became common for travelers to comment on the honeysuckle, roses, geraniums and carnations to be found round many cottage doors, contrasting markedly with the gardens of the French peasantry, which contained only apples and cabbages. William Thompson has estimated that in 1500 there "were perhaps 200 kinds of cultivated plants in England. Yet in 1839 the figure was put at 18,000. Nearly all our garden flowers arrived during the intervening years: in the sixteenth century tulips, hyacinths, anemones, crocuses; in the seventeenth Michael-

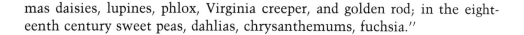

mas daisies, lupines, phlox, Virginia creeper, and golden rod; in the eight-eenth century sweet peas, dahlias, chrysanthemums, fuchsia.''

crocus

phlox

By the middle of the nineteenth century, the old-fashioned hardy peren-nials of the cottage garden were fast losing popularity with townspeople as they followed the fashion of the upper classes and planted gaudy geraniums and *Calceolaria.* ''The old favorites survived only in the garden of the coun-tryman, still poor in relation to the townsman, and in some old vicarage gardens whose owners had not shared the material advantage of the time,'' Roy Genders explains.

A nineteenth-century author, Mrs. Ewing, wrote in *Letters from a Little Garden* (1885) that in preceding decades head gardeners at the large estates had thrown herbaceous plants by the hundreds onto the compost pile to make way for the tender bedding plants of the new fashion. With this prevailing trend, it was only in the cottage gardens that the old flowers could be found. The planting of brightly colored exotics in ''bedding out'' gardens continued (at the expense of hardy perennials) in most of the landscapes of the British upper classes. Fortunately, the trend started to change as a number of pow-erful opponents halted the influence of this perhaps worst of all possible taste in gardening history. Gertrude Jekyll and William Robinson were two visionary gardeners who were greatly responsible for turning the tide against the garish garden schemes of the High Victorian era. At the end of the nineteenth century, Jekyll wrote in *Wood and Garden*:

> It is curious to look back at the old days of bedding out, when that and that only meant gardening to most people, and to remember how the fashion, beginning in the larger gardens, made its way like a great inundating wave, submerging the lesser ones, and almost drowning out the beauties of the many little flowery cottage plots of our English waysides. And one wonders how it all came about, and why the bedding system, admirable for its own purpose, should have thus outstepped its bounds, and have been allowed to run riot among gardens great and small throughout the land. But so it was, and for many years the fashion, for it was scarcely anything better, reigned supreme. It was well for all real lovers of flowers when some quarter of a century ago a strong champion [William Robinson] of the good old flowers arose, and fought strenuously to stay the devastating tide, and to restore the healthy liking for the good old garden flowers. Many soon followed, and now one may say that all England had flocked to the standard. Bedding as an all-prevailing fashion is now dead; the old garden-flowers are again honored and loved, and every encouragement is freely offered to those who will improve old kinds and bring forward others.

As the last of the big Victorian gardens were abandoned and a more sane gardening fashion returned, authors like Mrs. Ewing were able to write: "It is such little gardens that have kept for us the blue primroses, the highly fragrant summer roses, countless beautiful varieties of daffy-down-dillies, and all the host of sweet, various and hardy flowers which are now returning . . . from village to hall."

Other social factors were encouraging a greater respect for the ancient tradition of the cottage garden. Around the last quarter of the nineteenth century, many educated and influential people became concerned about some of the harmful effects of the Industrial Revolution. Age-old traditions, craftsmanship, and artistry were becoming lost in the new mechanical world. One reaction against this loss of the artistic tradition of the common people was the formation of the arts and crafts movement, which helped to keep alive many of the rustic handicrafts of the decreasing rural population. The arts and crafts movement, which included such strong supporters as William Morris, revived among the middle and upper classes many household institutions, such as the cottage garden tradition. Morris admired English rural life — especially the idealized life of the cottager. He urged his audience to use "good old English flowers" and to make gardens like those of the cottagers. William

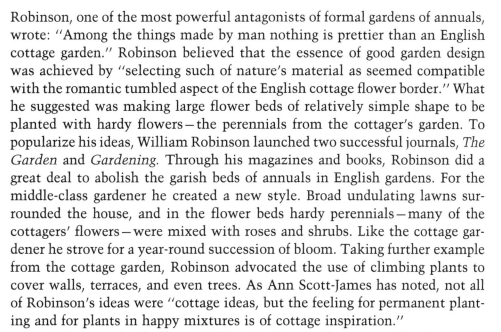

Robinson, one of the most powerful antagonists of formal gardens of annuals, wrote: "Among the things made by man nothing is prettier than an English cottage garden." Robinson believed that the essence of good garden design was achieved by "selecting such of nature's material as seemed compatible with the romantic tumbled aspect of the English cottage flower border." What he suggested was making large flower beds of relatively simple shape to be planted with hardy flowers—the perennials from the cottager's garden. To popularize his ideas, William Robinson launched two successful journals, *The Garden* and *Gardening.* Through his magazines and books, Robinson did a great deal to abolish the garish beds of annuals in English gardens. For the middle-class gardener he created a new style. Broad undulating lawns surrounded the house, and in the flower beds hardy perennials—many of the cottagers' flowers—were mixed with roses and shrubs. Like the cottage gardener he strove for a year-round succession of bloom. Taking further example from the cottage garden, Robinson advocated the use of climbing plants to cover walls, terraces, and even trees. As Ann Scott-James has noted, not all of Robinson's ideas were "cottage ideas, but the feeling for permanent planting and for plants in happy mixtures is of cottage inspiration."

In 1875 Gertrude Jekyll met William Robinson. She accepted his ideas with great enthusiasm. Indeed, she soon began to contribute to his gardening magazines. Jekyll became a celebrity in the horticultural world and soon was receiving many of her own commissions as a landscape designer. Jekyll made use of her training as a painter, taking the best of the cottage garden tradition and applying it to her landscape designs. As she wrote in *Wood and Garden:* "I have learnt much from the little cottage gardens that help to make our English waysides the prettiest in the temperate world. One can hardly go into the smallest cottage garden without learning or observing something new. It may be two plants growing beautifully together by some happy chance. . . . But eye and brain must be alert to receive the impression and studious to store it, to add to the horde of experiences."

As garden writer John Brooks has noted, Gertrude Jekyll was a "horticultural impressionist who saw gardening in terms of painting." In *Color in the Flower Garden*, Jekyll wrote, "Should it not be remembered that in setting a garden we are painting a picture—a picture of hundreds of feet or yards instead of so many inches, painted with living flowers seen by open daylight—so that to paint it rightly is a debt we owe to the beauty of the flowers and to the light of the sun; that the colors should be placed with careful forethought and deliberation, as a painter employs them on his picture, and not dropped in lifeless dabs, as he throws them on his palette."

Jekyll's main specialty was the herbaceous border, which she had studied in the gardens of the cottagers, where she had taken great pains to record harmonious combinations of plants. She designed her borders by placing the plants in drifts, avoiding stiff blocks of flowers. She also strongly advocated planting in masses rather than creating bitty gardens of dozens of different flowers. She had great aptitude for designing with foliage plants—among her favorites were hosta, bergenia, ornamental grasses, and silver plants like artemisia.

Though the professional relationship between Jekyll and Robinson was not long-lasting, during their collaborations she did exert a great deal of influence over Robinson's radical landscape concepts. As garden historian Edward Hyams has noted, "In the remoter parts of her gardens she followed Robinson, making wild gardens with woods and waters, and planting exotics in them; in the garden near the house she adopted the old English cottage garden, giving it a more sophisticated expression. In both she imposed a greater measure of careful order than did Robinson, but the latter was soon being influenced by her, so that he too accepted a measure of discipline and form. What Gertrude Jekyll excelled in was the choice, placing and juxtaposition of herbaceous plants to create a perfect floral and foliar harmony. . . . She was less hostile than Robinson to architectural features in a garden, and by her influence softened his hostility to such elements. Gertrude Jekyll's influence on Robinson and on the gardening of her times was important because Robinsonian enthusiasts were tending to abolish the garden altogether, replacing it with untutored countryside into which exotics were planted."

A more influential and permanent professional relationship developed in 1889 when Gertrude Jekyll met Edwin Landseer Lutyens, a young English architect. From the 1890s on, the partnership between Lutyens and Jekyll set a style that was to be known as the Surrey School. In essence, this was a harmonious arrangement of informal gardens within formal structures. She planted the spaces he designated for her within the overall pattern of the design. Lutyens' garden architecture was an extension of the house; he compartmentalized the landscape. It was the task of Jekyll, with appropriate plantings, to soften the sharp lines of his stone terraces, walls, and pergolas. Many other famous garden designers took the Jekyll-Lutyens techniques in other directions. Across England gardens were being divided into separate "rooms." These compartments created in the landscape, Susan Littlefield explains, "proved ideally suited to cottage gardens, which became a favorite theme. Vita Sackville-West's garden at Sissinghurst in Kent, for instance, looks to the cottage garden in its domestic scale and lush plantings, although it is a much more formal design. The compartment which she called her cottage garden includes a cottage, and a wealth of flowers."

Another world-famous English garden, Hidcote, was constructed at the beginning of this century by an American named Lawrence Johnston. Vita Sackville-West described Hidcote as "a cottage garden on the most glorified scale. . . . there is kind of a haphazard luxuriance, which of course comes neither by hap nor hazard at all."

Later in this century, many other influential garden innovators have perpetuated the ancient tradition of the cottage garden. Foremost among them is Margery Fish. This remarkable lady was a neighbor of mine, and I was fortunate enough to meet her before she died in 1969. Starting in 1937 at the age of forty, and for the next thirty years, Margery Fish made a remarkable garden at East Lambrook Manor in Somerset, a county in the west of England. She wrote in *Cottage Garden Flowers:*

> Nowhere in the world is there anything quite like the English cottage. In every village and hamlet in the land there are these little gardens, always gay and never garish, and so obviously loved. There are not so many now, alas . . . but the flowers remain, flowers that have come to be known as "cottage flowers" because of their simple steadfast qualities. The gardens themselves were usually small, sometimes only a slip between the cottage and the road, with a tiny patch behind. They were tidy without being prim and were always packed with flowers. No definite design went into their planting and the treasured flowers were put wherever there was room. There might be a myrtle, grown from a slip from grandmother's wedding bouquet, pinks from coveted slips, rosemary and lad's love, the great red peonies that last so well, and the crown imperials grown in a row. Wallflowers and snapdragons grew in the walls, and cheerful red and pink daisies played hide and seek between the shells that edged the path.

Margery Fish combined rare plants with old cottage garden favorites. She carefully selected her flowers so that something would be in bloom during the whole year—indeed one of her books, *A Flower for Every Day*, discusses plants that flower in each month of the year. Like her predecessors Gertrude Jekyll and Vita Sackville-West, Margery Fish made her garden into a series of distinct compartments, and in the cottager's style she clothed the stone walls of her ancient medieval house with a variety of colorful plants. Fish's style of gardening was much less complex than Jekyll's. Jekyll's gardens were brilliant, but in today's economy, impractical. We simply don't have the means to maintain such luxury. This is especially true of Jekyll's later collaborations with Lutyens, where an overexuberance of garden architecture makes such gardens impossible to construct and maintain in these expensive years of the twentieth century.

On the other hand, Margery Fish started her gardening career during World War II, when assistance (as for most of us today) would have meant hiring the occasional part-time helper. Fish's flower borders tend to be composed of more individual plants than Jekyll's gardens. They differed in other important ways. For instance, rather than planting in large drifts of flowers—the Jekyll trademark—Margery Fish made gardens that focused on the beauty of each plant. Jekyll had worked on a grand scale. For example, many times she would design garden borders that were planted with just Michaelmas daisies. Such a garden was very striking in the autumn, when these flowers were in full bloom, but would be boring for the rest of the year. This did not matter so much in Jekyll's large garden schemes, but in much smaller gardens, like those of Margery Fish, such principles would not work effectively. Working with about two acres, Fish wanted "every part of the garden to be interesting at every time of the year." She wrote in *We Made a Garden*: "White borders and white gardens are lovely and if there is enough room to indulge in such delights I am all for it. The beautiful silver and white garden at Sissinghurst is a delight, and there is nothing more beautiful than white and silver plants against somber old walls, such as courtyards and priory gardens. A gold and silver border is another luxury for the over-gardened, and one could have great fun finding just the right plants for it, but for most of us white and silver and gold must be woven into the tapestry of just one garden."

Before starting her own garden at East Lambrook Manor, Margery Fish laid down some goals and limitations, described in *We Made a Garden*: The landscape "must be as modest and unpretentious as the house, a cottage garden in fact, with crooked paths and unexpected corners. . . . The aim of all gardeners should be a garden that is always presentable—not a Ruth Draperish garden that has been or will be, but never is at its best. . . . A good bone structure must come first, with an intelligent use of evergreen plants so that the garden is always clothed, no matter what time of year. Flowers

holly

are an added delight, but a good garden is the garden you enjoy looking at even in the depths of winter. There ought never to be a moment when it is not pleasant and interesting. . . . My borders combine all aspects of gardening—shrubs, bulbs, foliage plants, even little patches of annuals to fill any bare spaces. Quite unorthodox, perhaps, but being a greedy woman I want something of everything, and in this way there is always something in bloom."

Since the years when Margery Fish created her remarkable gardens at East Lambrook Manor, many other outstanding designers have carried forward the tradition of the cottage garden. In England, John Brooks has created some of the most exciting gardens of the past decade. Brooks has been called "master of smaller gardens," and his landscapes are an extension of the house. In his designs, building and garden become united in happy harmony. Once he has defined his gardens with trees, shrubs, terraces, or pergolas, he creates decorative details by adding herbaceous and flowering plants. According to *Garden Design*, "He favors fullness—bold masses of plants with things spilling over paths and edges—and he prefers to use species that are native to or regionally identified with the area in which he is working."

Alan Bloom, one of Britain's greatest plantsmen, has done a tremendous amount to promote the use of hardy perennials worldwide. Indeed he has the largest range of garden flowers for sale in the world at his nursery in Norfolk. He is credited with inventing the "island" flower bed. The great advantage of this technique of displaying plants is that island flower beds favor viewing plants from all sides. And, of paramount importance to the modern gardener, island beds also allow easy maintenance. At his nursery in Bressingham, Bloom continues to give gardeners new varieties selected from favorite flowers. *Aconitum napellus* 'Bressingham Spire', *Ajuga metallica* 'Pink Elf', and *Astilbe* 'Bressingham Beauty' are but a few of the many plants he has given us. Alan Bloom is doing what many of the cottagers once did: he is selecting new varieties from old garden favorites. Bloom is presenting cottage gardens in island flower beds—borders that make the greatest visual impact in the garden. A good many of the plans in this book use the island border design.

Christopher Lloyd, one of the best horticulture writers of all time, is also a spendid garden designer. His mixed borders take the cottage garden tradition to a high degree of sophistication. His innovative ideas—like his ability to blend bulbs with herbaceous plants—provide inspiration for all.

Another giant among British horticulturists, Penelope Hobhouse, has applied painterly color theory to the garden. Taking direction from rules laid down by the French Impressionists, Hobhouse has applied their elaborate schemes of hues and tones to her gardens. She is in essence a modern Gertude Jekyll, but Hobhouse's schemes are practical and well suited to the limitations of the modern gardener.

Beth Chatto, another English gardener, has taken the luxuriance of the cottage garden tradition and applied it to her own property in Norfolk. The results are stunning. Chatto's water gardens are some of the best in the world.

What about the future of the cottage garden tradition? We can probably find the answer on this side of the Atlantic. Some very exciting gardens are being created by a Washington, D.C., company called Oehme, van Sweden & Associates, Inc. The two principals responsible for this innovative design firm are Wolfgang Oehme and James van Sweden. According to *The Washington Post* (Feb. 20, 1986), "Though van Sweden was trained in the Netherlands and Oehme in Germany, and their plant selection stresses European hybrids, their landscaping is recognized by horticulturists as being emphatically American." In an interview in *The Washington Gardener* (June 1984), Jim van Sweden stated: "We find ourselves riding the crest of the perennial wave—out front. . . . Planterly landscapes are moving away from the obsessive neatness and unrelieved evergreen of traditional American landscaping." In *Garden Design* Oehme, van Sweden & Associates describe their gardens as "dynamic places, organized as a series of layered spaces that become progressively less architectural as they move away from the house." It is worth recalling that in the last century, William Robinson was trying to create a similar type of landscape. Jim van Sweden describes the effect of his designs as looking "like big dried arrangements full of flowers, leaves, and grasses." In many of their designs Oehme, van Sweden try to achieve the disarray of the field or forest. The lushness in an Oehme, van Sweden garden is achieved

Wild-flower meadow. Garden-in-the-Woods, Framingham, Mass. *Photo by Robert Bottino.*

Dooryard garden. Capriland's Herb Farm, Coventry, Conn. *Photo by Jamake Highwater.*

Silver garden. Capriland's Herb Farm, Coventry, Conn. *Photo by Jamake Highwater.*

Woodland garden. Garden-in-the-Woods, Framingham, Mass. *Photo by John Williamson.*

Perennial borders. Sornberger Garden, Scotland, Conn.

Photo by Jamake Highwater.

Perennial garden. Haddon Hall, England. *Photo by Tom Todd, Taurgo Slides.*

Medieval garden. The first summer (1977) after I planted the garden: The Cloisters, The Metropolitan Museum of Art, New York, N.Y. *Photo by Tom Todd, Taurgo Slides.*

Damp garden — with *Primula japonica*. Redfield Garden, Scotland, Conn. *Photo by Dick Redfield.*

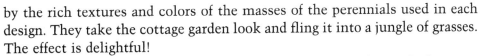

by the rich textures and colors of the masses of the perennials used in each design. They take the cottage garden look and fling it into a jungle of grasses. The effect is delightful!

Oehme, van Sweden aim to achieve a four-seasons garden—which critics have described as the new garden of the 1980s. Among their plantings, some of the principal perennials are tall ornamental grasses. These plants are becoming more and more common in landscape design, and tall grasses are certainly a trademark of Oehme, van Sweden designs. They make use of the giant grasses to create spaces—separate rooms in each of their gardens. Earlier designers like Gertrude Jekyll and Vita Sackville-West used evergreens to create the same effect, but the statuesque grasses Oehme, van Sweden use give a lightness to the design that cannot be achieved with denser barriers like conifers.

Oehme, van Sweden gardens have been described as romantic, but traditional romantic gardens relied on a great variety of plants, and if they fell short of that goal the result looked spotty. The romantic landscape as they interpret it uses fewer varieties of plants but arranges them in bolder groupings. The "less is more" directive makes a visual impact throughout the year. These designers try to magnify the unique features of an individual site. They have carried forward an old tradition—the concept that a garden should never be seen all at once, but should contain a number of surprises. Although the landscapes of these two designers can hardly be described as looking like cottage gardens, I think some of the lushness and apparent randomness of the plantings definitely carry with them the spirit of the cottager's garden.

There is no doubt that perennial gardens are here to stay. Large and small American nurseries are reporting record-breaking sales. A recent Gallup Poll survey has placed horticulture as the number one outdoor leisure activity of the American public. We now spend less time with time-honored traditions like vegetable gardening. Instead we are planting flower gardens. More American gardeners are buying perennials in favor of the traditional spring purchase of annuals. As a nation we are moving away from our earlier "throwaway" mentality. We restore old buildings rather than tear them down and build new ones, and we save and lovingly restore old antiques from grandmother's attic. In essence, Americans are becoming more European. We are beginning to appreciate things of lasting value. And what, if not that, is a perennial flower? The cottage gardeners of old were wise and, by necessity, frugal. They planted flowers that would live for a long time, perhaps longer than the gardener. Cottage gardeners created something of permanence in a world of impermanence. We Americans have now become like the great pioneers Jekyll, Morris, Robinson — we are turning away from a disposable society and are discovering the importance of tradition and things of lasting value. A garden of perennials will not only celebrate a time-honored tradition, it will provide something of joy and endurance. I think we can safely say the cottage garden tradition is alive and well and here to stay.

lilac

PERENNIAL GARDEN DESIGNS

GARDEN FOR SUN (I) *Colorful flowers for a sunny site*

This garden contains some classic perennials. Summer beauties like phlox, Oriental poppy, and Russell lupine form the backbone, and Siberian iris 'Caesar's Brother' provides magnificent foliage for the whole summer and fall. In June the spectacular blue-black blossoms of this iris almost make the rest of the flowers seem like a supporting cast. Some lovely small front-of-the-border perennials are also included in this plan. Outstanding is the dwarf white campanula, which forms small tufts. For the whole summer, this campanula is covered with little bell-shaped flowers. Another white-flowered perennial that adds grace to the plan is the Shasta daisy 'Little Miss Muffet'. This charmer grows only 10 inches high, and from June on produces masses of semi-double daisy-like flowers. For lovers of blue flowers, the prolific perennial *Stokesia* will be a favorite. Its light lavender-blue aster-like flowers appear in late August and stay until the middle of September. Other outstanding perennials in this island bed design include *Saponaria*, also known by the charming name of "bouncing Bet." Whatever you call it, this plant will delight you for the whole summer with myriads of double pink flowers. Whether you delight in tall stately perennials like phlox or prefer the rambunctious sprawling flowers like "bouncing Bet," you will get months of enjoyment from this sunny garden.

*6 *Achillea taygetea* 'Moonshine'—YARROW
5 *Artemisia schmidtiana* 'Silver Mound'—SILVER MOUND ARTEMISIA
3 *Campanula carpatica* var. *alba*—WHITE CARPATHIAN HAREBELL
10 *Chrysanthemum maximum* 'Little Miss Muffet'—SHASTA DAISY
3 *Geum x borisii*—AVENS
3 *Iris sibirica* 'Caesar's Brother'—SIBERIAN IRIS
3 *Lupinus* Russell Hybrid—RUSSELL LUPINE

3 *Nepeta x faassenii*—CATMINT
3 *Papaver orientale* 'Big Jim'—ORIENTAL POPPY
5 *Phlox paniculata* 'Bright Eyes'
5 *Phlox paniculata* 'Mt. Fuji'
3 *Salvia x superba* 'Blue Queen'
5 *Saponaria officinalis* 'Rosea Plena'—SOAPWORT
3 *Sedum spectabile* 'Autumn Joy'—STONECROP
5 *Solidago* 'Golden Dwarf'—GOLDENROD
3 *Stokesia laevis*—STOKES' ASTER

*Numbers in list are total quantities needed.
Numbers in the diagram indicate the quantity to be planted in each individual space.

GARDEN FOR SUN (I)

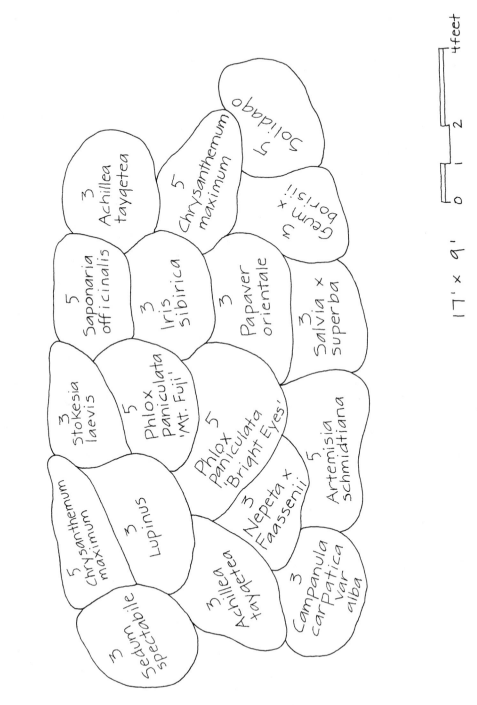

3
Achillea
taygetea

5
Chrysanthemum
maximum

5
Solidago

3
Geum ×
borisii

5
Saponaria
officinalis

3
Iris
sibirica

3
Papaver
orientale

3
Salvia ×
superba

3
Stokesia
laevis

5
Phlox
Paniculata
'Mt. Fuji'

5
Phlox
Paniculata
'Bright Eyes'

5
Artemisia
schmidtiana

5
Chrysanthemum
maximum

3
Lupinus

3
Nepeta ×
Faassenii

3
Sedum
spectabile

3
Achillea
taygetea

3
Campanula
carpatica
var
alba

17' × 9'

4 feet
0   1   2

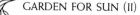

GARDEN FOR SUN (II) *Sunny flowers for spring, summer, and fall*

In this garden, three yuccas will provide a dramatic contrast to the less angular foliage of the other plants. This evergreen perennial adds a dynamic element to any garden, and its lovely white lily-like flowers are wonderful in June and July. Other remarkable plants form a curving ridge of varying height throughout the bed. At the front you will find patches of hardy English lavender. The variety selected, 'Munstead', grows only a foot high. From July until September, these sturdy plants have deep purple-blue flowers with an exquisite perfume. In the middle of the design is *Verbascum chaixii* 'Album', a perennial species of mullein. From June until September, this *Verbascum* sends up tall flower spikes. The blossoms are made up of white flowers, each bloom enhanced with a purple eye. Many special flowers have been included in this island bed. One in particular is cushion spurge, an outstanding early flowering perennial. In spring, the sight of it can be described as electric. In late May, the whole plant is covered with bright golden-green flower bracts — truly stunning, and a wonderful herald for the other colorful plants that will follow and continue to bloom until the fall.

*3 **Artemisia schmidtiana** 'Silver Mound' — SILVER MOUND ARTEMISIA
9 **Coreopsis grandiflora** 'Goldfink' — GOLDFINK COREOPSIS
6 **Echinops ritro** — GLOBE THISTLE
8 **Euphorbia epithymoides** — CUSHION SPURGE
3 **Gypsophila paniculata** 'Bristol Fairy' — BABY'S BREATH
6 **Lavandula angustifolia** 'Munstead' — MUNSTEAD LAVENDER

3 **Lythrum virgatum** 'Rose Queen' — LOOSESTRIFE
3 **Molinia caerulea** 'Variegata' — VARIEGATED PURPLE MOOR GRASS
1 **Papaver orientale** 'Helen Elizabeth' — ORIENTAL POPPY
9 **Sedum spectabile** 'Autumn Joy' — STONECROP
9 **Stachys byzantina** — LAMB'S EARS
3 **Verbascum chaixii** 'Album'
3 **Yucca filamentosa** 'Bright Edge'

*Numbers in list are total quantities needed.
Numbers in the diagram indicate the quantity to be planted in each individual space.

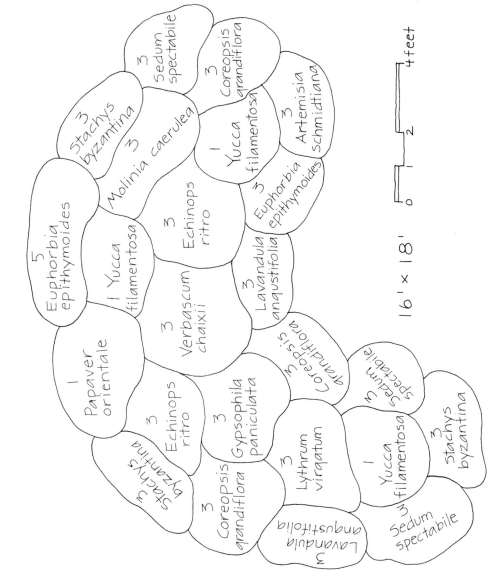

GARDEN FOR SUN (II)

5 Euphorbia epithymoides

1 Yucca filamentosa

Papaver orientale

3 Stachys byzantina

3 Molinia caerulea

3 Echinops ritro

3 Verbascum chaixii

3 Echinops ritro

3 Stachys byzantina

3 Coreopsis grandiflora

3 Gypsophila Paniculata

3 Lythrum virgatum

3 Lavandula angustifolia

3 Sedum spectabile

1 Yucca filamentosa

3 Stachys byzantina

3 Coreopsis grandiflora

Coreopsis grandiflora

1 Yucca filamentosa

3 Lavandula angustifolia

3 Euphorbia epithymoides

3 Artemisia schmidtiana

3 Coreopsis grandiflora

3 Sedum spectabile

16' × 18'

0   1   2   4 feet

GARDEN FOR SUN (II)

DESERT GARDEN   *An exotic garden of hardy "desert plants"*

To make a desert garden you do not have to live in an arid climate. Almost any sunny site with well-drained soil will provide the conditions necessary for cultivating these drought-resistant plants. This garden has an oval shape. Adding a number of rocks in groups will help to create the feeling of a desert landscape. A mulch of ¼-inch washed gravel—put down after all the flowers are planted—helps to contain the garden visually and also suppresses weeds. In the center of the graveled oval is a beach plum. This is a very lovely 6-foot tree that is often seen along coastlines and other botanically inhospitable places. In May, the beach plum is covered with white blossoms. *Yucca glauca*, with its tropical-looking pencil-thin foliage, provides year-round interest. Foliage plants like blue oats grass, 'Silver King' artemisia, and silver sage provide beauty for the whole growing season. And the flowers selected for this plan contribute vivid colors from early spring until fall. This collection of plants will surely inspire even the most conservative gardener to dig up a portion of lawn in order to create a desert garden.

*3 *Armeria maritima* 'Dusseldorf Pride'—SEA PINK
3 *Artemisia ludoviciana* 'Silver King'—SILVER KING ARTEMESIA
5 *Asclepias tuberosa*—BUTTERFLY MILKWEED
3 *Eryngium alpinum*
5 *Eryngium giganteum*
3 *Euphorbia griffithii* 'Fireglow'
3 *Gaillardia* x *grandiflora* 'Goblin'—BLANKETFLOWER
3 *Gypsophila paniculata* 'Bristol Fairy'—BABY'S BREATH
3 *Helianthemum nummelarium* 'Fire Dragon'
6 *Helictotrichon sempervirens*—BLUE OATS

3 *Iberis sempervirens* 'Autumn Snow'—CANDYTUFT
5 *Liatris scariosa*—BLAZING STAR
5 *Liatris scariosa* 'White Spire'—WHITE BLAZING STAR
3 *Oenothera missouriensis*—SUNDROP
3 *Opuntia humifusa*—PRICKLY PEAR CACTUS
3 *Penstemon barbatus* 'Prairie Fire'—BEARD'S TONGUE
1 *Prunus maritima*—BEACH PLUM
3 *Salvia argentia*—SILVER SAGE
3 *Yucca glauca*

*Numbers in list are total quantities needed.
Numbers in the diagram indicate the quantity to be planted in each individual space.

DESERT GARDEN

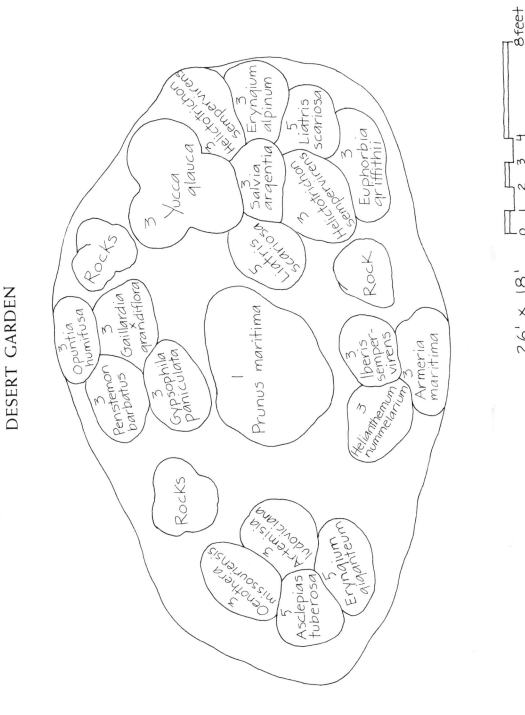

26' × 18'

8 feet

0 1 2 3 4

Heliotrichon sempervirens

3 Eryngium alpinum

5 Liatris scariosa

3 Yucca glauca

3 Salvia argentia

5 Heliotrichon sempervirens

3 Euphorbia griffithii

Rocks

5 Liatris scariosa

Rock

3 Opuntia humifusa

3 Gaillardia × grandiflora

Prunus maritima

3 Iberis semper- virens

3 Armeria maritima

3 Penstemon barbatus

3 Gypsophila paniculata

3 Helianthemum nummelarium

Rocks

3 Artemisia ludoviciana

3 Oenothera missourensis

5 Asclepias tuberosa

5 Eryngium giganteum

DESERT GARDEN

GARDEN FOR A SUNNY SITE *A little garden for a sunny site*

This gently curving flower bed contains some of the most beautiful perennials. One of the highlights is the blue Russell lupine—the pealike blossoms that cover these flowering spikes in June and July are unforgettable. A glorious accompaniment to lupines are Oriental poppies. In this plan, the 'Barr's White' poppy makes a beautiful companion for the blue Russell lupines. The blooms of this poppy are cup size, with paper-thin white petals. The shrubby purple sage is a perfect foliage plant to accompany many of these perennials, and looks especially good with the blue lupines and other plants in this border—notably the *Achillea* 'Moonshine'. The latter is one of the best late-summer flowering perennials. Its sulfur-yellow blooms last for weeks (if they are not picked by flower arrangers). A suitable companion to 'Moonshine', and included twice in this border, is *Sedum* 'Autumn Joy'. The fleshy stalks of this late-flowering perennial hold up huge flat heads of pink flowers. As these mature they become darker, finally turning brick red.

This flower border concentrates upon perennials that bloom in the summer and fall.

*6 *Achillea taygetea* 'Moonshine'—YARROW
3 *Artemisia absinthium* 'Lambrook Silver'—WORMWOOD
6 *Centranthus ruber*—RED VALERIAN
3 *Chrysanthemum maximum* 'Little Miss Muffet'—SHASTA DAISY
3 *Gaillardia x grandiflora* 'Goblin'—BLANKETFLOWER
3 *Lupinus* Russell Hybrid (blue)—RUSSELL LUPINE

3 *Nepeta x faassenii*—CATMINT
3 *Papaver orientale* 'Barr's White'—ORIENTAL POPPY
3 *Papaver orientale* 'Helen Elizabeth'—ORIENTAL POPPY
3 *Phlox paniculata* 'Mt. Fuji'
6 *Salvia officinalis* 'Pupurea'—PURPLE SAGE
3 *Salvia x superba* 'East Friesland'
8 *Sedum spectabile* 'Autumn Joy'—STONECROP

*Numbers in list are total quantities needed.
Numbers in the diagram indicate the quantity to be planted in each individual space.

GARDEN FOR A SUNNY SITE

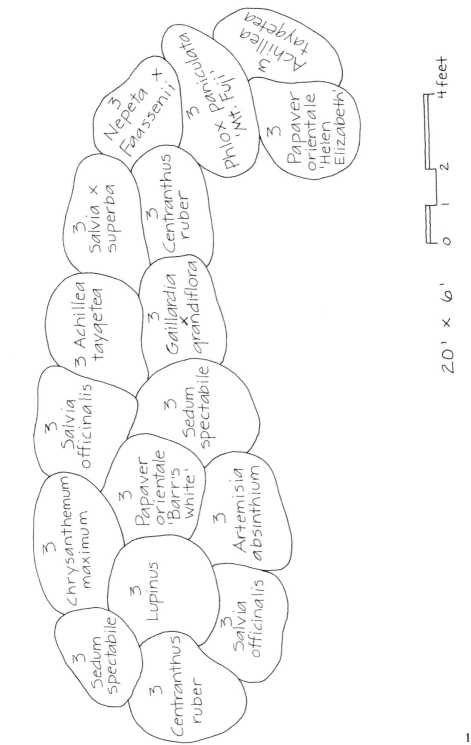

20' × 6'

0   1   2   4 feet

103

SHADE GARDEN *Year-round color for a shady site*

By adding some small evergreens like holly, a gloomy landscape can be converted into a verdant and cheerful garden even in a shady yard of modest size. This is especially true if evergreen perennials like Christmas fern and Baltic ivy are added. In winter and summer these plants will add greenery to the shady garden. In the center of this oval design, the shiny leaves of a red-berried holly provide the main focus all year round. (To have berries, the male cultivar of this holly, 'Blue Prince,' should be planted near the female, 'Blue Princess.') The garden plan will awaken in spring with the lovely flowers of the Labrador violet. And from spring until winter, the *Lamium* 'White Nancy' forms a dense mat of silvery foliage. The variegated Solomon's seal, with its tall, elegant white-edged leaves, dispels any gloom in this shady garden. *Hosta* 'Royal Standard' is chosen for this plan because it has attractive leaves all summer, and in August the tall stems of sweetly scented flowers will entice any onlookers into the garden. And from spring until fall, the *Corydalis* provide an indefatigable bouquet of yellow flowers.

*10 *Alchemilla mollis* — LADY'S MANTLE
 6 *Corydalis lutea* — YELLOW CORYDALIS
 6 *Dicentra eximia* 'Alba' — FRINGED BLEEDING
    HEART
 6 *Epimedium grandiflorum* 'Rose Queen'
 7 *Hedera helix* 'Baltica' — BALTIC IVY
 6 *Hosta* 'Royal Standard'
 1 *Ilex x meserveae* 'Blue Princess'
 3 *Iris sibirica* 'Flight of Butterflies' — SIBERIAN IRIS

 3 *Iris sibirica* 'Super Ego' — SIBERIAN IRIS
 8 *Lamium maculatum* 'White Nancy' — DEAD
    NETTLE
10 *Polygonatum odoratum thunbergii*
    'Variegatum' — VARIEGATED SOLOMON'S SEAL
 6 *Polystichum acrostichoides* — CHRISTMAS FERN
 3 *Pulmonaria saccharata* 'Argentea' — SILVER
    LUNGWORT
22 *Viola labradorica* — LABRADOR VIOLET

*Numbers in list are total quantities needed.
Numbers in the diagram indicate the quantity to be planted in each individual space.

SHADE GARDEN

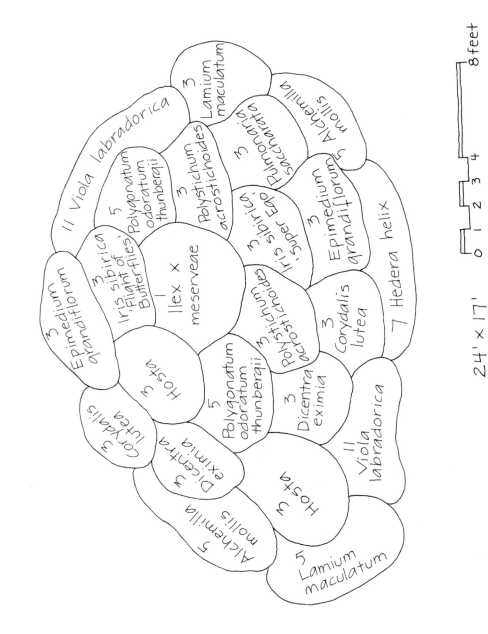

11 Viola labradorica

3 Lamium maculatum

5 Aichemilla mollis

3 Pulmonaria saccharata

5 Polygonatum odoratum thunbergii

3 Polystichum acrostichoides

3 Epimedium grandiflorum

3 Iris sibirica 'Super Ego'

3 Epimedium grandiflorum

3 Iris sibirica 'Flight of Butterflies'

1 Ilex × meserveae

7 Hedera helix

3 Corydalis lutea

3 Polystichum acrostichoides

5 Polygonatum odoratum thunbergii

3 Dicentra eximia

11 Viola labradorica

3 Hosta

3 Corydalis lutea

3 Dicentra eximia

3 Hosta

5 Lamium maculatum

5 Alchemilla mollis

24' × 17'

0 1 2 3 4   8 feet

GARDEN FOR LIGHT SHADE (I) *Islands of colorful flowers in dappled sunlight*

The plants for this semi-shaded garden will give enjoyment for much of the year. In April the bleeding hearts and Virginia bluebells provide color, and in September and October the Japanese anemones add glory with their stately white blooms. Another graceful flower included in this design is the astilbe. This shade-loving perennial is a winner in two ways. Its tall flower spikes are covered with hundreds of pink blossoms, giving the impression of extravagant feathery plumes. The other plus is its lovely shiny foliage, which lasts the whole summer. The hostas planted on both sides of the red astilbes provide perfect contrast. As members of the lily family, hostas are guaranteed to have spectacular blooms, but for me the chief merit of these perennials is the leaves. The hosta varieties chosen for this garden have striking foliage—some have yellow leaves while others have blue foliage. Both types of hosta make wonderful foils for astilbe.

This plan has a separate small bed planted with some surprises. The whole area is covered with *Lamium* 'White Nancy', a lovely ground cover with silver foliage, which grows only 6 inches high. Pretty Virginia bluebells are planted among the *Lamium*. In early April, their clusters of nodding blue flowers appear through the carpet of 'White Nancy'. The other surprise is Canada lilies. Their graceful stems will appear in the summer with stalks as tall as 7 feet covered with reddish-orange flowers.

*9 **Aegopodium podagraria var. variegatum**—
VARIEGATED BISHOP'S WEED
8 **Alchemilla mollis**—LADY'S MANTLE
3 **Anemone hupehensis japonica** 'September
Charm'—JAPANESE ANEMONE
6 **Astilbe x arendsii** 'Fanal'
3 **Cimicifuga racemosa**—BUGBANE
6 **Dicentra eximia** 'Alba'—FRINGED BLEEDING
HEART

3 **Hosta** 'Piedmont Gold'
6 **Hosta sieboldiana** 'Elegans'
12 **Lamium maculatum** 'White Nancy'—DEAD
NETTLE
5 **Lilium canadense**—CANADA LILY
3 **Mertensia virginica**—VIRGINIA BLUEBELLS
10 **Polystichum acrostichoides**—CHRISTMAS FERN

*Numbers in list are total quantities needed.
Numbers in the diagram indicate the quantity to be planted in each individual space.

GARDEN FOR LIGHT SHADE (I)

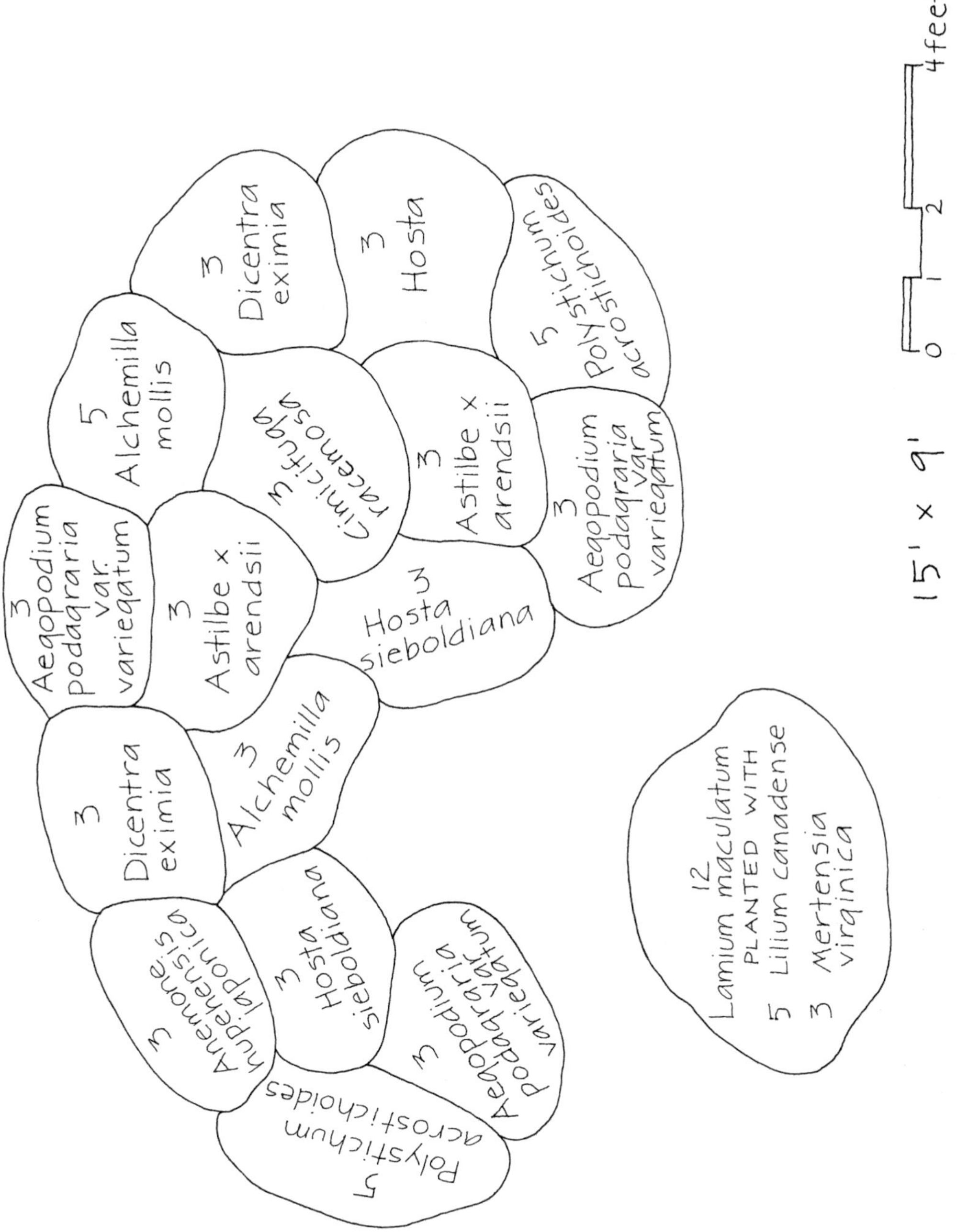

3
Dicentra
eximia

3
Hosta

5
Polystichum
acrostichoides

5
Alchemilla
mollis

3
Cimicifuga
racemosa

3
Astilbe ×
arendsii

3
Aegopodium
podagraria
var
variegatum

3
Aegopodium
podagraria
var.
variegatum

3
Astilbe ×
arendsii

3
Hosta
sieboldiana

3
Dicentra
eximia

3
Alchemilla
mollis

3
Anemonia
japonica

3
Hosta
sieboldiana

3
Aegopodium
podagraria
var
variegatum

5
Polystichum
acrostichoides

12
Lamium maculatum
PLANTED WITH
5 Lilium canadense
3 Mertensia
virginica

15' × 9'

0   1   2   4feet

GARDEN FOR LIGHT SHADE (II)   *The best blooms for light shade*

This plan is full of elegant flowers as well as beautiful foliage. The center of the garden boasts two shade-tolerant rose bushes. 'Ballerina' is a lovely rose that is covered with pink blooms in summer. The arching habit of this rose makes it look like a ballerina's skirt. Tall, stately yellow foxgloves make nice partners for the 'Ballerina' rose. Hostas, including the lovely yellow-leaved 'Gold Standard', provide interesting foliage for the whole summer. Other perennials with attractive leaves are featured in this plan: Silver lungwort, a personal favorite, is placed at the front of the border. This lovely perennial hugs the ground with its graceful silvery foliage. A popular geranium, 'Johnson's Blue', has been included in the design. In early summer, the open cup-shaped flowers of this geranium are a vivid blue.

When the last of the flowers fade in the fall, this garden will still be beautiful. Many of the foliage plants will not die down until late winter, and some perennials, like *Bergenia*, remain evergreen.

*6 *Alchemilla mollis* — LADY'S MANTLE
 6 *Astilbe tacquetii* 'Superba'
 6 *Athyrium goeringianum* — JAPANESE PAINTED
    FERN
 6 *Bergenia cordifolia*
10 *Chrysogonum virginianum* — GREEN-AND-GOLD
 3 *Corydalis lutea* — YELLOW CORYDALIS
 6 *Dicentra eximia* 'Alba' — FRINGED BLEEDING
    HEART
 6 *Digitalis grandiflora* — FOXGLOVE
 6 *Epimedium grandiflorum* 'Rose Queen'

 6 *Geranium* x 'Johnson's Blue' — CRANESBILL
 3 *Geum chiloense* 'Fire Opal' — AVENS
 6 *Hosta* 'Frances Williams'
 3 *Hosta* 'Gold Standard'
 3 *Hosta sieboldiana* 'Elegans'
 3 *Pulmonaria saccharata* 'Argentea' — SILVER
    LUNGWORT
 2 *Rosa* 'Ballerina' — ROSE
 6 *Salvia* x *superba* 'East Friesland'
 3 *Sedum spectabile* 'Autumn Joy' — STONECROP
 6 *Veronica teucrium* — SPEEDWELL

*Numbers in list are total quantities needed.
 Numbers in the diagram indicate the quantity to be planted in each individual space.

GARDEN FOR LIGHT SHADE (II)

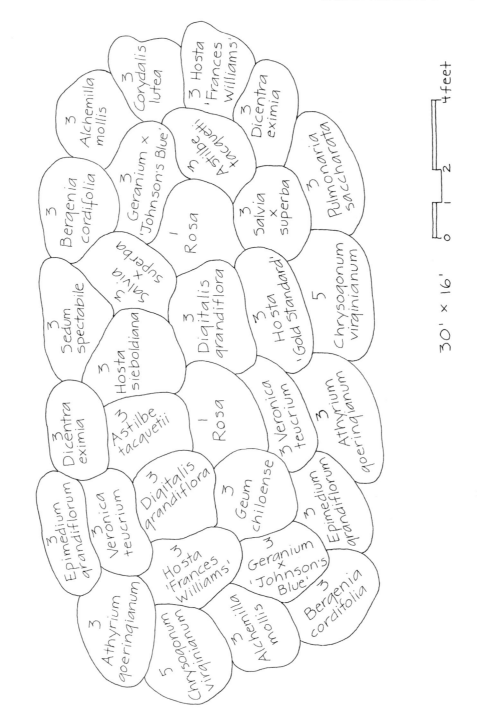

3 Alchemilla mollis

3 Corydalis lutea

3 Hosta 'Frances Williams'

3 Dicentra eximia

3 Bergenia cordifolia

3 Geranium × 'Johnson's Blue'

3 Astilbe tacquetii

1 Rosa

3 Salvia × superba

3 Pulmonaria saccharata

3 Sedum spectabile

3 Salvia × superba

3 Hosta sieboldiana

3 Digitalis grandiflora

3 Hosta 'Gold Standard'

5 Chrysogonum virginianum

3 Dicentra eximia

3 Astilbe tacquetii

1 Rosa

3 Veronica teucrium

3 Athyrium goeringianum

3 Epimedium grandiflorum

3 Veronica teucrium

3 Digitalis grandiflora

3 Geum chiloense

3 Epimedium grandiflorum

3 Athyrium goeringianum

3 Hosta 'Frances Williams'

3 Geranium × 'Johnson's Blue'

3 Bergenia cordifolia

5 Chrysogonum virginianum

3 Alchemilla mollis

30' × 16'

0 1 2 4 feet

GARDEN FOR HEAVY SHADE *Flowers that transform gloomy gardens*

Parts of the garden that are in heavy shade often present a problem, but gloom need not be the case. Many plants will grow in heavy shade, and the leaves and blossoms of these flowers can transform somber areas into delightful woodland glens. Areas of full shade are normally sites like north-facing borders backed by walls, trees, shrubs, or hedges. The light entering these gardens is usually indirect or filtered. The plants selected for this plan are some of the most shade-tolerant perennials. Garden flowers like hosta have been mixed with wild flowers and ferns. The outstanding foliage of many of these plants brightens up the dimmest garden. In this design the large island border is juxtaposed with a smaller circular garden which contains two lovely wild flowers: *Cornus canadensis*, a pretty member of the Dogwood family, acts as a weed-smothering ground cover. And amongst the *Cornus canadensis* I have included Virginia bluebell, one of the most beautiful spring flowers. Here is a garden that invites exploration and will dispel gloom from the shadiest landscape.

*5 **Asarum europaeum** — WILD GINGER
10 **Bergenia cordifolia**
36 **Cornus canadensis** — BUNCHBERRY
 3 **Digitalis grandiflora** — FOXGLOVE
 3 **Dryopteris goldiana** — GOLDIE'S FERN
 6 **Epimidium grandiflorum** 'Rose Queen'
 3 **Hosta** 'Piedmont Gold'
 3 **Hosta sieboldiana** 'Elegans'

 3 **Mertensia virginica** — VIRGINIA BLUEBELLS
 5 **Polygonatum odoratum thunbergii**
     'Variegatum' — VARIEGATED SOLOMON'S SEAL
 3 **Polystichum acrostichoides** — CHRISTMAS FERN
 9 **Pulmonaria saccharata** 'Argentea' — SILVER
     LUNGWORT
 5 **Shortia galacifolia** — OCONEE BELLS
 5 **Uvalaria perfoliata** — WOOD MERRYBELLS

wild ginger

*Numbers in list are total quantities needed.
Numbers in the diagram indicate the quantity to be planted in each individual space.

GARDEN FOR HEAVY SHADE

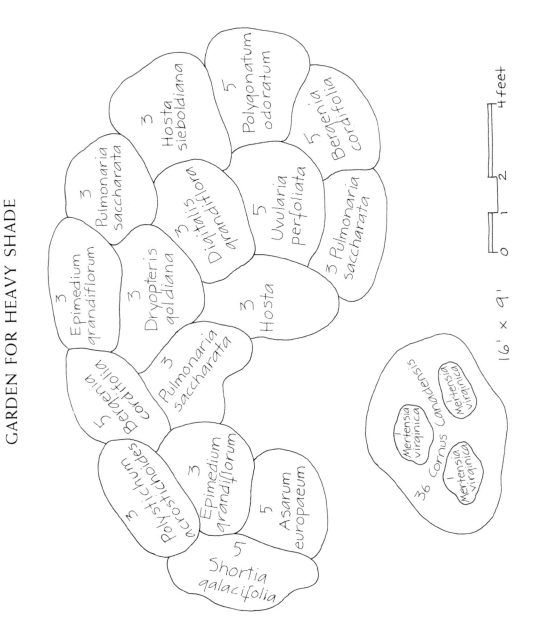

5 Polygonatum odoratum

3 Hosta sieboldiana

5 Bergenia cordifolia

3 Pulmonaria saccharata

3 Digitalis grandiflora

5 Uvularia perfoliata

3 Pulmonaria saccharata

3 Epimedium grandiflorum

3 Dryopteris goldiana

3 Hosta

5 Bergenia cordifolia

3 Pulmonaria saccharata

3 Polystichum acrostichoides

3 Epimedium grandiflorum

5 Asarum europaeum

5 Shortia galacifolia

36 Cornus canadensis

1 Mertensia virginica

1 Mertensia virginica

1 Mertensia virginica

16' × 9'

0 1 2 4 feet

GARDEN FOR HEAVY SHADE

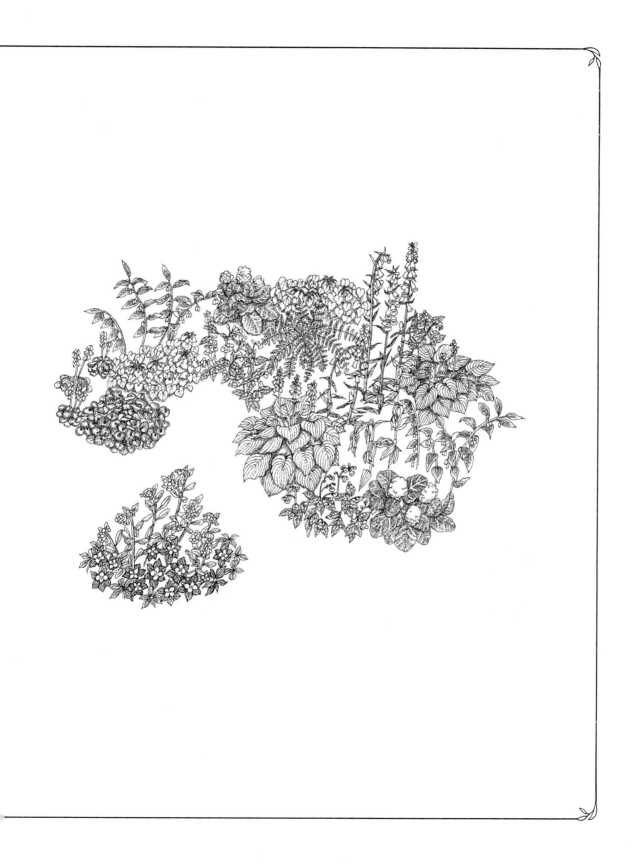

ENTRANCE GARDEN *An inviting dooryard garden of grasses, flowers, shrubs, and evergreens*

Dooryard gardens should be inviting and welcoming. This design, with a smoke tree dominating one of the borders, will provide year-round interest. The foliage of this tree is legendary. Purple leaves cover the whole tree, and in midsummer the feathery seed pods give it an unearthly appearance. Daylilies provide many months of color in this garden, and the golden marguerite will blossom all summer. On the other side of the pathway, *Cornus alba* 'Elegantissima' lends beauty in both summer and fall. The green foliage of this dogwood is marked with distinct white margins, and in winter, the blood-red stems are stunning. The tall zebra grass (*Miscanthus sinensis* 'Zebrinus') gives dramatic height to this part of the garden. This grass, as its name indicates, has blades marked by attractive white bands. In front of the zebra grass, a mugo pine is included. The compact rounded shape of this small evergreen makes a nice foil for the zebra grass. In front of the pine, Japanese blood grass makes a strong impact. Its scarlet stems are enhanced with a planting of the ebony-colored black mundo grass. This is an interesting garden for all seasons.

*3 *Achillea filipendulina* 'Coronation Gold' — YARROW
11 *Alchemilla mollis* — LADY'S MANTLE
 3 *Alcea rosea* — HOLLYHOCK
 3 *Anthemis tinctoria* 'Moonlight' — GOLDEN MARGUERITE
 3 *Artemisia ludoviciana* 'Valerie Finnis'
 3 *Calluna vulgaris* 'H. E. Beale' — HEATHER
 3 *Calluna vulgaris* 'Mrs. R. H. Gray' — HEATHER
 3 *Centranthus ruber* — RED VALERIAN
 1 *Clematis x jackmanii*
 1 *Cornus alba* 'Elegantissima' — RED TWIG DOGWOOD
 3 *Corydalis lutea* — YELLOW CORYDALIS
 1 *Cotinus coggygria* 'Royal Purple' — SMOKE TREE
 1 *Cynara cardunculus* — CARDOON
 6 *Eupatorium purpureum* — JOE-PYE WEED

 6 *Geranium x* 'Johnson's Blue' — CRANESBILL
 3 *Hemerocallis* 'Autumn Minaret' — DAYLILY
 3 *Hemerocallis* 'Christmas Carol' — DAYLILY
 3 *Hemerocallis* 'Frans Hals' — DAYLILY
 3 *Hemerocallis* 'Lamplighter' — DAYLILY
 3 *Hemerocallis* 'Winning Ways' — DAYLILY
 3 *Iberis sempervirens* 'Autumn Snow' — CANDYTUFT
 3 *Imperata cylindrica rubra* 'Red Baron' — JAPANESE BLOOD GRASS
 3 *Lavandula angustifolia* — ENGLISH LAVENDER
 1 *Miscanthus sinensis* 'Zebrinus' — ZEBRA GRASS
 7 *Ophiopogon planiscapus* 'Abaricus'
 3 *Phalaris arundinacea picta* — RIBBON GRASS
 3 *Pinus mugo var. mughus* — MUGO PINE
 3 *Verbascum bombyciferum*

*Numbers in list are total quantities needed.
Numbers in the diagram indicate the quantity to be planted in each individual space.

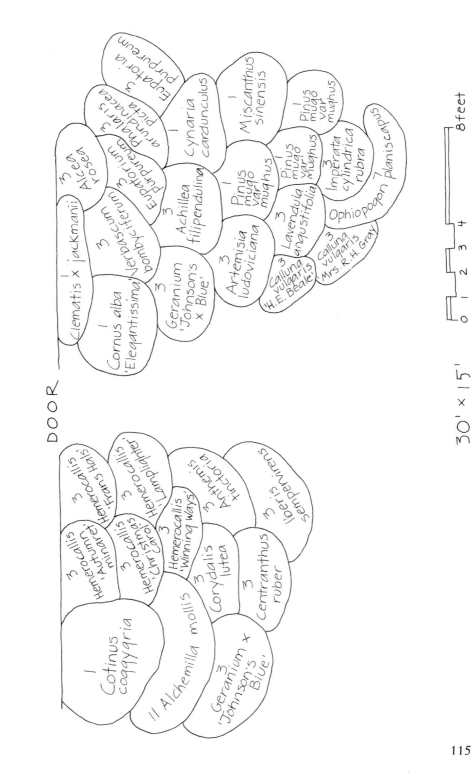

ENTRANCE GARDEN

DOOR

Upper plan:

- 3 Alcea rosea
- 1 Clematis x jackmanii
- 3 Phalaris arundinacea 'Picta'
- 3 Eupatorium purpureum
- 3 Verbascum bombyciferum
- 1 Cynaria cardunculus
- 1 Miscanthus sinensis
- 1 Pinus mugo var mughus
- 3 Achillea filipendulina
- 1 Pinus mugo var mughus
- 3 Pinus mugo var mughus
- 3 Imperata cylindrica rubra
- Cornus alba 'Elegantissima'
- 3 Geranium 'Johnson's x Blue'
- 3 Artemisia ludoviciana
- 3 Lavendula angustifolia
- 3 Calluna vulgaris 'H.E. Beale'
- 3 Calluna vulgaris 'Mrs. R.H. Gray'
- 7 Ophiopogon planiscapus

Lower plan:

- 3 Hemerocallis 'Frans Hals'
- 3 Hemerocallis 'Lamplighter'
- 3 Hemerocallis 'Autumn minaret'
- 3 Hemerocallis 'Christmas Carol'
- 3 Hemerocallis 'Winning ways'
- 3 Anthemis tinctoria
- 3 Iberis sempervirens
- 1 Cotinus coggygria
- 11 Alchemilla mollis
- 3 Corydalis lutea
- 3 Centranthus ruber
- 3 Geranium x 'Johnson's Blue'

30' × 15'

0 1 2 3 4 — 8 feet

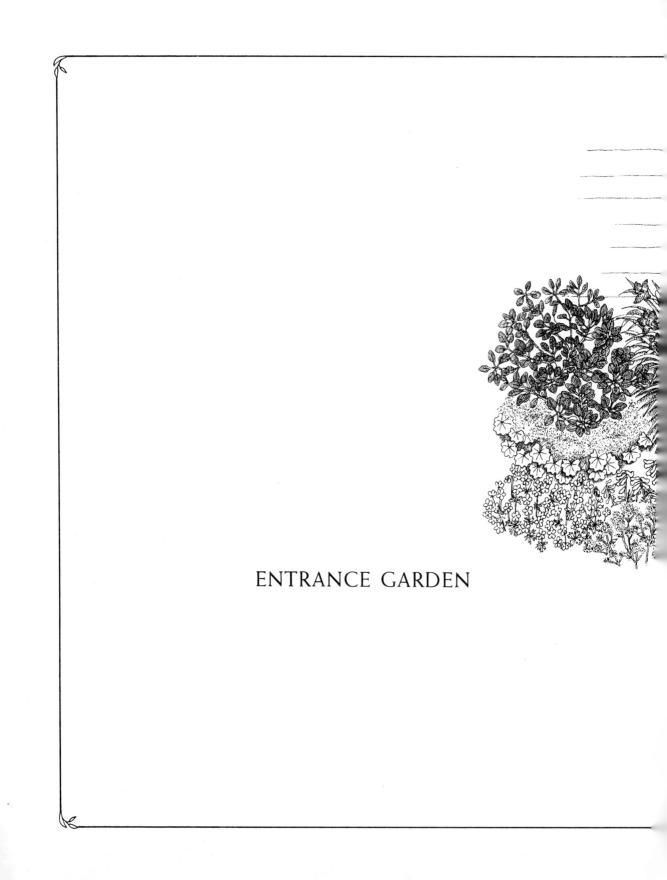

ENTRANCE GARDEN

LONG-BLOOMING FLOWER GARDEN FOR A SMALL YARD

A modest-size garden full of the most splendid blossoms

If your yard is not very large, this design for a small island flower bed is ideal. The plan contains plants that bloom for many weeks so that all summer long, this little garden adds color and interest to your landscape. *Gaura*, one of the perennials chosen for this design, blooms from June until October! Another plant in the plan, the golden marguerite, flowers almost as long. The perennials also include foliage plants like lady's mantle and 'Silver Mound' artemisia, which give beauty to the garden from spring until fall. Plant this garden in full sun.

lady's mantle

*20 ***Alchemilla mollis*** — LADY'S MANTLE
  3 ***Anthemia tinctoria*** — GOLDEN MARGUERITE
  9 ***Artemisia schmidtiana*** 'Silver Mound' — SILVER MOUND ARTEMISIA
  5 ***Callirhoe involucrata*** — POPPY MALLOW
 10 ***Chrysogonum virginianum*** — GREEN-AND-GOLD
  3 ***Echinacea purpurea*** — PURPLE CONEFLOWER
  6 ***Gaillardia* x *grandiflora*** 'Burgundy' — BLANKETFLOWER
  3 ***Gaura lindheimeri***
  3 ***Geranium sanguineum*** — CRANESBILL
 10 ***Liatris spicata*** 'Kobold' — BLAZING STAR
  3 ***Rudbeckia fulgida*** — BLACK-EYED SUSAN
  3 ***Sedum spectabile*** 'Autumn Joy' — STONECROP

*Numbers in list are total quantities needed.
Numbers in the diagram indicate the quantity to be planted in each individual space.

LONG-BLOOMING FLOWER GARDEN FOR A SMALL YARD

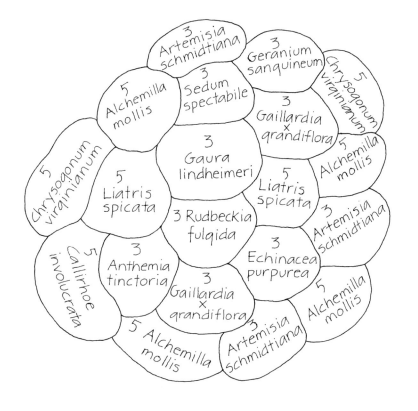

10' x 10'

0   1   2   4 feet

GARDEN FOR A DRY BED UNDER TREES

Barren, dry sites under large trees can become colorful gardens

The often dry, unsightly shady areas under trees like maples can become verdant and blossoming gardens with the addition of some ferns and other plants. This oval-shaped border can easily be adapted to your own site. Just remember that the taller plants, like the male fern, should be planted in the middle of the garden, and smaller plants, like the bird's-foot violet, should be cultivated at the edge of the bed. Plants with silver and green foliage, like the *Lamium* 'Beacon Silver' and variegated Solomon's seal, brighten gloomy areas. And the *Dicentra* 'Luxuriant', a perennial bleeding heart, provides a profusion of pink flowers all summer long. The *Helleborus corsicus* is a lovely evergreen perennial, almost like a bush. This variety of hellebore flowers very early in the year, and the blossoms, a lovely apple-green color, can last for up to eighteen weeks! Dainty drought-tolerant ferns, including maidenhair, are planted in bold clumps throughout this garden. Tiny hardy cyclamens add vivid splashes of color to the edges of this rounded flower bed.

*15 **Adiatum pedatum** — MAIDENHAIR FERN
  6 **Anemone hupehensis japonica** 'Queen Charlotte' — JAPANESE ANEMONE
  9 **Bergenia cordifolia**
 12 **Corydalis lutea** — YELLOW CORYDALIS
  5 **Cyclamen hederifolium**
  5 **Cyclamen purpurascens**
  6 **Dicentra eximia** 'Alba' — FRINGED BLEEDING HEART
  3 **Dicentra x** 'Luxuriant' — BLEEDING HEART
  6 **Digitalis grandiflora** — FOXGLOVE
 11 **Dryopteris felix-mas** — MALE FERN

  6 **Epimedium grandiflorum** 'Rose Queen'
  6 **Helleborus lividus corsicus** — CORSICAN HELLEBORE
  8 **Iris foetidissima** 'Lutea' — GLADWIN
 16 **Lamium maculatum** 'Beacon Silver' — DEAD NETTLE
  8 **Liriope muscari** 'Majestic' — LILY-TURF
  9 **Polygonatum odoratum thunbergii** 'Variegatum' — VARIEGATED SOLOMON'S SEAL
  9 **Polypodium virginianum** — ROCK POLYPODY
 15 **Viola pedata** — BIRD'S-FOOT VIOLET

*Numbers in list are total quantities needed.
Numbers in the diagram indicate the quantity to be planted in each individual space.

GARDEN FOR A DRY BED UNDER TREES

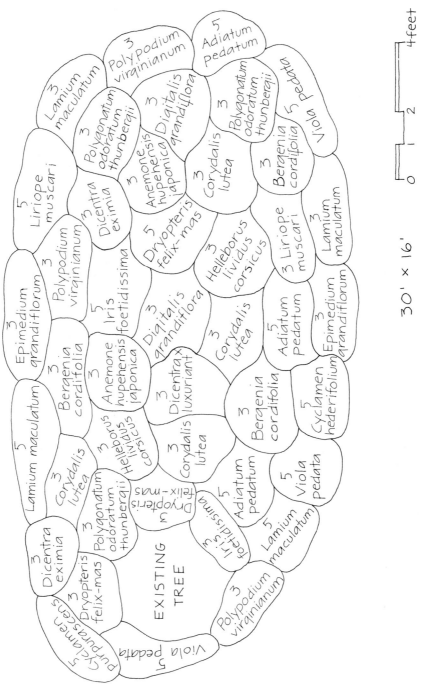

30' × 16'

0   1   2   4 feet

LARGE GARDEN FOR DAMP SOIL *Glorious flowers for a soggy landscape*

Home owners who have been frustrated in their attempts to create gardens with traditional flowers in areas of permanently damp soil should try this plan. A pathway meanders through the flower borders. Not only is this an attractive plan, but the path is also functional: nobody enjoys strolling through gardens with damp feet! The one tree included in this plan is a swamp cypress—a deciduous conifer that turns a lovely golden color in the fall. The leaves are very fine and do not litter the garden.

This damp-garden plan will provide interest for the whole growing season. In spring, the lovely yellow blossoms of marsh marigold unfold. Other early flowers include *Primula japonica,* which line the pathway. In May and early June, the 2-foot flowering spikes of the primulas bear whorls of blossoms, arranged in tiers. These flowers are indeed a spectacular sight in the sodden garden. Foliage plants, ferns, grasses, as well as many other perennials make this a spectacular garden. This is a plan for a sunny site.

*3 *Aconitum carmichaelii*—ACONITE, WOLFSBANE
3 *Acorus calamus*—SWEET FLAG
2 *Aruncus dioicus*—GOAT'S BEARD
9 *Astilbe chinensis* 'Pumila'
3 *Astilbe tacquetii* 'Superba'
6 *Caltha palustris*—MARSH MARIGOLD
6 *Eupatorium purpureum*—JOE-PYE WEED
6 *Glycera maxima* 'Variegata'—VARIEGATED MANNA GRASS
6 *Hosta* 'Frances Williams'
9 *Hosta* 'Gold Standard'
12 *Hosta sieboldiana* 'Elegans'
3 *Iris sibirica* 'Caesar's Brother'—SIBERIAN IRIS
6 *Ligularia stenocephala* 'The Rocket'
6 *Lobelia fulgens* 'Bee's Flame'
3 *Lobelia x vedrariensis*

6 *Mimulus cardinalis*—MONKEY MUSK
1 *Miscanthus sinensis* 'Variegatus'—VARIEGATED JAPANESE SILVER GRASS
2 *Miscanthus sinensis* 'Zebrinus'—ZEBRA GRASS
3 *Myosotis scorpioides*—FORGET-ME-NOT
2 *Osmunda regalis*—ROYAL FERN
9 *Peltiphyllum peltatum*—UMBRELLA PLANT
3 *Phalaris arundinacea picta*—RIBBON GRASS
12 *Polygonum* 'Border Jewel'
5 *Primula florindae*—HIMALAYAN COWSLIP
15 *Primula japonica*
1 *Rheum palmatum* 'Tanguticum'—ORNAMENTAL RHUBARB
3 *Rodgersia aesculifolia*
9 *Symphytum x uplandicum*—RUSSIAN COMFREY
1 *Taxodium distichum*—SWAMP CYPRESS

*Numbers in list are total quantities needed.
Numbers in the diagram indicate the quantity to be planted in each individual space.

LARGE GARDEN FOR DAMP SOIL

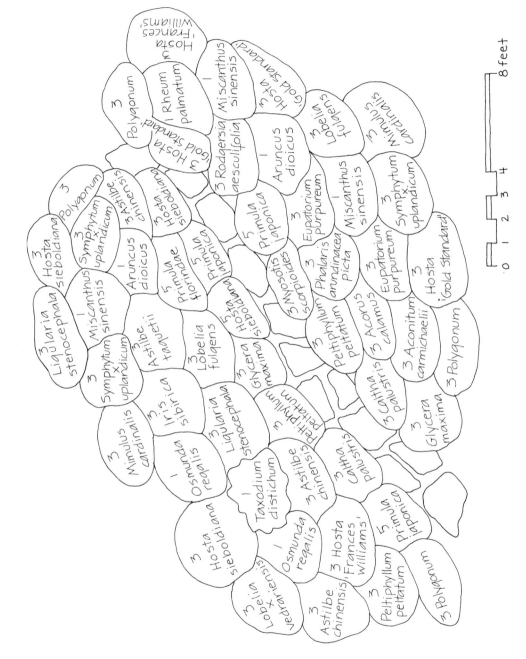

3 Hosta 'Frances Williams'

1 Rheum palmatum

3 Polygonum

3 Hosta 'Gold Standard'

3 Rodgersia aesculifolia

3 Miscanthus sinensis

1 Hosta 'Gold Standard'

1 Aruncus dioicus

3 Lobelia fulgens

3 Miscanthus sinensis

3 Mimulus cardinalis

3 Polygonum

3 Hosta sieboldiana

3 Symphytum x uplandicum

3 Astilbe chinensis

3 Hosta sieboldiana

5 Primula japonica

3 Eupatorium purpureum

3 Miscanthus sinensis

3 Symphytum x uplandicum

3 Ligularia stenocephala

1 Miscanthus sinensis

1 Aruncus dioicus

5 Primula florindae

5 Primula japonica

3 Eupatorium purpureum

3 Hosta 'Gold Standard'

3 Symphytum x uplandicum

1 Astilbe taquetii

3 Lobelia fulgens

5 Hosta sieboldiana

3 Myosotis scorpioides

3 Phalaris arundinacea 'Picta'

3 Eupatorium purpureum

3 Polygonum

3 Mimulus cardinalis

3 Iris sibirica

3 Ligularia stenocephala

3 Glyceria maxima

3 Peltiphyllum peltatum

3 Acorus calamus

3 Aconitum carmichaelii

3 Polygonum

1 Osmunda regalis

1 Taxodium distichum

3 Peltiphyllum peltatum

3 Caltha palustris

3 Glyceria maxima

3 Hosta sieboldiana

3 Lobelia vedrariensis

1 Osmunda regalis

3 Astilbe chinensis

3 Hosta 'Frances Williams'

5 Primula japonica

3 Astilbe chinensis

3 Caltha palustris

3 Peltiphyllum peltatum

3 Polygonum

SMALL GARDEN FOR A DAMP SITE *Graceful grasses and beautiful blooms for a damp garden site*

For a permanently damp site in the garden don't go to the expense of draining the soil—plant beautiful grasses and perennials that like damp feet. Flagstones provide access through this colorful island bed, and also keep your feet from getting wet! In the spring, the golden blossoms of marsh marigold will spill over the flagstones. For the whole summer, the tall banded leaves of the zebra grass rustle in the wind and delight you with their harlequin markings. The graceful foliage of the hosta adds a touch of elegance to this damp garden. And in summer, a walk through this border will be memorable as you inhale the fragrance of the sweet pepperbush. In late summer and early fall, nobody could possibly miss the deep blue spikes of the monkshood—this is one of the most magical of garden flowers.

*3 **Aconitum carmichaelii**—ACONITE, WOLFSBANE
1 **Aruncus dioicus**—GOAT'S BEARD
3 **Astilbe x arendsii** 'Fanal'
6 **Astilbe tacquetii** 'Superba'
3 **Caltha palustris**—MARSH MARIGOLD
1 **Clethra alnifolia** 'Pinkspire'—SWEET PEPPERBUSH
3 **Glycera maxima** 'Variegata'—VARIEGATED MANNA GRASS
3 **Hosta** 'Frances Williams'
6 **Hosta** 'Gold Standard'
3 **Iris sibirica** 'Caesar's Brother'—SIBERIAN IRIS
6 **Iris sibirica** 'Super Ego'—SIBERIAN IRIS
3 **Ligularia stenocephala** 'The Rocket'

6 **Lobelia cardinalis**—CARDINAL FLOWER
2 **Miscanthus sinensis** 'Zebrinus'—ZEBRA GRASS
3 **Monarda didyma** 'Cambridge Scarlet'—RED BERGAMOT
3 **Monarda didyma** 'Mahogany'
3 **Myosotis scorpioides**—FORGET-ME-NOT
1 **Myrica pensylvanica**—WAX MYRTLE
3 **Peltiphyllum peltatum**—UMBRELLA PLANT
6 **Polygonum** 'Border Jewel'
10 **Primula japonica**
3 **Rodgersia aesculifolia**
6 **Symphytum x uplandicum**—RUSSIAN COMFREY

*Numbers in list are total quantities needed.
Numbers in the diagram indicate the quantity to be planted in each individual space.

SMALL GARDEN FOR A DAMP SITE

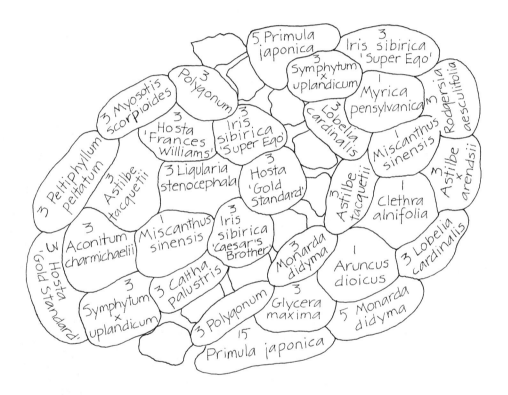

5 Primula japonica

3 Symphytum × uplandicum

3 Iris sibirica 'Super Ego'

1 Myrica pensylvanica

3 Rodgersia aesculifolia

3 Myosotis scorpioides

3 Polygonum

3 Lobelia cardinalis

3 Petiphyllum peltatum

3 Hosta 'Frances Williams'

3 Iris sibirica 'Super Ego'

1 Miscanthus sinensis

3 Astilbe × arendsii

3 Astilbe tacquetii

3 Ligularia stenocephala

3 Hosta 'Gold Standard'

3 Astilbe tacquetii

1 Clethra alnifolia

3 Hosta 'Gold Standard'

3 Aconitum charmichaelii

1 Miscanthus sinensis

3 Iris sibirica 'Caesar's Brother'

3 Monarda didyma

1 Aruncus dioicus

3 Lobelia cardinalis

3 Symphytum × uplandicum

3 Caltha palustris

3 Polygonum

3 Glycera maxima

5 Monarda didyma

15 Primula japonica

22' × 15'   0 1 2 3 4   8feet

SMALL GARDEN FOR A DAMP SITE

GRAND GARDEN *The ultimate garden of flowering perennials*

This is a large garden of flowering perennials and colorful foliage plants that is ideal for a sunny site. The plants chosen for this design make a strong statement in the landscape. In the middle of the island bed is a smoke tree. From late spring until late fall, this colorful tree is covered with rich purple leaves, and plumelike flowers appear in midsummer, giving it a cloudlike appearance. Colorful flowers and foliage plants form the basis of this design. Scotch thistle, a dramatic plant, adds architectural elegance for the whole season. A somewhat similar plant, the globe thistle, repeats this note at the other end of the garden. Other silver foliage plants, such as blue oats and 'Lambrook Silver' artemisia, provide blocks of silver in the design. Colorful perennials, including yarrow and peonies, contrast nicely with the silver foliage plants.

*5 *Achillea filipendulina* 'Coronation Gold' — YARROW
5 *Achillea taygetea* 'Moonshine' — YARROW
9 *Anaphalis triplinervis* — PEARLY EVERLASTING
6 *Artemisia absinthium* 'Lambrook Silver' — WORMWOOD
10 *Campanula carpatica* var. *alba* — WHITE CARPATHIAN HAREBELL
3 *Coreopsis verticillata* 'Moonbeam'
1 *Cotinus coggygria* 'Royal Purple' — SMOKE TREE
9 *Echinops ritro* — GLOBE THISTLE
10 *Euphorbia epithymoides* — CUSHION SPURGE
3 *Gypsophila paniculata* 'Bristol Fairy' — BABY'S BREATH
6 *Helictotrichon sempervirens* — BLUE OATS
9 *Lavandula angustifolia* 'Hidcote' — HIDCOTE LAVENDER
3 *Lupinus* Russell Hybrids — RUSSELL LUPINE

6 *Lythrum salicaria* 'Morden's Pink' — LOOSESTRIFE
6 *Nepeta faassenii* — CATMINT
6 *Onopordum acanthium* — SCOTCH THISTLE
1 *Paeonia* 'Sarah Bernhardt' — PEONY
3 *Papaver orientale* 'May Sadler' — ORIENTAL POPPY
3 *Phlox paniculata* 'Bright Eyes'
6 *Phlox paniculata* 'Mt. Fuji'
3 *Physostegia virginiana* — OBEDIENT PLANT
6 *Salvia argentia* — SILVER SAGE
3 *Salvia officinalis* 'Purpurea' — PURPLE SAGE
3 *Salvia x superba* 'East Friesland'
9 *Sedum spectabile* 'Autumn Joy' — STONECROP
3 *Solidago virgaurea* 'Golden Mosa' — GOLDENROD
10 *Stachys byzantina* — LAMB'S EARS
6 *Verbascum chaixii* 'Album'
1 *Yucca filamentosa* 'Bright Edge'

*Numbers in list are total quantities needed.
Numbers in the diagram indicate the quantity to be planted in each individual space.

GRAND GARDEN

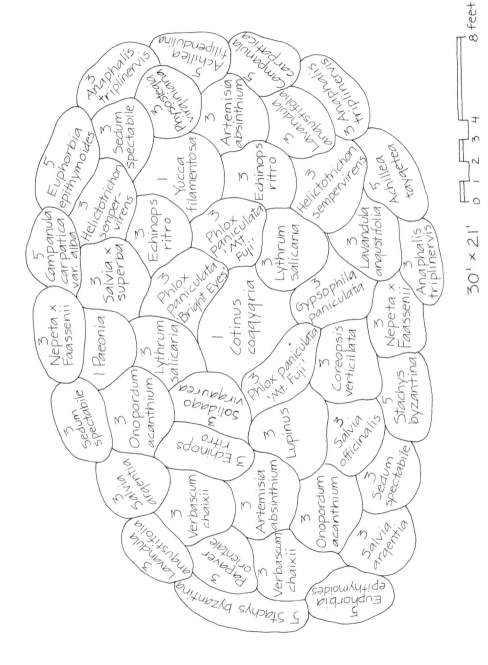

3 Anaphalis triplinervis
5 Achillea filipendulina
5 Campanula carpatica
5 Anaphalis triplinervis
5 Euphorbia epithymoides
3 Sedum spectabile
3 Physostegia virginiana
3 Artemisia absinthium
5 Lavandula angustifolia
3 Helictotrichon sempervirens
5 Achillea toyoetea
1 Yucca filamentosa
5 Echinops ritro
3 Campanula carpatica var. alba
5 Helictotrichon semper-virens
3 Echinops ritro
3 Salvia × superba
3 Phlox Paniculata 'Mt. Fuji'
3 Lythrum salicaria
3 Lavandula angustifolia
3 Anaphalis triplinervis
3 Nepeta × Faassenii
1 Paeonia
3 Phlox Paniculata 'Bright Eyes'
1 Cotinus coggygria
3 Gypsophila Paniculata
3 Nepeta × Faassenii
3 Lythrum salicaria
3 Coreopsis verticillata
5 Stachys byzantina
3 Sedum spectabile
3 Onopordum acanthium
3 Solidago virgaurea
1 Phlox Paniculata 'Mt. Fuji'
3 Salvia officinalis
3 Salvia argentea
3 Echinops ritro
3 Lupinus
3 Sedum spectabile
3 Verbascum chaixii
3 Artemisia absinthium
3 Onopordum acanthium
3 Salvia argentea
3 Lavandula angustifolia
3 Papaver orientale
3 Verbascum chaixii
5 Euphorbia epithymoides
5 Stachys byzantina

30' × 21'

0 1 2 3 4   8 feet

GRAND GARDEN

FALL GARDEN *Flowers that guarantee an Indian summer*

This design will enhance the autumnal garden with vivid late-blooming flowers. The island bed contains perennials that start blooming in summer and continue until fall. Many of these perennials, like *Coreopsis* 'Moonbeam' and *Achillea* 'Moonshine', flower for an incredibly long time. Plant this border where it will have the most effect, and when your neighbors' gardens are faded and dull, you will be enjoying blooms as late as November. This flower bed is for an area of full sun.

*15 ***Achillea taygetea*** 'Moonshine'—YARROW
  3 ***Aconitum carmichaelii***—ACONITE, WOLFSBANE
  6 ***Agapanthus umbellatus*** Headborne Hybrids—
    AFRICAN LILY
 10 ***Anemone hupehensis japonica*** 'September
    Charm'—JAPANESE ANEMONE
 10 ***Asclepias tuberosa***—BUTTERFLY MILKWEED
  9 ***Aster x frikartii*** 'Wonder of Staffa'—
    MICHAELMAS DAISY
  3 ***Aster novae-angliae*** 'Harrington's Pink'—NEW
    ENGLAND ASTER
  6 ***Boltonia asteroides*** 'Snowbank'
  1 ***Caryopteris x clandonensis***
  5 ***Ceratostigma plumbaginoides***—BLUE
    PLUMBAGO
  6 ***Coreopsis verticillata*** 'Moonbeam'
  6 ***Hemerocallis*** (any late-season red variety)
  3 ***Hemerocallis*** (any late-season yellow variety)

  3 ***Kniphofia uvaria*** 'Pfitzeri'—TORCH LILY
  3 ***Physostegia virginiana***—OBEDIENT PLANT
  9 ***Sedum spectabile*** 'Autumn Joy'—STONECROP
  5 ***Solidago virgaurea*** 'Golden Mosa'—
    GOLDENROD
  6 ***Stokesia laevis***—STOKE'S ASTER
  3 ***Stokesia laevis*** 'Alba'—STOKE'S ASTER
  3 ***Verbascum chaixii*** 'Album'

goldenrod

*Numbers in list are total quantities needed.
Numbers in the diagram indicate the quantity to be planted in each individual space.

FALL GARDEN

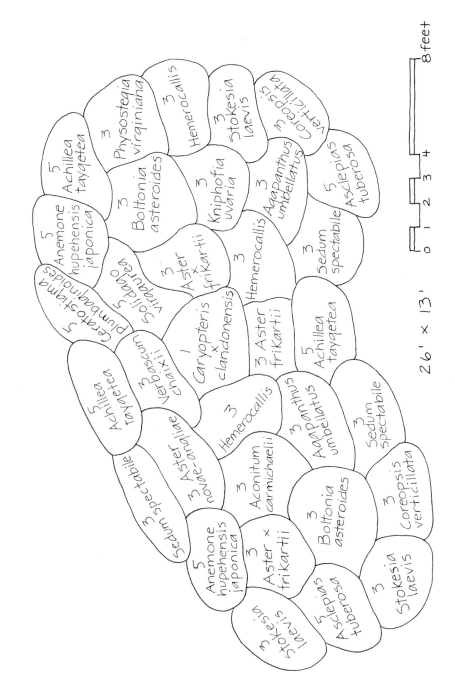

Achillea
taygetea
5

Anemone
hupehensis
japonica
5

Ceratostigma
plumbaginoides
5

Solidago
viragurea
5

Physostegia
virginiana
3

Boltonia
asteroides
3

Aster ×
frikartii
3

Hemerocallis
3

Hemerocallis
3

Stokesia
laevis
3

Kniphofia
uvaria
3

Caryopteris ×
clandonensis
1

Aster
frikartii
3

Agapanthus
umbellatus
3

Coreopsis
verticillata
3

Asclepias
tuberosa
5

Sedum
spectabile
3

Achillea
taygetea
5

Achillea
taygetea
5

Verbascum
chaixii
3

Hemerocallis
3

Agapanthus
umbellatus
3

Sedum
spectabile
3

Sedum spectabile
3

Aster
novae-angliae
3

Aconitum
carmichaelii
3

Boltonia
asteroides
3

Coreopsis
verticillata
3

Anemone
hupehensis
japonica
5

Aster ×
frikartii
3

Asclepias
tuberosa
5

Stokesia
laevis
3

Stokesia
laevis
3

26' × 13'

0 1 2 3 4   8 feet

TWIN ISLAND BEDS FOR A SUNNY SITE *Floral color in the sun*

This twin island plan not only invites strolling around the flower beds but also presents lovely views from all directions. The design combines flowers that have attractive blooms with those grown for the beauty of their foliage. *Nicotiana alata* 'Lime Green' is included in one of the borders. Although this plant is an annual, it will reseed itself. The emerald flowers release an exhilarating evening perfume, and the blossoms appear all summer long and continue until late fall. This design is for a site that has full sun.

*8 **Achillea ptarmica** 'The Pearl' — YARROW
10 **Ajuga reptans** 'Silver Beauty' — CARPET BUGLE
8 **Alchemilla mollis** — LADY'S MANTLE
6 **Artemisia canescens**
5 **Artemisia schmidtiana** 'Silver Mound' — SILVER MOUND ARTEMISIA
3 **Asclepias tuberosa** — BUTTERFLY MILKWEED
3 **Coreopsis grandiflora** 'Goldfink'
6 **Coreopsis verticillata** 'Moonbeam'
6 **Echinops ritro** — GLOBE THISTLE
6 **Geranium** x 'Johnson's Blue' — CRANESBILL
6 **Gypsophila paniculata** 'Bristol Fairy' — BABY'S BREATH
3 **Hemerocallis** 'Bright Banner'
3 **Hosta** 'Frances Williams'
6 **Hosta** 'Hadspan Blue'
3 **Kniphofia uvaria** 'Royal Standard' — TORCH LILY
3 **Lilium regale** — REGAL LILY
10 **Lobelia cardinalis** — CARDINAL FLOWER

3 **Mentha gentilis** 'Variegata' — GINGER MINT
10 **Nicotiana alata** 'Lime Green' — NIGHT-SCENTED TOBACCO
12 **Origanum vulgare** 'Aureum' — GOLDEN MARJORAM
6 **Penstemon barbatus** 'Prairie Fire' — BEARD'S TONGUE
6 **Polygonatum** 'Border Jewel' — BISTORT
10 **Solidago virgaurea** 'Golden Dwarf' — GOLDENROD

carpet bugle

*Numbers in list are total quantities needed.
Numbers in the diagram indicate the quantity to be planted in each individual space.

TWIN ISLAND BEDS FOR A SUNNY SITE

32' × 16'

8 feet

135

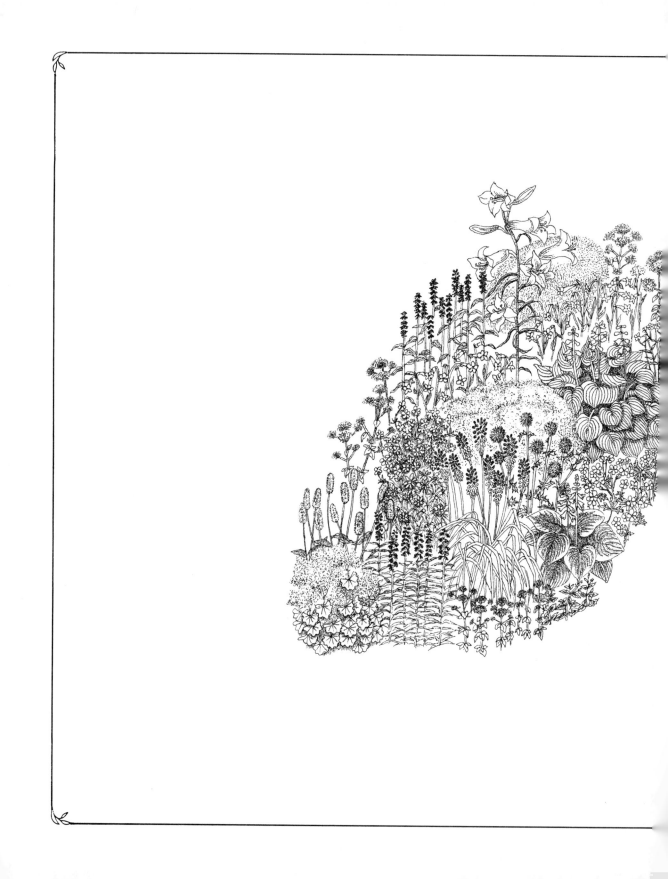

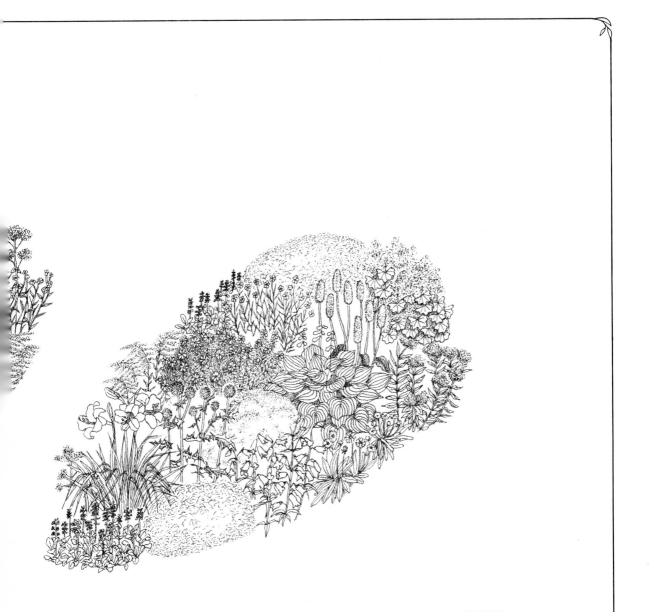

TWIN ISLAND BEDS FOR A SUNNY SITE

SPRING GARDEN *A garden full of the loveliest spring flowers*

After a long hard winter many people are impatient for the arrival of spring. This island garden contains some of the earliest and prettiest of spring flowers. At the center of the design a star magnolia is featured. In April and May, before the leaves appear, star-shaped white flowers cover this magnolia. Two *Hamamelis* 'Arnold Promise', a very early blooming variety of witch hazel, are also included in the plan. In some milder areas this tree will blossom in February. The flowers are quite a sight, each bloom consisting of masses of bright yellow ribbon-like petals. Some of the earliest flowers in this design are the double snowdrops—which are intermixed with plantings of *Viola labradorica*, a low-growing early-flowering violet. Although this garden is at its height in the spring, many of the flowers will also bloom in summer. And many of the early-blooming perennials will reflower in the fall.

*3 ***Alchemilla mollis*** — LADY'S MANTLE
6 ***Aquilegia chrysantha*** 'Silver Queen' — COLUMBINE
6 ***Aquilegia longissima*** 'Maxistar' — COLUMBINE
14 ***Bergenia cordifolia***
6 ***Corydalis lutea*** — YELLOW CORYDALIS
3 ***Dicentra eximia*** 'Alba' — FRINGED BLEEDING HEART
9 ***Dicentra*** x 'Luxuriant' — BLEEDING HEART
5 ***Doronicum caucasicum*** — LEOPARD'S BANE
9 ***Euphorbia epithymoides*** — CUSHION SPURGE
20 ***Galanthus nivalis*** 'Flore-Pleno' — DOUBLE SNOWDROP
13 ***Galium odoratum*** — SWEET WOODRUFF
6 ***Geranium*** x 'Johnson's Blue' — CRANESBILL
9 ***Geum*** x ***Borisii*** — AVENS

2 ***Hamamelis*** x ***intermedia*** 'Arnold Promise' — WITCH HAZEL
3 ***Iris pumilla*** — DWARF IRIS
3 ***Iris sibirica*** 'White Swirl' — SIBERIAN IRIS
1 ***Magnolia stellata*** — STAR MAGNOLIA
6 ***Mertensia virginica*** — VIRGINIA BLUEBELL
12 ***Polemonium caeruleum*** — JACOB'S LADDER
3 ***Polygonatum odoratum thunbergii*** 'Variegatum' — JAPANESE VARIEGATED SOLOMON'S SEAL
9 ***Pulmonaria saccharata*** 'Argentea' — SILVER LUNGWORT
6 ***Trillium grandiflorum*** — WHITE TRILLIUM
6 ***Trollius*** x ***cultorum*** 'Etna' — GLOBEFLOWER
10 ***Viola cucullata*** 'Freckles' — VIOLET
12 ***Viola labradorica*** — LABRADOR VIOLET

*Numbers in list are total quantities needed.
Numbers in the diagram indicate the quantity to be planted in each individual space.

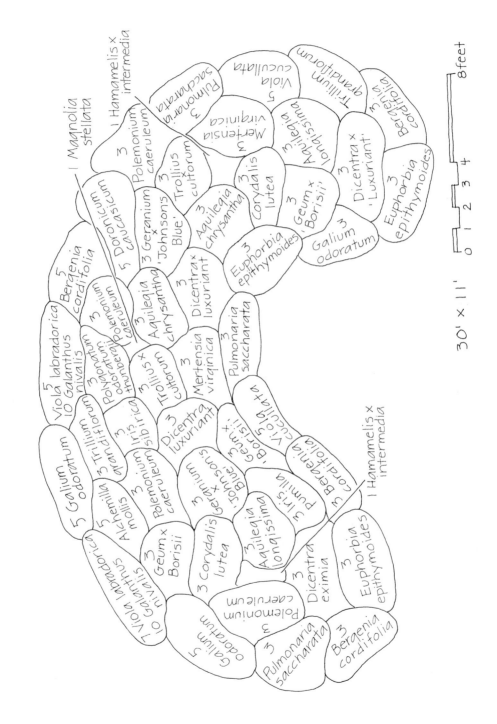

SPRING GARDEN

1 Magnolia stellata

1 Hamamelis × intermedia

3 Polemonium caeruleum

3 Pulmonaria saccharata

5 Trollius cultorum

3 Mertensia virginica

5 Viola cucullata

3 Aquilegia canadensis

1 Trillium grandiflorum

3 Bergenia cordifolia

3 Aquilegia chrysantha

3 Corydalis lutea

3 Geum × Borisii

3 Dicentra × 'Luxuriant'

3 Euphorbia epithymoides

3 Galium odoratum

5 Bergenia cordifolia

5 Doronicum caucasicum

5 Bergenia cordifolia

3 Geranium × 'Johnson's Blue'

3 Polemonium caeruleum

3 Aquilegia chrysantha

3 Dicentra × luxuriant

3 Euphorbia epithymoides

5 Galanthus nivalis

5 Viola labradorica

3 Polygonatum odoratum thunberaji

3 Trollius cultorum

3 Mertensia virginica

3 Pulmonaria saccharata

5 Galium odoratum

5 Alchemilla mollis

3 Trillium grandiflorum

3 Iris sibirica

3 Polemonium caeruleum

3 Dicentra luxuriant

3 Geum × 'Borisii'

3 Viola cucullata

3 Bergenia cordifolia

7 Viola labradorica

10 Galanthus nivalis

3 Geum × Borisii

3 Corydalis lutea

3 Geranium × 'Johnson's Blue'

3 Aquilegia longissima

3 Iris pumila

3 Dicentra eximia

3 Euphorbia epithymoides

5 Galium odoratum

3 Polemonium caeruleum

3 Pulmonaria saccharata

3 Bergenia cordifolia

1 Hamamelis × intermedia

30' × 11'

0 1 2 3 4   8 feet

SPRING GARDEN

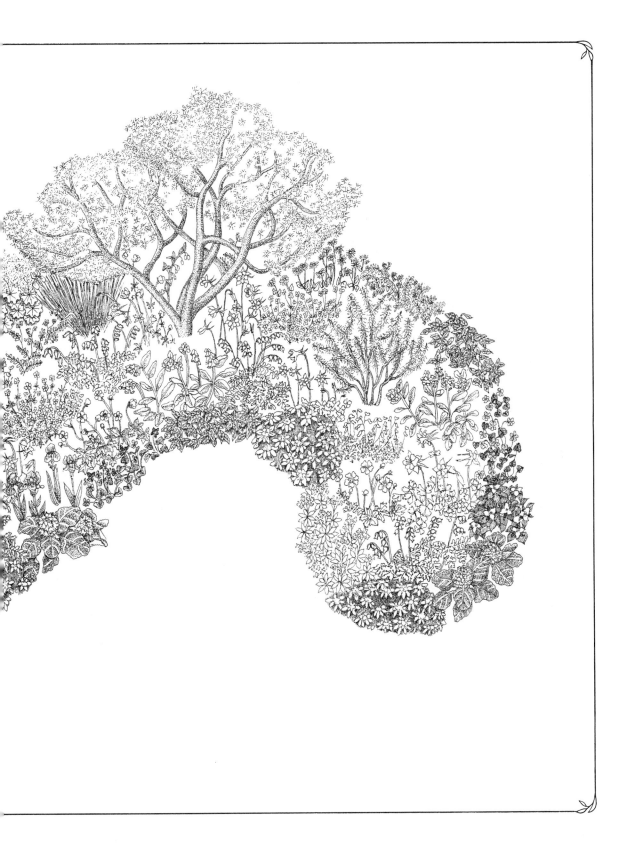

SEASIDE GARDEN *Seaside greenery for every season*

This plan of an enclosed garden is perfect for the front yard of a small beach house. A picket fence, covered at the front with climbing roses, surrounds the flowers and lawn. Against the house, two lovely trees — perfectly at home by the seaside — give height to the rear of the garden. The Russian olive bears silvery leaves and casts light shade. The other tree, the tamarisk, has delicate feathery leaves and in August, is covered with beautiful pink blossoms. Even when mature these trees are small, so they will not be overbearing when planted near a house. The moonlight broom, included by the fence in this design, will enhance the entrance. Many of the flowers chosen for this garden are foliage plants and grasses — artemisia, silver oats, miscanthus, and heather will provide beauty for much of the year. The other flowers were selected because they have long blooming seasons and because they thrive in maritime gardens. This is a garden plan for an open sunny site.

*6 *Alcea rosea* (red) — HOLLYHOCK
3 *Armeria maritima* 'Dusseldorf Pride' — SEA PINK
3 *Artemisia ludoviciana* 'Silver King' — SILVER KING ARTEMISIA
7 *Artemisia schmidtiana* 'Silver Mound' — SILVER MOUND ARTEMISIA
5 *Aurinia saxatilis* — BASKET-OF-GOLD
5 *Calluna vulgaris* 'H. E. Beale' — HEATHER
3 *Chrysanthemum maximum* 'Polaris' — SHASTA DAISY
2 *Cytisus x praecox* 'Moonlight' — MOONLIGHT BROOM
1 *Elaeagnus angustifolia* — RUSSIAN OLIVE
3 *Eryngium amethystinum*
3 *Eryngium giganteum*
3 *Helictotrichon sempervirens* — BLUE OATS
3 *Hemerocallis* 'Christmas Carol' — DAYLILY
3 *Hemerocallis* 'Constitution Island' — DAYLILY

3 *Hibiscus moscheutos* — ROSE MALLOW
3 *Hosta* 'Hadspan Blue'
3 *Lavandula angustifolia* — ENGLISH LAVENDER
5 *Limonium latifolium* — SEA LAVENDER
3 *Miscanthus sinensis* 'Purpurascens'
3 *Monarda didyma* 'Cambridge Scarlet' — RED BERGAMOT
1 *Myrica pensylvanica* — WAX MYRTLE
3 *Nepeta x faassenii* — CATMINT
1 *Pinus mugo var. mughus* — MUGO PINE
1 *Rosa banksiae* — BANKSIA ROSE
1 *Rosa* 'Climbing Cecile Brunner' — ROSE
6 *Santolina virens* — GREEN SANTOLINA
6 *Saponaria officinalis* 'Rosea-Plena' — SOAPWORT
3 *Sedum spectabile* 'Autumn Joy'
5 *Stachys byzantina* — LAMB'S EARS
1 *Tamarix ramosissima* 'Rosea' — TAMARISK

*Numbers in list are total quantities needed.
Numbers in the diagram indicate the quantity to be planted in each individual space.

SEASIDE GARDEN

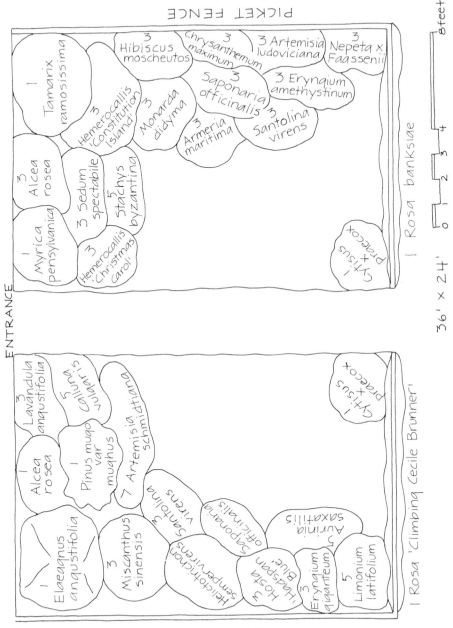

PICKET FENCE

ENTRANCE

1 Tamarix ramosissima

3 Hemerocallis 'Constitution Island'

Hibiscus moscheutos

3 Chrysanthemum maximum

3 Monarda didyma

3 Saponaria officinalis

3 Artemisia ludoviciana

3 Nepeta x Faassenii

3 Eryngium amethystinum

3 Armeria maritima

3 Santolina virens

3 Alcea rosea

3 Sedum spectabile

5 Stachys byzantina

Myrica pensylvania

3 Hemerocallis 'Christmas Carol'

Cytisus x praecox

1 Rosa banksiae

36' x 24'

8 feet
0 1 2 3 4

3 Lavandula angustifolia

3 Calluna vulgaris

7 Artemisia schmidtiana

Alcea rosea

1 Pinus mugo var mughus

Elaeagnus angustifolia

3 Miscanthus sinensis

3 Helictotrichon sempervirens

3 Santolina virens

3 Saponaria officinalis

3 Hosta 'Hadspen Blue'

3 Aurinia saxatilis

3 Eryngium giganteum

5 Limonium latifolium

Cytisus x praecox

1 Rosa 'Climbing Cecile Brunner'

PICKET FENCE

143

GARDEN OF FLOWERS FOR CUTTING

A lovely garden for enjoying outside, or for cutting and enjoying inside!

Flowers for cutting are too often grown in straight rows or are even hidden away in an odd corner of the vegetable garden. This plan is an attractive garden containing some of the best flowers for indoor arrangements—blossoms that last a long time when cut. Many of the perennials chosen are also suitable for drying. For flower-arranging enthusiasts, this garden will provide an abundant supply of some of the most beautiful foliage and blossoms.

*3 *Achillea filipendulina* 'Coronation Gold'—
  YARROW
9 *Achillea ptarmica* 'The Pearl'—YARROW
6 *Achillea taygetea* 'Moonshine'—YARROW
6 *Agapanthus umbellatus* 'Headborne Hybrids'—
  AFRICAN LILY
3 *Alchemilla mollis*—LADY'S MANTLE
3 *Artemisia lactiflora*—GHOST PLANT
3 *Artemisia ludoviciana* 'Valerie Finnis'
3 *Aster x frikartii* 'Wonder of Staffa'—
  MICHAELMAS DAISY
3 *Aster novae-angliae* 'Harrington's Pink'—NEW
  ENGLAND ASTER
3 *Astrantia major* 'Margery Fish'—MASTERWORT
9 *Briza media*—QUAKING GRASS
3 *Campanula percisifolia* 'Telham Beauty'—
  PEACH-LEAVED BELLFLOWER
5 *Catanache caerulea*—CUPID'S DART
3 *Centaurea macrocephala*—PERENNIAL
  CORNFLOWER
3 *Chrysanthemum maximum* 'Polaris'—SHASTA
  DAISY
3 *Coreopsis grandiflora* 'Sunburst'
3 *Delphinium* Belladonna Hybrids
3 *Dianthus x allwoodii* 'Doris'—CARNATION
3 *Echinops ritro*—GLOBE THISTLE
3 *Eryngium giganteum*
3 *Geum chiloense* 'Fire Opal'—AVENS

3 *Gypsophila paniculata* 'Bristol Fairy'—BABY'S
  BREATH
3 *Helianthus x multiflorus* 'Flore Pleno'—
  PERENNIAL SUNFLOWER
3 *Iris sibirica* 'Caesar's Bother'—SIBERIAN IRIS
3 *Iris sibirica* 'Super Ego'—SIBERIAN IRIS
3 *Kniphofia uvaria* 'Pfitzeri'—TORCH LILY
3 *Liatris spicata*—SPIKE GAYFEATHER
9 *Limonium latifolium*—SEA LAVENDER
6 *Lupinus* Russell Hybrids—LUPINE
9 *Lychnis chalcedonica*—MALTESE CROSS
3 *Monarda didyma* 'Cambridge Scarlet'—RED
  BERGAMOT
6 *Monarda didyma* 'Croftway Pink'—PINK
  BERGAMOT
6 *Nepeta x faassenii*—CATMINT
1 *Paeonia* 'Charlie's White'—PEONY
2 *Paeonia* 'Sarah Bernhardt'—PEONY
1 *Papaver orientale* 'Curlilocks'—ORIENTAL POPPY
1 *Papaver orientale* 'May Sadler'—ORIENTAL
  POPPY
3 *Phlox paniculata* 'Mt. Fuji'—PHLOX
3 *Phlox paniculata* 'Starfire'—PHLOX
3 *Physalis alkekengi*—CHINESE LANTERN
2 *Rosa polyantha* 'The Fairy'—ROSE
6 *Sedum spectabile* 'Autumn Joy'
3 *Solidago virgaurea* 'Golden Mosa'—GOLDENROD
3 *Stokesia laevis*—STOKE'S ASTER

*Numbers in list are total quantities needed.
 Numbers in the diagram indicate the quantity to be planted in each individual space.

GARDEN OF FLOWERS FOR CUTTING

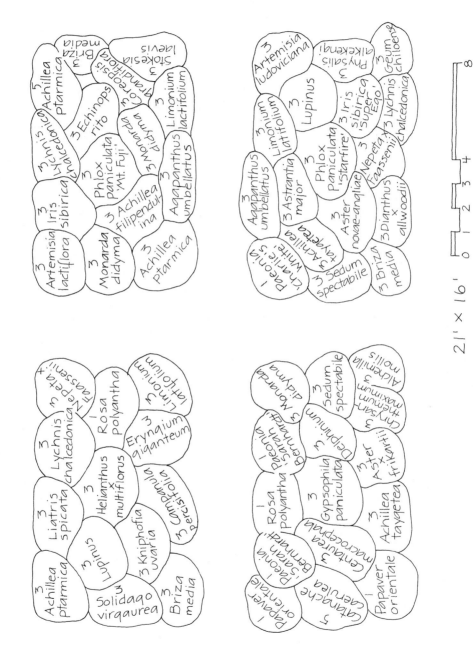

21' × 16'

145

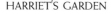

HARRIET'S GARDEN *A low-maintenance garden that can survive without pampering*

Harriet Choice, editor for "Garden Varieties," my syndicated garden column, is a weekend gardener. Her garden gets only periodic maintenance, and in summer it may not get any water other than what nature provides. This makes it difficult to plant the more fussy perennials. Harriet wanted a low-maintenance garden that includes plants with lovely blossoms. This is the plan I came up with. *Phlox subulata* give this garden a bright fanfare in the spring. Colorful blossoms continue well into fall, when *Sedum* 'Autumn Joy' and *Achillea* 'Moonshine' give an autumnal lushness to this easy-care garden. The lovely American native poppy mallow flowers from early summer until late fall with a minimum of care. As if that were not enough, the blossoms of poppy mallow are a lovely port-wine crimson. The evergreen foliage of *Yucca* 'Bright Edge' provides interest all through the season. This is also the perfect garden for people with "black thumbs." Harriet's garden is best in a sunny site.

daylily

*8 ***Achillea taygetea*** 'Moonshine' — YARROW
 3 ***Anthemis tinctoria*** — GOLDEN MARGUERITE
 6 ***Asclepias tuberosa*** — BUTTERFLY MILKWEED
16 ***Callirhoe involucrata*** — POPPY MALLOW
 6 ***Chrysopsis mariana*** — GOLDEN ASTER
16 ***Euphorbia epithymoides*** — CUSHION SPURGE
 3 ***Gaillardia x grandiflora*** 'Burgundy' —
    BLANKETFLOWER
 3 ***Hemerocallis*** 'Lamplighter' — DAYLILY
 5 ***Phlox subulata*** 'Emerald Blue' — MOSS PINKS
 5 ***Phlox subulata*** 'Pink Surprise' — MOSS PINKS
 5 ***Phlox subulata*** 'Red Wings' — MOSS PINKS
 6 ***Platycodon grandiflorus*** — BALLOON FLOWER
 3 ***Platycodon grandiflorus*** 'Alba' — BALLOON
    FLOWER
 9 ***Sedum spectabile*** 'Autumn Joy' — STONECROP
 3 ***Yucca filamentosa*** 'Bright Edge'

*Numbers in list are total quantities needed.
 Numbers in the diagram indicate the quantity to be planted in each individual space.

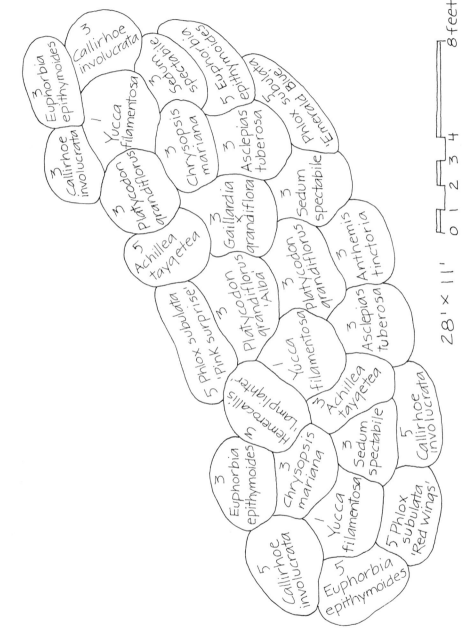

HARRIET'S GARDEN

3 Euphorbia epithymoides

3 Callirhoe involucrata

3 Callirhoe involucrata

1 Yucca filamentosa

3 Platycodon grandiflorus

5 Achillea taygetea

5 Phlox subulata 'Pink surprise'

3 Sedum spectabile

3 Chrysopsis mariana

3 Gaillardia x grandiflora

3 Platycodon grandiflorus 'Alba'

5 Euphorbia epithymoides

3 Asclepias tuberosa

3 Sedum spectabile

3 Platycodon grandiflorus

5 Phlox subulata 'Emerald Blue'

3 Anthemis tinctoria

3 Asclepias tuberosa

3 Euphorbia epithymoides

3 Hemerocallis 'Lamplighter'

1 Yucca filamentosa

3 Achillea taygetea

5 Callirhoe involucrata

3 Chrysopsis mariana

3 Sedum spectabile

5 Phlox subulata 'Red wings'

5 Callirhoe involucrata

1 Yucca filamentosa

5 Euphorbia epithymoides

28' × 11'

0 1 2 3 4   8 feet

FRAGRANT GARDEN   *Day and night, from late spring until fall, this garden will be sweetly scented*

Flowers are lovely, but if they are sweetly scented then they are indeed treasured. This little garden is surrounded by a simple wooden fence which allows climbing roses, wisteria, and sweet autumn clematis to ramble and ultimately to enclose the area. You will walk through the entrance and be overpowered with color and fragrance. A bench is provided in case you feel faint with delight! Two plants positioned near this wooden seat, night-scented tobacco and *Datura*, exhale their perfume in the evening. No garden could be more romantic. In May, you will be able to sit in the shade of the lilac, and both your eyes and your nose will be stimulated by its blossoms. Planted in the center of the grass are two lovely scented roses. And as if that were not enough, they are surrounded by perfumed violets. The entrance to this garden is "guarded" by a couple of sweetshrubs *(Calycanthus)*. These old favorites exude a spicy fragrance that will remind you of your grandmother's garden.

*6 ***Artemisia abrotanum*** — SOUTHERNWOOD
2 ***Calycanthus floridus*** — SWEETSHRUB
2 ***Clematis maximowicziana*** — SWEET AUTUMN CLEMATIS
6 ***Daphne cneorum*** — GARLAND FLOWER
2 ***Datura chlorantha***
6 ***Dianthus x allwoodii*** 'Doris' — CARNATION
12 ***Hemerocallis*** 'Hyperion' — DAYLILY
10 ***Hesperis matronalis*** — DAME'S VIOLET
6 ***Lavandula angustifolia*** — ENGLISH LAVENDER
12 ***Lilium regale*** — REGAL LILY
10 ***Lobularia maritima*** — SWEET ALYSSUM
1 ***Lonicera japonica*** 'Halliana' — HALL'S JAPANESE HONEYSUCKLE
10 ***Matthiola bicornis*** — NIGHT-SCENTED STOCK

6 ***Monarda didyma*** 'Cambridge Scarlet' — RED BERGAMOT
7 ***Nicotiana alata*** 'Lime Green' — NIGHT-SCENTED TOBACCO
4 ***Paeonia*** 'Sara Bernhardt' — PEONY
6 ***Phlox paniculata*** 'Bright Eyes'
6 ***Phlox paniculata*** 'Everest'
2 ***Ribes odoratum*** — CLOVE CURRANT
1 ***Rosa*** 'Chrysler Imperial' — ROSE
1 ***Rosa*** 'Climbing Etoile de Hollande' — ROSE
1 ***Rosa*** 'Madame Alfred Carriere' — ROSE
1 ***Rosa*** 'Madame Isaac Pereire' — ROSE
1 ***Syringa vulgaris*** 'Lavender Lady' — LILAC
24 ***Viola odorata*** — SWEET VIOLET
1 ***Wisteria sinensis*** — CHINESE WISTERIA

*Numbers in list are total quantities needed.
Numbers in the diagram indicate the quantity to be planted in each individual space.

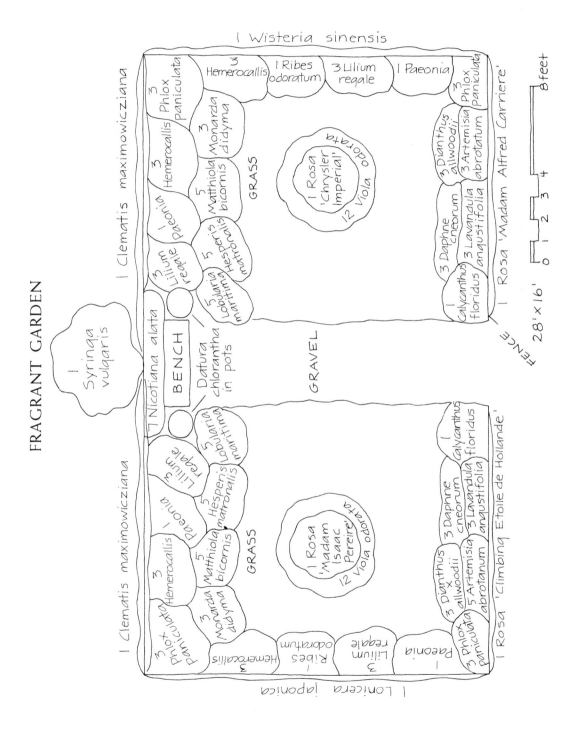

FRAGRANT GARDEN

SILVER GARDEN   *A silver garden to add rich elegance to the landscape*

If you have a sunny corner in your landscape, you might want to cultivate this garden of silver-leaved perennials. This collection of plants will provide enjoyment for the whole growing season. *Miscanthus sinensis* 'Variegatus' is featured in the center. This is a tall, stately grass that grows up to 7 feet and has elegant foliage striped with silver. Clustered around this two-tone grass is a collection of silver-leaved plants. In the four corners, plants of Scotch thistle make an imposing and beautiful statement. Crushed white marble chips set off these plants to their full advantage. This is a garden for a sunny site.

*6 *Achillea taygetea* 'Moonshine' — YARROW

10 *Allium caeruleum*

6 *Artemisia absinthium* 'Lambrook Silver' — WORMWOOD

16 *Artemisia schmidtiana* 'Silver Mound' — SILVER MOUND ARTEMISIA

12 *Echinops ritro* — GLOBE THISTLE

6 *Festuca ovina glauca* — BLUE FESCUE

2 *Gypsophila paniculata* 'Bristol Fairy' — BABY'S BREATH

6 *Helictotrichon sempervirens* — BLUE OATS

1 *Miscanthus sinensis* 'Variegatus' — VARIEGATED JAPANESE SILVER GRASS

4 *Onopordum acanthium* — SCOTCH THISTLE

6 *Ruta graveolens* — RUE

12 *Salvia argentia* — SILVER SAGE

6 *Salvia officinalis* — SAGE

6 *Santolina chamaecyparissus* — COTTON LAVENDER

12 *Stachys byzantina* — LAMB'S EARS

*Numbers in list are total quantities needed.
Numbers in the diagram indicate the quantity to be planted in each individual space.

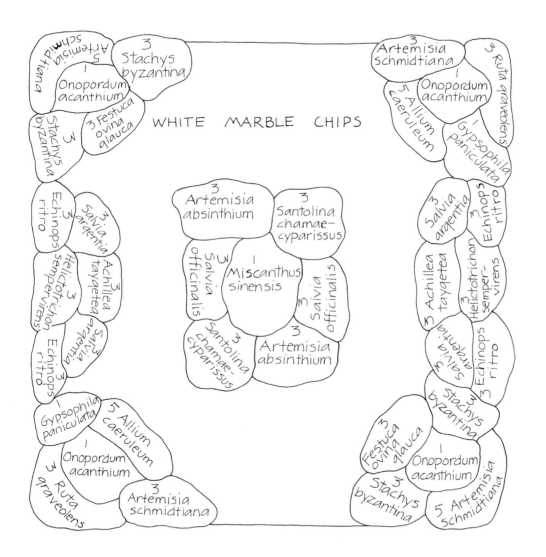

SILVER GARDEN

Artemisia schmidtiana

3 Stachys byzantina

5 Artemisia schmidtiana

1 Onopordum acanthium

3 Stachys byzantina

3 Festuca ovina glauca

WHITE MARBLE CHIPS

3 Artemisia schmidtiana

1 Onopordum acanthium

5 Allium caeruleum

3 Ruta graveolens

1 Gypsophila paniculata

3 Echinops rittro

3 Salvia argentia

3 Achillea tayaetea

3 Salvia argentia

3 Helictotrichon sempervirens

3 Echinops rittro

1 Gypsophila paniculata

5 Allium caeruleum

1 Onopordum acanthium

3 Ruta graveolens

3 Artemisia schmidtiana

3 Artemisia absinthium

3 Santolina chamae-cyparissus

3 Salvia officinalis

1 Miscanthus sinensis

3 Salvia officinalis

3 Santolina chamae-cyparissus

3 Artemisia absinthium

3 Salvia argentia

3 Achillea tayaetea

3 Helictotrichon sempervirens

3 Echinops rittro

3 Echinops rittro

3 Salvia argentia

3 Stachys byzantina

3 Festuca ovina glauca

1 Onopordum acanthium

3 Stachys byzantina

5 Artemisia schmidtiana

20' × 20'   0 1 2 3 4   8 feet

 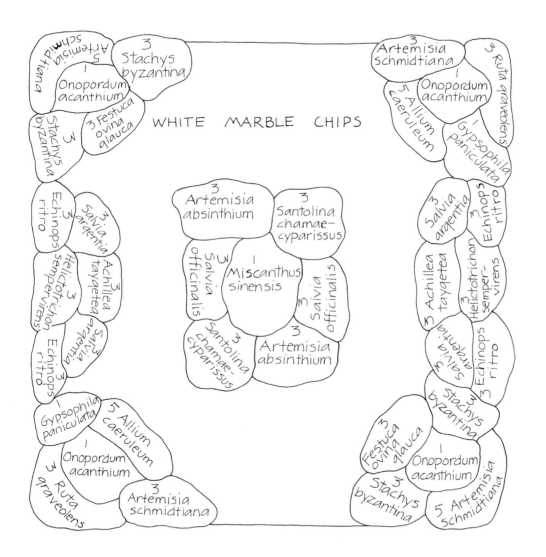

SILVER AND GOLD GARDEN *A rare combination of silver and gold blossoms and leaves*

This garden will be outstanding in any landscape. In the center is the long-blooming golden marguerite — a perennial that is literally covered with golden flowers for most of the summer. *Berberis* 'Aurea', one of the loveliest small shrubs, is covered from spring until fall with leaves that look as if they were made from beaten gold. Two sections of this plan contain *Salvia argentia*, with foliage the color of spun silver. This garden will provide enjoyment for much of the year, since the outstanding gold or silver leaves of these plants emerge in spring and last until the fall. This garden should be planted in full sun.

*6 **Achillea filipendulina** 'Coronation Gold' — YARROW

3 **Anthemis tinctoria** 'Moonlight' — GOLDEN MARGUERITE

3 **Artemisia canescens**

3 **Artemisia ludoviciana** 'Silver King' — SILVER KING ARTEMISIA

5 **Artemisia schmidtiana** 'Silver Mound' — SILVER MOUND ARTEMISIA

3 **Berberis thunbergii** 'Aurea' — GOLDEN BARBERRY

6 **Euphorbia epithymoides** — CUSHION SPURGE

6 **Gypsophila paniculata** 'Bristol Fairy' — BABY'S BREATH

10 **Lamiastrum galeobdolon** 'Herman's Pride'

5 **Lamium maculatum** 'White Nancy' — DEAD NETTLE

3 **Onopordum acanthium** — SCOTCH THISTLE

10 **Origanum vulgare** 'Aureum' — GOLDEN MARJORAM

3 **Ruta graveolens** — RUE

6 **Salvia argentia** — SILVER SAGE

3 **Salvia officinalis** 'Icterina' — GOLDEN SAGE

marjoram

*Numbers in list are total quantities needed.
Numbers in the diagram indicate the quantity to be planted in each individual space.

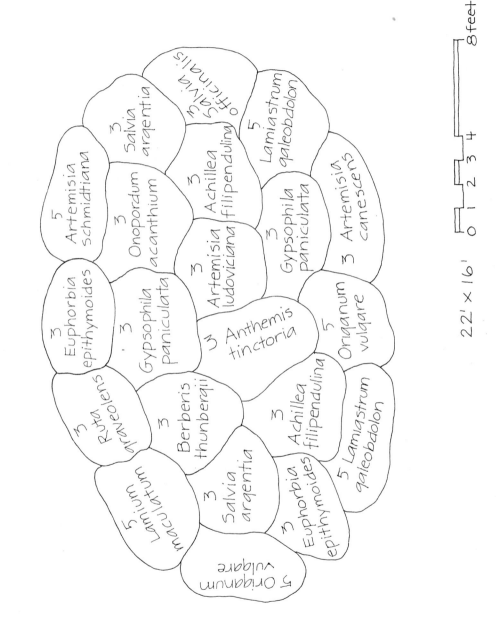

SILVER AND GOLD GARDEN

5 Artemisia schmidtiana

3 Salvia argentia

5 Salvia officinalis

5 Lamiastrum galeobdolon

3 Onopordum acanthium

5 Achillea filipendulina

3 Artemisia canescens

3 Gypsophila paniculata

3 Euphorbia epithymoides

3 Gypsophila paniculata

3 Artemisia ludoviciana

5 Gypsophila paniculata

3 Anthemis tinctoria

5 Origanum vulgare

3 Ruta graveolens

3 Berberis thunbergii

3 Achillea filipendulina

5 Lamiastrum galeobdolon

5 Lamium maculatum

3 Salvia argentia

3 Euphorbia epithymoides

5 Origanum vulgare

22' × 16'

0 1 2 3 4 8 feet

153

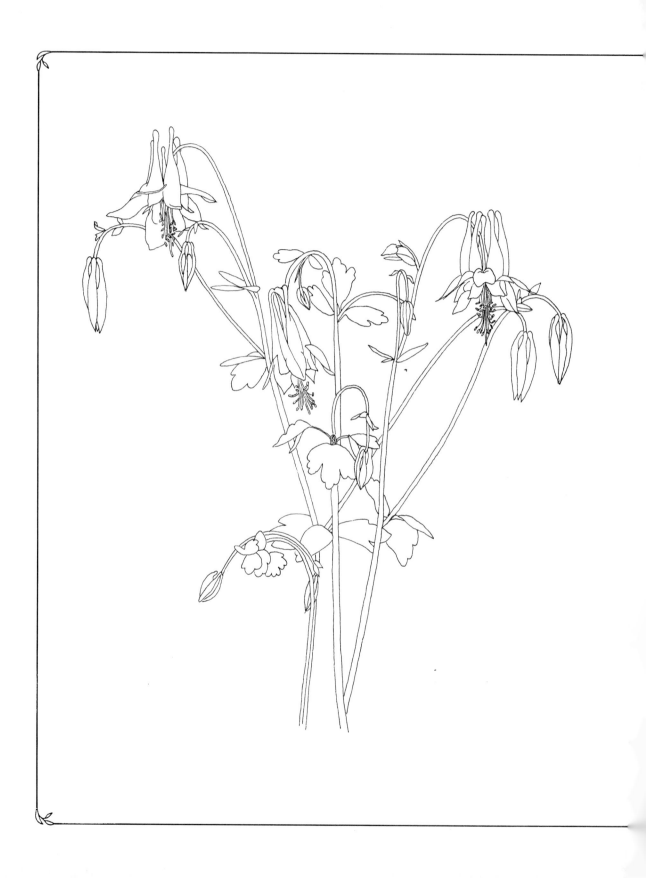

Chapter Four

THE WILD-FLOWER GARDEN

"The whole success of wild gardening depends on arranging bold
natural groups with a free hand." (*William Robinson*)

FROM COAST TO COAST naturalistic landscaping and its integral component, the wild-flower garden, are rapidly gaining popularity. For many
home owners these new gardens are a refreshing alternative to the manicured lawns and coiffured look of formal landscapes. Unfortunately, some
people think of a natural garden as little more than the unkempt yard of an
abandoned house. Others see it as a Rousseau landscape, rich and verdant,
with a sense of natural mystery. The basic elements of an informal garden
are maintenance-free ground covers, random plantings of annual and perennial flowers, and groupings of native or exotic trees. The primary objective
is to make the landscape look natural. If this is successful, the gardener's
handiwork is not apparent, as the authors of *Garden Design* explain: "Unlike
their Oriental counterpart, where nature is abstracted, the wild or woodland
garden celebrates the genius of the place—of nature's forms unchanged. Consequently, these gardens are both modest and romantic in their attitudes, for
rather than improving nature, the wild garden accentuates nature."

Naturalistic landscapes are especially appealing because the mind conjures
up promises of lush native-plant gardens that are care-free. The reality, however, is another matter. Native plants will not take care of themselves, especially when they are first established. Gertrude Jekyll, one of the great pioneers of naturalistic landscaping, stated: "Wild flower gardening is a
delightful, and in good hands a most desirable pursuit, but no kind of gardening is so difficult to do well, or is so full of pitfalls and of paths of peril.
Because it has in some measure become fashionable, and because it is under-
stood to mean the planting of exotics in wild places, unthinking people rush

to the conclusion that they can put any garden plants into any wild places, and that is wild gardening." This cautionary advice is as appropriate today as it was at the end of the nineteenth century. Perhaps more so, considering how many people now enjoy gardening. When designing a wild-flower garden one of the most important goals is to achieve a harmonious marriage between the natural features of the landscape and the plant material selected. The garden will be deemed a success if after completion and maturity it does not seem contrived, but looks as though it was the work of nature.

A naturalistic landscape can be comprised of other material besides native plants. When admitting an exotic species or cultivar into a wild setting, make sure that the new introduction is compatible with the harmony of the overall landscape. Remember, every plant, tree, and shrub is native to some region on earth, but when cultivated in another area, horticulturists generally call it an "exotic." It is a good policy to select exotic species from the same genus as the wild plants that you already have growing in a naturalistic landscape. Even if their native lands are far apart, different species from the same family generally look good when grown together. But make sure that the majority of plants used in the design are native to your particular area. The advantage of using local species is the fact that many are resistant to indigenous pests and diseases.

American wild flowers comprise a vast group—some attractive, some not. In the latter category are the so-called weeds, like dandelions and plantain, plants that we see in great abundance in both town and country. In the other category are many of the familiar flowers of garden borders, which are in fact native American plants. Goldenrod, aster, cosmos, coneflower, blanket-flower, and rudbeckia are all perennials indigenous to this continent. Many other flowers we consider American natives, like yarrow, Queen Anne's lace, oxeye daisy, and scarlet pimpernel, are in fact introductions from foreign lands. These plants found the soil and climate here so suitable that in a few centuries they have become some of the commonest wild flowers growing in the United States.

One of the attractive qualities of wild-flower gardens is the fact that once established, they are inexpensive and easy to maintain. But to achieve a stabilized landscape, careful planning and preparation must be made. Thought must be given to the plants selected. The chosen flowers and trees must be species that not only blend with the particular landscape but are suitable to the soil, light, and moisture conditions of the garden. For novices at wild-flower gardening, it might be best mainly to choose plants that are native to the region. Prevailing conditions of the garden should dictate the types of wild flowers selected from local flora. For instance, if you have sandy well-drained soil, choose species that thrive in dry conditions. Yucca, penstemon, poppy mallow, or blazing star would be appropriate. Conversely, if you have a heavy clay or poorly drained soil, you might consider growing wild flowers that are native to damp regions. Turtlehead, elephant head, cardinal flower, iris, and meadow beauty would be good choices.

Wild flowers can also be problem solvers for your garden. For example, if you have a hot spot in your yard—a south-facing dry slope or a sun-baked court—you might consider growing native plants from the arid regions of the American Southwest. Plants to consider would be desert mallow, desert marigold, or southwestern verbena. As wild-flower expert Henry Art suggests, when cultivating native plants, take direction from nature:

> In the east you might want to try planting jack-in-the-pulpit, wild ginger, spring beauty, trout lily, Dutchman's breeches, Solomon's seal, bloodroot, and trilliums in a deciduous woodland setting. In the Midwest, prairie species such as lead plant, butterfly weed, rattlesnake master, gayfeather, purple prairie clover, and purple coneflower mixed with appropriate native grasses create a stunning natural garden. Likewise the addition of goldfields, tidy tips, western shooting star, blazing star, golden stars, and blue dicks to grasslands on the West Coast mimics the natural landscape.

If these precautions are heeded, and if extra care is taken with upkeep for a couple of years after planting, from then on the wild-flower garden will require only periodic maintenance.

After researching the growing conditions on your particular site (soil type, shade areas, sun areas, wet areas, and so forth), start making a list of the wild flowers that can be cultivated there. A trip to a local botanical garden will

bloodroot

greatly help to decide what native species to select. When you have had some experience growing indigenous plants, you might want to be a little daring. Plants such as blue dicks, Indian pink, bitterroot, and golden stars are native to regions that have wet winters and springs but dry summers. During the hottest months of the year these plants become dormant. When grown in some of the eastern regions of the United States these perennials are susceptible to rot. To cultivate wild flowers that require summer drought in regions of high humidity it is necessary to cover the plants with plastic sheeting or glass just after they have become dormant. This protection keeps the underlying soil drier than that of the surrounding regions. Such horticultural experimentation is always worthwhile.

When growing wild flowers, a bit of daring can be rewarding. William Brumback, the plant propagator at the New England Wild Flower Society, once told me that if a plant doesn't do well in one spot, he tries it somewhere else, even in a place where he doesn't expect it to thrive. You never know!

Many people enjoy having both a formal garden and a naturalistic landscape. This can be achieved by confining the formal plantings to the area immediately around the house and establishing naturalistic areas farther away. The lawn can provide a gentle transition between the two zones. Near the house and the formal plantings, a close-cut lawn would be appropriate, while farther away a slightly shaggy lawn could gently merge into a wild-flower meadow. A number of these plans are presented in this chapter.

For converts to naturalistic landscaping the resources available today are excellent. All manner of native plants and seeds can be ordered from retail suppliers—including many species that have become scarce in the wild. With a little preparatory work, a rather uninteresting and time-consuming lawn can be converted into a flowery mead. Even barren and unproductive land can be transformed into a place of beauty. An old orchard, an overgrown shrub border, or a building lot that is supporting some trees can be converted into a woodland garden carpeted with a tapestry of wild flowers. Once established, wild gardens take much less maintenance than their formal counterparts. With so many pluses we may ask ourselves why it has taken so long for naturalistic plantings to become popular. Well, like any other art form, wild-flower gardening needed pioneer horticulturists who would champion its use in the domestic landscape. Years of proselytizing have at last succeeded—wild-flower gardens have become fashionable.

Naturalistic gardens are not an invention of the moment. They have an ancient history. The medieval period provides us with some of the first descriptions of wild-flower gardens. In the Middle Ages the basic type of landscape was the flowery mead. These flower-speckled meadows, usually enclosed, were created by planting wild flowers among low-growing grasses. One of the earliest descriptions of a "wild garden" was given by Boccaccio, the famous fourteenth-century Italian author. In the *Decameron*, Boccaccio mentions an extraordinary garden: "a plot of ground like a meadow, the grass of a deep green, spangled with a thousand different flowers." By looking at depictions in medieval art it seems that medieval "lawns" were fragrant carpets made by growing aromatic and sweetly scented herbs and wild flowers among the grasses. Geoffrey Chaucer, in the *Legend of Good Women*, provides us with a word picture of one of these delightful gardens.

> Upon the small, soft, sweet grass,
> That was with flowers sweet embroidered all,
> Of such sweetness, and such odor overall.

snowdrops

The landscape of the Middle Ages eventually changed. By the Renaissance the gardens of Europe had undergone a drastic metamorphosis. Flowery meads were abandoned and the garden evolved into a geometric landscape of knots and parterres. But some legacy of the wild gardens in the Middle Ages survived the vacillations of Renaissance fashion. A charming account of a flowery mead is preserved in the writings of Francis Bacon, the noted Elizabethan statesman and scientist. In his famous essay on gardens, Bacon suggested that at least one third of the garden heath (the wild part of the garden) should be "framed as much as possible to a natural wildness." He recommended that selected plants, such as primroses, violets, and strawberries, should be planted in the heath "here and there, not in any order." Other plants for this meadow were to be cultivated in "little heaps, in the nature of mole hills, to be set with wild thyme . . . pinks, germander, periwinkle, cowslips, daisies, bear's foot, and lily of the valley."

strawberry

After the Renaissance, the formal concepts of the French landscape gained popularity. Wild gardens all but vanished in Europe. Under the formidable hand of landscape architects such as Le Nôtre—master planner for the grounds of Versailles—"mere flowers" (let alone wild flowers) had no place in elegant gardens. English landscape architect Humphrey Repton later described the demise of naturalistic gardens in the seventeenth century: "Under the guidance of Le Nôtre and his disciples, the taste for nature in landscape gardening was totally banished or concealed by the work of art."

The "English landscape" movement of the eighteenth century was the next major innovation of garden architects. In this reaction against the formal landscapes of the French, proponents of the Romantic landscape advocated a return to naturalistic garden design. Humphrey Repton described his century's precepts for the ideal landscape: "In defining the shape of land or water we take nature as our model, and the highest perfection of landscape gardening is to imitate nature so judiciously that the influence of art shall never be detected." This philosophy—that all nature was a garden—gave rise to gardens that looked as though they always had been an intrinsic part of nature. The far-reaching influence of the Romantic landscape movement has been commented upon by a number of garden historians, including the authors of *Garden Design:* "As gardens became more natural and informal [in the eighteenth century], the geometry of previous landscapes was transposed into city planning throughout Europe and America. [And] it would not be until the middle and late nineteenth century that the informal, romantic notions of late eighteenth century English gardens would find their way into civic and residential planning."

In the nineteenth century, the English landscape movement lost its influence and a new style called the "gardenesque" evolved. The principal personality behind the gardenesque was a Scot named John Loudon. This new fashion stressed individual botanical specimens in sparse plantings. Anne Scott-James explains the gardenesque principle: "All the flowers were to bear individual scrutiny. . . . Loudon pressed for the cultivation of exotics, rarities and plants which were difficult to grow, especially the new species which were pouring in from all over the world. He wanted the maximum of variety in the garden and thought that a native [plant] was never as good as a foreign one." Although the gardenesque was a rather prim and formal approach to the landscape, it was at least tinged with some elements from the earlier naturalistic landscape movement of the eighteenth century.

The next period in garden history, the High Victorian, is yet another matter. The general refinement of the greenhouse, the improvements in heating these structures, and the ban in 1830 of the infamous British "glass tax" meant that every English estate and every middle-class gardener could afford a hothouse. Unfortunately these efficient greenhouses were used to raise outlandish plants. Coleus, pelargoniums, and lobelias—all in the most garish colors—were grown in astonishing numbers. And as soon as mild weather prevailed, these exotics were literally crammed into flower borders, geometric beds, and parterres. With no sense of color combination, the effect was nightmarish! Every new exotic grown under glass was placed in the garden along with all other botanical novelties. To make room for these tender new plants, other perennials—flowers that had been the backbone of the garden for years—were dug up and cast aside. This awful practice did have its critics, and one of the strongest was William Robinson, a self-educated Irishman who along with Gertrude Jekyll became a leading figure in late-nineteenth-century garden design. Robinson described this destruction of established perennials as a "rooting out of all the old favorites," further adding that "it was not uncommon to find the largest gardens in the country without a single hardy flower, all energies being devoted to the few exotics for the summer decoration."

In one of Robinson's best books, *The Wild Garden*, the author describes how a naturalistic garden could be made by establishing exotics in a wild English landscape. He wanted to show "how we may have more of the varied beauty of the hardy flowers than the most ardent admirer of the old style of gardening ever dreams of, by naturalizing many beautiful plants in our fields, outer parts of our pleasure grounds and in neglected places in almost every kind of garden. . . . They are the lilies, and bluebells, and foxgloves, and irises, and wild flowers, and columbines, and violets, and crane's-bills, and count-less pea-flowers, and moon daisies, and brambles, and cinquefoils, and evening primroses, and clematis, and honeysuckles, and Michaelmas daisies, and bindweeds, and forget-me-nots, and blue omphalodes, and primroses, and daylilies, and asphodels, and myriads of plants which form the flora of the northern or temperate regions of vast continents." Robinson's prolific writing did much to reeducate people about tasteful garden design. By the 1880s, the cluttered, garish, and vulgar gardens of the High Victorian period were waning in popularity. And under the direction of visionaries like Robinson and Jekyll, interest in wild gardens was once again established.

Today's wild-flower gardener can be inspired by reading English authors like Jekyll and Robinson, and also has the advantage of being able to purchase wild plants or seeds from more places in the world than those pioneers dreamed of!

WILD-FLOWER MEADOWS

Today one of the most popular forms of naturalistic landscaping is the wild-flower meadow. In ecological circles, "meadow" is a term applied to grassland which receives a high level of rainfall. Much of the eastern part of the United States contains typical meadow land. Prairies, on the other hand, are usually associated with dry areas in the Midwest. Various types of prairies exist—they are determined by the amount of moisture retained in the soil. For midwestern gardeners, many companies offer seed mixtures suitable to specific areas of the prairie belt (see the Suppliers list). Prairie seed mixes also do well in the gardens of eastern states, as do English wild-flower mixes. Southwestern plants need a hot dry summer, and therefore seeds of these species generally do not do well in the eastern states unless some special precautions are taken. For example, in my own wild-flower garden in Connecticut, I tried to grow the lovely Texas bluebonnet, but always with disappointing results.

Meadow gardens are a pleasant alternative to lawns. In my opinion, they present a more aesthetic approach to the domestic landscape. Once established, a flowery mead will require little maintenance—a sharp contrast to the traditional lawn. And a wild-flower meadow has the ecological bonus of attracting and being beneficial to wildlife. These flower-speckled fields are making a great impression on the American landscape, even in some unlikely areas. In Waukesha, Wisconsin, General Electric's Medical Systems replaced a large lawn with a prairie. The savings in maintenance cost is staggering. The lawn was annually costing General Electric $1500 per acre, whereas the prairie now can be maintained for only $25 per acre! In the summer of 1985, curators at the Storm King Art Center in Mountainville, New York, had the ingenious idea of presenting an Isamu Noguchi sculpture exhibition in a wild-flower meadow. In another instance, an important nationwide program called "Operation Wild Flower" is being sponsored by the federal government, state highway agencies, and the Council of State Garden Clubs. Started in 1973, this worthy project proposes to establish wild flowers along the highways and roads of America. It's nice to see leaders in government, art, and industry taking an interest in wild-flower gardens.

Meadows are the ideal choice for areas of full sun and poor soil—they will not do well in the shade. As with any garden installation, a meadow does not preclude maintenance. Upkeep entails pulling up certain unattractive or pernicious species of wild flowers. Dock, chickweed, and bindweed need to be eradicated. Like many plant sites in nature, the meadow is one stage in an ecological progression that ultimately culminates in a hardwood forest. Therefore be mindful, especially if you plant your meadow near woodland, to remove any maple, ash, or oak seedlings. Saplings will inevitably appear from time to time. If you don't remove them, in no time your carefully planted meadow will turn into a youthful woodland, and the meadow flowers, which need full sun, will not survive the competition from the young trees.

Before any serious thought is given to planting a wild-flower meadow, check with your local authorities. In some residential areas this particular kind of landscape is forbidden. If this is the case, you can get around this situation by a compromise. Plant the area open to public view with a more formal landscape, and behind the house (hidden from general view) cultivate a wild-flower meadow. And if over a number of years your flowery mead encroaches upon the formal garden, the gradual transformation of the whole landscape into a wild garden is not likely to be noticed—especially if it is well designed! The initial cost may be on the high side when you remove a lawn and establish a wild-flower meadow, but what you save on annual lawn maintenance will soon offset the cost, not to mention the time and drudgery saved by not having to mow a lawn in summer.

There are a number of approaches to installing a wild-flower meadow. The first thing to determine is your soil type (see Chapter One). Then before actually planting or seeding, great care should be taken to ensure that the soil is properly prepared and all perennial weeds are removed. (Methods for preparing the site are discussed in detail in Chapter One.)

Geographic location is going to determine the species of wild flowers that will do best in your garden. Commercial companies offer various seed mixes designed for different geographical areas. The term "wild-flower mixture" can be a very ambiguous description. These formulas contain seeds from both annual and perennial plants, sometimes even from garden hybrids. In some instances seeds are selected from plants that have a "wild-flower look." Many mail-order companies promise the gardener a meadow in about ninety days. Sure, this is possible – especially if the seed mixture is derived from annuals – but after a spectacular initial season, results the following year can be very disappointing, This is because many of these mixtures contain large quantities of seed from Europe, supplemented with seed collected in the western regions of the United States. In many parts of the country, plants grown from this supply will not set seed, or if they do, the scattered seed will not tolerate a harsh winter. Many of these commercial mixes contain seeds of plants not native to North America. And in some instances, the resulting annuals and perennials can be particularly invasive. Even some North American plants, when grown in another area, can become a nuisance and completely take over a wild-flower meadow. Avoid seed mixes, for instance, that contain *Tradescantia virginiana* (spiderwort) or *Lythrum salicaria* (purple loosestrife). Good seed mixes contain annuals that will give a colorful and prolonged display in the first year and perennials that will mature and impose a different and more permanent array of blossoms on the landscape in the second year.

Potential wild-flower meadow enthusiasts should heed the advice given by David Longland, Garden Director of the Garden in the Woods (New England Wild Flower Society): "Growing a meadow or naturalized lawn from a seed mixture can be difficult over large areas. Germination can be patchy if the seeded area is not properly prepared or watered, and it may take months or even years for seeds to become well established plants. Indigenous weeds can overtake meadow-mix seedlings, so this method often meets with dire results." Longland suggests sowing seed mixes in plots of less than 1000 square feet. Gardening in smaller areas allows for control of undesirable plants.

As early-blooming plants mature much quicker than later-flowering spe-

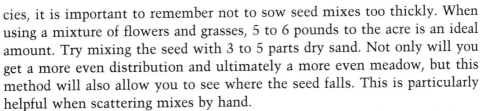

cies, it is important to remember not to sow seed mixes too thickly. When using a mixture of flowers and grasses, 5 to 6 pounds to the acre is an ideal amount. Try mixing the seed with 3 to 5 parts dry sand. Not only will you get a more even distribution and ultimately a more even meadow, but this method will also allow you to see where the seed falls. This is particularly helpful when scattering mixes by hand.

Some seed needs a cold period before it will germinate. These special germination requirements have been developed by plants over thousands of years. Chemical inhibitors ensure that each species germinates during optimum climatic conditions. Seeds from many northeastern American plants need a cold treatment before they will germinate—the lovely New England aster is an example. And even some northern species that do not require a definite cold treatment have higher germination rates when subjected to a winter freeze. Goldenrods are in this category. Therefore when sowing seeds selected for the Northeast, scatter them in the fall. Seed mixes for milder areas can be dispersed in the spring. The California poppy is a native of the West Coast of America. In its natural environment it is a perennial, but in colder areas like the Northeast, the California poppy has to be treated as an annual.

You will be able to exercise some control over the type of annuals that are going to be present in your wild-flower meadow: The first year, determine which flowers you like best and let these go to seed. Cut the seed heads off the flowers you don't like. Next year, your favorite annuals will appear in greater abundance.

Another method for establishing a meadow—one that is considered the best by the experts at the New England Wild Flower Society—is to plant mature wild flowers in a cleared area and sow native grass seed between the perennials. This grass seed is selected from species that have thin turf density and low growth. They bind the soil and act as a ground cover that suppresses weeds—including the aggressive species of grasses. Grasses have their own beauty which adds to the display of any wild-flower meadow, and the tall graceful stems give support for many wild flowers that would otherwise require staking. The following grasses are nonaggressive and will not crowd out flowers: little bluestem, sideoats grama, wild oats, June grass, and northern dropseed.

In early spring, clear the plot of ground, and as soon as all weeds are eradicated, plant selected native perennials. One plant every 3 to 4 square feet is ideal. After the flowers are in place, sow the grass seed over the entire area at double the recommended rate (25 pounds per acre). Make sure that the whole area is watered well during the next few weeks. (Summer watering is also important, especially during periods of drought.) If you need a design to work with, use the plan for the Prairie Garden or for the Sunny Wild-Flower Meadow. These gardens have a high density of wild flowers. To economize you could follow the layout but decrease the number of plants to one flower in each segment.

When planting a large meadow, using mature plants can be expensive. The alternative is to grow your own wild flowers from seed. If you decide to do this, clear the meadow site in early spring and sow native grass seed over the entire area at double the recommended rate. During the same month, or earlier if you have a greenhouse, sow selected wild flowers in flats. When the seedlings are large enough, they can be planted in individual pots or can be cultivated in rows in a part of the garden that acts as a temporary nursery. An ideal location is a section of the vegetable garden. After cultivating with a rototiller or hand-digging the chosen area, cover the soil with sheets of black plastic. This is a cheap and effective way of suppressing weeds. The wild-flower seedlings are then planted by making incisions into the plastic sheeting. By the fall you will have dozens of assorted plants, more than enough for a large meadow. The wild flowers can then be planted among the grass, either in the fall or in the following spring. Remember to plant small flowers at the front of the meadow and the taller ones either at the back or in the middle. A path can be made through the meadow by cutting with a lawn mower. Once established, the whole area will be a dense mass of grasses and wild flowers. Two mowings a year will be all the maintenance necessary. Cut the meadow at the end of the growing season, and leave the mowings where they fall. These not only supply mulch but also contain seeds that will germinate the next year. An early spring mowing helps to clear away any stubble left the previous November and scatters any remaining seeds. Some people enjoy the winter-dried flowers and grasses, and so for aesthetic reasons they cut their meadow only in the spring. If you decide to make one annual spring cutting, do it early, and make sure that last year's dried flower stalks are chopped up very fine. (A heavy layer of mulch will not have time to rot down and could impede the growth of early flowers.)

Favorite annuals and even some spring bulbs can be added to the meadow.

Early bulbs and flowers will not object to having later-blooming plants growing over them. Experiment with a wild-flower meadow. You will certainly have the time! Make a photographic record of your flowery mead, and keep accounts of any dull patches. These spots can be brightened by the addition of more flowers, planted in either the autumn or the following spring.

If for any reason you cannot get the ground cleared and sown with grasses early enough in the spring, then wait until fall. Native grasses do much better if planted in cool and moist weather conditions. Perennials can be planted anytime in the prepared ground, but if you plant these wild flowers in the summer, make sure that you water generously during the first season. In late fall, sow grass seed and cover the entire area with a half-inch layer of salt marsh hay. (This can be ordered from most garden centers.) When established, the grasses will comprise about two thirds of the meadow. If for any reason there is a delay between clearing the ground and planting the perennials and wild grass seed, then a temporary cover of annual rye grass or buckwheat can be used to protect the area from weed invasion until permanent species are planted.

Areas prone to erosion, such as steep hillsides and banks, can be planted with wild-flower meadows by establishing a temporary binding ground cover of oats. This is a method devised by Marie Sperka, an expert wild-flower grower. In August, gently rake the slope, and then for every 100 square feet spread 10 pounds of 10-10-10 commercial fertilizer. (The fertilizer helps the oats to become quickly established on the incline.) Next, broadcast oat seed over the whole area. Then lay a moderate mulch of salt marsh hay over the seeded slope. Wet the whole area with a gentle spray from a hose. (Heavy watering will just wash away the raked soil, seed, and fertilizer.) Finally, tamp down the whole area with a lawn roller. Or if you don't have one of these tools use a wooden board and apply compression by standing on the board. If your slope is in a very windy area, it would be advisable to take the precaution of pegging down the straw. Being planted in August, the oats will have too short a growing season to set seed. (If they were planted any earlier, the seed would mature and the oats would be a weed problem in next year's meadow.) By winter the dead stalks will be packed down by rain and snow, and next spring you will be able to insert wild-flower and grass seed into the oat mulch. Do not use rye seed because it will survive the winter and be a nuisance next year.

WOODLAND GARDENS

"To me a woodland garden is a garden made in a woodland setting, with most of the interloping undergrowth cleared away and the better woodland plants used where they can be seen without the clutter of ranker subjects." *(Margery Fish, 1964)*

As Margery Fish suggests, to create a wooded garden the first task is to remove pernicious brambles and rank undergrowth. This initial clearing will make room for choice small trees and shrubs. Overcrowding can make trees thin and spindly, and dense woodland will not allow enough light to reach plants and ferns that grow upon the forest floor. So thin out the woods, removing young trees and saplings and reserving the healthiest and most perfectly formed specimens. If there are oaks in the forest, keep as many as possible. These are ideal trees for growing among woodland flowers because their roots go far down into the soil and do not compete with shallow-rooted wild flowers. Oaks also give shade to these plants, and the dead leaves provide a good source of humus for the forest floor. To prevent any cut stumps from resprouting, either destroy them with a chemical stump killer or cut the tree to ground level and remove the bark to at least 3 inches below the ground. If you are attempting to create a woodland garden around a new house and want to save as many trees as possible from the ungentle hands of construction crews, make sure that heavy equipment is not driven over the roots of the existing trees. Do not let contractors dump piles of excavated soil around the trunks of trees. If all the trees are removed from a building site it will make life easy for the contractor and his crew, but for the home owner, future landscaping will cost a great deal more. It will be very expensive to plant trees just a fraction of the size of the original ones that were eradicated during construction.

When the woodland has been thinned out and unwanted plants and shrubs have been removed, attention must be given to the woodland floor. As forest soil is naturally rich in humus, it makes an ideal medium for shallow-rooted shade-loving perennials, which need a soil that is rich in both decaying organic matter and mycorrhizal fungus. So when planting woodland species, it is important to preserve as much of the forest soil as possible. To eradicate undesirable grasses and plants yet not disturb woodland soil, the following method is excellent. In spring take newspapers (five sheets thick) and spread them over the entire site. Water down the newspaper. (I do this as I go along since it prevents the paper from blowing away.) If no tap water is available near the woodland site, lay the paper after a rainy day, or even when it is raining. Spread a 2-inch-thick layer of salt marsh hay over the newspaper. And to speed the process of decay, add a sprinkling of commercial fertilizer over the entire site. As Marie Sperka points out, "If you are laying newspaper on a hillside, always start from the highest point and work downwards (the reverse of shingling a roof). You want to absorb the rain as it falls, rather than have it run downhill." By the next spring, unwanted grasses and plants beneath the newspaper will be dead. If there are still weeds in some areas, repeat the process in the troublesome spots. Because of the fertilizer used in this process it is better to wait until the fall before planting any wild flowers in the woodland. When ready for digging in perennials, remove sufficient mulch for the planting hole. Then without excavating too much soil, remove any dead root material and place the plant in the new hole, spread the roots, and then pile rich soil around the wild flower.

Shade-tolerant evergreens like rhododendron and mountain laurel are valuable shrubs for the woodland. These plants not only give the forest some color in winter, they also help to delineate the border of a woodland garden—and perhaps screen off a neighbor's yard or an ugly building. Evergreens are important accents in a woodland garden. They can be used as the focus around which wild flowers are grown. They also help to separate the woodland landscape into different "rooms" and make a wooded copse seem larger than it actually is.

azalea   rhododendron

WATER GARDENS

"Where there is a stream passing through the outskirts of the garden, there will be a happy prospect of delightful ways of arranging and enjoying the beautiful plants that love wet places. The least trickle of water, with a simple and clever arrangement of bold clumps of suitable plants, a pretty stream picture can be made. . . . The way to enjoy these beautiful things is to see one picture at a time; not to confuse the mind with a crowded jumble of too many interesting individuals, such as is usually seen in a water garden." *(Gertrude Jekyll)*

The range of botanical material available for planting around ponds, streams, and their margins is remarkable. Many aquatic plants are superb, not only because of their outstanding blossoms but also for their color and variety of foliage. These plants grow in habitats that range from deep water to the damp soil associated with the edges of ponds and watercourses. This range of growing conditions enables an incredible variety of plants to be cultivated in the concentrated area of a pond or stream, making the water-scape one of the most beautiful areas of the garden. And the striking and often vibrant foliage of aquatic plants has a strong effect on any landscape.

Even if you do not have a stream running through your property, you may be able to grow some of the loveliest water plants. If you think there is a potential site for aquatic plants in your garden, you need first to determine just how wet that particular area is. To do this, wait for a heavy rainfall, then immediately afterward note the spots in the garden where puddles appear. The areas surrounding these puddles will feel spongy when walked upon. If water still remains in the puddles after a week, stake these sites. Check these areas periodically, and if they remain spongy, you are in luck! These sections could be ideal areas for creating a marsh or bog garden. If after a few days the soil no longer feels spongy but does remain permanently moist, the area is potentially a perfect site for a wild-flower garden like the design in "Wild Flowers for a Damp Garden." Pinning down the source of water can be the deciding factor in determining what plants your garden will support. If moisture is provided by a high water table or underground spring, then your site will probably remain damp for the whole year. This area has the greatest possibilities for landscaping with water plants. On the other hand, if you have heavy clay soil, then you may have a damp site during the spring runoff, but by summer the land will almost certainly be totally dry. This area is probably not going to be suitable for moisture-loving plants.

Another important factor is light. Before planting the damp garden site, make sure that you select plants that will be satisfied with the amount of light they will receive in this location. And before designing your water garden, decide on the position of pathways. Water plants are fun, but not when you have to enjoy them with damp feet. Raise the levels of the paths through these areas by using gravel, flagstones, or pressure-treated lumber.

The next major landscape consideration for the wet meadow or marsh garden is the selection of suitable trees and shrubs. Many interesting species will thrive in these locations. Two good native trees ideally suited to wet soil are red maple *(Acer rubrum)* and bald cypress *(Taxodium distichum)*. The red maple is a hardy tree that can be grown in wet or moist soil. As its name suggests, this is a colorful tree. In the spring dozens of red blossoms create a scarlet haze, and in the fall the tree is covered with lovely crimson leaves. The bald cypress is the dominant tree of the Florida Everglades. It is extremely hardy and adaptable, being able to grow either in full sun or in high shade, in standing water or dry soil! In wet locations this tree produces attractive "cypress knees"—root projections that eventually surround the tree. Bald cypress is a perfect tree for the water garden.

The dawn redwood *(Metasequoia glyptostroboides)* is a lovely fast-growing deciduous conifer that thrives in the moist soil at the edge of a pool or streamside. The common larch *(Larix decidua)*, another deciduous conifer, is a good tree for planting in heavy clay soil or in a garden at the edge of marshland. Other trees to consider for the water garden are river birch, swamp white oak, Atlantic white cedar, black ash, and swamp cottonwood.

The list of attractive shrubs for the damp meadow and marsh is equally impressive. Choice specimens include the highly scented swamp azalea *(Rhododendron viscosum)*. Another, sweet pepperbush *(Clethra alnifolia)*, is a common shrub of North American swamp communities. In summer, scented white and pink flowers cover these bushes. The evergreen rosebay rhododendron *(Rhododendron maximum)* is another native shrub that is ideal for wet areas. Most of these delightful plants have been included in the garden designs in this chapter.

A marsh surrounded by cattails and rushes is a lovely sight. Equally lovely are the perennials suitable for the wet area of the garden. Early flowers for the damp landscape include an old-time favorite, forget-me-nots *(Myosotis scorpioides)*. In spring and early summer, tiny sky-blue flowers, each with a conspicuous yellow eye, make forget-me-nots one of the most attractive wild flowers. Another good perennial for a damp site is Virginia bluebells *(Mertensia virginica)*. In May, this plant bears tall stems covered with blossoms that change from delicate pink to bright porcelain blue. If you have a shady position with soil that is constantly moist, grow some native trilliums. In the right position these lovely flowers will soon establish thick colonies. In a damper site, the spring-flowering marsh marigold *(Caltha palustris)* will carpet a whole streamside with bright yellow flowers.

Summer plants for the water garden are equally impressive. For instance, bee balm *(Monarda didyma)*, a favorite flower of hummingbirds, displays lovely red blossoms from June until September. Another plant with scarlet blossoms, and one that blooms slightly later than bee balm, is cardinal flower *(Lobelia cardinalis)*. This gem is one of the most attractive perennials of both formal and wild gardens. Another native lobelia, *Lobelia siphilitica*, is covered with tall sky-blue flower spikes from September until the first frost.

As summer begins to change into autumn, the lovely white and pink flowers of turtleheads *(Chelone lyonii)* will begin to brighten a fading garden. Goldenrod, joe-pye weed, and swamp asters are end-of-season blossoms I always look forward to.

joe-pye weed

Many non-native plants can be included in the damp garden. Primroses, the gem of spring flowers, are ideally suited to the waterside garden. And since many iris need to be grown either in water or in very damp soil, they are ideal candidates for the water garden. Blue flag *(Iris versicolor)* and yellow flag *(I. pseudacorus)* should be included in the list of plants for a marsh or pond garden. A personal favorite non-native plant that grows happily by the waterside is astilbe. This is the perfect perennial for a shady damp site. In late June and early July this plant bears lovely dense fluffy spikes of flowers—the blossoms are available in many colors.

Many ferns are ideal plants for damp sites. One of the most notable is the giant ostrich fern. When it is grown in a moist situation, the fronds of this plant will reach over 4 feet high. Other impressive tall ferns suitable for the water garden are the cinnamon fern and the royal fern.

There are some marsh plants that can become invasive. Purple loosestrife (*Lythrum salicaria*) is one of the most attractive plants of damp sites, but its aggressive nature makes its inclusion in a water garden problematic. Cultivars of this plant tend to spread more slowly (see the Encyclopedia). Cattail is also an aggressive plant. For a small pond or other damp garden site, it is best to plant cattails in containers.

If you have a pond, stream, or marsh on your property and want to create a water garden, begin by analyzing your site. Decide what major trees and shrubs you would like to grow. If the area is covered with weeds, undesirable grasses, brambles, and other unattractive elements, first identify with wooden stakes any wild flowers that you want to keep. Then cut down and remove any large woody material. Next, follow the procedure described for creating a woodland garden: Cover the whole area with three to five sheets of newspaper. Dampen this down, then cover it with salt marsh hay. The plants that are going to be saved should be surrounded rather than covered with this mulch. Trees, shrubs, and perennials chosen to enhance the water garden can be planted anytime. Just remove an area of mulch and dig a hole big enough for the plant, then carefully surround the new specimen with the newspaper and straw. In about twelve months the newspaper and marsh hay will have rotted and the weeds buried underneath will have been destroyed. Planted perennials should have formed tight colonies. To prevent weeds from becoming established in bare patches in the future, use a suitable mulch.

MOSS GARDENS

"These plants are ideal for an area under large trees such as mature maples, where they provide year-around greenery with low maintenance." (*Gordon Emerson*)

In the right soil and light conditions moss makes an ideal substitute for the traditional grass lawn. Garden editors (myself included) at newspapers across the United States regularly receive letters asking for advice on eradicating moss from prized lawns. From the volume of letters received, it would seem that very few people know about the merits of moss gardening. Many gardeners spend a fortune trying to eradicate this tiny evergreen from shady patches of turf. Instead, learn a lesson from the tenacity of these mossy sites: change tactics and encourage moss, at the same time abandoning the attempt at growing grass in an area that is always going to be difficult. In my opinion, mossy turf is much more beautiful than grass. Moss has a texture like velvet, and when made into a lawn does not need fertilizer, cutting, edging, or spraying for pests and diseases. These ancient plants are diminutive, rarely exceeding an inch in height. Like grass, moss will tolerate foot traffic. But unlike grass, moss can stay green almost all year. In extreme drought mosses turn brown, but if given water, they will recover, in a matter of hours, to their former bright emerald-green color. Under similar stress, a grass lawn would take days to fully recover.

Acid soil, preferably with a pH of 5.5 or less, is generally preferred by moss. These plants also need good drainage—they will not tolerate soggy soil. In warm weather, if their roots are waterlogged, mosses will rot. If you plan to establish a moss lawn, first find a shady spot in the garden. The ideal soil is moist, compact, and drains well. Sandy soil that is on the coarse side is not good for a moss turf—the spores will not germinate where there is continual surface runoff.

With a soil testing kit, determine the pH of the site that you want to turn into a moss lawn. If the soil is not acid enough, add the required amounts of aluminum sulfate, ferrous sulfate, or sulfur (see table).

Acidifying the Soil

Starting pH	Desired pH	Treatment (pounds per 100 sq. ft.)		
		ALUMINUM SULFATE	FERROUS SULFATE	SULFUR
8.0	5.5	13.5	25.9	5.5
7.5	5.5	11.5	23.5	5.0
7.0	5.5	9.0	16.5	3.5
6.5	5.5	6.5	11.8	2.5
6.5	5.0	10.5	18.5	4.0

If there is some grass growing among the moss, when the pH is lowered to around 5.5, the turf will begin to die. For quick results, spread the required amount of either ferrous sulfate or aluminum sulfate over the lawn. In about two weeks the soil pH will have adjusted to the new level. Sulfur can be used instead of the other two chemicals—it is cheaper and less is needed—but it will take at least two months for the pH of the soil to adjust.

You don't have to do an enormous site—you can start off with a small patch. If you are happy with the results, next season increase the area of the moss garden. If the location chosen for the moss lawn already has patches of moss growing in it, altering the pH will encourage the moss to spread. If the area is devoid of moss, or you want to speed up the process in an area that has only small patches, then you can add plugs of moss from elsewhere. Do this in early spring when there is plenty of moisture and the weather is cool. Take small clumps of moss, gathered either from the wild or from a neighbor's garden. (If the latter is obsessed with manicured lawns, he will be grateful indeed.)

Moss, like any plant genus, is made up of numerous species. Some, like haircap moss *(Polytrichum commune)*, can grow to a height of 6 inches. But perhaps the best mosses for lawns are the ground-hugging varieties. One of the best species is cushion moss, a type often found growing in poor, acid soil. But any of the low mosses found on woodland floors will be suitable. A mixture of different species will give a beautiful pattern and texture to the garden site. Make a small hole in the soil and insert the new specimens. Be certain that there are no air spaces left between the moss and the soil. And most important, make sure that the new plantings are kept adequately moist for the next few weeks—at least until the mosses have had time to establish themselves in the new soil. When the moss has taken over an entire area, it will need very little care. Leaves that fall in the autumn must be carefully swept up with a flexible bamboo rake. (If left in place, these can rot and kill the underlying mosses.) Be on the lookout for aggressive weeds and tree saplings. Dandelion and thistles can destroy a carefully tended patch of moss, as can maple and ash seedlings. On the other hand, many rare and beautiful wild flowers can be established among the mosses. Ferns are also ideal companions for the moss lawn, and a pathway of stepping stones can enhance the whole area.

The ideas presented in this chapter can transform any garden, and it is hoped that some of the designs will encourage potential wild-flower gardeners. With some careful planning, a woodland setting can be made from just a couple of trees. A wild-flower meadow can be confined to the area adjoining a stone patio or terrace—making the observation of butterflies and birds another joy of summer. With just a little imagination, a plastic pool can become a water-lily pond surrounded by a miniature damp meadow. A fiberglass pond can also be filled with peat moss to create a bog garden that can be the highlight of the landscape. For those fortunate enough to have large gardens, and those with streams and ponds on their property, naturalistic landscaping is bounded only by the imagination. Wild flowers in any size garden give us pleasure and help us to appreciate some of the indigenous treasures we have growing in this magnificent and varied North American continent. Growing wild flowers that are native to our own geographic region puts us in touch with the seasonal rhythms. And as Henry Art says: "You may find a deeper sense of identity with the natural environment and develop a feeling of rootedness that is not possible when cultivating domesticated, horticultural varieties."

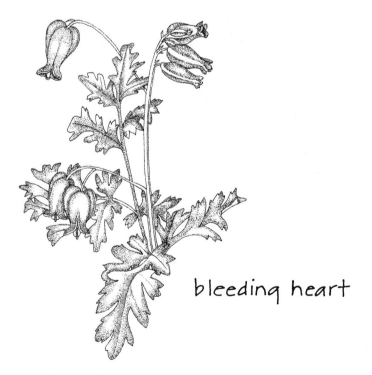

bleeding heart

WILD-FLOWER GARDEN DESIGNS

SECRET WILD-FLOWER GARDEN   *Your own secret Eden*

Surrounded by tall evergreen rhododendrons, this is a garden that will let you escape from the world and enjoy the harmony of a quiet grove of wild flowers. The rosebay rhododendrons that form this circular enclosure will eventually grow 16 feet high, but all the plants selected for the secret garden are species that will thrive in their shade. In this enclosed oasis, some early-blooming shrubs like flame azalea and pinxter flower are included, so on a May morning when seated on the wooden bench, you can be engulfed by these lovely blossoms. When you glance down to grass level, you will be able to admire the bloodroot. In spring, the delicious scent of the *Fothergilla*, planted just behind the bloodroot, will permeate the whole garden. And in the fall it will put on another magnificent show when the leaves turn scarlet. Oakleaf hydrangeas are planted behind the wooden bench. In late summer, these handsome shrubs will be covered with huge heads of white blossoms, which change to a lovely shade of pink as they mature. Also in summer, the regal Turk's-cap lily, planted by the entrance to the secret garden, will beckon onlookers into this mysterious grove.

*5 **Adiantum pedatum** — MAIDENHAIR FERN
6 **Aquilegia canadensis** — AMERICAN COLUMBINE
3 **Cypripedium calceolus pubescens** — YELLOW LADY'S SLIPPER
9 **Dicentra eximia** — FRINGED BLEEDING HEART
1 **Fothergilla major** — LARGE FOTHERGILLA
10 **Geranium maculatum** — WILD GERANIUM
3 **Hydrangea quercifolia** — OAKLEAF HYDRANGEA
3 **Lilium superbum** — TURK'S-CAP LILY
3 **Mertensia virginica** — VIRGINIA BLUEBELL

5 **Phlox divaricata** — BLUE WOOD PHLOX
9 **Polystichum acrostichoides** — CHRISTMAS FERN
1 **Rhododendron calendulaceum** — FLAME AZALEA
7 **Rhododendron maximum** — ROSEBAY RHODODENDRON
1 **Rhododendron periclymenoides** — PINXTER FLOWER
5 **Sanguinaria canadensis** — BLOODROOT
3 **Trillium grandiflorum** — WHITE TRILLIUM

*Numbers in list are total quantities needed.
 Numbers in the diagram indicate the quantity to be planted in each individual space.

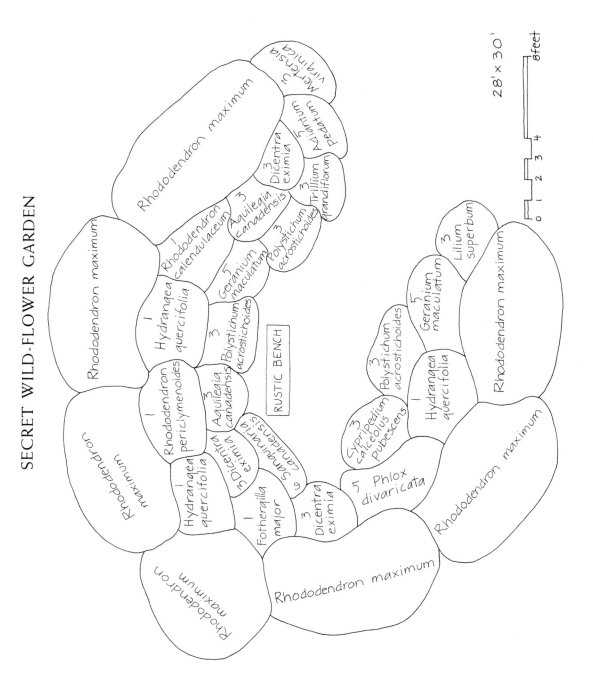

SECRET WILD-FLOWER GARDEN

Rhododendron maximum

3 Mertensia virginica

3 Dicentra eximia

3 Aquilegia canadensis

2 Adiantum pedatum

1 Rhododendron calendulaceum

3 Trillium grandiflorum

5 Geranium maculatum

3 Polystichum acrostichoides

Rhododendron maximum

1 Hydrangea quercifolia

3 Polystichum acrostichoides

RUSTIC BENCH

1 Rhododendron periclymenoides

3 Aquilegia canadensis

3 Cypripedium calceolus pubescens

3 Polystichum acrostichoides

5 Geranium maculatum

3 Lilium superbum

Rhododendron maximum

Rhododendron maximum

1 Hydrangea quercifolia

3 Dicentra eximia

6 Sanguinaria canadensis

1 Hydrangea quercifolia

1 Fothergilla major

3 Dicentra eximia

5 Phlox divaricata

Rhododendron maximum

Rhododendron maximum

Rhododendron maximum

28' × 30'

0 1 2 3 4 8feet

179

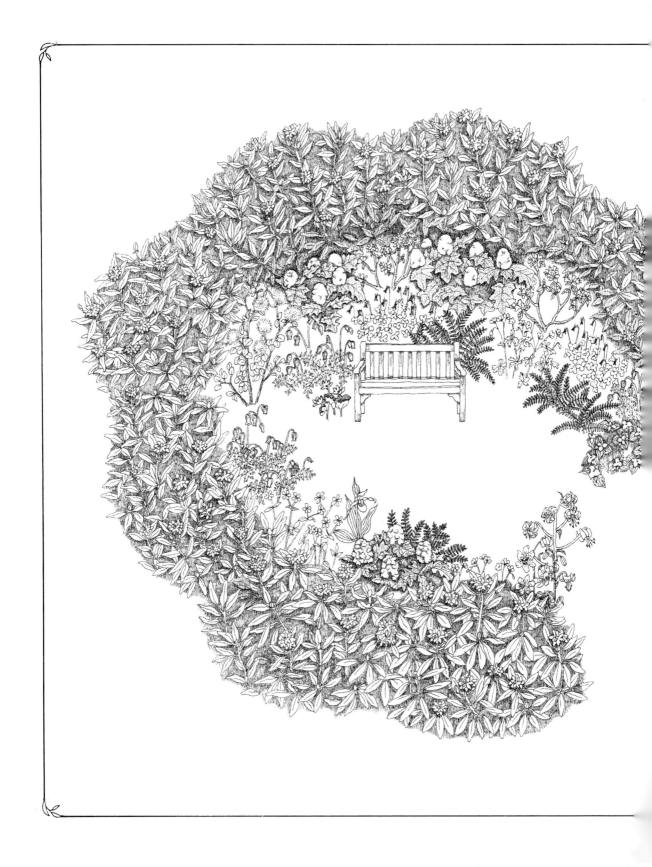

SECRET WILD-FLOWER GARDEN

WOODLAND GARDEN OF WILD FLOWERS *A mini woodland of wild flowers*

Even in a modest-size yard it is possible to create a small woodland wild-flower garden. The three canoe birch here form the "wood." Underneath this leafy canopy an assortment of beautiful perennials can be planted. In spring, a walk through this little garden will be a pleasure. Blue wood phlox, with their pale blue star-shaped flowers, are a cheery sight. Shooting star is another spring flower with blossoms as beautiful as its name suggests. So are the trilliums—in April and May these gorgeous flowers bear lovely triangular white blooms. As the season progresses, you will be able to enjoy other native blossoms. In June and July, the lovely Oconee bells display their dainty fringed white flowers. A mountain laurel is included in this plan, and in June, this spectacular evergreen shrub will add to the color of the wild flowers. Fall will bring other beautiful wild plants into bloom. In August and September, you will be able to admire the turtleheads when they produce their curious blooms on tall stalks. And providing greenery for the whole growing season is the delicate maidenhair fern. The Christmas fern keeps this woodland garden verdant even in winter, and also looks lovely under a canopy of bare white-branched birch trees.

*15 *Adiantum pedatum* — MAIDENHAIR FERN
  8 *Aquilegia canadensis* — AMERICAN COLUMBINE
  6 *Arisaema triphyllum* — JACK-IN-THE-PULPIT
  3 *Betula papyrifera* — CANOE BIRCH
  5 *Caulophyllum thalictroides* — BLUE COHOSH
  8 *Chelone lyonii* — PINK TURTLEHEAD
 13 *Chrysogonum virginianum* — GREEN-AND-GOLD
  8 *Cimicifuga racemosa* — BUGBANE
 12 *Dicentra eximia* — FRINGED BLEEDING HEART
  9 *Dodecatheon meadia* — SHOOTING STAR
 11 *Gillenia trifoliata* — BOWMAN'S ROOT
  1 *Kalmia latifolia* — MOUNTAIN LAUREL
  9 *Lobelia cardinalis* — CARDINAL FLOWER

  3 *Lobelia siphilitica* — GREAT BLUE LOBELIA
  3 *Mertensia virginica* — VIRGINIA BLUEBELL
 10 *Pachysandra procumbens* — ALLEGHENY SPURGE
 14 *Phlox divaricata* — BLUE WOOD PHLOX
  5 *Polygala paucifolia* — FRINGED POLYGALA
 10 *Polystichum acrostichoides* — CHRISTMAS FERN
 10 *Sanguinaria canadensis* — BLOODROOT
  8 *Shortia galacifolia* — OCONEE BELLS
  8 *Trillium grandiflorum* — WHITE TRILLIUM
  5 *Trollius laxus* — SPREADING GLOBEFLOWER
 10 *Uvularia sessilifolia* — LITTLE MERRYBELLS
  5 *Viola pedata* — BIRD'S-FOOT VIOLET

*Numbers in list are total quantities needed.
Numbers in the diagram indicate the quantity to be planted in each individual space.

WOODLAND GARDEN OF WILD FLOWERS

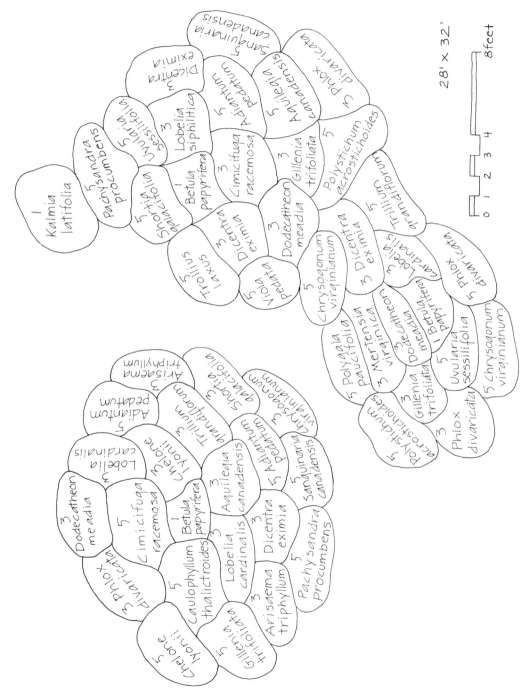

28' × 32'

8 feet

0 1 2 3 4

WOODLAND GARDEN OF WILD FLOWERS

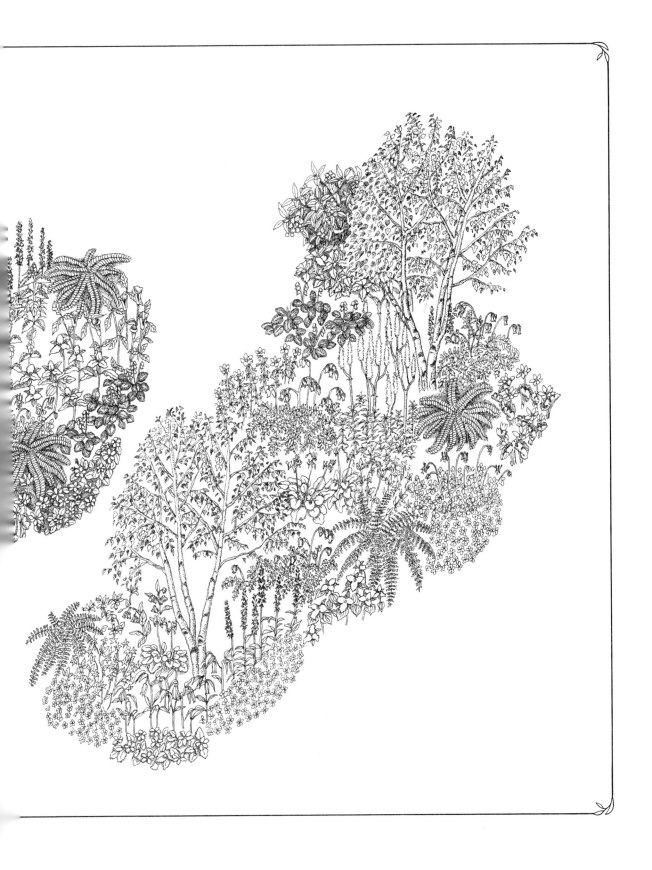

SUNNY WILD-FLOWER MEADOW *A trouble-free garden of wild flowers*

Once established, this lovely garden will be a tapestry of wild flowers. When the perennials have been planted, sow the entire area with 4 ounces of little bluestem. This attractive nonaggressive prairie grass will form neat tussocks which make a nice background for the wild flowers. In early summer the meadow comes into its own. A riot of colorful perennials gives zest to these two island beds even in late fall. The circular shape of the borders allows the wild flowers to be admired from all directions. It also allows the blooms to be picked with ease. Many of the plants in this design are favorite nectar flowers of butterflies—but perennials like butterfly weed will delight humans as much as butterflies. In fall, when neighbors' gardens have vanished from the landscape, you will still be enjoying late-flowering perennials like the asters, ironweed, and 'Golden Mosa' goldenrod. You will not be alone in your admiration for these autumn flowers—hummingbirds and butterflies will also appreciate them.

*3 *Amsonia tabernaemontana*—BLUE STAR
12 *Asclepias tuberosa*—BUTTERFLY MILKWEED
6 *Aster laevis*—SMOOTH ASTER
6 *Aster spectabilis*—SHOWY ASTER
3 *Baptisia australis*—BLUE FALSE INDIGO
6 *Boltonia asteroides* 'Snowbank'
9 *Chrysanthemum leucanthemum*—OXEYE DAISY
9 *Chrysopsis mariana*—GOLDEN ASTER
6 *Cichorium intybus*—CHICORY
6 *Coreopsis grandiflora* 'Sunburst'
9 *Echinacea purpurea*—PURPLE CONEFLOWER
3 *Helenium autumnale*—HELEN'S FLOWER

3 *Liatris pycnostachya*—PRAIRIE BLAZING STAR
3 *Liatris pycnostachya* 'Alba'—ALBINO PRAIRIE BLAZING STAR
6 *Lilium superbum*—TURK'S-CAP LILY
9 *Monarda didyma* 'Cambridge Scarlet'—RED BERGAMOT
9 *Rudbeckia fulgida*—BLACK-EYED SUSAN
6 *Silphium perfoliatum*—CUP-PLANT ROSINWEED
6 *Solidago virgaurea* 'Golden Mosa'—GOLDENROD
3 *Stokesia laevis*—STOKES' ASTER
6 *Vernonia noveboracensis*—IRONWEED

*Numbers in list are total quantities needed.
Numbers in the diagram indicate the quantity to be planted in each individual space.

SUNNY WILD-FLOWER MEADOW

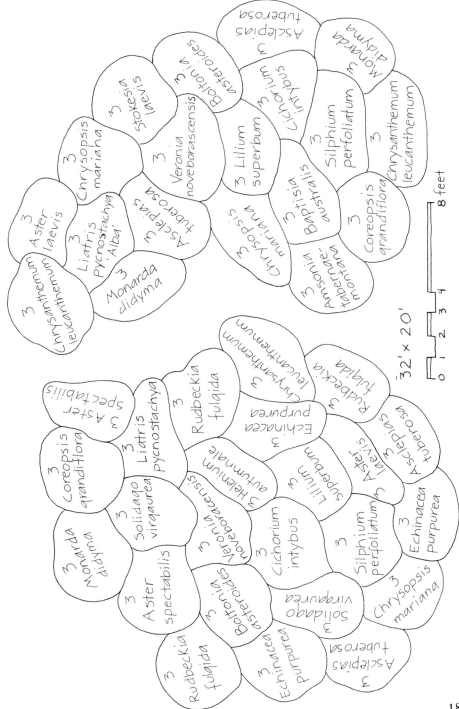

32' × 20'

8 feet

0 1 2 3 4

PRAIRIE GARDEN *Bring the great American prairie into your own garden*

This garden plan incorporates the most easily cultivated wild flowers of the American prairies. Install the plants in a cleared area first. Then sow 4 ounces of little bluestem grass seed between the wild flowers. This is a nonaggressive tussock-forming grass that will blend in with the prairie flowers. Planted in the middle of a lawn, this elegantly curving island border provides a delightful focal point for spring, summer, and fall. Once established, the prairie garden needs minimum maintenance—just an annual midwinter cutting of dried flower stalks. For smaller gardens, plant only half: divide the design in the middle and plant whichever half you like the best! This is a garden for all seasons. Early plants like columbine add colorful spring flowers. Soon after, in very quick succession, other perennials add their beauty. A summer favorite, prairie blazing star, bears rich spikes of long-lasting purple flowers. From summer to fall, the garden is a riot of color that ends with a great crescendo as the showy goldenrods, with their lovely yellow flowers, vie for attention with the blue asters.

*12 **Allium cernuum**—NODDING ONION
  2 **Amorpha canescens**—LEADPLANT
  6 **Anemone cylindrica**—THIMBLEWEED
  6 **Anemone patens**—PASQUEFLOWER
  9 **Aquilegia canadensis**—AMERICAN COLUMBINE
18 **Asclepias tuberosa**—BUTTERFLY MILKWEED
  3 **Aster azureus**—SKY BLUE ASTER
  6 **Aster ericoides**—HEATH ASTER
  3 **Aster laevis**—SMOOTH ASTER
  3 **Aster sericeus**—SILKY ASTER
  2 **Baptisia leucantha**—PRAIRIE FALSE INDIGO
  6 **Callirhoe triangulata**—POPPY MALLOW
12 **Coreopsis palmatum**—STIFF COREOPSIS
  2 **Desmodium canadense**—SHOWY TICK TREFOIL
  9 **Echinacea purpurea**—PURPLE CONEFLOWER
  6 **Eryngium yuccifolium**—RATTLESNAKE MASTER

15 **Geum triflorum**—PRAIRIE SMOKE
 9 **Liatris pycnostachya**—PRAIRIE BLAZING STAR
 6 **Ratibida pinnata**—YELLOW CONEFLOWER
 9 **Rudbeckia fulgida**—BLACK-EYED SUSAN
 1 **Silphium laciniatum**—COMPASS PLANT
 9 **Solidago speciosa**—SHOWY GOLDENROD
 9 **Vernonia fasciculata**—PRAIRIE IRONWEED

mallow

*Numbers in list are total quantities needed.
Numbers in the diagram indicate the quantity to be planted in each individual space.

PRAIRIE GARDEN

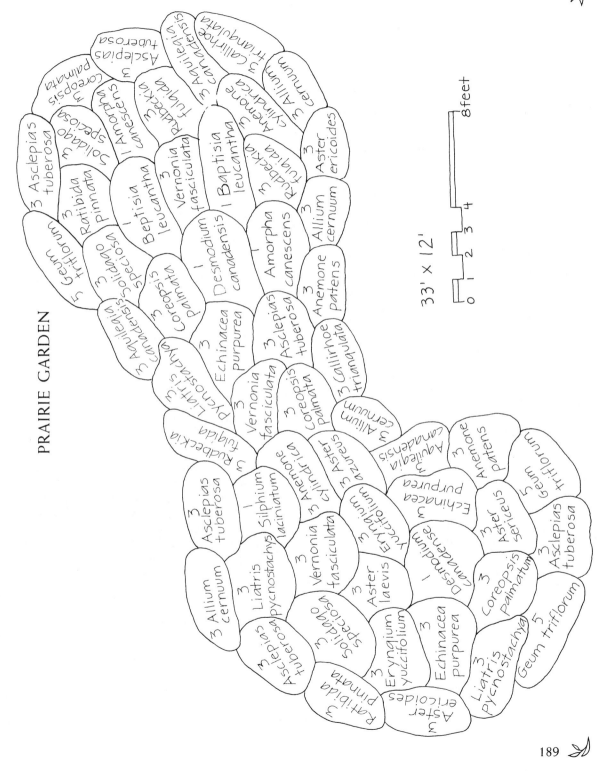

33' × 12'

0 1 2 3 4 8feet

WILD FLOWERS FOR A DAMP GARDEN *Colorful blooms that like damp feet*

This pretty collection of wild flowers invites strollers—the layout allows blossoms to be viewed on all sides. The swamp azalea, one of nature's most fragrant spring flowers, invites visitors into this enchanting garden. In summer, the lovely sweet pepperbush entices admirers with its spicy aroma. Marsh marigolds put forth their golden cups in the spring, and in summer the giant hibiscus, with dinner-plate-size blooms, vies for attention with the pretty pink loosestrife. Fall will be as beautiful, especially with the brilliant blossoms of the cardinal flowers. Tall stems of ironweed, crowned with blossoms of the richest purple, add great beauty to this garden in the autumn. A little pool reflects these lovely blossoms in its mirror-like surface. And floating upon the water, a fragrant water lily adds elegance.

*9 *Acorus calamus*—SWEET FLAG
9 *Caltha palustris*—MARSH MARIGOLD
3 *Carex pendula*—DROOPING SEDGE
1 *Cephalanthus occidentalis*—BUTTONBUSH
9 *Chelone lyonii*—PINK TURTLEHEAD
3 *Clethra alnifolia*—SWEET PEPPERBUSH
9 *Eupatorium purpureum*—JOE-PYE WEED
6 *Gentiana clausa*—CLOSED GENTIAN
2 *Hibiscus moscheutos*—ROSE MALLOW
18 *Iris pseudacorus*—YELLOW FLAG
11 *Iris versicolor*—BLUE FLAG
6 *Lilium canadense*—CANADA LILY
9 *Lilium superbum*—TURK'S-CAP LILY
21 *Lobelia cardinalis*—CARDINAL FLOWER
9 *Lobelia siphilitica*—GREAT BLUE LOBELIA
12 *Lychnis flos-cuculi*—RAGGED ROBIN

6 *Lysichiton americanum*—WESTERN SKUNK CABBAGE
9 *Lythrum salicaria* 'Morden's Pink'—LOOSESTRIFE
2 *Myrica pensylvanica*—WAX MYRTLE
1 *Nymphaea odorata*—FRAGRANT WHITE POND LILY
15 *Onoclea sensibilis*—SENSITIVE FERN
5 *Osmunda cinnamomea*—CINNAMON FERN
3 *Osmunda regalis*—ROYAL FERN
1 *Rhododendron viscosum*—SWAMP AZALEA
3 *Sagittaria latifolia*—ARROWHEAD
1 *Taxodium distichum*—SWAMP CYPRESS
6 *Veratrum viride*—WHITE HELLEBORE
3 *Vernonia noveboracensis*—IRONWEED
12 *Woodwardia virginica*—VIRGINIA CHAIN FERN

*Numbers in list are total quantities needed.
Numbers in the diagram indicate the quantity to be planted in each individual space.

WILD FLOWERS FOR A DAMP GARDEN

34' x 24'

8 feet
0 1 2 3 4

3 Clethra alnifolia

Osmunda cinnamomea

5 Iris versicolor

3 Onoclea sensibilis

3 Woodwardia virginica

Hibiscus moscheutos

3 Lilium canadense

3 Hibiscus moscheutos

3 Onoclea sensibilis

3 Lychnis flos-cuculi

3 Lobelia cardinalis

3 Lobelia cardinalis

3 Osmunda cinnamomea

3 Veratrum viride

3 Lilium canadense

Lysichiton americanum

3 Lychnis flos-cuculi

3 Onoclea sensibilis

3 Caltha palustris

3 Lythrum salicaria

3 Lilium superbum

1 Taxodium distichum

1 Veratrum viride

Veratrum viride

3 Lobelia cardinalis

1 Clethra alnifolia

1 Osmunda cinnamomea

3 Acorus calamus

1 Myrica pensyl-vanica

3 Lilium superbum

3 Iris pseudacorus

3 Lychnis flos-cuculi

3 Osmunda cinnamomea

Acorus calamus

1 Osmunda regalis

3 Sagittaria latifolia

3 Iris pseudacorus

3 Iris

3 Woodwardia virginica

1 Osmunda cinnamomea

3 Eupatorium purpureum

3 Eupatorium purpureum

3 Lobelia cardinalis

3 Onoclea sensibilis

3 Iris pseudacorus

3 Lobelia cardinalis

3 Iris versicolor

3 Lobelia siphilitica

GRASS

GRASS

POOL

1 Nymphea odorata

3 Carex pendula

3 Eupatorium purpureum

3 Lobelia cardinalis

1 Clethra alnifolia

3 Iris pseudacorus

3 Lilium superbum

3 Osmunda cinnamomea

3 Woodwardia virginica

3 Lythrum salicaria

1 Osmunda regalis

3 Clethra alnifolia

3 Chelone lyonii

3 Lobelia cardinalis

1 Myrica pensyl-vanica

3 Lythrum salicaria

3 Chelone lyonii

3 Lobelia siphilitica

3 Iris pseudacorus

3 Osmunda regalis

Lysichiton americanum

3 Lobelia siphilitica

3 Gentiana clausa

3 Chelone lyonii

3 Lobelia cardinalis

1 Cephalanthus occidentalis

Vernonia nove-boracensis

3 Lobelia siphilitica

3 Lychnis flos-cuculi

3 Woodwardia virginica

3 Chelone lyonii

3 Onoclea sensibilis

LONG BORDER OF WILD FLOWERS *A formal border of wild flowers*

For wild-flower enthusiasts with a small walled garden that is sunny, this design is ideal. For the whole summer and fall, this colorful garden backed by tall perennials will be a delight. The *Boltonia* 'Snowbank' that appears in two places in the design forms a bush that in late summer is literally covered in white star-shaped flowers. This display lasts for weeks! Competing with the *Boltonia* is the cup plant, a giant wild flower from the prairies. In July and August, handsome yellow daisies smother this perennial. The leaves form natural cups that delight the birds—providing them with a bathtub "au naturel"! *Amsonia,* with its ethereal blue flowers, is an eye-catcher at the front of the border. Its "bed fellow" in this design is the beautiful black-eyed Susan, a plant that needs no introduction.

*3 ***Achillea millefolium***—YARROW
 9 ***Amsonia tabernaemontana***—BLUE STAR
 3 ***Asclepias tuberosa***—BUTTERFLY MILKWEED
 2 ***Boltonia asteroides*** 'Snowbank'
 3 ***Chrysanthemum leucanthemum***—OXEYE DAISY
 3 ***Cichorium intybus***—CHICORY
 3 ***Daucus carota***—QUEEN ANNE'S LACE
 3 ***Echinacea purpurea***—PURPLE CONEFLOWER
 3 ***Helenium autumnale***—HELEN'S FLOWER
 6 ***Liatris pycnostachya***—PRAIRIE BLAZING STAR
 3 ***Lobelia cardinalis***—CARDINAL FLOWER
 3 ***Monarda didyma*** 'Cambridge Scarlet'—RED BERGAMOT

 3 ***Oenothera missouriensis***—SUNDROPS
 3 ***Rudbeckia fulgida***—BLACK-EYED SUSAN
 1 ***Silphium perfoliatum***—CUP-PLANT ROSINWEED
 3 ***Stokesia laevis***—STOKES' ASTER
 6 ***Vernonia noveboracensis***—IRONWEED

aster

*Numbers in list are total quantities needed.
 Numbers in the diagram indicate the quantity to be planted in each individual space.

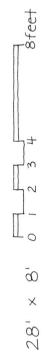

LONG BORDER OF WILD FLOWERS

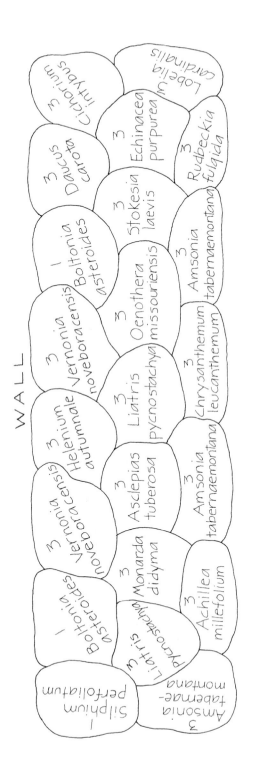

WALL

3 Cirsium altui...um

3 Daucus carota

3 Echinacea purpurea

Lobelia cardinalis

1 Boltonia asteroides

Stokesia laevis

3 Rudbeckia fulgida

3 Vernonia noveboracensis

3 Oenothera missouriensis

3 Amsonia tabernaemontana

3 Helenium autumnale

3 Liatris pycnostachya

3 Chrysanthemum leucanthemum

3 Vernonia noveboracensis

3 Asclepias tuberosa

3 Amsonia tabernaemontana

1 Boltonia asteroides

3 Monarda didyma

3 Achillea millefolium

3 Liatris pycnostachya

1 Silphium perfoliatum

3 Amsonia tabernae-montana

28' × 8'

0 1 2 3 4   8 feet

193

WILD FLOWERS FOR A SHADY GARDEN *A trove of wild flowers for a walled garden*

For wild-flower lovers with a modest-size walled garden, this plan for a border of native plants might be the answer. Smaller gardens, especially if confined by walls, can provide a shady oasis for some of the loveliest American wild flowers. From spring until fall, this border will provide both beauty and interest. In spring, the floral display gets off to a colorful start when wild columbine opens its red and yellow flowers. Not far behind, jack-in-the-pulpit emerges and displays its exotic-looking flowers. One of my favorite wild flowers, green-and-gold, is covered with golden daisies in spring and continues this floral exuberance until fall! Because green-and-gold is so generous with its blossoms, I have included two separate plantings at the front of this border. Tall plants at the back of the border include the late-summer-flowering cardinal flower. The bright scarlet stems are a delight in a shady garden. The companion to cardinal flower in this border is ostrich fern. Expect this beauty to unfold its 4-foot-long plumes for the whole summer! In the middle of the shady garden, plantings of red bergamot will add color and fragrance to this wild-flower border in time for the July 4th celebrations.

*6 *Adiantum pedatum* — MAIDENHAIR FERN
6 *Amsonia tabernaemontana* — BLUE STAR
6 *Aquilegia canadensis* — AMERICAN COLUMBINE
6 *Arisaema triphyllum* — JACK-IN-THE-PULPIT
3 *Chelone lyonii* — PINK TURTLEHEAD
9 *Chrysogonum virginianum* — GREEN-AND-GOLD
3 *Cimicifuga racemosa* — BUGBANE
9 *Dicentra eximia* — FRINGED BLEEDING HEART
3 *Dodecatheon meadia* — SHOOTING STAR
6 *Geranium maculatum* — WILD GERANIUM

6 *Lobelia cardinalis* — CARDINAL FLOWER
6 *Lobelia siphilitica* — GREAT BLUE LOBELIA
9 *Matteuccia pensylvanica* — OSTRICH FERN
6 *Monarda didyma* 'Cambridge Scarlet' — RED BERGAMOT
9 *Rudbeckia fulgida* — BLACK-EYED SUSAN
12 *Tiarella cordifolia* — FOAMFLOWER
3 *Tradescantia virginiana* — VIRGINIA SPIDERWORT
6 *Uvularia grandiflora* — BIG MERRYBELLS

*Numbers in list are total quantities needed.
Numbers in the diagram indicate the quantity to be planted in each individual space.

WILD FLOWERS FOR A SHADY GARDEN

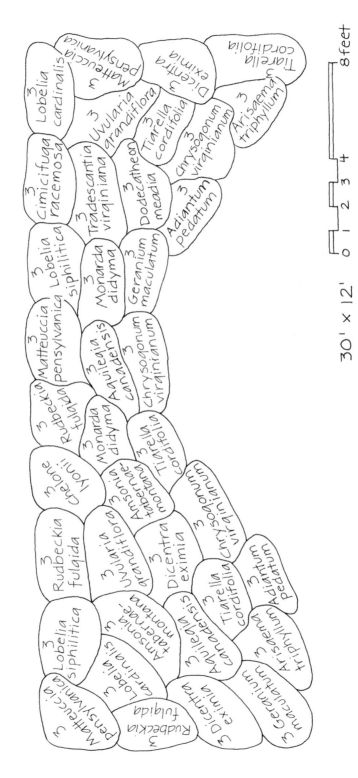

30' × 12'

8 feet

0 1 2 3 4

WILD FLOWERS FOR A SHADY GARDEN

Chapter Five

ENCYCLOPEDIA OF PLANTS

ACHILLEA (YARROW). Family: Compositae. Zones 3–10.

Although tolerant of many types of soil conditions, even poor rocky soil, *Achillea* like full sun.

Achillea filipendulina 'Coronation Gold'.

This is perhaps the most popular of the garden yarrows. 'Coronation Gold' is a vigorous plant that rarely needs staking. For much of the summer and early autumn, the 3-inch flat-topped blooms make a striking display with their mustard-yellow flowers. 'Coronation Gold' grows up to 3 feet.

Achillea millefolium (YARROW, MILFOIL).

This species of *Achillea* is the common yarrow of waysides. It grows 2 to 3 feet tall and bears white flowers for most of the summer. The flat round blossoms are made up of dozens of individual blooms. The whole plant emits a delicate aroma when crushed; the scent becomes stronger if the stems are dried. This is one of my favorite herbs, and in every country where I have resided, before summer's end I always make sure that my supply of dried yarrow is adequate for winter use. A tea made from a small handful of this herb, when sweetened with honey, makes an ex-

cellent beverage for winter colds and the flu.

Yarrow has been used by occultists for centuries. Stems are said to be good for divining the future, especially if they are placed under the pillow before retiring for the night. In the Middle Ages, witches were said to use yarrow sticks to fly through the air. Less sensational is the use of yarrow as a healing plant. In a discourse on this herb, the sixteenth-century herbalist Richard Banckes explained the medicinal uses of this wild flower: "King Achilles found this herb and with it he healed his men that were wounded with iron." The generic name identifies this herb with the famed warrior Achilles.

Achillea millefolium 'Fire King' bears 3-inch heads of rosy red flowers. 'Fire King' grows up to 2 feet and flowers from June to September.

Achillea ptarmica 'The Pearl'.

From June until October, this attractive cultivar bears double white flowers. 'The Pearl' grows up to 2 feet and is excellent for cutting.

Achillea taygetea 'Moonshine'.

In summer and for much of the fall, *Achillea* 'Moonshine' bears flat-topped canary-yellow flowers. Each blossom is 3 inches wide. In my opinion, this variety is the best *Achillea* for the perennial flower border. 'Moonshine' looks spectacular when planted with aconite or with *Sedum spectabile* 'Autumn Joy'.

ACONITUM (ACONITE, WOLFBANE, MONKSHOOD, QUEEN MOTHER OF POISONS). Family: Ranunculaceae. Zones 2–7.

Aconite is best grown in partial shade in deep, moist soil. If a good mulch is spread around the roots, however, it will grow in full sun. The name "wolfsbane" records the use of aconite as a poison. In Europe centuries ago, wolves were a common danger. To combat these predators, meat was laced with this highly poisonous plant and laid as bait. Aconite not only was used against animal pests but also has been used to poison humans. In imperial Rome, so many people used aconite to dispose of their enemies and opponents that the emperor Trajan forbade even the growing of wolfsbane. In fact, during his reign the cultivation of aconite was an offense punishable by death.

Aconite is a plant with an interesting mythology. The Roman historian and naturalist Pliny tells us that "aconite sprang out of the dog Cerberus when Hercules dragged him from the underworld." Pliny also believed that wolfsbane would neutralize the poison of a scorpion, and "even at a long distance" aconite's smell would kill rats and mice. Care should be taken when growing aconite, for as the Elizabethan herbalist William Turner stated, wolfsbane is "a most hastie poyson."

Aconitum carmichaelii.

If you can grow this plant in your area, by all means do so. The deep blue "helmet-like" flowers are a memorable sight in the autumnal garden. Since aconites are not damaged by light frost, they are perfect as a late-flowering perennial for northern gardens. *Aconitum carmichaelii* grows to a little over 3 feet. It is sometimes sold as *Aconitum fischeri.*

Aconitum napellus.

Aconitum napellus differs from *A. carmichaelii* in a number of ways: it is taller (4 feet), flowers a little earlier (July–August), and has more finely divided leaves. Both species of aconite are very beautiful plants.

ACORUS. Family: Araceae.

Acorus calamus (SWEET FLAG). Zones 3–10.

Sweet flag is a perennial that is usually found growing near water. The lance-shaped leaves as well as the roots have a pleasant, distinctive odor which is released when they are bruised. Centuries ago the inhabitants of castles and monasteries scattered the leaves of sweet flag on the stone floors. The foliage not only smelled nice, it helped to eliminate some of the vermin in those overcrowded and badly ventilated residences. The famous Greek physician Dioscorides wrote that sweet flag "helps the cough . . . the smoke thereof being taken at the mouth through a funnel." A later medieval herbal, the *Anglo-Saxon Herbal of Apuleius,* suggests the following: "That bees may not fly off take Acorus and hang it in the hive; then they will be content to stay, and will never depart." The anonymous author concludes that sweet flag "is seldom found, nor any man know it, except when it groweth and bloweth." Although sweet flag is generally found in shallow water and muddy riverbanks, if kept well watered, it will thrive in any rich garden soil. Plant this perennial in full sun. The aromatic leaves reach about 3 feet in height.

ADIANTUM. Family: Polypodiaceae.

Adiantum pedatum (MAIDENHAIR FERN, MAIDENHAIR). Zones 3–9.

This is one of the most beautiful of our native ferns. Emerald-green fan-shaped fronds can grow up to 2 feet high. The ebony stalks look almost too delicate for the leaves. Grow maidenhair fern in filtered sunlight in well-drained soil. If thickly planted, *Adiantum* will make a good ground cover.

AEGOPODIUM (GOUTWEED, BISHOP'S WEED). Family: Umbelliferae. Zones 3–9.

Aegopodium podagraria var. variegatum (VARIEGATED BISHOP'S WEED).

Although this plant can be invasive, if you are willing to keep an eye open for any excessive spreading, it is well worth using as a ground cover. The emerald-green leaves look as if they had been delicately brushed with white paint. This outstanding foliage is very useful to lighten up areas of shade. *A. podagraria variegatum* can also be grown in full sun. Variegated bishop's weed is cultivated for its attractive foliage—the flowers are uninteresting. Plants are 6 inches tall.

AGAPANTHUS (AFRICAN LILY, LILY-OF-THE-NILE). Family: Amaryllidaceae.

Agapanthus umbellatus 'Headborne Hybrids'. Zones 6–9.

Agapanthus umbellatus 'Headborne Hybrids' is the hardiest species of the genus. In late July and August, 2½-foot stems carry lovely blue lily flowers. Agapanthus (especially the hardier 'Headborne Hybrids') should be much more used than it is as a border perennial. This graceful lily is also an ideal plant for containerizing and growing on a patio. But if agapanthus are grown in a tub or flower pot, they will need fertilizer and plenty of water during the growing season. This extra care is worthwhile. Contented plants can bloom for sixty days or more. Plant agapanthus in full sun.

AGRIMONIA. Family: Rosaceae. Zones 3–8.

Agrimonia eupatoria (AGRIMONY, CHURCH STEEPLE).

Agrimony is a pretty herb that is pleasantly scented. From June until September this plant bears elegant yellow flower spikes, which, as the vernacular name suggests, look somewhat like a church steeple. Plant agrimony in full sun in any ordinary dry soil.

This perennial has been a medicinal herb since classical times. The Greek physician Galen said that agrimony was "very beneficial for the bowels." The later Anglo-Saxon herbalists recommended agrimony mixed with human blood and pounded frogs for internal bleeding! Medieval manuscripts are full of spells to be performed with the aid of agrimony. To enchant people and make them fall asleep, a medieval author recommended the following:

> Take agrimony a fair deal'
> And lay it under his head at night
>
> For of his sleep shall he not waken
> Till it from under his head taken.

The Elizabethan herbalist John Gerard had a more practical use for agrimony. He claimed that a tea made from the leaves "is good for them that have naughty livers." Agrimony is still used in modern herbal medicine as a mild astringent and tonic.

AJUGA (BUGLEWEED). Family: Labiatae. Zones 2–8.

Ajuga species and cultivars are fast-spreading low-growing plants that make ideal ground covers. Bugleweed grows best in sun or in light shade. It does not like waterlogged sites, so to avoid root rot diseases, give ajuga a well-drained soil.

Ajuga reptans (CARPET BUGLE).

This is a fast-growing plant that spreads by producing creeping stems. Each glossy leaf grows up to 2 to 4 inches long and they soon form dense carpets. In spring, 6-inch blue flower spikes rise above the foliage.

'Burgundy Glow' has multicolored foliage. The center of each leaf is suffused with rose and magenta, while margins are edged with cream. 'Silver Beauty' has gray-green foliage with a white edging. If you cannot find 'Silver Beauty', substitute 'Silver Carpet' (sometimes sold as 'Gray Lady').

ALCEA (HOLLYHOCK). Family: Malvaceae. Zones 3–8.

Alcea rosea (formerly *Althaea rosea,* and sometimes still sold under that name).

The hollyhock is a true cottage-garden flower, and happily, more of the old-fashioned garden hollyhocks are becoming available. For my taste, some of the newer varieties like 'Chater's Double' are a little overhybridized. Many mail-order nurseries are offering some of the old-fashioned single-blossomed type. These are lovely. In July, tall spikes reach up to 7 feet. The flowers are various colors; plants can have purple, white, pink, yellow, or red blooms. Although *Alcea rosea* is really a biennial, in a favorable position it will become a short-lived perennial. Cutting off faded flowers improves the longevity. Grow hollyhocks in full sun or partial shade, and try to protect from wind. In exposed sites you will have to stake them.

ALCHEMILLA. Family: Rosaceae. Zones 3–8.

Alchemilla mollis (LADY'S MANTLE).

Lady's mantle (also sold as *Alchemilla vulgaris*) is a low-growing perennial (6 to 12 inches) that bears attractive light green scallop-shaped leaves. Its spreading growth habit makes *Alchemilla* an excellent ground cover. In spring, greenish-yellow clusters of flowers appear. Lady's mantle can be cultivated in most soils and will grow in either sun or partial shade. The roundish leaves have the appearance of having been pleated, and with a little imagination this foliage does look like the folds of a medieval cloak—hence the name "lady's mantle."

The generic name of this herb informs us that the plant was used by alchemists. These occultists did not use the actual plants, but rather the jewel-like drops of early morning dew that collected on the leaves. This moisture was believed to have absorbed the magical qualities of the herb. As the sixteenth-century herbalist William Turner recorded: "In the night, it closeth itself together like a purse, and in the morning it is to be found full of dew." This magic water was used as an aphrodisiac and in other magical operations. Gerard recommends the whole plant "to keep down women's paps or dugs, and when they get too great or flaggy, it makes them lesser or harder."

ALLIUM (ONION). Family: Amaryllidaceae.

Allium caeruleum. Zones 3–9.

This stout plant grows 2 to 3 feet high. In spring, deep blue flowers appear. This hardy allium needs full sun.

Allium cernuum (NODDING ONION).
Zones 3–9.

In July this North American native produces large nodding globes of purplish to pink flowers. The plant matures at around 2 feet. Plant nodding onion in full sun in rich moist soil.

Allium sativum (GARLIC). Zones 3–10.

Garlic can be either a perennial or a biennial. The bulbs—made up of individual cloves—produce grasslike hollow green leaves. This foliage grows 1 foot tall, and in summer garlic bears attractive tight clusters of pink flowers.

Homer relates that it was garlic that Ulysses used to escape the enchantress Circe, who wished to turn him into a pig. The Roman naturalist Pliny thought highly of this herb: "Garlic has powerful properties, and is a great benefit against change of water and residence. It keeps off serpents and scorpions by its smell, and, as some have maintained, every kind of beast." I must agree with Pliny: garlic breath is unbearable! But modern research has shown that garlic does have some germicidal properties, so perhaps this herb would be useful against "change of water."

The use of garlic in food needs no explanation. And today *Allium sativum* is still used as a medicinal herb. Most health food shops sell deodorized garlic capsules.

Bulbs of garlic purchased at the local supermarket can be split apart and grown in the garden. Plant the cloves in early spring in a site that has full sun, 2 inches deep and 4 to 6 inches apart.

Allium schoenoprasum (CHIVES).
Zones 3–10.

Chives are not only one of the easiest perennials to grow, they are one of the most useful kitchen herbs. Plant chives in any good soil in full sun or part shade. They do well in a window box or even in a pot placed near a sunny window. In my own garden, I like to grow a number of clumps of chives. Some I allow to flower, and these I don't use in the kitchen as the stems become too coarse, but I very much enjoy their lovely lavender blooms. As an ornamental plant, chives are as nice as anything in the perennial border. Chives are one of the few herbs that lose flavor when dried, so to ensure a winter supply, place the cut herb in small plastic bags in the freezer. Chives are excellent when added to dips, blended with cream cheese or omelet mixes, or when used as a garnish for salads and tomato dishes.

ALOYSIA. Family: Verbenaceae.

Aloysia triphylla (formerly *Lippia citriodora*) (LEMON VERBENA). Zones 7–10.

This South American shrub is one of the most pleasantly aromatic plants that can be grown in the herb garden. When lightly bruised, the bright green leaves emit a delicious odor of sweet lemon. I have fond memories associated with this shrub. In my native county of Somerset, in the west of England, lemon verbena is hardy. The local dentist, who had the unfortunate name of Dr. Payne, had in his rather unkempt front garden the finest lemon verbena I've ever seen. The one delight—in fact, the only delight—of visiting Dr. Payne's surgery was being able to pick, crush, and inhale the fragrant leaves of that lemon verbena before sitting in his torture chair! And since lemon verbena is deciduous in England, I tried to plan my visits during the summer months.

Besides smelling nice, lemon verbena is excellent in the kitchen. The lemon fragrance enhances stews—even cakes—and placed in the cavity of a chicken before roasting, makes the most heavenly dish. If you want to be a tiny bit pretentious, use lemon verbena in finger bowls. Made into a tea, this herb is also a sovereign remedy for nausea and flatulence.

Lemon verbena appreciates a sunny position, and can be planted outside in Zones 7–10. In Zones 7–8, lemon verbena is deciduous, but in Zones 9 and 10 it is evergreen. In areas colder than Zone 7, keep plants in pots inside the house during winter. Do not move the lemon verbena outside again until all danger of frost has gone.

ALTHAEA. Family: Malvaceae.

Althaea officinalis (MARSHMALLOW, MORTIFICATION PLANT). Zones 5–8.

Although marshmallow, as its name suggests, is a herb found in marshes and other wet places, it will grow equally well in good garden soil. Grow it in full sun. Marshmallow belongs to the hollyhock family, and like other members of this genus, *Althaea officinalis* is a striking plant. In late summer, this tall perennial (3 to 4 feet) is covered with large pink flowers. The foliage of marshmallow is wonderful to touch—the leaves have the texture of finest velvet. Gummy starches and sugars extracted from the root of *Althaea officinalis* provided the main ingredient for the original marshmallow confection. Today this candy is made synthetically, and unfortunately never approaches the marvelous flavor of the original natural product. The other vernacular name of this herb, "mortification plant," records the use of marshmallow for treating septic wounds.

A medieval ritual used to prove an accused person's innocence required the suspect to hold a red-hot bar of iron. If guiltless, the ac-

cused suffered no serious burns. Accounts from the Middle Ages state that anointing the palms with an ointment made from marshmallow would allow the accused, irrespective of guilt or innocence, to escape unscathed from this torturous ordeal! Unfortunately, the medieval documents that recount this usage do not mention how the accused, presumably under lock and key, obtained the marshmallow ointment.

Marshmallow is still used today by medical herbalists. The leaves make an excellent poultice for leg ulcers; and made into a tea, the herb is an excellent remedy for coughs and bronchitis.

Althaea rosea. See *Alcea rosea.*

ALYSSUM SAXATILE. *See* Aurinia saxatilis.

AMORPHA (FALSE INDIGO). Family: Leguminosae.

Amorpha canescens (LEADPLANT). Zones 4–9.

This lovely shrublike plant of the prairies grows as tall as 3 feet. The woolly hairs that cover the plant give *Amorpha* a gray color—hence the name "leadplant." In summer the flowering spikes are covered with iridescent purple and orange blossoms. This is an adaptable plant that can be cultivated in a variety of soils, especially if the soil is well drained. Leadplant grows well on dry sandy sites. Cultivate *Amorpha* in full sun.

AMSONIA (BLUE STAR). Family: Apocynaceae.

Amsonia tabernaemontana. Zones 3–8.

In May and June this northeast coast native has terminal clusters of light blue star-shaped flowers. The narrow leaves of *Amsonia ta-*

bernaemontana give this perennial a willow-like appearance. Amsonia grows up to 3 feet and is equally at home in a perennial border, wild-flower meadow, or woodland garden. It likes ordinary garden soil, and can be grown in full sun or partial shade.

ANAPHALIS (EVERLASTING).
Family: Compositae.

Anaphalis triplinervis (PEARLY EVERLASTING). Zones 3–9.

Pearly everlasting is certainly not a garden extrovert, but the neat 1½-foot mounds of subtle silver-gray leaves make this a perfect choice for a silver garden, or a companion to more brightly colored perennials. Later in the summer, *Anaphalis* bears white "strawflowers." Bunches of these blooms are excellent for drying and using in floral arrangements. Grow pearly everlasting in full sun or light shade.

ANEMONE. Family: Ranunculaceae.

Anemone cylindrica (THIMBLEWEED). Zones 3–8.

This prairie flower is extremely drought resistant, so is a perfect perennial for dry soils. Thimbleweed grows up to 3 feet, and from May to July bears creamy white flowers that measure 1½ inches across. Unusual cone-shaped seed heads, which look like balls of cotton, make this plant attractive in late summer as well.

Anemone hupehensis japonica (also listed as *Anemone* x *hybrida*) (JAPANESE ANEMONE). Zones 5–8.

For the late summer and fall garden there is nothing quite like Japanese anemone. Graceful stems terminate with multiple buds and when these open—depending on the variety—have either single or double blossoms that measure up to 3 inches across. Grow Japanese anemone in light shade in moist well-drained soil. It needs protection from wind. In colder areas, before winter sets in, give the plant the advantage of a covering of mulch. These perennials generally grow up to 2½ feet, but in optimum conditions can become 5 feet tall.

'Queen Charlotte' has semi-double clear pink blossoms on 30-inch stems. 'September Charm' has delicate pink flowers shaded with rose and mauve on 30-inch stems.

Anemone patens (PASQUEFLOWER, PRAIRIE SMOKE). Zones 4–8.

This is a spring flower of the North American prairies. Pasqueflower is a low-growing perennial, rarely exceeding 6 inches in height, and has lavender to pale blue flowers with golden stamens. The blossoms measure 2 to 3 inches across. Mature seeds have attractive long feathery plumes which give the fruiting pasqueflower a misty appearance—hence the plant's other common name, "prairie smoke." *Anemone patens* can be grown in well-drained soil in full sun or light shade.

ANETHUM. Family: Umbelliferae.

Anethum graveolens (DILL, DILL WEED). Zones 3–10.

Dill is a hardy annual that can reach up to 5 feet. In early summer the delicate aromatic stems and find threadlike leaves are topped with lovely yellow umbels of flowers. Dill likes a sheltered sunny position in good well-drained soil. Protect this herb from wind, for the fragile stalks blow over in heavy gusts. Dill seed is best sown in a permanent position; it doesn't transplant well.

Testifying to the virtues of this herb, Richard Banckes, the sixteenth-century herbalist, wrote: "It assuageth rumblings in a man's womb [stomach] and wicked winds in the womb. Also, it destroyeth the yexing [hiccups]." Dill is still used in much of Europe as a tea to combat digestive ailments. This is one instance where the medieval use of a plant coincides with a modern use! In the kitchen, the whole herb, finely chopped or dried and pulverized, is used for flavoring vegetables, soups, and fish dishes. Dill seeds can be added to pickles and preservatives.

ANGELICA. Family: Umbelliferae.

Angelica archangelica (ANGELICA, HOLY GHOST PLANT). Zones 3–6.

In May, the tall (6-foot) majestic stems of angelica are topped by large round greenish flowers, made up of dozens of individual blooms. These blossoms last until July, when the giant seed heads appear. Angelica is normally a biennial plant; leaves are produced the first year and blossoms form in the following season. If all flowers are removed before going to seed, angelica will become a short-lived perennial that gets taller each year! The whole plant has a delicious warm aroma. Grow angelica in light shade in moist soil. Planted by itself in a wilder part of the garden, the stately appearance of angelica gives a note of grandeur to the landscape. Because of angelica's height, in more formal areas place it at the rear of the garden bed.

Our ancestors thought angelica had supernatural powers. They identified the herb with Michael the Archangel and with the Holy Ghost. People once believed that the roots of this benevolent plant would relieve all effects of intoxication, and that when angelica root was worn upon the body, the bearer was protected against the evil enchantments of witches and warlocks. According to the old herbals, when angelica root was placed

around the neck of an adolescent, all lusty feelings were dispelled!

Today young roots of angelica are candied for confections, and the seed is used for flavoring liquors.

ANTHEMIS. Family: Compositae.

Anthemis nobilis. See *Chamaemelum nobile.*

Anthemis tinctoria (GOLDEN MARGUERITE). Zones 3–9.

This is one of those marvelous perennials that will flower for the whole summer. As long as golden marguerite is in well-drained soil in full sun, it can be left pretty much alone. For non-gardeners who want perennial flowers in the garden, golden marguerite should be at the top of the list. For the whole growing season, golden daisy-like flowers, up to 2 inches across, cover the 2- to 3-foot bushy plants. The fernlike foliage adds to its beauty. If you take the time to remove dead flowers, the blossoms will keep appearing until the fall. Annual spring or fall division of these plants keeps clumps of golden marguerite from becoming leggy. *Anthemis tinctoria* 'Moonlight' is a hybrid with lovely pale yellow flowers.

ANTHRISCUS. Family: Umbelliferae.

Anthriscus cerefolium (CHERVIL). Zones 3–10.

Chervil is a quick-growing annual that will produce a crop from seed in just eight weeks. A delicate member of the parsley family, *Anthriscus cerefolium* is prized for its anise-flavored leaves. It prefers light shade and moist garden soil. Under favorable growing conditions, plants will reach 2 feet. As chervil does not like to be transplanted, sow the seed in a permanent site. Remove most flowers from the herb as soon as they form. (If allowed to blossom, chervil becomes coarse and loses its delicate flavor.) Leave just a few flowers to go to seed and supply future plants. This herb can also be grown inside as a pot plant.

Chervil is one of the *fines herbes* of French cuisine. It is wonderful in soups and sauces, but because of its delicate flavor, add it to cooked food only at the last minute. Chop this herb finely and sprinkle it upon salads, and add to egg, veal, fish, and poultry dishes. Chervil is also nice on sautéed vegetables.

AQUILEGIA (COLUMBINE). Family: Ranunculaceae. Zones 3–9.

These hardy perennials bloom in spring or early summer. The foliage forms ferny mounds and the flower stalks bear spurred blossoms held high above the leaves. Columbine grows best in light shade in moist well-drained soil, but except in the hottest regions, it can be grown successfully in full sun too.

Aquilegia canadensis (AMERICAN COLUMBINE).

This lovely American native grows up to 3 feet in height, and in late spring the blooms appear. Flowers are composed of an outer spurred ring of red petals, which encase an inner circle of yellow petals.

Aquilegia chrysantha 'Silver Queen'.

This is a lovely pure white columbine that grows up to 30 inches tall. 'Silver Queen' is a very bushy plant that flowers abundantly from spring until early summer.

Aquilegia longissima 'Maxistar'.

This 30-inch-tall columbine has lovely yellow flowers with long spurs, up to 4 inches! 'Maxistar' flowers from May until June.

ARISAEMA. Family: Araceae.

Arisaema triphyllum (JACK-IN-THE-PULPIT). Zones 4–8.

Jack-in-the-pulpit is a favorite spring wild flower. The unusual name is an apt description: the conspicuous blossom consists of a finger-like spadix (the "Jack") contained in the hooded green spathe (the "pulpit"). *Arisaema* blooms in late spring or early summer and has distinguishing foliage. The leaves are divided into three parts and are held high on tall stems. In late summer and early fall, attractive orange berries make the plant easily recognizable. Grow jack-in-the-pulpit in moist acid soil in partial shade. *Arisaema* reaches 1 to 3 feet.

ARMERIA (SEA PINK, THRIFT). Family: Plumbaginaceae.

Sea pinks are native to rocky coastal regions, where they cling to exposed cliffs. In spring their bright pink flowers bring the rocks alive with color. They thrive in full sun and in well-drained soil; damp soil rots the root crown. The foliage of *Armeria* forms grassy tufts, and in most regions these leaves remain evergreen.

Armeria maritima 'Dusseldorf Pride'. Zones 5–9.

In my opinion 'Dusseldorf Pride' is one of the best sea pinks—it is certainly one of the most floriferous. In May and June bright crimson globular flowers are held on 5-inch stalks over the grassy mounds.

ARTEMISIA. Family: Compositae.

Artemisia abrotanum (SOUTHERNWOOD, LAD'S LOVE). Zones 3–9.

For me this plant has many pleasant childhood associations. It is the first herb that I got to know and enjoy. My grandmother's ancient cottage in Anglesey, North Wales, boasted a fine herb garden, and the center of attraction was a very large bush of southernwood. As children we called this woody plant "rabbit tobacco." From it we would distill perfume, and with the sweet water of rabbit tobacco we would lavishly bathe every cat, dog, and goat that my grandmother owned.

Southernwood is a woody herb that grows about 3 feet tall. The finely divided leaves are very aromatic. In midsummer small yellow flowers cover the plant. Southernwood grows best in full sun in well-drained soil. To prevent the plant from becoming leggy, give it a good pruning in late spring.

To the medieval physician this herb was almost a panacea. For those people who had the annoying habit of speaking in their sleep, it was a sure cure. To quote the *English Leechbook:* "Take southernwood and stomp it, and mingle the juice with white wine or with vinegar, and give the sick to drink when he goeth to his bed, and it shall let [hinder] him from speaking in his sleep." For tingling in the ears, the following cure was recommended: "Take the juice of southernwood, and put it in the ear; and stop the ear with the leaves of the same herb, and drink the juice at evening and at noon, it shall heal the tingling." The 1491 edition of the *Hortus Sanitatis* includes southernwood among the entries. The author writes, "The smoke of this herb shall drive away snakes from the house." A few centuries later, the English herbalist Nicholas Culpeper recommended to male readers that "have their hair fallen and are bald" to mix the ashes of southernwood "with old salad oil." This concoction, Culpeper assured, would cause "the hair to grow again, either on the head or beard." Southernwood was sometimes called "lad's love" because when young men started courting they would rub the herb over their face with the hope of starting a manly beard.

Artemisia absinthium (WORMWOOD, ABSINTHE). Zones 3–9.

Wormwood is a tall shrubby perennial with lacy silver-gray leaves. With maturity the aromatic foliage becomes almost chalky. This distinctive coloration makes it a good choice for a contrast with other herbs in the garden. Wormwood grows to about 3 feet, but under the right conditions gets as high as 4 feet. At midsummer, tiny greenish flowers cover the herb. This is a very adaptable perennial that will grow in full sun or partial shade. Nor is it too particular about the type of soil it is cultivated in.

The name records the plant's medicinal use: for many centuries a strong infusion of this herb was used by physicians for ridding the intestinal tract of parasitic worms. The leaves of wormwood provide the distinctive flavor of vermouth, but its better-known association with alcohol is absinthe, a spirituous drink that contained large amounts of wormwood. This infamous beverage ruined the minds of those who imbibed more than the occasional tipple.

The authoritative and august Greek herbalist Dioscorides stated: "It seems also that being laid about ye chests, to keep ye garments uneaten," and "mixed with ink doth keep writings uneaten by mice." Centuries later, the Elizabethan herbalist John Gerard wrote: "Wormwood is good for poisoning by hemlock, and against the biting of the shrew mouse and the sea dragon"!

'Lambrook Silver' is a lovely form of wormwood introduced by Margery Fish—a beautiful foliage plant with much-divided silvery gray leaves.

Artemisia canescens. Zones 5–9.

This is a really lovely artemisia. The lacy silver-gray inward-curving foliage forms architectural mounds about 18 inches high. English garden writer Beth Chatto described this garden gem beautifully: "The finest filigree foliage . . . [stands] out in autumn as whitest and laciest of all grays."

Artemisia dracunculus (FRENCH TARRAGON). Zones 5–9.

Called by many the "king of herbs," tarragon is an indispensable kitchen seasoning. This noble plant is sometimes confused with the inferior-tasting Russian tarragon *(Artemisia dracunculoides).* Avoid growing this variety. If you are confused between the two tarragons, taste one of the leaves—by the spicy sharp bite, you will immediately know which is French tarragon. This herb is a herbaceous perennial that grows to about 2 feet. The branches are covered with long, narrow, dark green leaves. Although French tarragon produces some insignificant greenish flowers, these never set seed. Consequently, tarragon is propagated by stem or root cuttings. If you are offered seeds of tarragon, beware, for these will be the Russian variety. French tarragon does not like the very hot and humid summers of southern Florida and the Gulf Coast areas. Gourmets in those regions might try growing tarragon near a sunny window inside an air-conditioned house. In other areas, grow tarragon in full sun but try to provide a bit of shade.

Use this herb with chicken, shellfish, lobster, chicken salad, or any egg or cheese dishes. Tarragon is vital for making a classic béarnaise sauce.

Artemisia lactiflora (GHOST PLANT, WHITE MUGWORT). Zones 4–8.

This is a tall perennial that can reach 5 feet. It is one of the few artemisias that are grown for their flowers—most members of this family are cultivated for their silvery foliage. *Artemisia lactiflora* is sometimes called "ghost plant" because the foliage has a silvery down on both sides which gives the plant a somewhat skeletal appearance. Fragrant creamy white blossoms appear in summer on tall self-supporting stems. The leaves are dark green and deeply notched. The underside of the foliage is silvery. Ghost plant can be grown in damper soils than other species of artemisia can tolerate, and although best planted in full sun, *Artemisia lactiflora* will grow in light shade.

Artemisia ludoviciana 'Silver King' (SILVER KING ARTEMISIA). Zones 4–9.

There seems to be some confusion about the correct identity of this plant. True 'Silver King' is a tall 3- to 4-foot perennial. The leaves are the distinguishing factor: the upper foliage is thin and willow-like, while the lower leaves are sharply lobed. 'Silver King' is very popular for wreath making, and in the garden it is useful as a foil for other perennials. It combines especially well with *Eryngium giganteum:* the steely blue flowers look wonderful with the silvery foliage of 'Silver King'. Plant *Artemisia ludoviciana* in full sun. In warmer areas of the U.S., this plant can become invasive.

'Valerie Finnis', also listed as *Artemisia ludoviciana var. latiloba,* is one of my favorite silver plants. Although this particular artemisia is not very common in the U.S., it is well worth seeking out. It looks somewhat like a candelabrum: branches arch over and then send up new leafy shoots that are a wonderful shade of silver. 'Valerie Finnis' has much wider and longer foliage than most other hybrids or species of artemisia.

Artemisia schmidtiana 'Silver Mound' (SILVER MOUND ARTEMISIA). Zones 3–9.

This is perhaps the most popular of the artemisias. 'Silver Mound' forms delicate tufts of silky silvery leaves. The gossamer quality of these cushions—about 8 to 12 inches high and 12 inches across—adds beauty to any garden. Grow this species of artemisia in full sun in well-drained soil. If the soil is too rich, 'Silver Mound' tends to die back in the center or becomes less compact. This is a perfect perennial for edging pathways.

Artemisia vulgaris (MUGWORT). Zones 3–9.

Mugwort, a tall plant that reaches over 3 feet, is a common perennial of European hedgerows. The divided green leaves have a white undersurface. Small rusty yellow flowers appear in summer. Mugwort is easily cultivated, and will grow in full sun or part shade.

The strange name is derived from the use of this herb for flavoring ale. (Hops were not used for this purpose until the late fifteenth century.) Mugwort was considered a magical herb, especially if gathered on St. John's Eve (June 24). Plants obtained during this time would be hung over the lintel of a door, and according to Banckes's *Herbal* of 1525, "if it be within a house, there shall no wicked spirits abide." And "if a man bear this herb about him, he shall not be weary of traveling in his way." The *Anglo-Saxon Herbal of Apuleius* suggests using mugwort as a herbal styptic: "Take . . . young mugwort and red nettle tops, and temper therewith the powder of burnt salt; and lay to the wound and it shall staunch anon, on warrenty." As an alternative to this lengthy preparation the author informs the reader that "a hot dog's turd will do the same."

ARUNCUS (GOAT'S BEARD). Family: Roseaceae.

Aruncus dioicus. Zones 4–9.

Goat's beard is a hardy plant that in foliage and flower resembles a giant astilbe. A perfect site for this tall perennial is moist, well-drained soil, the sort of earth that is associated with the higher levels of a pond or stream bank, preferably in shade. Goat's beard can also be grown in the flower border, but make sure that the soil is rich in organic matter, and try to give the plant some shade. In a happy environment *Aruncus* will grow 6 to 7 feet tall, and from June until July it is covered with creamy white plumed flowers. Give *Aruncus* plenty of space to grow, because when mature this plant takes on shrublike proportions. In old gardens, one occasionally sees goat's beard plants that are sixteen years old and measure 6 feet across!

ASARUM (WILD GINGER, ASARABACCA). Family: Aristolochiaceae.

Asarum europaeum. Zones 4–8.

This low-growing evergreen perennial is cultivated for its glossy kidney-shaped foliage. Even in the shadiest of places, the shiny deep green leaves of asarabacca form dense 6-inch mats. Grow this plant in good rich soil. Wild ginger can be grown in light shade.

ASCLEPIAS. Family: Asclepiadaceae.

Asclepias tuberosa (BUTTERFLY MILKWEED, PLEURISY ROOT, BUTTERFLY PLANT). Zones 3–8.

On the prairies in summer, this native American plant is a marvelous sight. From July to early fall, the 1- to 3-foot stems are topped by dozens of tiny orange-yellow flowers. Plant butterfly milkweed in full sun in well-drained soil. In gardens north of Zone 6, many wildflower growers recommend giving this perennial a covering of mulch before winter. By pruning early blossoms, plants soon develop a more compact shrubby appearance and the flowering period is extended. As the name suggests, this is a plant that will attract butterflies to the garden.

This herb is used to treat infections of the respiratory tract, as is indicated by the vernacular name "pleurisy root." When the seed heads mature they become filled with silky down. This gift of nature was employed by our ancestors for filling pillows.

ASTER (MICHAELMAS DAISY). Family: Compositae.

Asters are wonderful for the late summer and fall garden. And after being neglected for so long, they are at last becoming much more widely used in American gardens.

Aster azureus (SKY BLUE ASTER). Zones 4–9.

As the name indicates, this prairie flower bears lovely light blue flowers, which appear in late summer. The foliage is attractive also—the arrow-shaped leaves are deep green to bluish in color. Sky blue aster grows 2 to 3 feet tall and should be planted in full sun in very dry or slightly moist soil.

Aster ericoides (HEATH ASTER). Zones 4–9.

I am always amazed to see heath aster growing in the most inhospitable places. In my own garden, the heath asters that grow in the very dry soil at the edge of a hemlock wood put on a wonderful autumn display, when myriads of tiny white daisies cover each plant. Heath aster looks inconspicuous all spring and summer—and you almost forget that the plant is in your garden—but then in September and October it comes into its glory. Heath aster is best when grown in drifts or largish blocks. It will grow in dry as well as moist soil and can be planted in full sun or part shade.

Aster x *frikartii* 'Wonder of Staffa'. Zones 5–9.

From July until September 'Wonder of Staffa' is covered with lavender blue daisy-like flowers, each blossom with a golden center. It forms neat 2½- to 3-foot clumps. Grow this aster in full sun in average well-drained garden soil.

Aster laevis (SMOOTH ASTER). Zones 4–9.

This is one of the best of the native asters. In September the 2-foot stems are covered with light blue flowers. Smooth asters like full sun and can be grown in average to moist soil.

Aster novae-angliae 'Harrington's Pink' (NEW ENGLAND ASTER). Zones 4–9.

This is an old garden favorite. In late summer and fall, tall 4-foot spikes bear a profusion of pink blossoms. Only the coldest frost affects this plant. 'Harrington's Pink' needs full sun.

Aster sericeus (SILKY ASTER). Zones 4–9.

This is a low-growing aster that reaches 1 to 2 feet in height. Large purplish flowers with curved petals appear in August and September. Silky aster likes full sun or light shade in soil that is on the dry side.

Aster spectabilis (SHOWY ASTER). Zones 4–9.

Showy aster is a wonderful fall bloomer. In September the foot-high stems are covered with lavender blue flowers. Grow this species in sun or light shade in dry soil.

ASTILBE (sometimes called *Spirea* in old gardening books). Family: Saxifragaceae. Zones 4–7.

Astilbes are attractive in both leaf and blossom. The arching plumes of flowers that surmount the delicately dissected shiny leaves give elegance to any garden. Astilbes should be cultivated in light shade in rich moist soil.

Astilbe x *arendsii* 'Fanal'.

In June and July this 2-foot astilbe bears dark red flowers. The foliage is an attractive reddish color.

Astilbe chinensis 'Pumila'.

This astilbe usually grows 8 to 12 inches tall. In August and September mauvish-pink flower spikes appear. *Astilbe chinensis* 'Pumila' will slowly spread into thick mats. This growth habit makes it very useful as a ground cover for shady sites.

Astilbe tacquetii 'Superba'.

This is my favorite astilbe; there are few more elegant flowers in the garden. In late summer, the large magenta flower spikes tower over the glossy ferny leaves. The sturdy 4-foot stems give majestic stature to the back of the flower border. In rich moist soil and light shade the flower spikes of *Astilbe tacquetii* 'Superba' last for weeks.

ASTRANTIA (MASTERWORT). Family: Umbelliferae.

Astrantia major 'Margery Fish'. Zones 4–8.

In May and June *Astrantia* bears white pink-tinged blooms. Each flower looks like a tiny posy and is held on a 2-foot stem. 'Margery Fish' is perfect for drying and for using in flower arrangements. Grow this *Astrantia* in well-drained soil in sun or partial shade.

ATHYRIUM. Family: Polypodiaceae.

Athyrium goeringianum 'Pictum' (JAPANESE PAINTED FERN). Zones 3–8.

This exotic and colorful hardy fern is the perfect plant for brightening dark places. Each of the 2-foot fronds is a subtle mixture of silver, gray-green, and wine-red. Grow Japanese painted fern in moist soil in light shade.

ATRIPLEX. Family: Chenopodiaceae.

Atriplex hortensis 'Rubra' (RED ORACH). Zones 3–10.

This hardy red annual will grow up to 5 or 6 feet in a season. Sow the seeds in light well-drained soil and give the plants plenty of moisture. For this little effort the gardener will be rewarded with a crop of succulent and tender leaves that are as delicious as spinach. Orach makes wonderful soup and adds flavor and color to summer salads. The bright red leaves make it attractive in the herb border. This herb can be invasive, so make sure flower heads are cut off before seeds ripen.

ATROPA. Family: Solanaceae.

Atropa belladonna (DEADLY NIGHTSHADE, BELLADONNA, DWALE). Zones 6–9.

Deadly nightshade is a tall perennial that reaches 5 feet at maturity. From June until late summer the brownish-purple bell-shaped flowers appear. The berries, about the size of a cherry, are initially green, then turn a shiny black. These highly toxic fruits are very sweet tasting (I once ate part of one) and so deadly nightshade should not be grown where children are about. Seven to nine berries will prove fatal. The rustic name for this fruit, "devil's cherries," bears witness to the toxicity of the berries. This is the timber rattlesnake of the plant world!

The name "nightshade" derives from an old superstition. It is said that at certain times this plant takes the form of an enchantress of exceeding loveliness, and that it is dangerous to look upon her. According to legend the plant belongs to the Devil, and Satan goes about trimming and tending deadly nightshade at his leisure. He can be diverted from its care only on Walpurgis Night (May 1), when he is preparing for the witches' sabbath. In medieval Europe, the fermented berries of belladonna were used by witches for the preparation of a hallucinogenic cream called *unguentum sabbati*. By vigorously rubbing their bodies with this cream, the witches believed they were flying through the air to join their companions at a satanic meeting! Fortunately today we have simpler means of transportation.

Atropa mandragora. See *Mandragora officinarum.*

AURINIA. Family: Cruciferae.

Aurinia saxatilis (BASKET-OF-GOLD). Zones 3–9.

Basket-of-gold is a low-growing perennial that reaches up to 12 inches and in spring is covered with bright yellow flowers. *Aurinia saxatilis* needs very well drained soil and does best when planted in full sun—rock gardens and gravelly sandy soil are ideal sites.

AZALEA NUDIFLORA. See *Rhododendron periclymenoides.*

B

BAPTISIA. Family: Leguminosae. Zones 3–8.

Baptisia australis (BLUE FALSE INDIGO).

This is a tall perennial that reaches 4 to 6 feet. In June, *Baptisia australis* bears blue flower spikes. The attractive foliage is gray-green. Grow *Baptisia* in moist lime-free soil in full sun or partial shade.

Baptisia leucantha (PRAIRIE FALSE INDIGO).

Prairie false indigo grows up to 4 feet, with attractive cones of white flowers appearing in June. *Baptisia leucantha* is a slow-growing but very long-lived prairie flower. Grow this *Baptisia* species in full sun to partial shade, in moist to moderately dry soil.

BELLIS (DAISY). Family: Compositae.

Bellis perennis (ENGLISH DAISY). Zones 4–9.

As children we used to make garlands of these enchanting flowers and with them celebrate mock weddings which, as five- or six-year-olds, we took very seriously! The garlands were made by piercing the thin stem of each daisy with a fingernail and threading another daisy into this slit. Such extravagance was permissible, for in England this daisy is one of the most plentiful flowers—especially in lawns. (*Bellis perennis* is also abundant in the lawns of northwestern American gardeners.)

Bellis perennis is a small herbaceous plant, 1 to 6 inches tall, that from spring until fall bears tiny white flowers with yellow centers. Cultivate *Bellis perennis* in full sun to light shade, in moist soil.

The word "daisy" is a corruption of "day's eye," a reference to the flower's opening in sunshine and closing at night. The Elizabethan herbalist and gardener John Gerard wrote: "The leaves of daisy used amongst other potherbs do make the belly soluble ... the juice of the leaves snift up into the nostrils, purgeth the head mightily of foul and filthy slimie humors.... The same given to little dogs with milk keepeth them from growing great." If daisy juice could keep Fido small, *Bellis perennis* would be the wonder plant for city dwellers! Thompson & Morgan sells the seed of *Bellis perennis* (but they make no canine claims for daisy juice).

BERBERIS (BARBERRY). Family: Berberidaceae.

Berberis thunbergii 'Aurea' (GOLDEN BARBERRY, YELLOW JAPANESE BARBERRY). Zones 4–9.

Every gardener should find a place for this shrub—yellow Japanese barberry is one of the best golden plants available. From late spring until fall, small golden oval leaves cover these bushes. In sunlight the shrubs look as if they were made from burnished gold. Yellow Japanese barberry is a small slow-growing deciduous shrub that matures at 2 feet. *Berberis* are thorny plants, so handle them with respect. Grow golden barberry in full sun or light shade, in moist well-drained soil.

BERGENIA. Family: Saxifragaceae.

Bergenia cordifolia. Zones 3–8.

This evergreen perennial is one of the most useful plants for shady areas. The thick leathery leaves of *Bergenia* can measure up to 1 foot across. A red tinge adds to the beauty of the foliage, and often this color deepens during the winter. In spring, spikes of pink flowers appear. Grow this plant in shade or in a moist well-drained soil to which lime has been added. If the soil is moist enough, *Bergenia* will grow in full sun, but try to protect it from the midday sun. Watch for slugs eating the leaves; use poison bait to control them.

BETULA (BIRCH). Family: Betulaceae.

Betula papyrifera (CANOE BIRCH, PAPER BIRCH). Zones 2–8.

Winter or summer, the birch is a beautiful tree. The enchanting snow-white bark sets off the delicate light green leaves in summer, in fall the leaves put on a spectacular show as they turn a brilliant yellow, and in winter the beauty of naked birches is legendary. *Betula papyrifera* is a deciduous tree that matures at around 40 to 60 feet. Grow canoe birch in full sun in well-drained soil. For warmer areas (Zones 7–8), European white birch *(Betula pendula)* or river birch *(Betula nigra)* would be a better choice. Local garden centers will recommend the best variety for your area.

Be on the lookout for two insect pests that affect these trees: bronze birch borer and birch leaf miner. If leaves start to be covered with what looks like white scribbles, you have leaf miner. Birch borer is indicated by small holes in stems or branches, and foliage that wilts even when the soil is moist. Garden centers carry products that provide easy means of control.

BOLTONIA. Family: Compositae.

Boltonia asteroides 'Snowbank'. Zones 4–9.

My first experience with *Boltonia* was very surprising. A small plant purchased in the spring grew at an astonishing rate. And although this perennial looked neat and compact, it did nothing extraordinary for the whole summer — except grow. Then suddenly in early autumn my 4-foot "bush" of *Boltonia* started to open its white daisy-like flowers. Although nothing spectacular at first, in a few weeks the *Boltonia* stole the show from other late-blooming perennials. Myriad white daisies made 'Snowbank' look like a Christmas tree. Of all plants grown in the garden, I think *Boltonia asteroides* 'Snowbank' is the ugly duckling that becomes a swan! Not only does this perennial look spectacular in bloom but it also flowers for many weeks. 'Snowbank' has stiff stems that need no support. It is a roomy perennial, so give the plants plenty of space. Grow *Boltonia* in full sun in either moist or dry soil.

BORAGO. Family: Boraginaceae.

Borago officinalis (BORAGE, COOL TANKARD). Zones 3–10.

Borage is a cheerful annual for the herb garden, the sky-blue flowers with black centers making this one of the few herbs with a really attractive flower. The delicate blossoms contrast with the coarse hairy leaves, giving the impression of a delicate ballerina with hairy legs! The strong stems of borage grow to 3 feet. Plant this herb in full sun in any well-drained soil.

Although today borage is cultivated in the herb garden mainly for its beauty, the cucumber-flavored leaves are delicious in summer drinks, alcoholic and otherwise. The vernacular name "cool tankard" records this practice. Some people recommend the leaves of borage in salads, but I find them much too coarse for this purpose. As a matter of fact, it's like swallowing sandpaper! A medieval English herbal praises borage for its ability to bestow joviality upon all those who ingest it: "Its virtue is to engender good blood, and to make a man light and merry, and ruddy of cheer," according to the *English Leechbook*. So great was the ability of borage to drive away melancholy that the ancients wrote: "If your wife or children, your father and mother, your brother and sister and all your friends were to die under your very eyes, you would find it impossible to shed a single tear over them." The fainthearted should take note: drinking borage juice is said to make the most timid person have the courage of a lion!

BRIZA. Family: Gramineae.

Briza media (QUAKING GRASS). Zones 4–8.

Quaking grass is one of the most beautiful of the small grasses. From June until August the curious loose flowers rise above the grassy tufts and shimmer with the slightest breeze. Quaking grass grows up to 3 feet. Cultivate this perennial ornamental grass in poorish soil in full sun; rich earth makes it too coarse.

C

CALENDULA. Family: Compositae.

Calendula officinalis (MARIGOLD, POT MARIGOLD). Zones 2–10.

No herb garden should be without marigolds (not to be confused with French or African marigolds—varieties of *Tagetes*). The large bright orange and yellow flowers, which appear in early summer and continue until late fall, are one of the highlights of the herbal border. This annual is easy to grow and will thrive in full sun in any reasonable garden soil. The flowers, borne on foot-long stems, open and close with the sun. Sometimes on a cloudy day marigolds will not open their blossoms at all. The freshly picked petals are delicious in salads, soups, and stews. Marigold flowers infused in hot water, like tea, make a wonderful extract—excellent for healing chapped hands, reducing varicose veins, and eliminating thread veins on the face. The ointment, either homemade or purchased, works equally well. And I have successfully used this preparation for minor burns and insect stings. In times past the bright yellow flowers of marigold were used as a substitute for costly saffron . . . and considering the current price of saffron, it's not a bad idea today. In earlier centuries the yellow dye from marigolds was used as a cosmetic, a practice recorded in the vitriolic writings of William Turner, a famous Elizabethan herbalist: "Some use marigold to make their hair yellow with the flowers of this herb, not being content with the natural color which God has given them." This cantankerous fellow was expelled from the kingdom more than once, and it's not too hard to see why!

CALLIRHOE. Family: Malvaceae. Zones 3–10.

Callirhoe involucrata (POPPY MALLOW, WINE-CUPS, ROSE POPPY MALLOW).

Poppy mallow is a remarkable plant. Some years ago a friend sent me seeds of *Callirhoe* and ever since I have treasured this perennial.

Poppy mallow is a prostrate plant that spreads fairly slowly. The flowers, as the name "wine-cups" indicates, are a lovely port color. There are some perennials that bloom all summer—poppy mallow is one of these. Since this plant hugs the ground, to take full advantage of the colorful blossoms, grow poppy mallow along a pathway or let it sprawl over a low wall. *Callirhoe* is a drought-resistant plant, so it is a perfect flower for low-maintenance gardens. Grow it in full sun in well-drained soil.

Callirhoe triangulata.

This midwestern native of the prairies has triangular leaves, with 2-inch deep purple blooms that appear in summer. This perennial prefers sandy and loose loamy soils.

CALLUNA (HEATHER). Family: Ericaceae. Zones 3–8.

The heathers are shrubby evergreen plants that flower for a long period, usually between July and November. This is a favorite plant of my childhood. I can remember the exhilarating feeling of trekking over the heather on a Scottish moor in the fall when the flowers make these unearthly areas ablaze with color. To create this same effect it is best to plant *Calluna* in masses—generous blocks that will stand out in the landscape. Bunches of Scottish heather that I picked in the fall to adorn the bumpers of our car would keep their color a whole year—even longer if not tied to the front of a car! Grow these plants in full sun in well-drained sandy soil to which some peat moss has been added. Heathers are ideal plants for coastal areas.

Calluna vulgaris.

Calluna vulgaris 'H. E. Beale' is a spreading heather that reaches 2 feet in height. It bears double pink flowers from August to November. 'Mrs. R. H. Gray' is a dwarf heather, only 4 inches tall, that bears pink flowers in August and September. 'Silver Queen' has nice woolly silver foliage which contrasts well with the dark pink flowers that cover the plants in August and September. 'Silver Queen' grows up to 1 foot.

CALTHA. Family: Ranunculaceae.

Caltha palustris (MARSH MARIGOLD). Zones 3–9.

This moisture-loving perennial has attractive roundish glossy, fleshy leaves. In spring, the whole plant is covered with large golden cup-shaped flowers. Although the marsh marigold is found in the wild along stream banks and ponds, it will adapt to good moist garden soil. Except when *Caltha* is planted in very moist ground, try to give it some light shade. Marsh marigolds grow 12 to 18 inches high.

CALYCANTHUS. Family: Calycanthaceae.

Calycanthus floridus (SWEETSHRUB). Zones 4–8.

This is an old-fashioned sweet-smelling shrub with deep burgundy flowers in May and June. These blossoms are very fragrant, as are the leaves when crushed. *Calycanthus* is a neat shrub that at maturity will reach 6 to 9 feet. For smaller garden areas, it can be pruned to a more compact shape. Grow *Calycanthus* in sun or light shade in rich well-drained soil.

CAMPANULA (BELLFLOWER). Family: Campanulaceae.

Campanulas are a very diverse group of plants recognizable by their attractive bell-shaped flowers. They vary in size from dwarf species to campanulas that are 3 feet tall. All bell-flowers need a somewhat rich well-drained soil. Many species and varieties bloom for the whole summer and continue flowering well into the fall.

Campanula carpatica var. *alba* (WHITE CARPATHIAN HAREBELL). Zones 3–8.

In late spring and for much of the summer this foot-high plant is covered with open white bell-shaped flowers. The crinkled pointed foliage forms little semi-evergreen mounds. Grow this species in full sun or partial shade.

Campanula lactiflora 'Superba'. Zones 5–8.

This tall campanula reaches 3 feet. The violet-blue inch-wide flowers appear in June and July. Grow *Campanula lactiflora* 'Superba' in full sun or partial shade.

Campanula medium (CANTERBURY BELLS). Zones 3–8.

This is a biennial campanula that grows 2 to 4 feet high. The violet-blue flowers are fairly large 2-inch-long bells that appear in midsummer. Grow Canterbury bells in sun or partial shade, in ordinary garden soil.

Campanula percisifolia 'Telham Beauty' (PEACH-LEAVED BELLFLOWER). Zones 3–8.

Peach-leaved bellflower grows 2 to 3 feet tall. From June to August showy terminals of bright blue or white flowers appear. These blossoms are cup-shaped and are very conspicuous. Grow this species in full sun or partial shade.

Campanula rotundifolia (HAREBELL, BLUEBELLS OF SCOTLAND, WITCH'S THIMBLE). Zones 3–8.

From June until September, this low-growing perennial bears lovely sky-blue bell-shaped flowers. Harebell spreads up to 18 inches wide and grows 12 inches high. Cultivate this plant in well-drained soil in sun or partial shade.

Harebell was a flower of sorcerers, goblins, and witches. The vernacular name "witch's thimble" indicates its occult connections, but so do the other names. The close association between hare and witch has long been established—the hare was one of the favorite guises of the witch, who chose to turn herself into this animal to escape pursuers and speed her on her way. As for the harebell's other name, as Geoffrey Grigson points out, "Bluebell of Scotland or no, it was also the Old Man's Bell, the Devil's Bell, which was not to be picked. . . . In Ireland this dangerous and fine etched plant is sometimes *Mearacan Puca*, thimble of the puca or goblin; and it was a fairy plant in the south-west of England, however much it now has been airyfairy'd."

CAREX. Family: Cyperaceae.

Carex pendula (DROOPING SEDGE). Zones 4–9.

This attractive semi-evergreen 2-foot sedge is ideal for a shady, moist part of the garden. Drooping sedge has a graceful arching habit. The flowering spikes appear in May and June.

CARYOPTERIS. Family: Verbenaceae.

Caryopteris x *clandonensis*. Zones 5–9.

From August until frost, this low-growing shrub is covered with fringed powdery blue blossoms. *Caryopteris* grows 2 to 3 feet tall, and when crushed, the silvery green foliage releases a pleasant aroma. Grow this shrub in full sun in well-drained soil. In colder areas *Caryopteris* is sometimes killed back to ground level. If this happens, cut away the

dead wood before new growth emerges in the spring. In very cold areas (Zone 4 or low Zone 5), cut the shrub to the ground in early winter, and cover the stumps with mulch.

CATANANCHE. Family: Compositae.

Catananche caerulea (CUPID'S DART). Zones 5–9.

Cupid's dart is rather like a perennial cornflower. In July and August the 2-foot plants are covered with blue daisies. These blossoms are everlasting and so are perfect for dried flower arrangements. Cupid's dart needs to be grown in full sun in well-drained soil. To have an impact on a flower border, *Catananche* should be planted in blocks of three to five plants.

CAULOPHYLLUM. Family: Berberidaceae.

Caulophyllum thalictroides (BLUE COHOSH). Zones 3–8.

This hardy native American flower is grown for its bright blue berries, which appear in late summer. Blue cohosh spreads rapidly, and the plants grow 1 to 3 feet high. The fruiting plants are most outstanding when they are grown in a mass in a woodland-type setting. Grow blue cohosh in shade in moist soil. Abundant moisture is essential.

CENTAUREA. Family: Compositae.

Centaurea macrocephala (PERENNIAL CORNFLOWER). Zones 3–8.

This tall perennial reaches 4 feet. In June and July, large bright yellow thistle-like flowers on stiff stems make it outstanding in the garden. Grow perennial cornflower in full sun to partial shade, in well-drained soil.

CENTRANTHUS. Family: Valerianaceae.

Centranthus ruber (RED VALERIAN).
Zones 5–9.

Anybody who travels in the British Isles in summer cannot help but notice that the stone walls of medieval castles are often alive with colorful flowers. On careful observation it will be seen that these plants actually thrive in the ancient stone mortar! Chances are, you have just been introduced to red valerian. But take heart, you don't have to own a castle to cultivate *Centranthus ruber* successfully. From July to August the 3-foot plants of red valerian bear lovely clusters of pinkish-red flowers. If dead flower spikes are removed, *Centranthus* will bloom again in the fall. Grow red valerian in full sun or partial shade, in well-drained soil. This plant can be established in stone walls or in flower borders, and it looks very good sprawling by pathways.

CEPHALANTHUS. Family: Rubiaceae.

Cephalanthus occidentalis (BUTTONBUSH).
Zones 4–9.

Buttonbush is a neat little shrub for the damp part of the garden. A lovely native plant, it is not used enough in American gardens. From mid-July, for four to six weeks, attractive sphere-shaped flowers cover the bush. These orbs are large and make the buttonbush look like a decorated Christmas tree! *Cephalanthus* generally reaches 3 to 5 feet. Cultivate it in full sun. It will not do well in dry soil.

CERATOSTIGMA. Family: Plumbaginaceae.

Ceratostigma plumbaginoides (BLUE PLUMBAGO). Zones 6–10.

From August to October this low-growing perennial bears lovely, intense gentian-blue flowers. In the fall, the foliage turns a deep mahogany color. *Ceratostigma* is only 6 to 12 inches tall. Cultivate blue plumbago in full sun or partial shade, in well-drained soil. In a protective part of the garden and with the help of winter mulch, it will survive in Zone 5 regions. But even in Zone 6 areas a protective mulch is advisable.

CHAMAEMELUM. Family: Compositae.
Zones 3–10.

Chamaemelum nobile (formerly *Anthemis nobilis*) (ROMAN CHAMOMILE).

True chamomile can easily be grown from seed. A spring sowing will give an abundant harvest by midsummer. This low-growing perennial creeps over the garden border, and in summer it sends up foot-long branching stems that are topped with daisy-like flowers. Chamomile prefers full sun, although plants will tolerate some shade. The blossoms and finely cut leaves have a delicious smell of apples. For the whole summer, white flowers cover the stems.

For centuries this benign herb has given relief from a great assortment of ailments. It is a wonder cure for digestion problems, summer diarrhea, stomach spasms, and plain old tummy ache. A beverage made by infusing about thirty chamomile flowers in a teapot makes a wonderful bedtime drink which will relax the body and promote sleep. And if we can believe the gypsy herb-women, chamomile tea prevents nightmares. Roman chamomile is an ideal ground cover for dry areas—sites that if planted with grass would turn brown in the summer heat. Chamomile will also tolerate acid soils and even a certain amount of shade.

Walking on a chamomile "lawn" is indeed an experience; a delicious apple fragrance is released with every step. If you are seriously thinking about one of these aromatic lawns, try to locate *Chamaemelum nobile* 'Treneague' or *Chamaemelum nobile* 'Flore Pleno'. The former is non-flowering, and since it never needs cutting, it is considered by many to be the best variety of Roman chamomile for making into a lawn. The other cultivar, 'Flore Pleno', does need an occasional cutting, but it bears on its short stems the most fragrant double flower. Whatever variety you choose, remember that a chamomile lawn will not stand the traffic that normal grass will tolerate, and it will be necessary to do some occasional hand weeding. My best advice is to choose a small area. If it is a success, then next season, you can expand your lawn.

In the Middle Ages, chamomile was widely used for strewing on stone and wood floors. When crushed underfoot, the pleasant fragrance must have been a relief after the musty smells of the castle and monastery. In his herbal, John Gerard sums up the use of chamomile in Elizabethan England: "Oil of chamomile is exceedingly good against all mannor of aches and pains . . . against coldness in the stomach, sore belching, voideth wind . . . used in baths provoketh sweat, rarifieth the skin and openeth the pores . . . is a remedy against all wearisomeness." The old herbalists recommended chamomile infusions for headache and migraine. On a personal note, I find a hot bath containing a strong brew of chamomile flowers wonderfully relaxing after a hard day's work. I learned about the chamomile soak from the writings of the seventeenth-century herbalist Nicholas Culpeper:

"Bathing with chamomile removes weariness and eases pain to whatever part it is employed."

CHELIDONIUM. Family: Papaveraceae.

Chelidonium majus (CELANDINE, CELANDINE POPPY, GREATER CELANDINE). Zones 5–9.

Celandine grows 1 to 3 feet tall and throughout summer bears bright yellow flowers. It was once used for removing warts (the country names "felonwort" and "wartwort" record this practice). To carry out this operation a piece of celandine was simply broken off the main plant and the thick orange juice that exudes from the stem was applied to the offending growth. A medieval volume on magic, *The Book of Secrets* of Albertus Magnus, tells the reader that if celandine is mixed "with the heart of a mole, he shall overcome all his enemies, and all matters on suite, and shal put away all debate." Furthermore, the author of this weighty tome tells gullible readers, if celandine is "put on the head of a sick man, if he shal die, he shall sing with a loud voice, if not, he shal weep." Grow celandine in full sun or light shade, in any type of soil except waterlogged ground.

CHELONE. Family: Scrophulariaceae.

Chelone lyonii (PINK TURTLEHEAD). Zones 4–9.

This is a lovely late-blooming perennial that is perfect for waterside gardens. At the end of summer or in early fall snapdragon-type pink flowers appear. *Chelone lyonii* grows 2 to 3 feet tall and in a few seasons will form dense colonies. Grow pink turtlehead in full sun or partial shade, in moist soil.

CHENOPODIUM. Family: Chenopodiaceae.

Chenopodium bonus-henricus (GOOD KING HENRY, MERCURY). Zones 3–10.

Good King Henry is a hardy and robust perennial that grows up to 2 feet. The foliage is arrow-shaped, and in June insignificant green blossoms appear on long spikes. Good King Henry is easy to grow; any well-drained soil is suitable, and some shade is preferred.

The name of this herb has nothing to do with a monarch. It is given to the plant to distinguish it from a somewhat similar, but poisonous, dye plant—Bad Henry *(Mercurialis perennis)*. Good King Henry was a favorite vegetable in the Middle Ages; like spinach, it was served with melted butter. This herb is still good to include on a modern menu.

CHRYSANTHEMUM. Family: Compositae.

Chrysanthemum balsamita (COSTMARY, ALECOST, BIBLE-LEAF). Zones 6–9.

The vernacular names of this plant, "alecost" and "Bible-leaf," record two of *Chrysanthemum balsamita*'s ancient uses: ale making and page marking. Bible reading and swigging beer were two favorite pastimes of medieval monks, so it is only appropriate that these ecclesiastics should name one of their favorite plants after those occupations. The name "costmary" is in honor of the Virgin Mary. The Madonna claimed many plants for her own, and *Chrysanthemum balsamita* is included in the list.

Alecost has a nice smell—a mixture of mint, lemon, and balsam. Because of this, it was strewn onto the stone floors of castles and monasteries. The Elizabethan herbalist John Gerard recommends alecost for "warming and drying the brain."

Costmary is a sprawling perennial with silvery leaves that grows to 3 feet. In late summer small button-like yellow flowers appear. Grow alecost in full sun in dry well-drained soil. Use the leaves in making potpourri, or do what the medieval monks did: scatter them on the floor!

Chrysanthemum leucanthemum (OXEYE DAISY, MOON DAISY, MARGUERITE). Zones 3–9.

The oxeye daisy is an erect, slightly branched perennial that grows 2 feet tall. Throughout the summer this herb bears numerous white daisy flowers with yellow centers.

Midsummer's day, as the sun approached the solstice, was a special celebration for our European ancestors, a time of powerful magic. And among the important activities during this occasion of great solar power, the gathering of herbs was deemed essential. Any plants flowering at that time were considered magical. Because the oxeye daisy blooms at midsummer it became a powerful plant, a herb that could provide protection against supernatural forces. Its vernacular English name, "tunder flower" or "thunder flower," records an ancient rustic belief that if the oxeye daisy was grown on the roof of a house or barn, the building would be protected from lightning. The otherworldly aura surrounding the oxeye daisy was passed on through the centuries. John Petchey, the seventeenth-century herbalist, stated that the blossoms of this herb "cast forth beams of brightness." In herbal medicine this plant has been used for night sweats, coughs, and bronchial catarrhs. Oxeye daisy is easy to grow in the garden. Plant it in full sun in well-drained soil.

Chrysanthemum maximum 'Little Miss Muffet' (SHASTA DAISY). Zones 4–9.

Shasta daisies like to be planted in full sun in rich soil. From June until August, lovely semi-double daisies cover this 14-inch plant. 'Little Miss Muffet' is the perfect choice for the front of the flower border. To extend the flowering period, remove dead flowers. All Shasta daisies are best divided every other year: dig up mature plants, discard the center roots, and replant only those with vigorous outer root systems. For Shasta daisies to retain their prolific blossoming during summer, this drastic splitting is essential. In Zones 4–5, give Shasta daisies a winter protection of mulch.

'Polaris' is one of the most popular Shasta daisies. In June and July, the 2-foot plants bloom prolifically. Each daisy has a yellow center.

Chrysanthemum parthenium (FEVERFEW). Zones 4–9.

Feverfew is an erect branched perennial that grows 10 to 24 inches high. In summer it produces white daisy flowers with golden centers. Feverfew is easily grown in the herb garden, in full sun in any reasonable soil.

The name "feverfew" is derived from *febris*, the Latin word for fever, and *fugere*, the Latin word that means "to chase away." Before the advent of the modern pharmaceutical industry, feverfew was used by all households not only as a cure for fevers but as a relief from headaches. It was the aspirin of the herbal era. The medieval medical book *Hortus Sanitatis* states that feverfew when "mixed with wine . . . will make women faithful and lighthearted." A little later, the Elizabethan herbalist John Gerard recommended feverfew "for them that are giddie in the head."

Chrysanthemum segetum (CORN MARIGOLD). Zones 3–10.

For centuries corn marigold has been considered a beautiful flower. It is one of the plants depicted most often in the Metropolitan Museum of Art's famous late-fifteenth-century Unicorn Tapestries. Although the corn marigold is an annual, it will reseed itself and appear in the garden year after year. *Chrysanthemum segetum* forms neat 18- to 14-inch bushlike mounds. From late May until really heavy frost, this garden gem is literally covered with golden yellow semi-double daisies. The bluish tinge of the foliage adds to the beauty of the plant.

I have successfully used this flower in formal borders, lining pathways, and in a wildflower meadow. Do try to grow this exquisite wild flower. Seed can easily be obtained from Chiltern Seed in England (see the Suppliers list).

CHRYSOGONUM. Family: Compositae.

Chrysogonum virginianum (GREEN-AND-GOLD, GOLDENSTAR). Zones 5–9.

Green-and-gold is a lovely ground cover adaptable to both sun and shade. In more northerly gardens *Chrysogonum* will flower from spring until fall. In hotter regions of the country, it will generally blossom only in the spring. Green-and-gold is 8 inches tall; the flowers are yellow and star-shaped. Although it can be grown in full sun, *Chrysogonum* will bloom most prolifically if planted in light shade. Grow green-and-gold in rich moist soil.

CHRYSOPSIS. Family: Compositae.

Chrysopsis mariana (GOLDEN ASTER, MARYLAND GOLDEN ASTER). Zones 4–9.

The fall-blooming golden aster has a daisy-like flower. *Chrysopsis* is similar in appearance to an aster, but has what no aster has—a yellow flower. For gardeners in hot climates who do not have great success with Michaelmas daisies, *Chrysopsis* is the answer. It grows 1½ to 3 feet tall and should be planted in full sun or light shade in any type of garden soil.

CICHORIUM. Family: Compositae.

Cichorium intybus (CHICORY, SUCCORY). Zones 3–10.

We have all seen the beautiful spikes of sky-blue chicory flowers along our highways. From July until September, the 3- to 6-foot stems of this wayside perennial are covered with blossoms that open and close with the daylight. Our ancestors ascribed various magical properties to this plant: The occult powers of chicory would enable anybody who carried the flowers to become invisible. And if it was held against locked doors or caskets they would immediately spring open! But such wonders could be performed only if certain procedures were followed: The aspiring witch or warlock had to gather chicory on St. James's Day (July 25), either at midday or at midnight, and a golden knife had to be used. If the task was not done in perfect silence, the chicory gatherer would immediately be struck dead. But perhaps these rituals were worth the danger, for according to the medieval *Book of Secrets* of Albertus Magnus, if you rubbed chicory juice collected on this

special occasion all over your body, you could "obtain the favor of great persons." It would seem that chicory is the undiscovered herb of lobbyists on Capitol Hill! Grow chicory in full sun in any garden soil.

CIMICIFUGA. Family: Ranunculaceae.

Cimicifuga racemosa (BUGBANE, BLACK COHOSH). Zones 2–4.

Don't be put off by the name. Bugbane is a lovely perennial—perfect for shady gardens, even deeply shaded ones. In July and August white wandlike blossoms, often called "fairy candles," appear on this 4- to 5-foot perennial. The only blemish on this otherwise perfect wild flower is the odor of the blossom. But take heart, the smell is also disliked by insects—hence the English name for *Cimicifuga*, "bugbane"! Nobody will notice the odor (except biting insects) if *Cimicifuga* is planted at the back of a flower border. The leaves of bugbane are attractive—deep green and ferny. *Cimicifuga* is an ideal perennial for the back of the shady flower border or a woodland setting. If the garden soil is rich and moist, bugbane can also be planted in full sun.

CLEMATIS. Family: Ranunculaceae.

These lovely plants have been called "queen of the climbers," an apt description for such long-blooming vines. Clematis can be grown in either full sun or light shade. What it needs most of all is cool roots in a soil that is never too wet or too dry. So when planting clematis take extra care when preparing the soil: Add either peat moss, leaf mold, or garden compost. Some sand will help with drainage. When it is planted, cover the ground around the clematis with a few inches of mulch; this will help to keep the roots cool and retain moisture. Because the stems of clematis are rather twiggy and brittle, give the plants some sort of support.

Clematis x *jackmanii.* Zones 5–8.

From June until September this 12-foot clematis has large deep plum-blue flowers.

Clematis maximowicziana (also sold as *Clematis paniculata*) (SWEET AUTUMN CLEMATIS). Zones 5–9.

A gardening friend who has problems pronouncing this Latin nightmare calls *Clematis maximowicziana* "Clematis Molly the Witch." If you want to impress gardening friends, favorite aunts, or loan officers, try saying "maxi-mow-vitz-iana." This is the closest a human voice can come to the correct pronunciation of *maximowicziana*!

Sweet autumn clematis is a vigorous climber that can grow up to 30 feet. When it flowers, in the fall, it is covered with fragrant 1-inch white blooms. After blossoming, sweet autumn clematis bears lovely silver seed heads—these are perfect for use in flower arranging.

CLETHRA. Family: Clethraceae.

Clethra alnifolia (SWEET PEPPERBUSH, SUMMERSWEET). Zones 3–8.

I once carried a containerized sweet pepperbush in the back of my car. The fragrance was unforgettable—a sort of sweet clove smell, definitely not pepper! But enjoyment of this shrub is not confined to the inside of an automobile. Throughout August the rich sweet aroma of *Clethra* blossoms is released from the spikes of white flowers. Although at maturity sweet pepperbush reaches 5 to 8 feet and measures 6 feet across, it can be kept smaller with clipping. Grow *Clethra* in full sun in acid soil.

Clethra alnifolia 'Pinkspire' has pink flowers and blooms longer, from July to September.

COLCHICUM. Family: Liliaceae.

Colchicum autumnale (AUTUMN CROCUS, NAKED LADIES). Zones 3–9.

This charming plant is not really a crocus but rather a member of the lily family. Planted in a mass, it can transform an area of your garden into a field of gossamer-pink blossoms. Like magic, these ethereal vase-shaped flowers appear out of the ground during September and October. Because the dainty blossoms are leafless, English rustics call the autumn crocus "naked ladies." The French call them *dame sans chemise* ("lady without a dress"), and the more earthy German horticulturists refer to them as *nackende Huren* ("naked whore"). My favorite name is the one we used in my native Somerset: "naked nannies"! The nakedness of the plant so perplexed an early nineteenth-century gardener that he wrote, "I have pitied this plant a thousand times. Its blossom rises out of the ground in the most forlorn conditions possible without a sheath, a fence, a calyx, or even a leaf to protect it: and that not in the spring, to be visited by summer suns, but under the disadvantages of the declining year" (as quoted in Grigson).

The modern gardener is no longer perplexed by the late bloom of the autumn crocus; instead we can contemplate the beauty of its delicate petals. Autumn crocus is an ideal choice for brightening a corner of lawn, a patch of flower garden, or a faded window box. Purchase the bulbs in August or September and plant them in small clumps of six or more. For best results, dig a planting hole about 1 foot deep, mix the soil with good compost, and return this rich mixture to the hole; then plant the bulbs 3 to 4 inches deep.

CONIUM. Family: Umbelliferae.

Conium maculatum (POISON HEMLOCK). Zones 3–8.

This is a tall biennial that can reach 6 feet. Poison hemlock belongs to the Umbelliferae family, a large group that includes such plants as Queen Anne's lace and sweet cicely. The strong fetid odor emitted from all parts of the herb and the red spots on the stems easily distinguish the poisonous hemlock from harmless members of the Umbelliferae family. These unpleasant exhalations are caused by coniine, a poisonous alkaloid. The smell is strongly reminiscent of mice. In his writings, the Greek physician Dioscorides mentions the poisonous properties of hemlock: "This is also of ye venomous herbs, killing by its coldness." Dioscorides used hemlock externally for "wanton dreamers, and seed shedder." He recommended hemlock "smeared on about ye stones [testicles]." Women did not escape his prescriptions. According to Dioscorides, this herb would "forbid ye breasts to grow great in the time of virginity." Anatomical charms have certainly changed in the past eighteen hundred years!

Some medieval physicians used hemlock internally as an anesthetic. One English manuscript from the fifteenth century, the *English Leechbook*, suggests that "to put a man to sleep, that he may be treated or cut, two spoonfuls of hemlock juice are mixed with a gallon of wine." The patient is then given the poisoned wine to drink. And in the author's own words, "he shall sleep soon." After a gallon of booze, never mind the hemlock—I should think an ox would find it difficult not to sleep. It's not surprising that few survived medieval surgery! To cultivate hemlock in the herb garden, grow it in moist soil in sun or partial shade. Great care should be taken in handling this plant.

COREOPSIS (TICKSEED). Family: Compositae.

Coreopsis are very easy plants to cultivate— all should be grown in full sun, and they are not particular about the type of soil. Coreopsis flowers during the summer.

Coreopsis grandiflora 'Goldfink'. Zones 4–9.

'Goldfink' is a small compact plant, reaching only 9 inches in height. From June to August this miniature perennial is covered with golden-yellow flowers. *Coreopsis grandiflora* 'Sunburst' is 20 inches tall and has bright yellow 2-inch semi-double flowers from June until August. This is a drought-resistant plant.

Coreopsis palmatum (STIFF COREOPSIS). Zones 4–9.

In July, bright yellow flowers adorn this 2- to 3-foot coreopsis. Stiff coreopsis is a plant of the prairies, and so will tolerate very dry soil.

Coreopsis verticillata 'Moonbeam'. Zones 3–9.

This is one of the prettiest perennials in the flower garden. For the whole summer and much of the autumn, delicate lacy foliage is covered with lovely open light yellow star-shaped flowers. 'Moonbeam' forms compact "bushes" that grow up to 18 inches. This is one of the easiest garden flowers to cultivate. 'Moonbeam' is perfect for planting by pathways, and it can even be grown in a hanging basket.

CORIANDRUM. Family: Umbelliferae.

Coriandrum sativum (CORIANDER).
Zones 3–10.

Coriander is a feathery annual that grows to about 1½ feet. In appearance it is not unlike Italian parsley. Coriander is fairly easy to grow except in hot, humid regions like Florida and the Gulf Coast, where it is best grown on a window ledge inside an air-conditioned room. In other parts of the country cultivate this herb in full sun in well-drained soil. Try to find a protected site; the thin stems are prone to wind damage. Sow the seeds when all danger of frost has passed.

Coriander provides two distinct seasonings. The seeds have a delightful aroma somewhat like oranges, and are ideal for curries, breads, and cakes. The leaves, on the other hand, don't have quite the same perfume. The old herbalists mention that the foliage of coriander smells like bedbugs. Having never shared my slumber with those insects, I can't verify the truth of this! But whatever perfume they emit, their effect on the taste buds is another matter. Coriander leaves add a wonderful pungency to Chinese, Mexican, and Middle Eastern cuisines. Dioscorides, the Greek herbalist from the first century A.D., advised against overindulging in coriander: "Being taken too much of it disturbs ye understanding dangerously." In the Middle Ages, the opposite advice was given by the German herbalist Peter Schoeffer. In his *Her-*

barius Latinus he wrote, "Coriander taken with vinegar soon after dining heavily, prohibits vapors from rising to the head"!

CORNUS (DOGWOOD). Family: Cornaceae.

Cornus alba 'Elegantissima' (RED TWIG DOGWOOD). Zones 2–8.

This is a shrub for all seasons, but red twig dogwood is especially beautiful in the winter, when the dark red stems can be set off against a snowy landscape. 'Elegantissima' grows up to 8 feet. In spring the dark green foliage appears—the silvery white margins on the leaves make them outstanding—followed by attractive flowers in June. This shrub can be grown in sun or partial shade, in moist well-drained soil.

Cornus canadensis (BUNCHBERRY).
Zones 3–8.

This Lilliputian member of the dogwood family is only 4 to 6 inches tall, but bunchberry bears the characteristic and beautiful flowers that many taller members of the dogwood family have. Bunchberry is a semi-evergreen ground cover that, in the right conditions, can form dense colonies. In early summer the whorls of leaves are crowned with greenish-white flowers. In the fall it bears attractive red fruit. Grow *Cornus canadensis* in shade, in cool moist soil.

CORYDALIS. Family: Fumariaceae.

Corydalis lutea (YELLOW CORYDALIS).
Zones 5–10.

For brightening a shady part of the garden, no plant could be better than yellow corydalis. From spring to fall this graceful perennial is covered with yellow tubular flowers, and fernlike foliage adds to its beauty. Yellow corydalis is a very adaptable plant, and although it does best in light shade, it will grow well in both full sun and deep shade. The only requirement is well-drained soil—little fuss for a beautiful and multipurpose perennial. With occasional watering, I have successfully grown this plant in a dry shady area under a maple tree. Yellow corydalis will establish itself in rich pockets of soil in old stone walls. It looks outstanding planted against rocks.

COTINUS. Family: Anacardiaceae.

Cotinus coggygria 'Royal Purple' (SMOKE TREE). Zones 5–8.

'Royal Purple' is one of the most attractive deciduous trees for the garden. In spring it is covered with lovely deep purple foliage, and in August the smoky plumelike flowers give it the appearance of being enveloped in a dense billowy pink cloud. *Cotinus*, which matures at 10 to 15 feet, is an ideal tree for a patio or lawn specimen. Grow a smoke tree in full sun, in any garden soil. *Cotinus* does extremely well in infertile, dry soil. Trees planted in the fall are occasionally slow to leaf out the following spring, but be patient—the wait will be well worthwhile.

COTONEASTER. Family: Rosaceae.

Cotoneaster horizontalis (ROCKSPRAY COTONEASTER). Zones 5–9.

For graceful form there is nothing quite like this 2-foot shrub. The branches grow in arching tiers, and on each fanlike branch the twigs are arranged in a herringbone pattern, bearing attractive glossy green leaves. In milder areas the foliage remains on the plant all year. In colder zones, rockspray cotoneaster is deciduous. In these areas, the leaves turn lovely orange and red colors before dropping. In May *Cotoneaster horizontalis* is covered with small pink flowers, and by August showy scarlet berries dot the branches. The red fruit remains until late November. Give this plant full sun and any reasonable garden soil.

CRATAEGUS. Family: Rosaceae.

Crataegus monogyna (HAWTHORN, MAY, HAGTHORN). Zones 4–8.

The white and reddish flowers of hawthorn that deck the English countryside during the month of May are indeed a spectacular sight. And equal to the color of the blossoms is their heady perfume—unless the observer gets too close and is overcome by a fragrance that is unpleasantly strong.

The late spring flowering of the hawthorn coincided with May Day celebrations, important rites that celebrated the time of year when spring finally changed to summer. May Eve was also Walpurgis Night, next to Halloween the most important date on the witch's calendar. For these reasons our European ancestors considered the hawthorn a supernatural tree. The hawthorn's malevolent associations are very ancient, and derive from the tree's connection with the cult of the Greek goddess Maia. It was under an arbor of hawthorn that this deity wove her hellish enchantments. (The hawthorn has other uses outside the witch's garden. The scarlet berries have been used for a long time for angina and other heart conditions.)

The hawthorn grows to 25 or 30 feet and has a spread of 15 to 20 feet. For small gardens, *Crataegus* can be kept in bounds by pruning, or even made into a hedge. Grow hawthorn in ordinary garden soil in a sunny site. It will also tolerate light shade.

CYCLAMEN. Family: Primulaceae.

A number of hardy cyclamens are available to gardeners. These lovely members of the primrose family are beautiful in flower as well as leaf. Cyclamens are purchased as roundish corms—bulbs that look a little like flattened buns. And many people (myself included) have been confused about which side to plant upward. Find the side with the most curve: this is the side that will send out roots, so plant the corms with this side down. Cyclamens need only shallow cultivation, so bury the bulbs about 2 inches deep and 4 inches apart. Cyclamens are best planted by pathways or in areas where their small but lovely flowers will be appreciated. Rock gardens and the front of shady borders are also ideal locations. They like good moist garden loam, preferably soil that has been enriched with organic matter.

Cyclamen hederifolium (formerly *Cyclamen neapolitanum*). Zones 5–8.

This species flowers in late summer and early autumn, when dozens of pink butterfly-like blossoms appear from each corm. These little blooms have a dark spot in the center. The deep green foliage is dotted with silver.

Cyclamen purpurascens (formerly *Cyclamen europaeum*) (ALPINE VIOLET). Zones 5–8.

In late summer and early autumn, sweetly scented rose-red butterfly-like flowers appear. These small blossoms are held on 6-inch stalks. The kidney-shaped foliage is very beautiful—the leaves are a mottled silvery green and last for most of the season.

CYNARA. Family: Compositae.

Cynara cardunculus (CARDOON). Zones 8–10.

If you grow cardoon in your garden, expect many "oohs" and "ahhs" from visitors who are being introduced to *Cynara cardunculus* for the first time. This is a very grand plant with an outstanding architectural form that makes a bold statement in any landscape. At maturity the cardoon reaches 6 feet, with the silver fanlike leaves creating a giant vase. In late summer, the flowers tower above the stiff gray foliage. *Cynara* is a close relative of the artichoke, and like its edible kin, the cardoon has huge thistle-like flower heads. Blue petals crown each fist-size blossom. In colder areas of the country, the cardoon either can be dug up and stored in damp sand in the basement or greenhouse before really cold weather sets in, or it can be treated as an annual. If seed is sown inside in February or March, small plants can be placed in the garden at the end of spring. By late summer they will have reached maturity. I enjoy cardoon in my Connecticut (Zone 5) garden until Christmas. When mature, they tolerate fairly cold weather. You can purchase cardoon from Well-Sweep Herb Farm or you can buy seeds from Chiltern Seeds (see Suppliers list). Grow cardoon in full sun, in rich moist soil.

CYPRIPEDIUM. Family: Orchidaceae.

Cypripedium calceolus pubescens (YELLOW LADY'S SLIPPER). Zones 3–9.

It is always pleasing when the most attractive member of a genus is the easiest variety to grow. This is true in the case of yellow lady's slipper. From May to June, this beautiful native orchid sends up 2-foot leafy stems topped with little golden pouches—the "slippers." Each bloom has two long curled brown petal segments which hang down from the yellow pouches.

Correct planting is essential for the healthy growth of lady's slippers. Make sure that the growing tip of the *Cypripedium* is planted just below the soil surface, and cover newly planted yellow lady's slippers with a light pine needle or leaf mulch. These orchids prefer growing in woodland soil, but if you cannot provide this, try to plant *Cypripedium* in acid soil rich in humus. Yellow lady's slipper prefers to be planted in shade.

CYTISUS (BROOM). Family: Leguminosae. Zones 5–8.

Broom is a deciduous shrub with evergreen branches, which grows to 5 to 8 feet. In spring the whole plant is covered with yellow flowers. Plant broom in full sun in well-drained soil. This shrub tolerates windy, sandy coastal conditions.

Cytisus praecox 'Moonlight' (MOONLIGHT BROOM).

In May, moonlight broom is a spectacular sight, with sulfur-yellow pealike flowers literally covering the 8-foot bushes.

In the Middle Ages, broom was considered magical, a herb that could be used by malevolent forces or against them. A thirteenth-century poem tells of a wife consulting a spirit in the broom to find out if her husband is faithful:

> Tell me, being in the broom,
> Teach me what to do
> That my husband
> Have me true.

Somewhat vitriolically, the broom spirit answers the wife's plea:

> When your tongue is still
> You'll have your will.

"Its virtue," says Richard Banckes, "is good to Knit bones and sinues together." In modern times, extract of broom has been used as a diuretic.

D

DAPHNE. Family: Thymelaeaceae.

Daphne cneorum (GARLAND FLOWER). Zones 5–7.

Garland flower is a low-growing evergreen that has an unforgettable fragrance. In April and May, scented pinkish flowers cover the 6- to 12-inch plants. *Daphne cneorum* slowly spreads outward. Planted 2 feet apart, it will eventually form a dense aromatic carpet. Garland flower needs full sun or light shade, and should be grown in well-drained moist soil. Once established, it resents being moved or being given any sort of pruning. Mulch around these plants to keep the roots cool and moist.

DATURA. Family: Solanaceae.

Datura chlorantha. Zones 9–10.

For heady perfume during summer nights, plant *Datura chlorantha*, for only in the warm night air do these flowers release their scent. Enjoy this perennial in a special fragrance garden or grow it in a pot or tub. If a containerized datura is placed by a window or door, wafts of the rich sweet scent can enter the house in the evenings. *Datura chlorantha* is a shrubby plant that reaches up to 10 feet. From July until November it is covered with exquisite trumpet-shaped blooms. These flowers are double and light yellow in color.

In frost-free parts of the country, datura can be left outside year-round. In colder regions, prune the plants severely and keep them indoors over the winter. They will be happy if kept by a window. To save indoor space, I cut my plants back and replant them in smaller winter pots. If you keep a datura in the house during the cold months, give it a minimum amount of water; this helps keep the plant dormant. When all danger of frost is past, plant it outside again. Grow *Datura chlorantha* in an enriched moist soil.

Datura stramonium (THORN APPLE, ANGEL'S TRUMPET, JIMSONWEED). Zones 3–10.

Thorn apple is an attractive annual that from midsummer to fall bears lovely white trumpet-shaped flowers. After pollination a large spiny seed capsule develops, which eventually splits open to reveal black seeds. Thorn apple can grow up to 4 feet but generally reaches only about 2 feet. To cultivate it in the herb garden, plant thorn apple seed after all danger of frost is past. Sow the seed in good rich soil, preferably in a sheltered position.

The poisonous qualities of this herb were described by the Greek herbalist Dioscorides: "The root being drunk with wine ye quantity of a dragm, hath ye power to effect not un-pleasant fantasies. But two dragms being drunk, make one beside himself for three days, and four being drunk kill him." The seventeenth-century English herbalist John Petchey mentions that thorn apple seed crushed and administered in beer causes insanity for twenty-four hours, and was given by criminals to those they intended to rob. Petchey also wrote: "Wenches give half a dram of it to their Lovers, in beer or wine. Some are so skilled in dosing of it, that they can make men mad for as many hours as they please." The Elizabethan herbalist John Gerard recommended thorn apple made into an ointment to cure "all manor of burnings or scauldings, as well of fire, water, boiling lead, gun powder, and that which comes by lightening." A modern English medical herbalist, Dr. Malcolm Stewart, suggests that thorn apple "may be applied externally as a poultice to reduce local pain."

DAUCUS. Family: Umbelliferae.

Daucus carota (QUEEN ANNE'S LACE, WILD CARROT). Zones 3–10.

One of our most attractive wild flowers, Queen Anne's lace is a biennial, which means that leaves will be produced the first year and flowers the second. Once you have Queen Anne's lace in the garden, allow the plants to self-seed. *Daucus carota*, the ancestor of the modern carrot, has fernlike leaves, grows 4 to 5 feet tall, and flowers from June until August. These lovely blooms, made from hundreds of small white blossoms, look like bird's nests. Queen Anne's lace will grow in almost any soil but prefers a well-drained site. Grow *Daucus carota* in full sun or in a position that will receive full sunshine for at least half the day.

DELPHINIUM. Family: Ranunculaceae.

Delphinium Belladonna Hybrids. Zones 3–7.

Delphiniums are lovely flowers, and if your climate allows, do by all means grow these beautiful plants. The Belladonna Hybrids are some of the easiest delphiniums to cultivate. They also tolerate warmer climates than other varieties of delphinium. Belladonna Hybrids grow 3 to 5 feet tall, and if dead heads are removed, will bloom all summer. They are available in a number of colors, the most popular being 'Bellamosum' (dark blue), 'Belladonna' (light blue), and 'Casa Blanca' (white). Delphiniums can be grown in full sun or very light shade. They need a moist rich well-drained soil. When planting delphiniums, add rotted compost and a handful of superphosphate to the soil. To conserve moisture in summer, give delphiniums a mulch. No delphinium will do well in a windy site — even in sheltered parts of the garden, plants will probably need staking. But this little effort is worthwhile.

DESMODIUM. Family: Leguminosae.

Desmodium canadense (SHOWY TICK TREFOIL, CANADA TICKSEED). Zones 3–8.

Canada tickseed is a robust hardy perennial that grows up to 5 feet. In midsummer, attractive yellow pealike flowers cover the branches. Grow showy tick trefoil in full sun or in light shade, in moist soil.

DIANTHUS (CARNATION, PINK).
Family: Caryophyllaceae.

Carnations are favorite garden flowers. They are also ideal for cutting and using in arrangements — frequent picking encourages prolific blossoming. Many *Dianthus* species and varieties have fragrant flowers, and they have attractive silvery evergreen foliage. Cultivate *Dianthus* in alkaline well-drained soil. If your soil is acid, add a handful of garden lime to the area before planting.

Dianthus x *allwoodii* 'Doris'. Zones 4–8.

This is a very fragrant carnation that reaches 12 to 15 inches. The large semi-double flowers are light pink with a deeper pink center. 'Doris' is a very prolific bloomer.

Dianthus caryophyllus (CLOVE CARNATION, CLOVE PINK, GILLYFLOWER). Zones 5–7.

Clove carnation is a low-growing short-lived perennial that has attractive narrow silver-gray foliage. In midsummer, strongly scented pink blossoms cover the plant. As clove carnation grows only 9 inches high, it is an ideal perennial for planting at the front of a garden border. The flowers of this lovely plant have a strong odor of cloves.

Wine flavored with carnation blossoms was a popular beverage in the Middle Ages. The Elizabethan herbalist John Gerard recommends making a conserve from carnation flowers and sugar. This, he states, "is exceedingly cordial, and wonderfully above measure doth comfort the heart, being eaten now and then." Clove carnation blossoms are perfectly harmless, so can be added to salads and drinks. Or if not used in the kitchen, the deliciously scented flowers are wonderful when dried and put into a potpourri mixture.

DICENTRA (BLEEDING HEART).
Family: Fumariaceae. Zones 3–9.

The following *Dicentra* should be grown in semi-shade in rich moist soil. They do not like windy sites.

Dicentra eximia (FRINGED BLEEDING HEART).

From April until September, rose-pink heart-shaped flowers appear on this foot-high perennial. The attractive fernlike leaves are a grayish green. To keep plants flowering prolifically, remove dead blooms. *Dicentra eximia* 'Alba' has fernlike blue-gray foliage and in spring the whole plant is covered with pure white "bleeding hearts."

Dicentra x 'Luxuriant'.

This is one of the loveliest plants for the garden—it is certainly one of the longest blooming. From late April to October, cherry-red flowers are carried on long stalks over the ferny foliage. 'Luxuriant' grows 12 to 18 inches high.

DIGITALIS (FOXGLOVE).
Family: Scrophulariaceae. Zones 4–8.

Cultivate foxgloves in well-drained soil in partial shade. If flower stalks are cut off before they go to seed, the plants will bloom again. However, when growing biennial varieties of *Digitalis*, to ensure continued supply in the garden let some blossoms go to seed.

Digitalis grandiflora (also called *Digitalis ambigua*).

This is a true perennial foxglove that grows to 3 feet and in June and July bears spikes of hanging yellow flowers.

Digitalis purpurea (PURPLE FOXGLOVE, FAIRY'S HAT).

This tall biennial is common in lime-free soils throughout northern Europe. Purple foxglove grows as tall as 5 feet. Most of the leaves are concentrated in a tight circle at the base of the flower spike. In early summer,

drooping purple blossoms freckled with dark spots cover the tall spikes.

Purple foxglove is a plant well steeped in superstition and magic. As Geoffrey Grigson notes, "As usual, this plant of the fairies was powerful in their hands against you, or in your hands against them, provided you took the risk of gathering it. Fairies are supposed to have given the corollas of their powerful plant to the fox"—hence the vernacular name of this plant. "Wearing these foxgloves, the fox could then sneak in magic silence up to the poultry or away from men." This herb had other occult uses: If you suspected that your child had been substituted by a changeling (fairy child), then all you had to do was rub the juice of the foxglove on the babe. If the infant was not human it would vanish and your real baby would appear.

Outside the witch's garden the foxglove has other uses. An extremely important heart stimulant, digitalis, comes from the leaves of this plant.

Digitalis purpurea 'Excelsior' hybrids are covered with numerous blossoms in June and July. The pastel-colored flowers are carried on side branches that stand out from the main 4-foot stem. Although 'Excelsior' hybrids are biennial, they readily reseed themselves. This is a stunning plant that should be included in every garden.

DIPSACUS. Family: Dipsaceae.

Dipsacus fullonum (TEASEL). Zones 3–10.

Teasel is a biennial that grows 4 to 5 feet high. It has a rigid furrowed stem, and in summer blue prickly flower heads crown the branches. When dried, these are most attractive in flower arrangements. In his herbal *De Materia Medica*, the ancient Greek herbalist

Dioscorides aptly described the teasel: "On ye top of ye stalk at every shoot one head like a hedgehog somewhat long and prickly." In past centuries teasel was used for carding wool; the comblike heads were passed through raw wool, straightening the fibers and making spinning possible. Grow teasel in full sun or partial shade in any type of garden soil.

DODECATHEON. Family: Primulaceae.

Dodecatheon meadia (SHOOTING STAR).
Zones 4–8.

Shooting star is a lovely spring flower that grows between 1 and 2 feet tall and blooms from April to June. The inch-long pendant blossoms are rose-pink or lavender. And with a little bit of imagination, they do look like falling stars—hence the lovely common name. Grow *Dodecatheon* in full sun or light shade. It occurs naturally in both woodland settings and open prairies, so it is a plant that will tolerate a wide variety of soils. But in spring, the period of active growth, shooting star seems to need moist soil. So if you are cultivating *Dodecatheon* in drier soil, make sure that plants receive ample moisture in April and May.

DORONICUM. Family: Compositae.

Doronicum caucasicum (LEOPARD'S BANE).
Zones 4–7.

Leopard's bane is a lovely spring flower. In April and May this 18-inch plant is covered with large bright daisies. *Doronicum* also has attractive foliage; the leaves are serrated and are heart-shaped. Leopard's bane goes dormant in summer, and the foliage vanishes. To hide this bare spot in the garden, plant some annuals. I cover the naked soil around *Doron-*

icum with the green-flowered night-scented tobacco, *Nicotiana alata* 'Lime Green'. In my Zone 5 garden, this annual tolerates many cold spells and is still blooming in November. *Doronicum* can be grown in full sun or partial shade. Give these perennials rich moist soil.

DRYOPTERIS. Family: Polypodiaceae.

Dryopteris felix-mas (MALE FERN).
Zones 4–9.

This is the best fern for dry shady sites. Large fronds extend 3 to 4 feet. Male ferns will grow in almost every type of soil except boggy ground, so long as they are in the shade.

Dryopteris goldiana (GOLDIE'S FERN).
Zones 4–9.

This giant fern has fronds that are 1½ feet wide and 4 feet long! New foliage has a pleasant yellowish tinge. Grow Goldie's fern in shade, in rich moist soil.

E

ECHINACEA. Family: Compositae.

Echinacea purpurea (sometimes listed as *Rudbeckia purpurea*) (PURPLE CONEFLOWER).
Zones 3–9.

Purple coneflower is a handsome plant with large pink petals clustered around a dark central cone—like a large pink daisy wearing a top hat! It grows to 4 feet and flowers during the summer months—some years, from July to September. Grow *Echinacea* in full sun, in rich well-drained soil.

ECHINOPS (GLOBE THISTLE).
Family: Compositae. Zones 3–8.

Echinops ritro (also listed in catalogues as 'Taplow Blue').

This impressive perennial is ideal for the back of the flower border or the center of an island garden. In July and September steely blue spheres rise on 4-foot stems above the thistle-like silver-gray leaves. Grow *Echinops* in full sun or partial shade, in average well-drained soil.

ECHIUM. Family: Boraginaceae.

Echium vulgare (VIPER'S BUGLOSS). Zones 4–10.

This is one of my favorite English wild flowers. As a child I first discovered viper's bugloss growing on sand dunes along the rugged coast of northern Wales. For the whole summer, *Echium* forms stiff mounds that are literally covered with blossoms. The purple buds open slowly to violet flowers, and the blossoms last for many weeks. Two to 3 feet tall, viper's bugloss is a biennial, but occasionally will be a short-lived perennial. Bees adore this plant. Cultivate viper's bugloss in full sun in well-drained soil. It is drought resistant and excellent for seaside gardens.

ELAEAGNUS. Family: Elaeagnaceae.

Elaeagnus angustifolia (RUSSIAN OLIVE). Zones 2–8.

Russian olive is a fast-growing deciduous tree—shrubby and round-headed in form—that matures at 20 to 25 feet. It is ideal for cold, hot, or very dry garden areas. It will even tolerate salt spray. *Elaeagnus angustifolia* is a perfect problem solver for difficult spots in any landscape.

Not only is Russian olive one of the most adaptable small trees, it is also one of the most beautiful. The willow-like dark green leaves have a silver undersurface, and in early summer the tree is covered with greenish-yellow flowers. When the blossoms ripen, the small yellow oval fruit provides winter food for birds. Grow Russian olive in full sun.

ENDYMION. Family: Liliaceae.

Endymion nonscriptus (ENGLISH BLUEBELL). Zones 5–8.

McClure & Zimmerman, rare-bulb specialists in Chicago, have at last made this lovely flower available to American gardeners. In spring, the lusty pointed glossy leaves of the bluebell appear, and from these grassy clumps arise foot-high stems. Delicately suspended from these fleshy stalks are dozens of small azure-blue bell-shaped flowers. The lip of each bell gently curves back. Plant bluebells in moist well-drained soil, in sun or light shade.

In the Unicorn Tapestries at The Cloisters in New York City, the English bluebell is depicted next to the unicorn, which is chained to a pomegranate tree inside a wooden enclosure. (These world-famous medieval textiles illustrate the hunt and capture of a unicorn.) The generic name of the bluebell is *Endymion*, and this name associates it with the lover of the Greek moon goddess, Selene. According to legend, Selene placed her beloved, Endymion, in a perpetual sleep so that his beauty and strength would not fade. The unicorn was considered by medieval people to be a lunar creature. Perhaps the designer of the Unicorn Tapestries, aware of this fable, placed the bluebell next to the unicorn to make an allusion to this legend.

EPIMEDIUM. Family: Berberidaceae.

Epimedium grandiflorum 'Rose Queen'.
Zones 5–8.

Epimedium are slow-growing dense creeping perennials. They have broad shieldlike leaves that are delicately suspended from 9-inch stalks. In late summer, the foliage turns a lovely reddish color, and in milder areas the plant is evergreen. In May, sprays of large rose-colored flowers appear. The blossoms are spurred and very showy. Grow *Epimedium* in light or heavy shade, in deep moist soil. This perennial is perfect for lining shady pathways or for planting under trees or shrubs.

ERYNGIUM (ERYNGO). Family: Umbelliferae.

For hundreds of years *Eryngium* has enjoyed great popularity because it was credited with being one of nature's aphrodisiacs. "Marvelous is the characteristics reported of it," wrote the Roman naturalist Pliny. "Its roots grow into the likeness of one sex or the other. . . . Should the male form come into possession of men, they become lovable in the eyes of women." Pliny concludes his account by stating that "taken beforehand it keeps off the after effects of wine"! Elizabethan herbalist John Gerard wrote that the roots of eryngo "preserved with sugar . . . are exceedingly good to be given unto old and aged people that are consumed and withered with age. . . . They are also good for other sorts of people that have no delight or appetite to venerie, nourishing and restoring the aged, and amending the defects of nature in the younger." By all accounts, *Eryngium* is quite a remarkable plant! To cultivate *Eryngium*, plant it in full sun in well-drained soil.

Eryngium alpinum. Zones 3–8.

This very beautiful perennial grows just over 2 feet. The basal foliage is light green and heart shaped. In summer, gun-metal blue flowers are borne on blue stems. The cone-shaped flower heads are surrounded by an exquisite lacy ruff.

Eryngium amethystinum. Zones 2–7.

Eryngium amethystinum is a 2-foot-high perennial that blooms in July and August. Its thistle-like flowers are surrounded by bluish bracts.

Eryngium giganteum. Zones 5–8.

This is the easiest *Eryngium* to cultivate. Stiff stems reaching 2 to 3 feet carry lovely silver-gray blossoms and foliage. The conelike flowers are surrounded by metallic-looking leafy bracts. *Eryngium giganteum* flowers in late summer or early fall. This is a very variable plant, sometimes an annual, other times a long-lived perennial. But even if the plants you grow turn out to be annuals, don't worry; before the end of the year, dozens of seedlings will surround the original plant. This attractive plant looks splendid when grown with artemisia.

Eryngium planum. Zones 5–8.

This is a 3-foot perennial with small blue flowers. Although not as flamboyant as the other species, it is a prolific bloomer and very easy to grow. *Eryngium planum* is one of the most commonly available species of eryngo.

Eryngium yuccifolium (RATTLESNAKE MASTER). Zones 4–8.

This is a strange-looking perennial from the prairies and open woods of the eastern United States. In July and August the long yucca-like foliage is surmounted by tall stems that bear roundish white flowers. *Eryngium yuccifolium* grows 3 to 4 feet high. It is called "rattlesnake master" because it was once thought that a tea brewed from the root would cure rattlesnake bites.

EUPATORIUM. Family: Compositae.

Eupatorium coelestinum (MISTFLOWER, BLUE BONESET). Zones 5–8.

This bushy perennial grows up to 3 feet. It is covered with compact clusters of light lavender flowers from August until frost. Grow *Eupatorium coelestinum* in full sun to partial shade, in well-drained moist soil.

Eupatorium purpureum (JOE-PYE WEED, SWEET JOE-PYE WEED). Zones 4–9.

Joe-pye weed is a native perennial that is not used enough in American gardens (in England it is much more appreciated). From July until September large branching stems of magenta blossoms appear on a plant that can reach over 6 feet. When a number are grown together, the misty flowers and dark stems create a handsome effect. Grow this plant in full sun, in moist soil.

EUPHORBIA. Family: Euphorbiaceae.

Euphorbia epithymoides (sometimes listed as *Euphorbia polychroma*) (CUSHION SPURGE). Zones 4–10.

When this plant flowers in the spring it is electrifying. Cushion spurge forms neat and attractive mounds, which in May are literally covered with sulfur-yellow flower bracts. The color is rather like that of yellow "magic markers." It is not vulgar—more shockingly delightful!

Grow cushion spurge in full sun to partial shade, in well-drained soil.

Euphorbia griffithii 'Fireglow'. Zones 5–9.

This attractive plant is 3 feet tall, and in June, fiery red flower bracts cover the top of the stems. In colder areas give this plant the protection of a winter mulch. Grow this *Euphorbia* in full sun or partial shade, in well-drained soil.

F

FESTUCA. Family: Gramineae.

Festuca ovina glauca (BLUE FESCUE). Zones 4–9.

This is a lovely evergreen grass. The thin rigid blue spikes of blue fescue grow 10 inches high and form neat tussocks. Everyone who sees this grass for the first time immediately wants to have it for their own flower bed. It is ideal for the "silver garden," the front of a border, or for growing as a ground cover. Grow blue fescue in full sun in well-drained soil. It will grow in shade, but some of the blue will be lost from the foliage.

FILIPENDULA. Family: Rosaceae.

Filipendula ulmaria (MEADOWSWEET, QUEEN OF THE MEADOW). Zones 3–9.

Meadowsweet is one of my favorite herbs of childhood. In England, and in other temperate areas of Europe, it is a common waterside plant, and patches of meadowsweet provide a spectacular sight in the summertime. Fresh or dried, this herb has a wonderful fragrance that will freshen up a kitchen or a smoky room. I am in good company in my high opinion of meadowsweet: This was a popular herb with Queen Elizabeth I. Seventeenth-century herbalist John Parkinson wrote that Her Majesty "did more desire it than any other sweet herb to strew her chambers withal," Meadowsweet grows 2 to 3 feet tall, with delicate fernlike leaves on the stems. Most of the foliage is concentrated in a rosette at the base of the plant. In summer, clusters of fluffy white blossoms appear. This plant is best grown in a moist and shady part of the garden, but it will grow in full sun if the soil has been enriched with good compost.

In 1839, salicylic acid (aspirin) was first discovered in the buds of this important herb. Meadowsweet was originally given the Latin name *Spiraeae ulmaria.* The word "aspirin," meaning "from spiraea," records the importance of this herb as a medicinal plant. A tea made from the flowers is perfect for treating heartburn, acidity, and fevers. A tisane of meadowsweet is also helpful for treating diarrhea. Elizabethan herbalist John Gerard wrote: "The leaves and flowers far excel all other strowing herbs, for to decke up houses, to strowe in chambers, hals, and the banketting houses in sommer time; for the smell thereof maketh the hart merrie, delighteth the senses: neither doth it cause headach, or lothsomnesse to meate, as some sweet smelling herbes do."

FOENICULUM. Family: Umbelliferae. Zones 7–10.

Foeniculum vulgare. (FENNEL, GREEN FENNEL).

In England, and in milder part of the United States, fennel is a perennial. But in colder parts of North America, it is grown as an annual. There are a number of different varieties of this herb. All of them smell strongly of licorice, and have small yellow flowers and graceful feathery leaves. All types of fennel grow in full sun in any good garden soil. If you are going to harvest only the leaves of green fennel, not the seeds, remove the flowers as soon as they start to form.

Among fennel's reputed virtues was the ability to bestow longevity and courage. This made the herb popular with Roman soldiers, who added fennel seed to their bread during campaigns. In medieval households fennel was used for cooking fish, as a potherb, and for strewing on the floor as a flea deterrent. According to the *English Leechbook,* physicians in the Middle Ages prescribed fennel for the following uses: "This herb do fill women's breast with milk and are used for the wombling of the stomach or for those that desire to break wind or vomit." Hung over the lintel of a doorway, fennel would drive any evil spirits away, and if the seeds were placed in a keyhole, no ghost could enter the building. In the modern household, fennel can be employed in more mundane matters. This herb is excellent with fish dishes, chicken, stews, and herb breads. Fennel is supposed to be an appetite suppressant. Seventeenth-century herbalist Nicholas Culpeper wrote that all parts of the plant "are used in drink or broth to make people lean who are too fat."

Foeniculum vulgare var. *dulce* (Florence fennel or finochio) is really a vegetable grown for its edible bulbous leaf base, and strictly speaking, should not be included in the herb garden.

Foeniculum vulgare purpureum (bronze fennel) has lovely dark copper leaves. Bronze fennel is equally at home in the herb garden and in the flower border. Remove the flowers to preserve the lovely foliage. Bronze fennel can be used as a substitute for common fennel but is not as strongly flavored.

FOTHERGILLA. Family: Hamamelidaceae.

Fothergilla major (LARGE FOTHERGILLA). Zones 5–8.

This is a lovely spring-flowering shrub that matures at 6 to 10 feet. In growth it is neat and rounded. In late April and early May, inch-long white "bottle brush" blossoms with a lovely honey scent cover the tips of the branches. In fall the tree is equally beautiful, as the foliage turns brilliant yellow and orange-red. Grow *Fothergilla* in full sun in well-drained soil. It will grow in partial shade, but the fall colors will not be as vivid.

FRAGARIA (STRAWBERRY). Family: Rosaceae.

Fragaria vesca (WILD STRAWBERRY). Zones 4–9.

The wild strawberry is an attractive plant that looks lovely edging pathways or naturalized in open woodland. *Fragaria vesca* is a bushy plant without runners. It starts flowering in June and continues until fall. The strawberries are found on the plants all summer long. Elizabethan herbalist John Gerard thought highly of wild strawberry. He recommended drinking the distilled water from strawberries with white wine: "good against the passion of the heart." This beverage, he tells his readers, would "renew the spirits, and make the heart merry." Grow wild strawberry in rich moist soil, in full sun or partial shade.

G

GAILLARDIA (BLANKETFLOWER). Family: Compositae. Zones 3–9.

Blanketflower should be grown in rich well-drained soil in full sun. It is drought resistant and so is a good choice for people who cannot devote much time to their garden. Gaillardias are excellent as cut flowers. If you find the gaillardia growing in a different spot from that of the previous season, be assured that it hasn't pulled up its roots and moved. The center of the plant has died out and new plants have sprung up from the peripheral root system. This tends to happen every few years with blanketflower.

Gaillardia x *grandiflora*.

From June to August, *Gaillardia* x *grandiflora* 'Burgundy' has large 3-inch wine-red blossoms. These daisy-like blooms are held on 30-inch stems.

'Goblin' is a dwarf blanketflower. From July until frost, deep red blooms bordered with yellow cover this 12-inch plant.

GALANTHUS (SNOWDROP). Family: Amaryllidaceae.

Galanthus nivalis 'Flore-Pleno' (DOUBLE SNOWDROP). Zones 3–8.

Everybody loves snowdrops, the flowers that tell impatient gardeners that spring is on its way. Well, there is an even better flower—the double snowdrop. Plant *Galanthus* in early fall or late summer. Snowdrops prefer light shade, but can be grown in full sun. Give them a "woodsy" moist well-drained soil. Under trees and shrubs and lining pathways are perfect sites for these early flowers. Plant 3 inches deep and space 3 inches apart.

GALIUM. Family: Rubiaceae.

Galium odoratum (SWEET WOODRUFF).
Zones 3–8.

Sweet woodruff is an excellent ground cover for shady spots. Whorls of star-shaped chartreuse-green leaves form dense 6-inch-high mats. In April and May little white flowers appear above the leaves. Sweet woodruff, especially when dry, has a delightful odor of new-mown hay. When added to white wine, sweet woodruff tastes pleasant too. This is especially popular in Germany, where May wine is made by infusing the leaves of woodruff in Moselle or other white wines. Grow *Galium odoratum* in partial shade in moist well-drained soil.

Galium verum (LADY'S BEDSTRAW).
Zones 3–6.

Lady's bedstraw is a sprawling perennial that grows from 1 to 3 feet tall. From spring to late summer, tiny clusters of yellow flowers cover the main stems. The foliage is arranged in whorls on the branches. The curious common name refers to the story that this was the plant that the Virgin lay upon when giving birth to Jesus. In another legend, Mary used bracken fern as bedding, but this arrogant plant refused to acknowledge the Christ Child. For this sin bracken lost its flowers. Meanwhile, a plant of lady's bedstraw, just blossoming when Jesus was born, welcomed the babe — and miraculously its white flowers were changed into golden blossoms. A less romantic tale relates that lady's bedstraw was the only flower in the stable that the donkey did not eat, and so the Virgin had no other alternative for bedding!

Plant *Galium verum* in sun or partial shade in any reasonable garden soil. Lady's bedstraw

looks good in a rock garden or lining pathways and is ideal for woodland settings.

GAURA. Family: Onagraceae.

Gaura lindheimeri. Zones 5–9.

Gaura is a drought-resistant perennial that blooms from early summer until frost. By the end of the season, this vase-shaped plant may have reached 5 feet. Elegant wandlike stems bear delicate white flowers. The spear-shaped leaves are concentrated at the base of the plant. The secret of success with *Gaura* is to make sure that it has very well drained soil. To grow this perennial in heavy soil, add plenty of sand to improve drainage. Grow *Gaura* in full sun. In Zones 5–6, give it the protection of a winter mulch.

GENTIANA (GENTIAN). Family: Gentianaceae.

Gentiana clausa (CLOSED GENTIAN, BOTTLE GENTIAN). Zones 4–8.

This is surely one of America's most beautiful wild flowers. This distinctive gentian has closed flowers — blooms that never fully open. The blossoms are an intense blue and occur in clusters at the tips of the stems. This sprawling perennial is 1 to 3 feet tall and flowers in September or October. Grow closed gentians in partial shade or full sun, in moist or wet soil.

GERANIUM (CRANESBILL). Family: Geraniaceae.

In the main, geraniums are adaptable hardy perennials. Do not confuse these cold-resistant plants with the frost-tender geraniums usually associated with window boxes. Cranesbills, so named because the seed heads look like the beak of a crane, are wonderful flowers for the perennial garden. Their flat lobed foliage is also very striking. Sometimes the leaves are finely divided.

Geranium x 'Johnson's Blue'. Zones 4–8.

In spring or early summer, this lovely hybrid has vivid blue cup-shaped flowers. 'Johnson's Blue' grows up to 1 foot. Grow this geranium in sun or partial shade.

Geranium maculatum (WILD GERANIUM). Zones 4–8.

This lovely North American native flowers in the spring. *Geranium maculatum* grows up to 2 feet high and has inch-wide pale lilac blossoms. Grow this geranium in sun or partial shade.

Geranium pratense (MEADOW CRANESBILL). Zones 4–8.

This lovely English wild flower has beautiful clear blue flowers. Meadow cranesbill grows up to 2½ feet high and blooms from July until September. *Geranium pratense* prefers semi-shade.

Geranium sanguineum. Zones 3–8.

From May until September, this foot-high geranium bears lovely wine-colored blossoms. *Geranium sanguineum* is very accommodating: it will thrive in full sun, partial shade, or fairly heavy shade. As long as it receives water, it is not too particular about the soil it is grown in.

GEUM (AVENS). Family: Rosaceae.

Grow geums in full sun to partial shade, in rich well-drained soil.

Geum x *borisii*. Zones 4–8.

From May to June, pure orange flowers are borne on foot-high stalks above a dense cluster of hairy leaves. Even after June, *Geum* x

borisii continues to bloom sporadically; sometimes flowers appear on the plant as late as October. Silky down covers the foliage.

Geum chiloense 'Fire Opal'. Zones 5–9.

This geum blooms mainly from late May until July, and will flower again in the fall, although not prolifically. 'Fire Opal' grows up to 2 feet. The double blossoms are scarlet.

Geum triflorum (PRAIRIE SMOKE). Zones 4–8.

In April this foot-high perennial bears drooping pink flowers. As the blossoms mature they give rise to attractive tasseled seed heads, which give the whole plant a smoky effect. Grow *Geum triflorum* in full sun in moist well-drained soil.

GILLENIA. Family: Rosaceae.

Gillenia trifoliata (BOWMAN'S ROOT). Zones 3–8.

This is a woodland perennial that grows 2 to 3 feet tall. In early summer, inch-long pink to red flowers form loose clusters. The stems are massed and have attractive triple-lobed leaves. Although a single plant of Bowman's root would not make a great impression in the garden, a small colony of three to five plants makes a nice show, especially in a woodland setting. Bowman's root prefers partial shade, but can be grown in full sun. Give *Gillenia* a humus-rich moist soil.

GLYCERA. Family: Gramineae.

Glycera maxima 'Variegata' (VARIEGATED MANNA GRASS). Zones 5–8.

For the waterside, there is no better foliage plant than variegated manna grass. Initially, new spring leaves are deep pink, then as they mature, the foliage becomes creamy yellow on green. The leaves eventually grow to 3 to

4 feet in length. The intense variegation of this grass makes it visually outstanding in a garden—even from a distance. *Glycera maxima* 'Variegata' is very adaptable; it will actually grow in shallow water, or it can be cultivated in any moist garden soil. If variegated manna grass is planted in water, be careful that it does not become invasive. Grow this plant in full sun.

GYPSOPHILA. Family: Caryophyllaceae.

Gypsophila paniculata 'Bristol Fairy' (BABY'S BREATH). Zones 3–9.

This ethereal plant will eventually become a large cloudlike mass of tiny double white flowers. 'Bristol Fairy' grows to 3 feet and flowers for the whole of the summer. Dried gypsophila is wonderful in arrangements—one plant will satisfy the most industrious florist. Baby's breath should be grown in full sun in well-drained soil. It likes lime, so unless your garden soil is already alkaline, add some garden lime to the planting soil. Gypsophila resents being moved, so take this into account when you plant it.

H

HAMAMELIS (WITCH HAZEL). Family: Hamamilidaceae.

Hamamelis x *intermedia* 'Arnold Promise'. Zones 5–8.

In early spring, before the leaves emerge, this small tree is covered with fragrant yellow blossoms. 'Arnold Promise' can bloom as early as February, even when the temperature is freezing! The flowers appear in loose clus-

ters along the branches, each bloom a bundle of tiny primrose-yellow ribbons. 'Arnold Promise' is a vase-shaped tree that matures at around 20 feet. In the fall the foliage of this *Hamamelis* turns brilliant orange. In order to enjoy the rich perfume on cold spring mornings, 'Arnold Promise' should be planted near the house or a frequented pathway.

HEDERA (IVY). Family: Araliaceae.

Hedera helix 'Baltica' (BALTIC IVY). Zones 4–9.

Ivy is an attractive low-growing evergreen that, contrary to popular belief, will thrive in sun. This dense climber is ideal for planting under trees or for covering walls. Baltic ivy is useful for controlling erosion on steep banks, or for planting where an evergreen ground cover is needed. Although *Hedera* prefers indirect light, when established it will grow either in full sun or in dense shade. If it is cultivated in heavy shade the growth will be slow. Ivy prefers well-drained soil and likes to be planted in areas of high light intensity. 'Baltica' is one of the hardiest ivies, but will survive in Zone 4 areas only in very protected spots.

HELENIUM (HELEN'S FLOWER). Family: Compositae.

Helenium autumnale. Zones 3–10.

Helenium is an attractive late-blooming perennial. In August and September, Helen's flower bears large yellow daisy-like blooms, each with a raised central "pom-pom." *Helenium autumnale* grows between 2 and 6 feet tall. Many garden varieties of *Helenium* are available. Grow them in full sun, in moist soil. *Helenium* will adapt to quite wet soil, so it is a good choice for a permanently damp part of the garden.

HELIANTHEMUM (ROCKROSE). Family: Cistaceae.

Rockrose is a semi-evergreen shrub that thrives in sun-baked conditions, in well-drained limy soil. Grow these plants in a rock garden, desert garden, or let them sprawl over a low wall. To keep plants healthy and to ensure prolific blooming, shear *Helianthemum* after flowering.

Helianthemum nummularium 'Fire Dragon.' Zones 5–9.

This 10-inch plant spreads to a little under 2 feet across. The bushy shrubs are covered with attractive silvery gray foliage. From May to June, large coppery red blossoms cover 'Fire Dragon'.

HELIANTHUS (PERENNIAL SUNFLOWER). Family: Compositae.

Helianthus x *multiflorus* 'Flore Pleno'. Zones 4–9.

This is a 6-foot perennial sunflower that has double blooms—flowers that resemble yellow dahlia blossoms. *Helianthus multiflorus* 'Flore Pleno' is perfect for planting at the back of a perennial border or for placing in the middle of an island garden. Wherever you grow this magnificent plant, it will be noticeable from quite a distance! Perennial sunflower flowers in late summer and early autumn. Grow this "botanical behemoth" in full sun in moist well-drained soil.

HELICHRYSUM. Family: Compositae.

Helichrysum angustifolium (CURRY PLANT). Zones 8–10.

This is a lovely shrub to grow in the herb garden. When mature, curry plant will reach 2 feet. All parts of the plant exude a delightful odor of sweet curry. Since this is a half-hardy shrub, in areas of cold winters, curry plant is best grown in a pot. In late spring when all danger of frost has passed, the containerized herb can be placed on a patio or sunk into the earth in the herb garden. Remember, of course, to move the curry plant back inside before the first frost. The silver foliage of this plant is magnificent. Mustard-yellow blossoms appear in summer. Grow curry plant in well-drained sunny sites. This herb is used primarily for making potpourri, and the dried flowers are used in scented herb wreaths.

HELICTOTRICHON. Family: Gramineae.

Helictotrichon sempervirens (BLUE OATS). Zones 4–8.

The only dumb thing about this grass is its name! How could anybody call such a beautiful plant "blue oats"? Surely it's a name more suitable for horse feed than for one of nature's most elegant grasses! The 2-foot, almost metallic-looking leaves form graceful arching clumps. In June the flowering plumes make this grass look even more elegant—if that is possible. *Helictotrichon* looks wonderful in the "silver garden" or really anywhere, as long as it can be seen. Grow this perennial in full sun, in dry or in well-drained soil.

HELIOTROPIUM. Family: Boraginaceae. Zones 9–10.

Heliotropium arborescens (sometimes listed as *Heliotropium peruvianum*) (HELIOTROPE, TURNSOLE, CHERRY PIE).

Heliotrope is a lovely old-fashioned herb that can perfume a whole room with a delicious "cherry pie" scent. This is a tender perennial shrub, so unless you have a greenhouse or live in Zones 9–10, it is best cultivated as an annual. The bushy plant grows about a foot tall, and the tiny violet blossoms have a most appealing scent. Heliotrope is an adaptable plant. Providing the soil is kept moist, it will grow in any garden, in full sun or partial shade. Just for the scent alone, this herb is a delight. A homeopathic extract has been used to treat hoarseness of voice, or what used to be called "clergyman's throat."

HELLEBORUS (HELLEBORE).
Family: Ranunculaceae.

For the jewel in the winter crown, I would choose hellebores. And fortunately for American gardeners, these lovely members of the buttercup family are becoming more available from garden centers and mail-order companies. All hellebores appreciate some shade, especially in summer.

Helleborus lividus corsicus (CORSICAN HELLEBORE). Zones 5–9.

This is the largest of the hellebores, reaching 3 feet. The lovely spiny evergreen leaves remind me of holly foliage. The blossoms, which appear as soon as the snow melts, are borne on long arching branches. The large flowers are a lovely emerald-green and, miraculously, last for twelve to sixteen weeks. Grow Corsican hellebore in light shade or deep shade, in rich moist soil.

In colder zones, make sure that you plant *Helleborus lividus corsicus* in a protected spot. Cold wind can severely burn the lovely foliage of these perennials. In my Connecticut (Zone 5) garden, before winter sets in, I spray the leaves with an antidessicant (available at all garden centers).

Helleborus niger (CHRISTMAS ROSE, BLACK HELLEBORE). Zones 3–8.

Christmas rose is a perennial that grows up to 12 inches tall. From midwinter to midspring, this leathery evergreen produces attractive white flowers. The blooms remind me of an orchid—the large blossoms consist of stiff, pure white petals, each with a golden center. If you cannot resist picking some of the flowers of your Christmas rose, don't feel guilty; they will last a very long time in water. *Helleborus niger* is best grown in light shade, in a rich soil high in organic matter.

This herb is known as black hellebore because of the ebony color of the roots—the part employed by herbalists. In the early herbals, entries for Christmas rose were invariably included with white hellebore *(Veratrum album)*—which is not a hellebore at all but in fact a member of the lily family. The physicians of past centuries considered the black hellebore and the white hellebore to be identical in their therapeutic properties. To the ancient herbalists, black hellebore was a magical plant, a herb that demanded special precautions before collecting. The Roman naturalist Pliny outlined these procedures: "First a circle is drawn around it with a sword; then the man who is going to cut it looks to the east with a prayer that the gods will grant him permission to do so. He also keeps on the lookout for a flying eagle—for generally one is present when men cut [the hellebore]—and if an eagle flies near, it is a sign that the gatherer will die in the year." The hellebores are strong purgatives, as Pliny warns; "furthermore, even when the Hellebore proved successful, the various colors of the vomits are terrifying to see, and after the vomit comes the worry of watching the stools." Pliny then warns who should not take hellebore internally: "Never prescribe for old people or children, or for those who are soft and effeminate in body and mind, or for the thin and delicate." It is a curative of "giddiness, melancholia, insanity and wild distraction. . . . Care must be taken, even with happy treatment not to administer Hellebore on a cloudy day; for to do so is followed by unbearable torture." Although not intentionally, Elizabethan herbalist John Gerard gives a humorous account of the medical uses of white and black hellebore: "A purgation of Hellebore is good for mad and furious men, for melancholy, dull, or heavy persons . . . and briefly for all those that are . . . molested with melancholy. . . . This strong medicine made of white hellebore ought not to be given inwardly unto delicate bodies without greate correction, but may be more safely given unto country people which feed grossely, and have hard, tough, and strong bodies."

HEMEROCALLIS (DAYLILY). Family: Liliaceae. Zones 3–10.

Although *Hemerocallis* have blooms that last only a day, as the English name indicates, the blooms are prolific. Daylilies are the most adaptable of all garden perennials. They will grow in full sun or semi-shade, and are both heat and drought resistant. Very few garden pests bother these tough plants. By carefully selecting a number of different varieties, you can have daylilies in bloom from June to October. Once established, these hardy perennials will form weed-smothering mats. A daylily bed is perhaps the perfect solution for a low-maintenance garden. Grow *Hemerocallis* in any garden soil. Although daylilies bloom most prolifically in full sun, they are never

disappointing when grown in light shade, especially if you plant varieties that have flowers with more delicate pastel colors. These plants can be moved anytime. Because daylilies come in such a variety of colors— there are literally hundreds to choose from— in a number of the garden plans, I have not specified varieties of *Hemerocallis*. In these instances I have indicated colors that would be appropriate to the design, and gardeners can choose their own favorites.

'Autumn Minaret' is a tall daylily (5 feet) that blooms in September. The long branched stems carry yellow flowers that have a distinct red flush. Planted in masses, this variety is perfect in the center of an island border.

'Bright Banner' is one of my favorite daylilies. From mid-July until September this 42-inch plant has gold blooms that are edged with red.

'Christmas Carol' has lovely velvety crimson-red blooms with green hearts. This daylily grows up to 3 feet and blooms in August.

'Constitution Island' blooms from mid-July to early September. The light gold deeply ruffled flowers are borne on 28-inch stems.

'Evergold' blooms from mid-July until September. Ruffled deep gold flowers grow on 40-inch stems.

'Frans Hals' has bicolored blossoms. Striking red and yellow flowers grow on 24-inch stems. 'Frans Hals' blooms in September.

'Hyperion' is an old garden favorite. Not only are the pale lemon flowers lovely, but these blossoms are very fragrant. Blooms appear on 42-inch stems. 'Hyperion' flowers around midsummer.

'Lamplighter' has bright velvety red flowers with yellow hearts. The blooms appear on 32-inch stems. 'Lamplighter' flowers in August, and the blossoms stay open in the evening.

'Winning Ways' has greenish-yellow flowers. At the center of each bloom is a green heart. From mid-July to mid-August, 'Winning Ways' carries these blossoms on 26-inch stems.

HESPERIS (ROCKET). Family: Cruciferae.

Hesperis matronalis (DAME'S VIOLET, SWEET ROCKET). Zones 4–8.

This is a lovely plant with fragrant phloxlike flowers. The Elizabethan herbalist and fiery Protestant William Turner remarked that rocket, especially the seed, "quickens nature and excites the passions." According to Turner this seed was also indispensable for "bitings of the shrew-mouse and other venomous beasts."

Sweet rocket grows between 2 and 3 feet tall, and from mid-spring until midsummer the plants are covered with loose clusters of fragrant flowers. These blossoms vary in color; sometimes plants will have purple or violet blooms, other times the flowers will be white. To extend the blooming period until fall, remove dead flower heads. Grow dame's rocket in moist well-drained soil, in full sun or light shade. Although dame's rocket is a short-lived perennial, it readily reseeds itself. No self-respecting fragrance garden should be without sweet rocket.

HIBISCUS. Family: Malvaceae.

Hibiscus moscheutos (ROSE MALLOW). Zones 5–10.

One blossom of the rose mallow would make a perfect boutonniere for the Jolly Green Giant—the flowers are dinner-plate size! This mammoth perennial grows to 7 feet. In late summer or early fall, rose mallow bears lovely 12-inch hollyhock-like flowers. These blooms can be either white, pink, or red. Needless to say, care must be taken before imposing this hibiscus on the garden—rose mallow is not a plant for a window box! Grow *Hibiscus moscheutos* in full sun in damp soil. It will take a limited amount of shade and will grow in drier soils.

HOSTA (PLANTAIN LILY, FUNKIA). Family: Liliaceae. Zones 3–9.

The large heart-shaped leaves of hosta provide interest in the garden from spring until fall. Some varieties have dainty foliage—leaves under 6 inches—while other hosta have huge tropical-looking leaves, measured in feet. As members of the Lily family, hosta have attractive flowers, and many varieties have scented blossoms. Today, gardeners are fortunate in that hosta are available in every shade of blue, green, and gold. Amongst perennials for a shady site, hosta is first choice. But a number can be grown in full sun, especially in more northern gardens. 'Royal Standard' is included in this category. Grow these lovely perennials in rich moist soil.

'Frances Williams' is an 18-inch hosta with handsome blue-green foliage that is heavily veined and quilted. A distinct yellow band lines the margin of each leaf. At maturity 'Frances Williams' forms a large 3 × 4-foot clump. In summer this gilded hosta has fragrant flowers. The blossoms have a faint lavender tinge.

'Gold Standard' has pleated golden leaves gently edged with blue-green. My bank balance is the only factor that stops my buying more of these lovely hosta. 'Gold Standard' deserves its name: at the back of a shady border, this 3-foot golden gem is a stunning sight. As these plants mature, especially if they are planted in areas of lighter shade, the gold foliage mellows and becomes burnished. 'Gold Standard' flowers in summer and has lavender blooms.

'Hadspan Blue' is my favorite blue hosta. The large rounded leaves have tapering points, and the blue foliage has a surface powdering—like a dusting of confectioner's sugar! This makes the color more intense. 'Hadspan Blue' flowers in August; these blossoms are lavender colored.

'Piedmont Gold' is 24 to 30 inches tall and has pleated golden heart-shaped leaves with undulating margins. Attractive white flowers appear in August.

'Royal Standard' has light green leaves with a lovely waxy sheen. The foliage is large, and forms mounds measuring up to 2 feet. In August and September, fragrant white blossoms add to the beauty of this hosta. 'Royal Standard' will grow in shade or in full sun.

Hosta sieboldiana 'Elegans'.

For many people this variety is the first choice when selecting a blue hosta. The large nicely rounded leaves form 2½-foot mounds. In summer, fragrant light lavender flowers rise above the foliage. 'Elegans' can be grown in full sun, but in shade, the blue color is more pronounced.

HYDRANGEA. Family: Saxifragaceae.

Hydrangea quercifolia (OAKLEAF HYDRANGEA). Zones 5–9.

In both summer and fall, the very large oak-shaped leaves make this an attractive deciduous shrub. In the autumn, the deep red and purple foliage is quite lovely. Large blooms appear in June and July. These cone-shaped clusters of lacy white flowers last a long time, and before fading turn a lovely deep pink. Oakleaf hydrangea grows 6 to 8 feet high and has a spread of 6 feet. This shrub can be grown in sun or shade. If grown in shady areas, the fall color will not be as intense, and blossoms will be fewer. Oakleaf hydrangea likes moist well-drained soil.

HYOSCYAMUS. Family: Solanaceae.

Hyoscyamus niger (HENBANE). Zones 3–10.

Henbane can be either an annual or a biennial. This herb grows about 2 to 3 feet tall and has sticky, hairy leaves with a disagreeable odor. In summer, the stems bear curious cream-colored flowers, each bloom streaked with purple veins. The ripe seed pods have a distinct serrated outer edge that looks very much like the points on a crown. Plant henbane in well-drained soil in full sun.

This is a highly poisonous plant. The classical herbalists were aware of the toxic properties of henbane. Pliny wrote: "All kinds [of henbane] cause insanity and giddiness. . . . It has the character of wine, therefore injures the head and brain." Elizabethan herbalist John Gerard recommended henbane for "inflammation of the stones [testicles] and other secret parts. . . . To wash the feet in the decoction [boiled extract] causeth sleep . . . and also the often smelling of the flowers." He warned against the poisonous qualities of this herb: "The leaves, seed, and juice taken inwardly causeth an unquiet sleep like unto the sleep of drunkenesse, which continueth long, and is deadly to the party." Gerard ends his discussion of henbane with an amusing story: "The seed is used by montibank tooth-drawers which runne about the country, for to cause worms come forth of men's teeth, by burning it in a chafing dish with coals, the party holding his mouth over the fumes thereof: but some crafty companions to gaine money convey small lute strings into the water, persuading the patient that those small creeping beasts come out of his mouth or other parts which he intended to ease."

HYPERICUM. Family: Hypericaceae.

Hypericum perforatum (ST.-JOHN'S-WORT). Zones 4–9.

St.-John's-wort is a branched perennnial that grows to 3 feet. From mid to late summer, star-shaped yellow flowers make this a most attractive herb. Grow this plant in light shade in any good garden soil.

In the past, St.-John's-wort was a magical herb, one that would protect humans, livestock, and buildings from supernatural forces. The fresh juice of St.-John's-wort turns red with exposure to air, and Christian symbolists identified this secretion with the blood of St. John. The fact that this herb flowers around the feast of St. John (June 24) further aided the allegorists. The plant therefore became known as St.-John's-wort, and if collected on the festival of this important divine, the herb would inherit supernatural properties. According to Banckes's *Herbal* of 1525: "The virtue of it is thus. If it be putte in a mannes house there shall come no wycked spryte therein." In the Middle Ages it was believed that by simply smelling the leaves even the insane could be cured. The foliage and the flowering tops of St.-John's-wort have strong antiseptic qualities, and because of this it is useful for treating wounds and inflammations.

HYSSOPUS. Family: Labiatae.

Hyssopus officinalis (HYSSOP). Zones 3–7.

Hyssop is a bushy shrub that grows to 2 feet. The woody stems bear small pointed leaves, and in summer, lovely blue flowers cover the whole plant. In mild areas this herb is evergreen. Because of the ease with which it can be clipped, hyssop makes a good low hedge for the herb garden. It will grow in poor soils but needs full sun.

Sixteenth-century English herbalist Richard Banckes wrote that the virtue of hyssop is found in the fact that "if a man take the juice thereof and put it in his mouth, it will heal all manner evils in the mouth . . . if it be drunken green or in powder, it maketh a man well colored." Hyssop's pungent aromatic flavor was much enjoyed in the medieval kitchen and was added to soups, stews, and stuffings. Today hyssop is still widely employed as a tea for alleviating chest disorders, colds, coughs, sore throats, and fevers. A recipe "for old coughs" given by Elizabethan herbalist John Gerard can be tried today. He recommends a brew made from hyssop, "figges, water, honey, and rue." Many gardeners grow hyssop because it is such a good bee plant.

I

IBERIS (CANDYTUFT). Family: Cruciferae. Zones 3–9.

Perennial candytuft is a compact little evergreen plant that is ideal for lining pathways, planting in rock gardens, or for growing at the front of a flower border. Grow candytuft in full sun, in rich well-drained soil.

Iberis sempervirens 'Autumn Snow'.

'Autumn Snow' is a perennial candytuft that forms neat 8-inch evergreen mounds. In spring the plants are covered with tight clusters of white flowers, and they will bloom again in the fall.

ILEX (HOLLY). Family: Aquifoliaceae.

Ilex x *meserveae* 'Blue Prince' and 'Blue Princess'. Zones 4–9.

Being an Englishman, I have always loved the red-berried evergreen hollies so common in my native land. For years I resented the fact that I could not grow these lovely trees in my Connecticut garden because of the severe New England climate. So now every time I see sturdy bushes of 'Blue Prince' and 'Blue Princess' holly growing in cold parts of America, I offer a moment of silent praise for Kathleen Meserve, the plantswoman who produced this excellent weather-resistant strain. In the early 1970s, using her kitchen windowsill for a nursery, this remarkable woman bred evergreen hollies that were hardy to −20° F.—one of the most astounding horticultural achievements in recent years. 'Blue Princess' and 'Blue Prince' deserve their aristocratic names. 'Blue Princess' reaches about 12 feet, bears proper holly leaves (dark green and prickly), and is covered with bright red berries. The lady's consort, 'Blue Prince', is also exceptional: for three months, this tree bears an abundance of pinkish white flowers. But you can't choose just one. The female will not produce berries without having a pollinating member of the opposite sex nearby. Who said gardens were without lust! Grow these hollies in sun or partial shade, in moist well-drained acid soil.

IMPERATA. Family: Gramineae.

Imperata cylindrica rubra 'Red Baron' (JAPANESE BLOOD GRASS). Zones 5–9.

If you like red, then Japanese blood grass, the "scarlet woman" of the grass world, is for you. Although this is not a gigantic grass, it will be outstanding in any landscape. The 2-foot blades have a wonderful scarlet hue, and when sunlight shines through the foliage, the plants seem almost unearthly. Grow Japanese blood grass in full sun. In colder regions, protect it with a winter mulch.

INULA. Family: Compositae.

Inula helenium (ELECAMPANE, HELEN'S FLOWER). Zones 3–8.

Elecampane is a tall, stately herb that grows to more than 6 feet. The lower, basal leaves are large, while the upper foliage is much smaller. In midsummer plants are covered with small yellow daisy-like flowers. Elecampane is best grown in sun or semi-shade, in moist soil.

In charming Elizabethan prose, John Gerard tells the legend of this herb: "Some report that this plant took the name Helenium of Helena wife to Menelaus, who had her hands full of it when Paris stole her away into Phrygia." The Roman naturalist Pliny thought very highly of elecampane and recommended it as much as possible: "Let no day pass without eating some roots of Inula, considered to help the digestion and cause mirth." This Roman author recommended elecampane as a valuable cosmetic, aphrodisiac, and stimulant: "Helenium, which had its origin, as I have said, in the tears of Helen, is believed to preserve physical charm, and to keep unimpaired the fresh complexion of our women.

Moreover, it is supposed that by its use, they gain a kind of attractiveness and sex appeal. Taken in wine ... it is attributed with the power of stimulating gaiety, and of banishing sorrow." In medieval Europe elecampane was used as a cure for seasickness. For centuries elecampane has also been used for treating chest disorders. Today, in modern herbal medicine, this herb is still used for coughs and respiratory disorders.

IRIS. Family: Iridaceae.

Iris foetidissima 'Lutea' (GLADWIN, ROAST BEEF PLANT). Zones 5–9.

This is one of the handsomest fall plants. Gladwin is an 18-inch evergreen iris with dark green leaves. In the autumn it bears large pods, and when they ripen, they split apart and reveal bright scarlet seeds. These vivid berries are arranged in double rows and look like strings of scarlet pearls. When torn, the leaf blades of Gladwin emit a curious odor of roast beef, hence the country name "roast beef plant" for this perennial. The flowers of *Iris foetidissima* 'Lutea' appear in late spring; blossoms are a smoky gold color. Grow this iris in part shade in well-drained soil. Gladwin looks especially good when planted in a mass under deciduous trees. Flower arrangers will love the fruiting seed heads.

Iris germanica (GERMAN IRIS; "BEARDED IRIS" in most catalogues). Zones 4–8.

German iris flower in May and June. They vary tremendously in height—some reach only 4 inches, others grow to 4 feet—and are available in every possible color. Grow *Iris germanica* in full sun or partial shade, in average well-drained soil.

Iris pseudacorus (YELLOW FLAG). Zones 5–8.

This lovely iris is perfect for naturalizing along the margins of ponds or streams. Yellow flag will be quite happy if planted in a few inches of standing water or in the squelchy soil of the bank. Alternatively, this adaptable plant can be grown in fairly moist garden soil. Grow yellow flag in full sun.

In June and July, *Iris pseudacorus* bears lovely yellow fleur-de-lis blossoms. Plants grow to 3 feet.

Iris pumilla (DWARF IRIS, DWARF BEARDED IRIS). Zones 4–8.

This 4- to 8-inch garden gem flowers from late April to mid-May. Blossoms are varied—they are either yellow, lilac, or white. The leaves get a little longer after the iris has bloomed. Dwarf iris is a good plant for the rock garden or for the front of a flower border. Grow it in full sun in well-drained humus-rich soil.

Iris sibirica (SIBERIAN IRIS). Zones 3–8.

Siberian iris flower in June and July. The dainty blossoms appear on the top of the stems. Grow these lovely iris in full sun in average well-drained soil.

'Caesar's Brother' is one of the best of the Siberian iris. It has midnight-purple flowers on 30-inch stems.

'Flight of Butterflies' has bicolored blossoms about 2 inches across; the upper petals are veined with red-violet, and the three downward-curving petals are very light blue. 'Flight of Butterflies' grows to 3 feet.

'Ruffled Velvet', a 30-inch Siberian iris, has attractive deep plum blossoms. The downward-curving petals have gold in the center.

'Super Ego' has a bicolored flower with sky-blue upper petals which contrast beautifully with the purple and veined downward-pointing petals. 'Super Ego' grows to 30 inches.

'White Swirl' is a truly beautiful flower with pure white blossoms, each bloom having a streak of yellow at the throat. 'White Swirl' grows to 34 inches.

Iris versicolor (BLUE FLAG). Zones 4–8.

Blue flag is a perennial native to the eastern and midwestern United States. This 3-foot iris is a wetland species, ideal for the bog garden, margins of ponds and streams, or a permanently damp part of the landscape. In May, blue fleur-de-lis blossoms appear. Grow *Iris versicolor* in full sun. A number of attractive varieties are available.

J

JUNIPERUS (JUNIPER). Family: Cupressaceae.

Juniperus horizontalis 'Wiltonii' (WILTON CARPET JUNIPER). Zones 3–9.

This creeping conifer eventually forms a dense evergreen mat, and when established, does indeed look like a blue rug! The foliage is an attractive blue-gray. *Juniperus horizontalis* 'Wiltonii' is the slowest-growing of all the blue carpet junipers, and so it is good for small low-maintenance gardens. Grow *Juniperus horizontalis* 'Wiltonii' in full sun, in well-drained soil.

K

KALMIA (LAUREL). Family: Ericaceae.

Kalmia latifolia (MOUNTAIN LAUREL). Zones 4–9.

This lovely evergreen shrub matures at around 8 to 10 feet and attains a spread of 10 feet. In the wild, specimens can get even larger. Mountain laurel is a neat, compact shrub that is one of the glories of the garden in June. Clusters of attractive pink to white buds slowly open into beautiful cup-shaped blooms. Dozens of blooms make each cluster of flowers a living posy. Mountain laurel thrives in partial shade to full sun and likes moist, acid soil. Some of the best stands of *Kalmia latifolia* I have ever seen were those growing in peat moss at the edge of a bog. Older, leggy specimens can be cut to the ground and will resprout from the base.

KNIPHOFIA (formerly *Tritoma*) (TORCH LILY). Family: Liliaceae. Zones 5–9.

As children we called these attractive perennials "red hot pokers," and indeed the thick tapering spikes, tipped with fiery flowers, do look like heated irons. Many gardening books and catalogues still list them as *Tritoma*, a name much easier to pronounce than *Kniphofia*! (The latter is pronounced "ny-fo-fee-uh.") Red hot pokers flower in the summer or fall, and are best planted in full sun to partial shade, in rich well-drained soil. In colder areas they should have the protection of a winter mulch.

Kniphofia uvaria.

'Pfitzeri'. This lovely perennial flowers in September and October; blossoms are a deep orange. 'Pfitzeri' grows to 3 feet.

'Royal Standard' bears lovely bicolored flowers in August and September. Blooms start opening at the bottom of the flower spike and continue to the tip. The flowers are red initially, and as they open they turn yellow. 'Royal Standard' grows to 3 feet.

L

LAMIASTRUM. Family: Labiatae.

Lamiastrum galeobdolon 'Herman's Pride'. Zones 3–9.

The crinkly green leaves of this plant look as if they had been carefully dabbed with silver paint. 'Herman's Pride' is a spreading foot-high perennial that provides good ground cover in shady sites. In May and June, whorls of yellow snapdragon-like flowers appear amongst the leaves. Grow *Lamiastrum* in partial shade to full shade, in well-drained soil.

LAMIUM (DEAD NETTLE). Family: Labiatae. Zones 3–9.

Lamium maculatum.

For a shady site there is no better ground cover than *Lamium maculatum.* Grow these two varieties in average garden soil. They will both tolerate dry shade.

'Beacon Silver' has silver leaves, delicately edged with green, which brighten up the gloomiest shady garden. From April to October, attractive pink flowers appear on 6-inch stalks.

'White Nancy' is not as readily available as 'Beacon Silver', but I think it is a prettier plant. The leaves are slightly smaller, more silvery, and have a wider green margin than 'Beacon Silver'. 'White Nancy' also seems a little more robust. As the name indicates, this is a white-flowering *Lamium maculatum.*

LAURUS. Family: Lauraceae. Zones 8–10.

Laurus nobilis (SWEET BAY, LAUREL, BAY TREE).

Sweet bay is a lovely aromatic evergreen tree. The sweetly scented leaves are one of the main ingredients of *bouquet garni*, an essential part of classic French cuisine. Bay is indigenous to the Mediterranean regions, where it grows as high as 40 to 60 feet. As an outdoor tree in the United States, bay is hardy only in Zones 8–10. Mature trees in the South are a spectacular sight. In other areas this herb is best grown in a tub or large pot and moved outside only when the weather is mild. Make sure that the potted bay is given some protection from strong sun and harsh winds. As this tree responds to clipping, it is often used as a topiary ornament.

The Greeks and Romans believed that if bay was hung over the lintel of a house, lightning strikes would be averted. The Roman naturalist Pliny relates the merits of bay: "The laurel alone of all shrubs planted by man and received into our houses is never struck by lightning. . . . Those anointed with it are shunned by all venomous animals." Pliny also recommends bay for an unsightly complexion: "Pounded and applied at night [it] removes pimples and itching." The word "baccalaureate," meaning "laurel berries," came into being in the ancient world when scholars and poets of merit were crowned with bay. "The berries," noted Elizabethan herbalist John Gerard, "are good against wearisomenesse . . . or wast away humors." He further added that this herb "stires up decayed appetitie, takes away the loathing of meat. . . . It is reported that common drunkards were accustomed to eat in the morning fasting two leaves [of bay] thereof against drunkednesse." In the modern household, bay is indispensable in the kitchen. Add the leaves to soups, stews, pâté, marinades, even custard puddings.

LAVANDULA (LAVENDER). Family: Labiatae.

There are over twenty species of lavender available; most are not hardy except in Zones 9–10. For colder regions, English lavender and its varieties are the best for growing outside. Plant the following hardy lavenders in full sun in well-drained soil.

The ancients sprinkled flowers of this herb into their bath water. ("Lavender" derives from *lavare*, the Latin verb meaning "to wash.") Clothes were also cleaned in lavender water, and although this delightful practice has been abandoned, the now obsolete word for laundress, "lavender," preserves the association. A recipe for an interesting beverage is given in the fifteenth-century *English Leechbook* "for trembling hands and hands that fall asleep. Take Lavender and Primrose, and seeth them in ale, and drink it." Another fifteenth-century herbal, the *Hortus Sanitatis*, has much to say about lavender: "The mother of God was very fond of lavender flowers because of their virtue in protecting clothes from dirty filthy beasts." "Lavender," says the Elizabethan herbalist John Gerard, "is of a thin substance, consisting of many arie and spiritual parts. Therefore it is good to be given any way against the cold diseases of the heart . . . to them that have the falling

sickness, and that use to swoone much." Gerard also considered lavender invaluable for "the panting and passion of the heart." Today lavender blossoms are still prized for their scent. On occasion I use lavender tea as a remedy for headaches.

Lavandula angustifolia (sometimes called *Lavandula vera, Lavandula spica,* or *Lavandula officinalis*) (ENGLISH LAVENDER). Zones 5–9.

This herb is a bushy perennial that grows to 3 feet. In summer it is covered with lovely aromatic spikes of mauve flowers.

'Hidcote' is the most popular of the many cultivars derived from English lavender. Sometimes sold as *Lavandula nana atropurpurea*, it is a compact plant that grows to about 2 feet and makes a good hedge. The blossoms are violet and highly scented.

'Munstead' is a compact variety of English lavender—it reaches only 1 to 2 feet. The flowers are deep blue and are ideal for drying.

'Twickel Purple' is outstanding among the taller varieties of English lavender. This plant has deep lavender flowers and grows to 36 inches. In Zones 5–6 'Twickel Purple' should be given a winter mulch.

LEONURUS. Family: Labiatae.

Leonurus cardiaca (MOTHERWORT). Zones 5–8.

Motherwort is a stout leafy perennial that grows to 4 feet. From June until September, whorls of pinkish flowers decorate the tall flower spikes. Plant motherwort in full sun, in light well-drained soil to which some lime has been added.

The ancient herbalists used this plant for making the heart merry and strong. Motherwort was also employed for hysterical conditions and swooning. When this herb was hung over the lintel of the door it was said to prevent evil spirits from entering the house. Seventeenth-century English herbalist Nicholas Culpeper thought highly of motherwort: "There is no better herb to drive melancholy vapors from the heart, to strengthen it and make the mind cheerful, blithe and merry."

LEVISTICUM. Family: Umbelliferae.

Levisticum officinale (LOVAGE). Zones 3–9.

This tall, branched, leafy perennial grows to 5 feet. In June and July, plants bear flat circular blooms made up of dozens of tiny yellow flowers. The whole herb looks a bit like a large celery plant. Lovage will grow in most regions of the United States, with the exception of southern Florida and the Gulf States, where year-round warm conditions prevent the winter freeze necessary for lovage to complete its growing cycle. In other areas, plant lovage in either full sun or partial shade. This herb prefers a rich moist soil.

Lovage is strongly aromatic. "It is good for the stomach," wrote the Roman naturalist Pliny, "likewise for convulsions and flatulence." A cordial made from lovage roots is still used by Europeans for upset stomachs. According to the *English Leechbook*, all one had to do to cure "trembling hands, and hands asleep," was wash with lovage "when thou goest to bed, as hot as thou mayest suffer." Elizabethan herbalist John Gerard advocated lovage as a cosmetic: "The distilled water of lovage clereth the sight, and putteth away all spots, lentils, freckles, and redness of the face, if they be often washed therewith." Cold lovage tea would have the same effect and might be worth trying if you have spots or freckles you want to get rid of.

Lovage is one of the most useful herbs for the modern kitchen. Its strong celery flavor is wonderful in stews and soups. A personal favorite is spinach and bacon salad with chopped lovage leaves.

LIATRIS (BLAZING STAR, GAYFEATHER). Family: Compositae. Zones 3–8.

These lovely plants from the prairies need full sun and deep soil that is well drained.

Liatris pycnostachya (PRAIRIE BLAZING STAR, KANSAS GAYFEATHER).

In midsummer, 4-foot flower spikes rise from a tight cluster of narrow leaves. The top foot of these shoots is covered with rosy purple flowers. Buds begin to open at the top of the spike and continue downward until the whole blossom is fully opened.

Liatris pycnostachya 'Alba' (ALBINO PRAIRIE BLAZING STAR) is a white form.

Liatris scariosa.

This drought-resistant perennial is similar to *Liatris pycnostachya* except that the flowers are a little darker and *Liatris scariosa* grows a little taller (4 to 6 feet). 'White Spire' is a white form of *Liatris scariosa*.

Liatris spicata (SPIKE GAYFEATHER).

From July until September, deep purple flowers top the 3-foot flower spikes. This is a drought-resistant plant.

Liatris spicata 'Kobold' is a much smaller *Liatris*, reaching only 18 to 24 inches. The reddish-lilac flowers appear from July to September. The smaller size of 'Kobold' makes it an ideal choice for planting at the front of a flower border.

LIGULARIA. Family: Compositae.

Ligularia stenocephala 'The Rocket' (also listed as *Ligularia* x *przewalskii*). Zones 3–8.

This perennial is perfect for planting in the damp soil associated with a pond or stream, or in a permanently damp part of the garden. 'The Rocket' deserves its impressive name: from summer to early fall, the 5-foot ebony stems are covered with bright yellow flowers. Complementing the lovely blossoms are the handsome rounded leaves, which have jagged edges and are streaked with purple veins. Grow 'The Rocket' in partial shade.

LILIUM (LILY). Family: Liliaceae. Zones 3–8.

Lilium canadense (CANADA LILY).

Canada lily is one of America's most beautiful wild flowers. In June, drooping yellow bell-shaped flowers are borne in clusters on 5-foot stems. The inside of each blossom is orange, and each bloom is speckled with dark spots. Canada lily prefers moist soil, where it can be grown in full sun. In drier soil, provide this lily with some shade. Plant Canada lilies 6 to 8 inches deep and 1 foot apart.

Lilium candidum (MADONNA LILY).

This lily grows 4 to 5 feet tall. In summer the fragrant blossoms appear, pure white and trumpet shaped. Plant the bulbs in early fall in good soil in a position of full sun. Make each hole only about 2 inches deep (this sounds shallow, but it is the correct depth for Madonna lilies). Space bulbs 1 foot apart.

For centuries the lovely Madonna lily has been enjoyed in the garden for its beauty and for the bulb's medicinal qualities. Incorrectly, some modern writers have said that gardeners in the Middle Ages grew only plants that were useful, and never considered growing flowers for their beauty alone. The following description by medieval author Bartholomaeus Anglicus (Bartholomew The Englishman) puts this notion in true perspective: "The lily is next to the rose in worthiness and nobleness. . . . Nothing is more gracious than the lily in fairness of color, in sweetness of smell and in effect of working virtue."

Many early writers suggested using the bulb of the Madonna lily for curing bites of poisonous reptiles. Walahfrid Strabo, a monk from the Middle Ages, praised this herb for its antivenom properties:

> If a snake treacherous and wily
> As it is by nature, plants with deadly
>   tongue its parcel
> Of venom in you, sending grim death
>   through the unseen wound
> To the innermost vaults of the heart—
>   then crush lilies with a weighty pestle
>   and drink the wine.
> Now place the pulp on the top of the livid
>   spot where the snake' tongue jabbed;
> Then indeed you will learn for yourself
>   the wonderful power
> This antidote has. Nor is that all: this
>   same pulp of crushed lily is good for
>   limbs that are twisted awry.

A claim made by the Greek physician Dioscorides should interest modern beauticians: "It cleareth ye face and makes them without wrinkles." Crescenzi, a medieval author, also had a cosmetic use for this herb: Madonna lily "will cause the hair to grow in used up places." John Gerard, the famous Elizabethan herbalist, gave an ample list for the medicinal uses of this plant. The following is amusing: "It ripeneth apothumes [boils] in the flanks, coming of venery and such like."

Lilium regale (REGAL LILY).

This lily grows to 6 feet tall and in July has fragrant white flowers. The blooms are up to 6 inches long, funnel shaped, and hang straight out from the stem. Plant regal lilies in full sun to partial shade, in humusy well-drained soil. Plant the bulbs 6 to 9 inches deep and 1 foot apart.

Lilium superbum (TURK'S-CAP LILY).

This distinctive lily blooms in July and August. Brown-spotted orange flowers hang from the 3- to 6-foot stems. Their lovely petals curve upward, and red anthers add to their beauty. Grow Turk's cap lilies in moist soil in partial shade. If the roots are mulched, *Lilium superbum* can be grown in full sun. Plant bulbs 6 inches deep and 1 foot apart.

LIMONIUM (SEA LAVENDER). Family: Plumbaginaceae.

Limonium latifolium. Zones 3–8.

This pretty flower from coastal areas is one of the best blooms for drying and using in decoration. *Limonium latifolium* flowers from July until September, when lavender-blue flowers appear on 18-inch stems. The blossoms are tiny but numerous and are borne on fanlike branches. Grow this perennial in full sun in well-drained soil.

LIPPIA CITRIODORA. See *Aloysia triphylla.*

LIRIOPE (LILY-TURF). Family: Liliaceae.

Liriope muscari 'Majestic'. Zones 5–9.

This member of the Lily family produces evergreen grasslike tufts of leaves. From August to September, large lavender flowers appear on 15-inch spikes. Liriope is an ideal perennial for planting under trees. Zone 5 conditions stretch the hardiness of this perennial; in colder areas grow 'Majestic' in a more protected site. Plant lily-turf in partial or deep shade, in well-drained soil.

LOBELIA. Family: Lobeliaceae.

Lobelia cardinalis (CARDINAL FLOWER). Zones 4–8.

Of all garden plants this perennial displays the most intense scarlet petals. Indeed, the name "cardinal flower" refers to the blossom's likeness to the scarlet of a cardinal's robe. From July until early fall, *Lobelia cardinalis* produces lovely stems of crimson flowers. Although in the wild cardinal flower is most often encountered near the edges of ponds and streams, it is quite at home at the back of a flower border, where the lovely 3-foot flower spikes can be appreciated. Cardinal flower is an adaptable plant and can be grown in sun or shade. A good covering of leaf mulch around the base retains moisture during summer, and in winter protects the somewhat frost-sensitive roots.

Lobelia fulgens 'Bee's Flame'. Zones 5–8.

This lobelia is similar to cardinal flower but grows a little taller (3 to 4 feet) and has attractive dark purple stems and foliage. If anything, the flowers of 'Bee's Flame' are more vivid than those of *Lobelia cardinalis*. The color of this perennial is not for the timid! Grow 'Bee's Flame' in moist soil in light shade. In Zones 5–6, this lobelia needs the protection of a winter mulch.

Lobelia siphilitica (GREAT BLUE LOBELIA). Zones 4–8.

In August and September this lobelia bears bright blue flowers on 3-foot stems. *Lobelia siphilitica* prefers semi-shade, but in moist soil it can be grown in full sun.

Lobelia x *vedrariensis*. Zones 5–8.

A lovely flower, from September to late October *Lobelia* x *vedrariensis* bears violet blossoms on long stems. By accident I planted some seedlings of this lobelia under a maple tree in fairly dry soil. The mistake has proved a great success—*Lobelia* x *vedrariensis* not only thrives in this soil, but in this particular garden, flowers even as late as early November. Other late-flowering perennials such as Japanese anemone succumb to frost well before the *Lobelia* x *vedrariensis*. This lobelia can also be grown in full sun in a moister soil.

LOBULARIA. Family: Cruciferae.

Lobularia maritima (SWEET ALYSSUM). Zones 9–10.

Even though this is a perennial native to southern Europe, it is generally treated as an annual. In the mildest areas of the United States, Zones 9–10, sweet alyssum is perennial. In other areas sow alyssum outside after the last spring frost. For the whole summer, this much-branched foot-high plant bears numerous tiny white, purple, lilac, or pink flowers. These blooms are very fragrant. Grow sweet alyssum in full sun in average soil, and cut off dead flowers to encourage more blooms. *Lobularia* is very good for edging pathways or flower borders.

LONICERA (HONEYSUCKLE). Family: Caprifoliaceae.

Lonicera japonica 'Halliana' (HALL'S JAPANESE HONEYSUCKLE). Zones 4–9.

This is a vigorous climber that can reach 15 feet. From midsummer to early fall, lovely pure white flowers cover the plant, and as the blooms mature they change to yellow. The blossoms are very fragrant, especially on warm evenings. In milder zones, Hall's Japanese honeysuckle is evergreen. Grow this climber in full sun or partial shade, in moist well-drained garden soil. This honeysuckle is useful for planting on banks to prevent erosion.

Lonicera periclymenum (HONEYSUCKLE, WOODBINE). Zones 5–9.

Honeysuckle is a common woodland climber that is native to the temperate regions of Europe and Asia. The plant is called woodbine because it is commonly found tightly wrapped around trees. This deciduous vine can grow to 20 feet. Fragrant yellow flowers appear in summer, followed by red berries. For best results, grow wild honeysuckle in rich soil in a slightly shaded position. Like most species of *Lonicera*, it looks most attractive if trained upon a support or if grown over an arbor or wall.

The Elizabethan herbalist John Gerard wrote: "The ripe seed gathered and dried in the shadow and drunke ... fourty days together, doth waste and consume way the hardness of the spleene and removeth wearisomenesse, helpeth the shortnesse and difficultie of breathing, cureth the hicket [hiccup]." In the seventeenth century, another English herbalist, Nicholas Culpeper, mentioned that honeysuckle made into a conserve "should be kept in every gentlewomens house." This, he assured his readers, cures asthma, "takes away the evil of the spleen: provokes urine, procures speedy delivery of women in travail. . . . If you make use of it as an ointment, it will clear the skin of morphew [scabs], freckles, and sunburnings, or whatever else discolors it, and then the maids will love it." For curing afflictions of the skin, an infusion of the flowering tops of honeysuckle is still used externally as an astringent and antiseptic.

LUPINUS (LUPINE). Family: Leguminosae.

Lupinus Russell Hybrids. Zones 4–8.

Lupines are floral aristocrats that should be included in the landscape more often. With a few precautions, in June and July these stately plants can become the focus of the perennial garden. Give lupines lime-free soil and plenty of moisture, and try to provide some protection from hot, desiccating summer winds. The flowers of Russell lupines come in many shades, but whatever color is chosen, the pea-like blossoms that cover the flowering spikes are unforgettable. Remember to remove all spent flower heads to encourage a second blossoming.

LYCHNIS (CAMPION). Family: Caryophyllaceae.

Lychnis chalcedonica (MALTESE CROSS). Zones 3–8.

In June and July, this 2½-foot perennial bears lovely scarlet cruciform flowers, which do indeed look like a Maltese cross. Grow this plant in full sun, in moist well-drained soil.

Lychnis flos-cuculi (RAGGED ROBIN). Zones 3–8.

This lovely English wild flower is a delight to have in any garden. Ragged robin is a bushy perennial that matures at 2 to 3 feet. In spring, purplish-pink tassel-like blossoms bring the plant alive with color. The flowers look as if each petal has been snipped with scissors — the ragged appearance of the blooms is charming. Although this *Lychnis* is usually found in damp meadows, it can easily be grown in moist soil in the flower garden. Ragged robin will usually flower again in the fall.

LYSICHITON. Family: Araceae.

Lysichiton americanum (WESTERN SKUNK CABBAGE). Zones 4–9.

Don't be put off by the name. Although this plant is in the same family as eastern skunk cabbage, its appearance is very different: *Lysichiton americanum* is a beautiful perennial. In spring, before the leaves uncurl, 2-foot-long yellow arum-like flowers appear. Later the giant leaves unfold. These are stiff and dark and reach 2 feet in height. Western skunk cabbage can be grown in shallow water (3 inches) or in soil that is constantly moist. The plant takes some time to establish itself in a new location, but the wait is well worthwhile.

LYTHRUM (LOOSESTRIFE). Family: Lythraceae. Zones 3–9.

Speeding down the highways of northeastern America in our automobiles, many of us have admired the tall stands of purple flowers that appear wherever the soil is moist. As a wild plant loosestrife is lovely but all too invasive. Fortunately a number of cultivars are available. In summer or early fall, loosestrife has showy spikes of pink or purple blooms. Willow-like foliage adds to its beauty. Grow these perennials in sun in any rich moist garden soil. *Lythrum* are lovely by a pond or stream but are equally happy in wild-flower meadows or flower borders.

Lythrum salicaria 'Morden's Pink'.

'Morden's Pink' is a 3-foot bushy perennial that is covered with pink flowers from June until September.

Lythrum virgatum 'Rose Queen'.

From June until August the 30-inch spikes of this *Lythrum* are covered with pink flowers. 'Rose Queen' is slightly smaller than 'Morden's Pink', and many people think more refined.

M

MAGNOLIA. Family: Magnoliaceae.

Magnolia stellata (STAR MAGNOLIA). Zones 3–8.

In spring, before the leaves appear, dozens of large pure white star-shaped blossoms make this tree a dazzling sight. When mature, *Magnolia stellata* reaches 15 feet in height and has an equivalent spread. This is a very branched shrubby tree, ideal for planting on patios or as a lawn specimen. Grow this magnolia in full sun to light shade, in rich acid soil.

MALVA (MALLOW). Family: Malvaceae.

Malva sylvestris (MALLOW, COMMON MALLOW). Zones 3–9.

This common European plant has coarse hairy ivy-like leaves, and from May to August it bears pinkish purple flowers. Mallow grows from 1½ to 3 feet high. Plant this herb in full sun in any reasonable garden soil.

The Roman author Pliny had much to say about the mallow: "They are efficacious against every sort of sting, especially those of scorpions, wasps and similar creatures, and those of the shrew-mouse. . . . A leaf placed on a scorpion paralyses it. . . . Whoever swallows daily half a ladle of the juice . . . will be immune to all diseases. . . . Mallows are so aphrodisiac . . . that the seeds . . . sprinkled for the treatment of women, stimulate their sexual desire to a definite degree." Pliny advises administering the juice "in doses of three ladles to sufferers from melancholia and in doses of four to those who are raving." Pliny's Greek contemporary Dioscorides says that the stalks of mallow "are profitable for the entrails and the bladder." This eminent herbalist had many applications for this plant. He suggested that the herb should be used for "stinging of bees and wasps." More remarkable was Dioscorides' suggestion that if a man is anointed with mallow "he remains unstrikable." Mallow was used in medieval Europe as a potherb, except, according to the *English Leechbook*, in the month of February, when it was "venomous." The author of this herbal recommends a plaster made of mallows for "swelling of a man's cods [testicles]." In this book mallows are also prescribed as a dentifrice: "To clean [teeth] and make them white. Take the root of mallows and rub thy teeth and gums therewith. And after that take a rough cloth, and rub thy teeth therewith."

Today mallow is made into a soothing poultice, and when taken internally, it is used to treat coughs and bronchitis.

MANDRAGORA (MANDRAKE). Family: Solanaceae. Zones 6–10.

Mandragora officinarum (formerly *Atropa mandragora*) (MANDRAKE, SATAN'S APPLE).

This member of the Nightshade family is native to southern Europe. Mandrake, a perennial, has a rosette of wrinkled dark green leaves that emerge from the crown and grow to about 12 inches. The flowers appear in the spring (sometimes fall) and are greenish yellow or sometimes purplish. Mandrake blossoms appear either singly or in clusters. The branching root of this herb can measure to 3 or 4 feet long! Grow mandrake in a sheltered position with some shade. Because the roots go far down into the ground, the soil needs to be rich and well dug. Give a protection of mulch before winter, or in areas north of Zone 6 you may want to bring plants inside before winter.

By infusing the root bark in water or wine, the ancients employed mandrake as an anesthetic before and after surgery. The Roman physician Pliny recommended that the surgeon give the patient a piece of root to chew before operating. In the eleventh-century *Anglo-Saxon Herbal of Apuleius,* the author mentions the supernatural qualities of mandrake: "For witlessness, that is the devil sickness, or demonical possession, take the body of the same wort, mandrake, by the weight of three pennies, administer the drink in warm water as he may find most convenient; soon he will be healed. . . . If any see some heavy mischief in his home, let him take this wort mandragora, into the middle of the house, as much of it as he may have with him, he compelleth all evil out of the house."

Since ancient times, because of the humanoid shape of the root, mandrake was thought to have magical properties. In past centuries people believed that digging up this herb was a dangerous operation. The herbalists thought the mandrake would scream with such an awful sound when pulled from the ground that the gatherer would be immediately struck dead. (According to one medieval source, if a sinful man approached the herb, the mandrake would flee immedi-

ately, but if he could encircle it quickly with an iron implement, it would prevent the mandrake from escaping. Early writers mentioned that this plant grew under gallows, and could easily be found at night because it shone like a lamp. A male mandrake would appear under a gibbet that had hanged a man and conversely a female plant would grow under a hanged woman.) So to obtain this magical herb the surrounding earth was first loosened with an implement made of ivory or iron. This had to be done during the last light of dusk, and three circles had to be drawn around the mandrake with a magical sword. With a length of rope, a hungry dog would then be tied to the root. A dish of meat was placed a little beyond the reach of the animal, and when the dog strained to get the food the mandrake would be pulled from the earth. Unfortunately, because of the screeching of the mandrake, the poor dog would die immediately. But the crafty herbalist would be unharmed, because he had taken the precaution of stopping his ears with wax, and as a safeguard blew on a trumpet as the root was pulled up. (I've seen stranger things than this in Central Park!) Once obtained, the plant could be used for all sorts of magical operations. If placed under the pillow at night, mandrake would answer all questions. It had to be kept in a box and be given four milk baths annually. The resulting fluid was highly prized, and sprinkled about the home would bring good fortune.

MARRUBIUM (HOREHOUND). Family: Labiatae.

Marrubium vulgare (HOREHOUND, WHITE HOREHOUND). Zones 3–10.

This herb is a bushy gray perennial with branching stems that grow to about a foot in height. Horehound flowers from June until September. Cultivate it in full sun in any good garden soil.

The Greek physician Dioscorides advised horehound for "ye venomous beast bitten, and to such as have drunk some deadly thing." Over one thousand years ago, the poet monk Walahfrid Strabo urged that the unsavory flavor of this herb be ignored since the virtues of the plant were legion.

> Horehound comes next, and what shall I
>   say of this
> Powerful worker? A precious herb, though
>   biting
> And sharp on the tongue where it tastes
>   so unlike
> Its scent: for whereas the scent is sweet,
>   the taste
> Is not sweet at all. Yet taken in a draft,
> For all its nastiness it assuages pain
> In the chest, and most when drunk still
>   warm from the fire
> And ladled out quickly to close the meal.
>   If ever
> A vicious stepmother mixes in your drink
> Subtle poisons, or makes a treacherous
>   dish
> Of lethal aconite for you, don't waste a
>   moment—
> Take a dose of wholesome horehound; that
> Will counteract the danger you suspect.

The eleventh-century *Anglo-Saxon Herbal of Apuleius* gives a horehound recipe that is used today: "For colds in the head, and in case a man hreaks [hacks] heavily, it will heal them wonderfully." Although exceedingly bitter tasting, horehound is still used today for chest ailments.

MATTEUCCIA. Family: Polypodiaceae.

Matteuccia pensylvanica (OSTRICH FERN). Zones 2–9.

In the wild, this spectacular native American fern can reach as high as 8 to 10 feet, but normally in garden conditions it grows to about 4 to 5 feet. The huge leaves are like giant ostrich plumes. This fern likes very moist conditions, so waterside places are ideal. Ostrich fern will also grow in moist garden soil, especially if the roots are well mulched. If you grow *Matteuccia* in a garden border, do not let the soil dry out. In very damp sites this fern can be grown in full sun; in other areas, cultivate in light shade.

MATTHIOLA (STOCK). Family: Cruciferae.

Matthiola bicornis (NIGHT-SCENTED STOCK). Zones 3–10.

Although this is a humble annual, for the whole summer the evening fragrance from night-scented stock is quite delectable. *Matthiola bicornis* is especially enchanting when placed by a window or near a door, where the warm night air will carry the perfume into the house. Small lilac flowers appear on bushy 15-inch stems.

MELISSA. Family: Labiatae.

Melissa officinalis (BALM, LEMON BALM). Zones 4–10.

This is a bushy, hairy aromatic perennial that smells of lemons and grows 3 feet high. Balm is one of the easiest herbs to cultivate—plant it in full sun in any reasonable garden soil. Bees have a great affinity for this herb. The Greek name of the plant, *melissa*, means bee. The Roman naturalist Pliny mentions the affinity between these insects and lemon balm:

"If hives are rubbed over with Melissophyllum [balm] . . . the bees will not fly away, for the flower gives them great pleasure. . . . With besoms made of this plant, swarms are controlled with the greatest ease." According to Pliny, if the beekeeper is careless, lemon balm "is also a most effective remedy for the sting of bees, wasps and similar insects." Lemon balm was much praised by Avicenna, a famous Arab physician of the Middle Ages. He wrote that balm "maketh the heart merry and strengthened the vital spirits." Another important work from the medieval period, the *Hortus Sanitatis*, states: "The dried leaves laid on top of the head will draw out the congestion and leave one lightheaded." In the sixteenth century, an Oxford don, Thomas Cogan, wrote about a distilled water, the main ingredient of which was balm. This, he said, was useful for students because they were susceptible to melancholy, and this herb dispersed heaviness of the mind and increased the memory.

The herb was believed to have great power. The Elizabethan herbalist John Gerard wrote: "It is of so great virtue, that though it be but tied to his sword that have been given the wound, it stauncheth the blood." The sixteenth-century author of the *Grete Herbal* tells his readers that "wine, Melisse [balm] is sodden in, is good to keep one from swooning if the cause is cold." Much later, but equally promising, is an entry in the *London Dispensary*, dated 1696: "An essence of balm given in Canary wine, every morning will renew youth, strengthen the brain, relieve lanquishing nature and prevent baldness." If we can believe these reports, lemon balm seems to be the undiscovered miracle drug of the millennium!

Melissa is a good herb for the summer garden: the spicy leaves are wonderful in cool drinks, and rubbed on the skin will relieve irritation from insect bites and stings. In the kitchen, lemon balm is good in stuffings for roast chicken and veal. This herb also adds a zesty flavor to fruit salads. A tea made from lemon balm is beneficial against nausea and upset stomachs. In many countries this beverage is also recommended for treating anxiety and depression. Dried balm is wonderful in potpourri mixes, herb baths, and pillows.

Melissa officinalis 'Aureus' (GOLDEN LEMON BALM) has gold-edged leaves. The bright foliage looks particularly good in shady places.

MENTHA (MINT). Family: Labiatae.

No herb garden should be without mint. These versatile and strongly scented plants provide a great assortment of seasonings for both food and drink. Mints do best when planted in light shade in fairly rich soil. Because the roots can be very invasive, it is best to restrain these vigorous plants by growing them in a bottomless pot or by enclosing them with half-buried bricks or tiles. For lustier foliage remove the flowers as soon as they form. Most mints are susceptible to a disfiguring fungus called rust. Dull reddish powder appears upon the stalks, and where the infection occurs, and the stems swell. To eradicate the disease, cover the dried-out mint stalks with straw in the fall and burn them. This will kill the fungus spores but will not damage the roots.

The ancient herbalists used mints widely. Dioscorides wrote that mints "provoke lust . . . and being laid to ye forehead it pacifyeth headaches . . . being applied to women before conjunction does work conception, and being rubbed on it makes smooth a rough tongue." Anticipating a more modern use, Pliny wrote: "The smell of mint by itself refreshes our spirits and its flavor gives zest to food; for this reason, it is a familiar ingredient in our sauces." Pliny further recommended mint for scholars, adding that garlands made of plaited mint delight the soul, therefore are good for the mind. Describing the enormous number of species of mints, the medieval gardener Walahfrid Strabo commented that there are as many kinds of this herb as fishes in the Indian Ocean or sparks that fly from Mount Etna. Strabo recommended mint tea for ailments of the throat:

> If a man who is often troubled with
>   hoarseness wets his dry
> Throat in julep of mint, the roughness
>   will go and the tone come clear.

Today, as in previous centuries, a breath smelling of mint is considered very desirable. The fifteenth-century *English Leechbook* instructs the reader: "For the mouth that stinketh. Take juice of black mint . . . and put it into thy nostrils."

In the modern kitchen mint is used in a variety of dishes. Used fresh or dried, this herb is excellent as a sauce for lamb, in yogurt, green peas, fruit punches, and of course mint julep. In summer, mint sorbets are a delicious treat. Mint tea is perfect for stimulating the appetite, easing upset stomachs, and curing nervous headaches.

Mentha gentilis 'Variegata' (GINGER MINT). Zones 6–9.

This is a lovely variegated mint, with golden veins lacing the green leaves. *Mentha gentalis* 'Variegata' grows 1½ to 2 feet tall and has a spicy smell of ginger.

Mentha x *piperita* (PEPPERMINT). Zones 4–9. Peppermint is immediately recognizable by its unique smell. The 2-foot stems of this herb have a reddish hue. In summer, dense flower spikes of violet blossoms appear.

Mentha x *piperita* 'Citrata' (EAU DE COLOGNE MINT). Zones 4–9.

This strongly scented mint has a very pleasant smell of old-fashioned eau de cologne. The egg-shaped leaves are edged with purple.

Mentha pulegium (PENNYROYAL). Zones 8–10.

The leaves of this creeping mint are oval. From July to October, small whorls of lilac flowers appear on the stems. Pennyroyal is not hardy in areas north of Zone 8, although even in Zone 6 it can survive outside if it is given a good covering of mulch before winter.

In his herbal, the *Hortulus*, the medieval monk Walahfrid Strabo extols the virtue of pennyroyal.

> Believe me, my friend, if you cook some
>   pennyroyal
> And use it as a potion or poultice, it will
>   cure
> A heavy stomach . . .
> To prevent heat from harming your head,
>   put a sprig of pennyroyal behind your
>   ear.

The *Anglo-Saxon Herbal of Apuleius* recommends this herb for seasickness: "Let him take this same wort Pulegium [pennyroyal], and Wormwood, let him pound them together with oil and with vinegar, let him smear himself therewith frequently." A medieval book on magic, *The Book of Secrets* of Albertus Magnus, lists some of the properties of pennyroyal: "If the [pennyroyal] . . . be put into a vessel of bees, the bees shall never fly away, but they shall gather together there. And if the bees be drowned and look as if they were dead, if they be put into the aforesaid confection, they shall recover their life in a litel time, as by the space of one hour." The sixteenth-century herbalist Richard Banckes stated that pennyroyal should be gathered "in the time of flowering," and that "it may be kept in its virtue all a year. . . . For a cold humor in the head, take powder of it to the grievance without any liquor." In the medieval period pennyroyal was scattered upon the floors to destroy flies and other vermin.

Mentha x *rotundifolia* (APPLE MINT, ROUND-LEAVED MINT). Zones 5–9.

Apple mint has attractive roundish leaves that are covered with soft white down. Because of the haunting fragrance of sweet apples emitted when the plant is bruised, this is a favorite mint. This tall herb can grow 3 feet high. In midsummer, flowering spikes appear. Initially these are grayish white, but as the blossoms mature they deepen in color, turning shades of violet. Apple mint is very resistant to rust disease.

Mentha spicata (SPEARMINT, GARDEN MINT). Zones 4–9.

Of all culinary mints, spearmint is the most popular. This strongly flavored herb grows between 1 and 2 feet high, with hairless leaves almost 2 inches long. In summer, violet flower spikes appear. Of all mints, spearmint is the most prone to rust fungus.

MENYANTHES. Family: Gentianaceae.

Menyanthes trifoliata (BUCKBEAN, BOGBEAN). Zones 2–9.

This showy native American plant is ideal for planting in shallow water or in very wet soil. Attractive clover-like foliage arises from creeping rootstock. In May and June, dense

clusters of white flowers, gently tinged with pink, appear on 1½-foot stems. Grow this aquatic plant in full sun.

MERTENSIA. Family: Boraginaceae.

Mertensia virginica (VIRGINIA BLUEBELL). Zones 3–8.

The buds of Virginia bluebell appear pink, but when open they are a lovely sky-blue. This 18- to 24-inch plant flowers from March to May. The only drawback to this beautiful wild flower is that the foliage dies back in the summer. If planted in a woodland garden, this will not be important. In more formal flower beds, either plant some annuals over the bare spot or surround *Mertensia* with later-blooming perennials like hosta. Virginia bluebells should be grown in light to full shade, in rich moist soil.

MIMULUS (MONKEY MUSK, MONKEY FLOWER). Family: Scrophulariaceae.

Mimulus cardinalis. Zones 4–8.

Monkey musk should be included in all waterside plantings. It is a short-lived perennial, but when grown by water in moist soil it will readily self-sow. In fact, if not kept in check, it can take over a large area in no time. From midsummer on, *Mimulus cardinalis* is covered with brilliant scarlet and yellow snapdragon-like flowers. This perennial grows a foot high and can be cultivated in any damp soil.

MISCANTHUS. Family: Gramineae.

Miscanthus sinensis.

Miscanthus sinensis 'purpurascens' grows in Zones 4–9 and reaches 3 to 4 feet. In late summer the arching foliage of this grass turns lovely shades of purple and red. Grayish plumes of seed heads appear in late summer and fall. Grow *Miscanthus sinensis* 'purpur-ascens' in full sun. Most soils are fine for cultivating this grass.

Miscanthus sinensis 'Variegatus' (VARIE-GATED JAPANESE SILVER GRASS) has green and buff-yellow variegated foliage. The tall leaves reach 5 to 7 feet. Grow it in Zones 5–9, in sun or partial shade, in any reasonable soil. This plant looks excellent by the water's edge.

Miscanthus sinensis 'Zebrinus' (ZEBRA GRASS), is very tropical looking, and therefore it is especially welcome in gardens in colder regions. Bold clumps of the tall arching leaves can reach 8 feet. Individual leaves are made outstanding by horizontal golden bands. At the end of the growing season this plant has an added bonus: in October and November tall plumes of flowers rise above the leaves. Grow zebra grass in Zones 5–9, in full sun in damp or moist soil. In colder regions this plant takes time to produce new spring foliage — be patient!

MOLINIA. Family: Gramineae.

Molinia caerulea 'Variegata' (VARIEGATED PURPLE MOOR GRASS). Zones 5–9.

This ornamental grass is exquisite. The narrow arching green leaves are delicately edged with cream. In the fall, fountain-like flowers rise above the 2-foot mounds. These blooms are very showy and tinted with purple. Variegated purple moor grass will grow in a very moist site and can also be cultivated in drier soils. Grow this adaptable grass in full sun or part shade.

MONARDA (BERGAMOT). Family: Labiatae.

Monarda didyma (RED BERGAMOT, BEE BALM, OSWEGO TEA). Zones 4–10.

Throughout the summer this hardy North American native bears attractive brightly col-ored flowers. These large blossoms are about 2 inches across and are highly favored by hummingbirds and bumblebees. The whole plant reaches about 2 feet, and all parts (but especially the leaves) are strongly aromatic. Plant bergamot in full sun, in soil that is rich in organic matter. If the soil is poor, add rotted compost or manure. This plant will also grow in light shade.

After the Boston Tea Party of 1773, patriotic Americans no longer drank Indian tea. Instead, they used a beverage brewed from bergamot, which not only proved pleasant but also had the stimulating properties of tea. The British soon discovered the trick, tried it themselves, and found it to be delightful. Although they did not abandon their traditional teas, they added bergamot to an Indian tea, creating the popular "Earl Grey" blend. *Monarda* can give a delightful fragrance to fruit cups and summer drinks. Bergamot can also be taken as a beverage to relieve nausea and menstrual pains. The dried blossoms are used in potpourri.

'Cambridge Scarlet' is covered with brilliant scarlet flowers from late June until September. This is a 40-inch perennial.

'Croftway Pink', a lovely soft pink bergamot, blooms about the same time as 'Cambridge Scarlet' and is also the same height.

'Mahogany' flowers a little longer than other varieties of *Monarda*. It reaches 3½ feet and is a deep wine-red. A very desirable plant.

MYOSOTIS (FORGET-ME-NOT). Family: Boraginaceae. Zones 3–10.

Myosotis scorpioides (formerly *Myosotis palustris*).

German folklore provides an explanation for the name of this plant. According to a popular tale, a reckless but gallant knight, full of ardor for his sweetheart, was determined to retrieve some lovely blue flowers from the Danube's deep water for his beloved. The love-blind knight leaped into the river before removing his heavy armor. As the poor fellow sank to a watery grave, he cried out to his lady: *"Vergiss mich nicht!"* ("Forget me not!"). From late spring to early fall, the forget-me-not's sky-blue flowers enhance any pond or stream. *Myosotis* is happy in wet soil or in water just a few inches deep. It prefers partial shade, but if the soil is very moist this perennial can be planted in full sun.

MYRICA. Family: Myricaceae.

Myrica pensylvanica (WAX MYRTLE, BAYBERRY, CANDLEBERRY). Zones 2–6.

Wax myrtle is a native American shrub which, depending on the location, will grow up to 6 feet tall. In May pale green flowers appear. The aromatic leaves are evergreen in mild climates, but in colder areas, this shrub is deciduous. The fruit and the leathery foliage are covered with aromatic waxy secretions. Bayberry does best in full sun and in dry sandy infertile soil. As this is an ocean plant, it is very tolerant of salt spray—which makes wax myrtle an ideal choice for planting near roads that are salted in winter. *Myrica* also can be pruned into a hedge.

The ripe berries are boiled to extract the bayberry wax used in candlemaking and soap manufacture. This wax can be extracted on a small scale by boiling the berries in a large pan. When the liquid is cooled, the wax floats to the surface and soon hardens. To ensure berry formation, both male and female plants are needed.

When chewed, bayberry bark will ease the pain of toothache. A tea made from the leaves is used to treat diarrhea and fevers.

MYRRHIS. Family: Umbelliferae.

Myrrhis odorata (SWEET CICELY).
Zones 4–10.

For me sweet cicely is another herb of childhood memories. A favorite aunt lived in the beautiful rugged limestone country around Matlock in the Derbyshire hills. Summer vacations there were always enjoyable because of the rich flora of the surrounding woods and mountains. One of the commonest wild flowers of this area was sweet cicely—every streamside and riverbank was enhanced with the graceful and delicate foliage of this useful herb. Walking along a watercourse where sweet cicely grows abundantly is indeed an experience. The rich anise scent of the herb permeated our clothes, our hands, even our hair. We soon discovered that handfuls of this plant are excellent for rubbing upon the fur of dogs—especially after they had rolled in cow manure! Sweet cicely is a perennial that grows to 3 to 4 feet. The feathery green leaves, with their downy undersides, are very soft to touch. White flowers are produced in May and June, then large black seeds appear. Plant sweet cicely in moist soil in a shady position. This herb will grow in full sun, but make sure the soil is enriched with organic material and protect the roots by covering the soil with mulch. Keep plants well watered in summer.

Elizabethan herbalist John Gerard called sweet cicely "great chervil." This plant was highly regarded by Gerard, who wrote: "Held to be one of the pot-herbes, it is pleasant to the stomach and taste.... It hath in it a certaine windinesse, by means whereof it procureth lust.... The roots are ... most excellent in sallad, if they be boyled and after dressed as a cunning Cooke knoweth how better than my selfe. [Sweet cicely] is very good for old people that are dull and without courage; it rejoyceth and comforteth the heart, and increaseth their lust and strength." Sweet cicely was not only used in the kitchen but was employed as a polish, made by grinding the seeds with wax. When used on furniture, it imparted an aromatic scent to the wood. And yet another use of sweet cicely: to keep attentive during long sermons, congregations chewed the seeds of this herb.

N

NEPETA (CATMINT, CATNIP). Family: Labiatae. Zones 3–8.

"Catmint also has the power to counteract the poisons of serpents," instructs Pliny, the Roman naturalist. "The smoke and smell of burning catmint drives them away; so those about to sleep in fear of snakes had better place catmint under the bed clothes." Centuries later, Elizabethan herbalist John Gerard, obviously an admirer of cats, wrote that these animals "are very much delighted, for the smell of it is splendid to them, that they rub themselves upon it and wallow and tumble in it, and also feed on the branches and leaves greedily." For humans, this wise herbalist recommended catmint "for them that be busted inwardly by means of some fall from a high place, and that are very much bruised." The doctors of past centuries suggested that chewing the roots would make the

most timid person aggressive. Researchers have observed that smoking the leaves of catmint produce a mild "high"; perhaps this is what cats and timid people experience! A tea made from this herb is beneficial for diarrhea and the common cold. Externally, catmint is useful for bruises, cuts, and abrasions.

Nepeta cataria.

This catmint is a herbaceous perennial with heart-shaped leaves and square stems. The herb grows 3 to 4 feet tall, and in late summer white blossoms appear. Catmint is easy to grow. Plant it in a sunny position in moist soil. This herb will tolerate some shade.

Nepeta x faassenii (GARDEN CATMINT).

Garden catmint is a smaller variety that reaches 12 to 18 inches. In July and August, the plants are covered with billowy lavender flowers.

NICOTIANA. Family: Solanaceae.

Nicotiana alata 'Lime Green' (NIGHT-SCENTED TOBACCO). Zones 3–10.

I can hardly think of this lovely plant as an annual. Once planted, 'Lime Green' self-seeds year after year but doesn't become too invasive. This is one of the very few plants that actually has green flowers—the blossoms are a lovely light lime color. In my Connecticut garden I find that 'Lime Green' will appear in early summer and continue flowering in sheltered parts of the garden until November! Tall spikes, up to 4 feet, are covered with trumpet-like flowers. At night, these blossoms are deliciously fragrant. Night-scented tobacco will grow in sun or partial shade, in most garden soils.

NYMPHAEA (WATER LILY). Family: Nymphaeaceae. Zones 4–10.

In natural ponds, hardy water lilies can be planted in the soil at the bottom. Press the tubers into the mud, making sure that you keep them horizontal, where they will be covered with 6 to 18 inches of water. As long as their roots do not freeze, hardy water lilies can be grown in any outdoor pool or pond.

In an artificial pool, water lilies are best cultivated in plastic containers—small laundry baskets are ideal. Fill the container with a mixture of three parts garden soil and one part well-rotted cow manure. If you have problems getting the cow manure, mix an average-size bucket of garden soil with a couple of handfuls of dried blood and two handfuls of bonemeal, mix well, and use that instead. Place the water lily horizontally in the container just below the surface of the soil. Next, put a couple of inches of gravel over the soil. The basket can now be carefully lowered into the pool and placed where the water is 6 to 18 inches deep. Remember that although these lilies can be kept outside all winter, the roots must not freeze. If you are considering constructing an artificial pool, make it at least 2 feet deep. Water lilies need as much sunlight as possible.

Nymphaea odorata (FRAGRANT WHITE POND LILY).

This is a lovely native water lily that appears throughout the United States and southern Canada. For the whole summer, lovely fragrant blooms float upon the surface of the water. The white blooms can be fully 6 inches wide, and each blossom has a yellow center. If you have any problem getting *Nymphaea odorata*, look in aquatic-plant catalogues, which offer a wide selection of hardy white water lilies.

O

OCIMUM (BASIL). Family: Labiatae. Zones 3–10.

This ancient plant is steeped in folklore. The Roman author Pliny counseled that basil should be sown with cursing and ranting. According to the classical and medieval herbalists, basil was a paradox. They believed that this plant could both engender venomous beasts and also be used as an antidote to their bites and stings. Pliny mentioned that basil mixed with vinegar "is good for fainting," and that "being aphrodisiac, [it] is also administered to horses and mares at the time of service." For being jolly and happy, the Elizabethan herbalist John Gerard suggested eating basil seeds, as they "cureth the infirmities of the heart, taketh away sorrowfulness which causeth melancholy, and maketh a man merry and glad."

In the modern kitchen basil has many uses. The classic combination is with tomatoes. And this herb is essential to many Italian dishes. Try it with salads, dressings, chicken, and egg and rice dishes. Sliced tomato lightly dressed with salt, oil, and vinegar, then sprinkled with chopped purple basil, is a personal favorite.

Ocimum basilicum (BASIL, GREEN BASIL).

Basil is an aromatic plant that reaches up to 2 feet. In temperate areas it is usually treated as an annual. To cultivate basil, grow the herb in full sun in well-drained organically rich garden soil. Sow the seed in the ground as soon as all danger of frost has passed. If you do not have a garden, you can grow this herb in a pot near a sunny window. To make bushier plants, pinch off the flowering tops as soon as they appear.

Ocimum basilicum 'Dark Opal', called purple basil or red basil, has wonderful deep red foliage—leaves that are attractive in the flower border, or when used for garnishing dishes.

OENOTHERA. Family: Onagraceae.

Oenothera missouriensis (SUNDROP, OZARK SUNDROP). Zones 4–9.

This is a plant for full sun and well-drained, even sandy, soil. Sundrops are in the same family as the evening primrose, but they bloom in the daylight, not at night. Sundrops are hardy, drought-resistant, and can tolerate poor soil. This is a trailing plant that grows to 10 inches high. From June until August, lovely 4-inch lemon-yellow cuplike flowers cover the plants. Sundrop is the perfect perennial for the front of a border or for a rock garden.

ONOCLEA. Family: Polypodiaceae.

Onoclea sensibilis (SENSITIVE FERN). Zones 2–10.

This adaptable fern will grow in full sun or shade, and although it prefers moist soils, *Onoclea* will grow in drier areas. Sensitive fern—so called because the fronds succumb to the first frost—has attractive foliage. The fronds grow to 3 feet and are broadly segmented.

ONOPORDUM. Family: Compositae.

Onopordum acanthium (SCOTCH THISTLE, SILVER THISTLE). Zones 4–9.

I could not imagine my garden without this spectacular plant. Scotch thistles are majestic in appearance and make a decided impression on the landscape. The first year, *Onopordum* creates a huge rosette of spiny silvery leaves. These are most attractive, and look as if they have been covered with silky cobwebs. The following year, gigantic branched, rigid, 6- to 8-foot stems climb into the air. These silver spikes are covered with spiny projections and feltlike down. As if this were not enough, the tops of the spires are crowned with lilac flowers. In twilight and on moonlit nights, these plants take on a spectral appearance. Although Scotch thistle is a biennial, it reseeds freely. Once you have this plant in your garden you will not want to be without it. Scotch thistle will grow in any type of soil but needs full sun.

OPHIOPOGON. Family: Liliaceae.

Ophiopogon planiscapus 'Arabicus'. Zones 6–10.

This is a very desirable evergreen perennial (also sometimes called *Ophiopogon planiscapus* 'Nigrescens'). The narrow grasslike leaves grow in dense clumps, and are almost jet black. Tiny pink bell-like flowers appear in summer, followed by shiny black berries. The dark carpet effect of this perennial is very effective at the front of borders. Grow *Ophiopogon* in sun or shade in well-drained soil. This is a drought-tolerant plant.

OPUNTIA. Family: Cactaceae.

Opuntia humifusa (PRICKLY PEAR CACTUS). Zones 5–9.

This hardy cactus has flat spiny cactus pads. In June and July, attractive 3-inch yellow roselike blooms appear on the prickly pads. Plant this 10-inch cactus in full sun in sandy well-drained soil. In colder areas, the pads look shriveled after a hard winter, but by early summer prickly pear will have recovered.

ORIGANUM (MARJORAM). Family: Labiatae.

In Greece and Rome this plant was dedicated to Hymen, the god of marriage, and marjoram was worn at weddings in his honor. In medieval Europe the aromatic leaves of this herb were put into all odoriferous ointments, waters, and powders, and were used extensively as a flavoring in broths and meats. The Elizabethan herbalist John Gerard informed his readers that marjoram is a good remedy against "cold diseases of the brain and head, being taken any way to your best liking; put up the nostrils it provoketh sneezing and draweth much baggage plegme. . . . It draweth away waterish humors, and is used in medicines against poison." Gerard also prescribed marjoram for those "as are given to overmuch sighing."

Origanum majorana (SWEET MARJORAM, KNOTTED MARJORAM). Zones 9–10.

The scientific name of this herb, *Origanum majorana*, is derived from two Greek words. *Origanum* comes from *oranos*, meaning joy or happiness, and marjoram from *oros*, which means mountain. Combined, they mean "joy of the mountain," an apt description for this lovely plant of rocky places. Although sweet marjoram is a perennial, it is usually treated as an annual, for only in the mildest areas (Zones 9 and 10) will it survive outside during the winter. Sweet marjoram reaches 10 to 12 inches, and from midsummer to fall, knotlike clusters of flowers appear. Plant this herb in full sun in well-drained soil. The addition of lime to the soil is beneficial for all marjorams.

Origanum vulgare (WILD MARJORAM, OREGANO). Zones 3–10.

Wild marjoram is a very variable hardy perennial that will grow as tall as 24 inches. In summer and autumn it produces clusters of rose-purple flowers. Grow this herb under the same conditions as sweet marjoram. Make sure that in the summer, plants of wild marjoram are cut back. This ensures new leaf growth and prevents this perennial from getting leggy.

Origanum vulgare 'Aureum' is a lovely golden form of wild marjoram. Grow this perennial in full sun; shady sites pale the coloration. Golden marjoram grows to 8 inches and slowly spreads into a thick carpet. In summer, spikes of purple flowers rise 6 inches above the leaves. In milder parts of the country golden marjoram is evergreen—or more correctly, evergold!

OSMUNDA. Family: Osmundaceae. Zones 2–9.

Osmunda cinnamomea (CINNAMON FERN, FIDDLEHEADS).

By the side of a pond or in other moist areas, this majestic fern can grow to 6 feet. And although cinnamon fern prefers damp areas, it can be grown in moist garden soil, where it will reach 2 to 3 feet. Mature fronds are covered with an attractive cinnamon-colored wool—hence the English name for this fern. *Osmunda cinnamomea* prefers light shade but will grow in areas that receive up to six hours of direct sunlight a day, especially if these are damp sites.

Osmunda regalis (ROYAL FERN).

"Osmund Royal" sounds like the name of a character from a novel by Anthony Trollope or Oscar Wilde, but in fact it is one of the vernacular names of the majestic royal fern. *Osmunda* is one of the names of the Scandinavian god Thor. This thunder-wielding god had great respect for people who carried branches of his sacred fern, and spared such mortals from his fearsome lightning bolts. Whether planted as a protection against lightning or for its aesthetic value, royal fern looks spectacular when grown by a pond or stream. The tall, graceful fronds of this native North American plant double their impact when reflected in water. The majesty of this fern is depleted when it is planted too close to other plants, however, so give it room to grow. Allow a large clump to dominate one side of the waterscape. Royal fern grows to 6 feet. If planted by water, *Osmunda regalis* can tolerate full sun. In drier soil give this fern some shade.

P

PACHYSANDRA. Family: Buxaceae.

Pachysandra procumbens (ALLEGHENY SPURGE). Zones 5–9.

This is the native North American pachysandra. Allegheny spurge is a good ground cover, although in colder regions it is deciduous. It grows to a foot in height, and in spring bears spikes of attractive white to pink fragrant blossoms. Grow this perennial in humus-enriched soil, in shade.

PAEONIA (PEONY). Family: Paeoniaceae. Zones 2–8.

Peonies are hardy perennials that with a little initial care will live in the garden for many, many years. Grow peonies in full sun, in well-dug soil rich in organic matter. These plants will tolerate some shade. In areas of acid ground add some lime to the soil. Make sure that the "eyes" (growing tips on the roots) are planted exactly 1½ inches below soil level, and once they are planted, avoid moving peonies.

The genus *Paeonia* is named after the Greek physician Paeon. According to legend, with the aid of this plant, this doctor cured Pluto and the other gods of wounds received during the Trojan War. Writing in the first century A.D., Pliny asserted that it was best to collect peonies "at nighttime because the woodpecker of Mars, should he see the act, will attack the eyes in its defense." He considered that this plant had supernatural powers that "prevents the mocking delusions that fauns bring on us in our sleep." In ancient times it was thought that the peony arose from emanations of moonbeams. And, like the moon, this perennial was believed to shine at night. This light, according to these ancient authorities, drove away evil spirits and would also protect shepherds and their flocks from dangerous animals. Claudius Aelianus, a Roman author living in the first century A.D., wrote of the magical properties of the peony: "It groweth upon high rocks . . .

which opening in the summer solstice, doth yield in the night time a certain fairy, as it were, sparkling brightness and light." Both the root and the seed of peonies were deemed magical. The eleventh-century *Anglo-Saxon Herbal of Apuleius* mentions that seeds "of peony shine in the nighttime like a candle, and that plenty of it is in the right season found out and gathered by the shepherds." In the Middle Ages the seed was used to cure nightmares or melancholic dreams. The seeds were either drunk in wine or strung as necklaces and worn as a charm against evil spirits. According to these physicians, if the seed of the peony was laid upon a lunatic, in no time he would be cured!

'Charlie's White' has double white blossoms that appear in May and early June and are borne on 42-inch stems.

'Prince of Darkness' is covered with strongly fragrant deep red blossoms in May.

'Sarah Bernhardt' has scented blooms with deep pink petals. This 34-inch peony blooms in late June.

Paeonia officinalis 'Rubra Plena' (MEMORIAL DAY PEONY).

This old-fashioned peony has been cultivated in gardens for centuries. In May and June, this 2-foot perennial has deep red double blooms.

PANICUM (PANIC GRASS). Family: Gramineae.

Panicum virgatum 'Rotstrahbusch' (RED SWITCH GRASS). Zones 4–9.

This 3- to 4-foot grass is best cultivated in a sunny site, in well-drained soil. The charm of this grass is in its neat upright growth habit and the red color of the leaves. In the summer the tips of the leaves are deep crimson. By fall, the foliage becomes a rich oxblood color.

PAPAVER (POPPY). Family: Papaveraceae.

The soporific properties of the poppy have been known for centuries. In legend, the goddess Ceres drank poppy juice to ease her sorrow at the abduction of her daughter Persephone. The sixteenth-century author of *The Grete Herbal* states that "the quantity of a grain . . . of opium taken in the body mortifieth all the wits of man in such a manner that he feeleth no pain and causeth him to sleep." The late fourteenth-century herbal *Agnus Castus* recommended poppy for treating migraine. The author suggests mixing the herb with olive oil and rubbing it on the forehead. Tincture of opium, called laudanum, was first prepared early in the sixteenth century by the Swiss alchemist Paracelsus, who infused crude opium in wine alcohol.

Papaver orientale (ORIENTAL POPPY). Zones 3–8.

The cup-size blooms of the Oriental poppy are tissue-paper thin. Many varieties are streaked with midnight black in the center. Most Oriental poppies bloom in May and June, and grow to 2½ to 3 feet. It is a shame that such a lovely flower as the poppy should fade totally when finished flowering. By July, even the leaves have vanished. But fortunately the great British plantswoman Gertrude Jekyll found a solution to this problem by sowing annual gypsophila *(Gypsophila elegans)* near the poppy in spring. When the poppy fades, the pretty gypsophila will replace it. If you don't like baby's breath, daylilies can serve the same purpose—just plant the poppies close by. Grow Oriental poppies in full sun in any well-drained soil. When planting these perennials, make sure that the growing crown (the point where the leaves emerge) is 3 inches below the soil level.

'Barr's White' is a lovely white poppy with purple-black spots at the base of the flowers.

'Big Jim' is the best red available, a lovely fire-engine color.

'Curlilocks' is a personal favorite. The flowers are vermilion and the petals are serrated. The center of each bloom is ebony. 'Curlilocks' blooms for a long time, May to July. The 30-inch stems are entirely self-supporting.

'Helen Elizabeth' is covered with salmon-pink flowers in May.

'May Sadler' is a poppy no garden should be without. Finest pink blooms are enhanced with a jet-black center.

PELARGONIUM (SCENTED GERANIUMS). Family: Geraniaceae. Zones 9–10.

These are often called geraniums, but technically speaking they are pelargoniums. These remarkable plants from the South African Cape not only are attractive in shape but have delightfully fragrant leaves. Many of these scented geraniums have variegated foliage. Planted outside in summer, pelargoniums make a wonderful, fragrant hedge. These are tender plants, so only in the mildest regions (Zones 9–10) can pelargoniums to be left out all winter. But wintering them indoors is no problem. They make wonderful house plants that can be grown on any window ledge. Small pelargoniums grown outside after all danger of frost is past will have become large specimens by midsummer, in some cases over 3 feet tall. Rose, peppermint, and lemon are the three most common species of scented geraniums. As the name suggests, they are highly scented. In each of these major groups are dozens of varieties. All of these scented geraniums are wonderful to add to potpourri. Add the fresh foliage to puddings, cakes, teas, and flavored butter.

Pelargonium crispum (LEMON PELARGONIUM).

The lemon-scented pelargoniums grow up to 3 feet high. Their stiff leaves have an exquisite lemon aroma. 'Mable Gray' is one of the best varieties for a strong citrus odor—excellent for potpourri.

Pelargonium graveolens 'Attar of Roses'.

'Attar of Roses' is a tall plant with stiff lobed leaves. When slightly bruised, this foliage emits a delightful scent of roses.

Pelargonium tomentosum (PEPPERMINT GERANIUM).

The peppermint geraniums are trailing plants with wonderful velvety emerald-green leaves. When the foliage is gently crushed, a strong odor of mint permeates the air.

PELTIPHYLLUM. Family: Saxifragaceae.

Peltiphyllum peltatum (UMBRELLA PLANT). Zones 5–8.

This northwestern native is perfect for the borders of a water garden and will grow in sun or shade. In April, the pale starry-pink blossoms appear before the leaves have unfurled. And as soon as the blossoms fade, the tropical-looking foliage appears, parasol-shaped and borne on 2-foot stems. Each leaf is a foot in diameter, quite an impressive sight by a stream or pond. In fall, the foliage turns a coppery bronze, and as an additional benefit umbrella plant is useful for preventing the erosion of slippery, muddy banks.

PENNISETUM. Family: Gramineae.

Pennisetum alopecuroides (ROSE FOUNTAIN GRASS). Zones 4–9.

This is one of the most graceful of the ornamental grasses. Mature plants form neat 2-foot mounds of thin arching leaves, and from July until September, 3-foot flowering spikes appear. These are lovely; each spike is tipped with a silvery rose wheatlike bloom. The blossoms are delicate and soft and last well into winter. In full bloom and in the right light, rose fountain grass does look like shimmering jets of water. Grow this ornamental grass in full sun in any well-drained soil.

PENSTEMON (BEARD'S TONGUE). Family: Scrophulariaceae. Zones 3–9.

Penstemon barbatus 'Prairie Fire'.

From July until frost, 'Prairie Fire' bears orange-red spikes of flowers. The blooms are tubular and appear on the tips of the stems. Plants reach about 2 feet. Grow *Penstemon* in full sun in well-drained soil. Damp soil will rot these plants.

PETROSELINUM. Family: Umbelliferae.

Petroselinum crispum (PARSLEY). Zones 3–10.

Parsley is a hardy biennial that grows to 3 feet. The leaves are divided, and flowers appear in summer as clusters of greenish-yellow blossoms. This herb was dedicated by the Greeks to Persephone, goddess of the underworld, and they made wreaths of parsley for adorning the tombs of their dead. Because parsley germinates slowly, there is a superstition that the seeds of this herb must go to the devil nine times before it can germinate. Parsley was used extensively in medieval kitchens and was included in any dish that required herbs. The medieval herbalist Richard Banckes praised this plant: Parsley "multiplyeth greatly mans blood . . . comforteth the heart and stomach. And is good in pottage and to stop [stuff] chickens." A little later, Elizabethan herbalist John Gerard recommended "the root or seeds" of this herb, "boiled in ale and drunken" for casting "forth strong venome or poison" or for "breaking and wasting away winde." In earlier centuries, it was recommended that the seed be sprinkled over the head three times a year to prevent baldness. A rather contradictory proverb on the cultivation of parsley is that it grows best for the wicked, for an honest man, or where the mistress is master.

PHALARIS. Family: Gramineae.

Phalaris arundinacea picta (RIBBON GRASS, GARDENER'S GARTERS). Zones 3–9.

This handsome grass is a vigorous perennial that tolerates a wide variety of sites—both damp and dry soils. In damp areas, *Phalaris* can become invasive. The foliage of this ornamental grass is variegated, with green and white bands. Leaves grow up to 3 feet.

PHLOX. Family: Polemoniaceae.

Phlox divaricata (BLUE WOOD PHLOX, WILD SWEET WILLIAM). Zones 3–8.

This woodland perennial is ideal for moist soil and light shade. In May the foot-high plant is covered with loose clusters of pale white, blue, or lilac flowers. Blossoms are star-shaped.

Phlox paniculata. Zones 3–4.

These are the border phlox, plants that in summer display tall stems (3 to 4 feet) tipped with clusters of fragrant flowers. No herbaceous border would be complete without these perennials. They require a rich well-drained soil, full sun or light shade, and plenty of water during the summer. Border phlox do not do well in windy parts of the garden. They are susceptible to mildew, but there are mildew-resistant varieties available. To help prevent this unsightly fungal infection, plant *Phlox paniculata* at least 2 feet apart. If mildew does occur, spray the leaves with a fungicide every fortnight. For lustier blossoms, thin out the shoots each spring: leave about three stems on each crown, and remove the rest of the shoots by pinching them off with the fingers. To keep border phlox vigorous, roots should be divided every three or four years: dig up the whole plant, save the sections that are farthest away from the center of the root ball, and discard the rest. Seedlings set by border phlox should be removed; these will not be true to the parent's variety, but will be reversions to the less attractive species. Border phlox flower during July and August; sometimes they will bloom again in the fall. In Zone 3, border phlox will need some winter protection.

'Bright Eyes' is a lovely pink phlox with a red eye.

'Everest' has pure white flowers, and at the center of each blossom is a rose-colored eye.

'Mt. Fuji' is the best of all white phlox.

'Starfire' is a brilliant deep red phlox.

Phlox subulata (MOSS PINK). Zones 3–8.

These are low-growing evergreen spring-flowering phlox, which make a colorful ground cover. When in flower, *Phlox subulata* is literally covered with blossoms. Plant moss pinks in full sun in well-drained soil. The

plants form spreading clumps that grow 3 to 8 inches high. *Phlox subulata* is a drought-resistant perennial.

'Emerald Blue' is a lovely light blue phlox with rich green foliage.

'Pink Surprise' is one mass of soft pink blossoms in the spring.

'Red Wings' is a lovely deep red, almost crimson, phlox.

PHYSALIS. Family: Solanaceae.

Physalis alkekengi (CHINESE LANTERN, WINTER CHERRY). Zones 2–7.

This 2-foot perennial is grown not for its flowers but for the lovely pumpkin-orange seed capsules. These attractive pods appear in the fall and really do look like Chinese lanterns. *Physalis* was a very popular plant in medieval and Renaissance Europe and is illustrated in almost all the early herbals. William Turner, an Elizabethan herbalist, mentions Chinese lantern in his *New Herball:* "It hath fruyte in little sede vessells lyke unto bladders round and red lyke gold . . . whyche the garland makers use in making garlandes." The seed pods of the Chinese lantern are still used to make dried flower arrangements. Grow this perennial in full sun, in rich moist well-drained soil.

PHYSOSTEGIA (OBEDIENT PLANT, FALSE DRAGONHEAD). Family: Labiatae.

Physostegia virginiana. Zones 4–9.

Obedient plant provides attractive blooms late in the season. From August until October, bright pink snapdragon-shaped flowers appear on the square stems. *Physostegia* is called "obedient plant" because when the stalk of a blossom is moved, it will remain in its new position. Divide plants of *Physostegia* every two or three years. Grow them in full sun or partial shade, in average moist soil. *Physostegia* can also be grown in fairly damp soil.

PINUS (PINE). Family: Pinaceae.

Pinus mugo var. *mughus* (MUGO PINE). Zones 2–7.

Mugo pine is a many-branched evergreen that will mature as a 6-foot bun-shaped mound. This conifer is a very neat and attractive pine, perfect for smaller gardens. Cultivate mugo pine in full sun, in well-drained moist soil.

PLATYCODON (BALLOON FLOWER). Family: Campanulaceae. Zones 3–9.

Platycodon grandiflorus.

Platycodon is an attractive perennial that grows to 2 feet and flowers in July and August. The buds are balloon-shaped. When these flower, the blooms look like blue star-shaped cups. Blossoms are held on stiff stems. Grow *Platycodon* in full sun or partial shade, in light fertile soil. If you are transplanting these flowers, remove as much earth as possible around the root ball and try not to sever the tap roots. 'Alba' is a white form of the species.

POLEMONIUM. Family: Polemoniaceae.

Polemonium caeruleum (JACOB'S LADDER, GREEK VALERIAN). Zones 4–9.

Jacob's ladder is a graceful perennial that in May and June produces terminal clusters of bell-shaped blue flowers. *Polemonium* grows to 3 feet. The foliage is attractive; the leaves look like the rungs of a ladder—hence the English name. Grow it in partial shade or full sun, in rich moist well-drained soil.

POLYGALA (MILKWORT). Family: Polygalaceae.

Polygala paucifolia (FRINGED POLYGALA, GAYWINGS). Zones 2–8.

This North American wild flower is perfect for moist areas in light or deep shade, where it will form loose colonies that grow only 6 inches high. In May and June, this trailing plant bears exquisite pink orchid-like flowers. Each blossom is tinged with purple and has a fringed lip. The "wings" of the blossoms look like tiny birds in flight.

POLYGONATUM (SOLOMON'S SEAL). Family: Liliaceae.

Polygonatum odoratum thunbergii 'Variegatum' (JAPANESE VARIEGATED SOLOMON'S SEAL). Zones 3–9.

In shady areas, few plants look as attractive as Japanese variegated Solomon's seal. The great charm of this perennial is the variegated leaves. The foliage arches gracefully like a fern frond, and on each side of the stalk, oval leaves are arranged in pairs. The leaves are green with a yellow edge. From April until June, white fragrant bell-shaped flowers hang from the arching stems. Plants grow to 3 feet. Grow this *Polygonatum* in shade, in moist rich soil.

POLYGONUM. Family: Polygonaceae.

Polygonum bistorta (BISTORT). Zones 3–8.

Bistort is a perennial plant that occurs in damp meadows and has a reddish serpentine root. In spring, the 2- to 3-foot flowering spikes are covered with pink blossoms. Bistort prefers a moist soil and a slightly shaded site.

The Roman naturalist Pliny wrote that bistort "dissipates the effect of drunkeness. The fumes arising from it when it burns keep away serpents, especially asps, or makes them so tipsy that they are in a state of torpor." In the Middle Ages, a pudding made from bistort was eaten as a spring rejuvenative. The medieval French herbal *Le Grant Herbier* promises the reader that "an electuary of powdered bistort . . . and of aromatic spices . . . aids conception for it brings comfort to the retentive quality of the womb." Today bistort is used as a tea for diarrhea and as a gargle for gingivitis. The strong styptic quality of the roots makes this herb useful for staunching bleeding. Young shoots can be boiled and enjoyed as spring greens.

Polygonum 'Border Jewel' is an excellent ground cover with glossy lance-shaped green leaves. In the fall, this foliage turns an attractive red. The flowers appear in late May, each stem tipped with a tight cluster of pink blossoms. Plants soon form thick colonies that grow to 6 inches high. 'Border Jewel' is an adaptable plant that will grow in damp soil by a waterside or in ordinary moist garden soil. Grow this *Polygonum* in full sun or light shade.

POLYPODIUM. Family: Polypodiaceae.

Polypodium virginianum (ROCK POLYPODY). Zones 3–8.

Rock polypody is an attractive evergreen fern that will stay verdant even in Zone 3 winters. Fronds are lance-shaped and consist of individual tongue-shaped leaflets. Rock polypody forms dense mats which look most attractive by pathways, in woodland settings, planted on walls, or allowed to sprawl over tree stumps. Grow this fern in shade in moist soil. Rock polypody matures at around 10 inches.

POLYSTICHUM. Family: Polypodiaceae.

Polystichum acrostichoides (CHRISTMAS FERN). Zones 2–8.

Christmas fern is an evergreen that has attractive lobed fronds which can grow to 3 feet long. Plant Christmas ferns in moist soil in light shade. If the soil is rich and if enough moisture is present, this fern can be grown in full sun.

PONTEDERIA. Family: Pontederiaceae.

Pontederia cordata (PICKERELWEED). Zones 3–9.

Pickerelweed grows in the shallow water of a stream or pond and is at its best in late summer and early fall. The blossoming spikes can grow as high as 4 feet and are tipped with light blue orchid-like flowers. The attractive leaves are heart shaped. Pickerelweed can also be grown in boggy soil. Grow this perennial in full sun.

POTERIUM. Family: Rosaceae.

Poterium sanguisorba (formerly *Sanguisorba minor*) (BURNET, SALAD BURNET). Zones 3–10.

Salad burnet is a hardy perennial that grows up to 2 feet high. In early summer, thimble-shaped reddish flowers appear. Grow this herb in full sun in well-drained soil.

As the name suggests, this herb is used in salads. The tender cucumber-flavored leaves are the parts used. The sixteenth-century herbalist John Gerard recommended adding this herb to food: "In salads . . . it is thought to make the heart merry and glad, as also being put into wine, to which it yieldeth a certain grace in the drinking."

PRIMULA (PRIMROSE). Family: Primulaceae.

Members of the genus *Primula* delight the eye as well as the nose. Many of these are ideal for banks of streams and the damp margins of ponds. And, provided you have a continually damp soil, some of the best are the candelabra primulas, so called because the flowers are arranged in circular tiers. *Primula florindae* and *Primula japonica* are among this group.

Primula florindae (HIMALAYAN COWSLIP). Zones 5–8.

From midsummer on, these deliciously nutmeg-scented primulas produce flowering spikes that grow up to 4 feet high. The loose balls of sulfur-yellow to reddish flowers that top the stalks are composed of up to fifty individual blossoms. The broad leaves of the Himalayan cowslip grow thickly and help to suppress weeds. This primula is ideal for brookside, pond, or bog garden—any area of permanently damp soil. It will grow both in full sun and in partial shade.

Primula japonica. Zones 5–8.

This is one of the easiest candelabra primulas to cultivate. *Primula japonica* will thrive in either full sun or partial shade and grows to 2 feet. The flowers have a good color range: white, pink, purple, and red. Once established, this primula will readily self-sow. *Primula japonica* generally flowers in May and June, but will sometimes flower again in the fall.

Primula vulgaris (ENGLISH PRIMROSE). Zones 5–8.

In spring, from a rosette of wrinkled leaves, arise delicately fragrant pale yellow flowers. These early blooms are held on 6-inch stalks.

Grow English primroses in rich moist soil, in light shade.

PRUNUS. Family: Rosaceae.

Prunus maritima (BEACH PLUM). Zones 2–8.

This hardy tree will grow well in adverse conditions. Beach plum, as its name indicates, is an ideal candidate for seashore gardens. It will also thrive in non-maritime conditions, especially if planted in light sandy soil in full sun. For this reason I like to include beach plum in my "desert gardens." *Prunus maritima* is a small, nicely rounded tree that matures at 6 feet. In May, the branches are liberally sprinkled with lovely white blossoms. In the fall, small plums delight the birds, or if you are quick enough, will make a delightful jelly. Beach plum is a handsome tree very suitable for the small garden.

PULMONARIA. Family: Boraginaceae. Zones 3–8.

Pulmonaria officinalis (LUNGWORT, JERUSALEM COWSLIP).

Lungwort is a striking herb with spotted evergreen leaves (except in colder regions). This spring-flowering perennial bears blue blossoms that turn pink as they mature. Lungwort grows up to about 1 foot. This plant is easy to cultivate. Grow it in moist soil in a lightly or heavily shaded position.

Because of the lung-shaped foliage and white blotches on the leaves, this herb was used to treat pulmonary disorders. Apparently the leaves have the appearance of unhealthy lungs. This association between plant and human organ was interpreted by the early herbalists as a heaven-sent sign that the herb was a cure for all lung disorders. (If a plant had the appearance of any part of the human body it was believed that it could cure any disease of that particular member. This theory was called the doctrine of signatures and is explained by a seventeenth-century herbalist, William Coles: "God gave such herbs for the use of men and hath given them particular signatures whereby a man may read even in legible characters of them.") Lungwort is still used today by modern herbalists for disorders of the chest.

Pulmonaria saccharata 'Argentea' (SILVER LUNGWORT).

Although not very many growers stock this particular lungwort, it is well worth the effort to find a supplier. In my opinion this is one of the best silver foliage plants available. Tight clusters of leaves hug the ground. The silver spots on the foliage merge so that only a gentle ripple of green shows through; other leaves are entirely silver; and some leaves even have a green margin. I enjoy silver lungwort at the front of a shady border, where the plants will form a weed-smothering colony. In my Zone 5 garden, leaves remain attractive until December; in milder areas silver lungwort will remain evergreen. Cultivation is the same as for *P. officinalis*.

R

RATIBIDA. Family: Compositae.

Ratibida pinnata (YELLOW CONEFLOWER). Zones 3–8.

This is a lovely prairie plant that grows to 5 feet. In midsummer, it is covered with large yellow flowers, daisy-like blossoms that surround a dark central cone. *Ratibida pinnata* is an adaptable plant that can be grown in both moist and dry soil. Give yellow coneflower full sun.

RHEUM (RHUBARB). Family: Polygonaceae.

Rheum palmatum 'Tanguticum' (ORNAMENTAL RHUBARB). Zones 5–9.

This is one of those hardy perennials that look very much like an exotic jungle plant— a boon to gardeners in temperate areas. It is ideal for the large garden. *Rheum palmatum* 'Tanguticum' has broad, deeply cut applegreen leaves that grow up to 3 feet across. Equally impressive are the pink flowers that appear in June and July and rise high above the leaves on 6-foot spikes. 'Tanguticum' does best in deeply dug soil that is rich in organic matter. Although these plants like damp soil, they will not tolerate being permanently immersed in water.

RHODODENDRON. Family: Ericaceae.

Rhododendron calendulaceum (FLAME AZALEA). Zones 5–9.

This lovely deciduous rhododendron matures at 4 to 10 feet. As the name "flame azalea" suggests, this is a brightly colored shrub. It flowers in late May or early June, and the blooms can be either orange-red, yellow, or scarlet. The flowers are funnel-shaped and appear in bunches at the tips of the branches. Grow this plant in light shade in moist acid well-drained soil.

Rhododendron maximum (ROSEBAY RHODODENDRON). Zones 3–9.

This is the evergreen that landscapers refer to as "Rhodo Max." For making a tall dense screen in a shady area there are not many plants better than rosebay rhododendron. It is also fast growing, gaining between 8 and 12 inches a year and maturing at around 16 feet. In June and July *Rhododendron maximum* has small white to pale pink flowers. Grow it in moist soil, in dappled or deep shade, but not in a very windy site. I have moved these rhododendrons in the middle of summer and have never lost a plant.

Rhododendron periclymenoides (PINXTER FLOWER, PINK AZALEA). Zones 3–9.

Pinxter flower is a branching shrub that reaches 5 to 7 feet and has lovely light green foliage. In May, before the leaves have unfolded, funnel-shaped clusters of pink flowers appear at the tips of the branches. These blooms are only slightly fragrant. Grow pinxter flower in dry coarse soil in light shade—a rocky ledge is a good site. (Pinxter flower is sometimes listed as *R. nudiflorum* or as *Azalea nudiflora.*)

Rhododendron viscosum (SWAMP AZALEA). Zones 4–9.

This is one of my favorite native shrubs, which I first discovered when riding my bicycle through a state forest. A whole grove at the edge of a swamp made the still summer air intoxicating with a rich sweet clove perfume.

Swamp azalea is a deciduous plant that matures at around 8 feet. In July, white or pink flowers appear. These fragrant blossoms form clusters and resemble the flowers of honeysuckle. Swamp azalea needs a wet, soggy soil and should be planted in light shade.

RIBES. Family: Saxifragaceae.

Ribes odoratum (CLOVE CURRANT, BUFFALO CURRANT). Zones 4–7.

This a lovely addition to the scented garden. In April, fragrant yellow blossoms cover the arching 8-foot canes of this flowering currant. The blooms are strongly perfumed with a delicious clove smell. In June and July, black berries add to the beauty of this shrub. Grow clove currant in full sun in any good garden soil.

RODGERSIA. Family: Saxifragaceae.

Rodgersia aesculifolia. Zones 5–8.

This is a majestic perennial ideal for marshy ground. In optimum growing conditions these plants reach 4 feet. The outstanding feature of *Rodgersia aesculifolia* is its horse chestnut–like leaves, each one held on a long stalk, with a bronze sheen that is most striking. In June and July, creamy white to pink clusters of flowers add to the beauty of this plant. For *Rodgersia* to grow well in full sun, it should be planted in a permanently moist site, but if given some shade, it can be grown farther away from the source of water.

Like a fussy customer in a restaurant, *Rodgersia* is a little particular about where it is placed. My friends accept this fastidious quality in me, so I cannot deny this eccentricity in one of my favorite plants. If any *Rodgersia* languishes in earth that is too wet or too dry, I just dig it up and move it to what I hope will be a more suitable site. It is well worth this little trouble.

ROSA (ROSE). Family: Rosaceae.

The rose is one of the oldest of the cultivated garden flowers. In his thirteenth-century

herbal, *De Proprietatibus Rerum*, Bartholomaeus Anglicus gives a poetic description of
the rose: "Among all flowers of the world the
flower of the rose is chief and bearest ye
praise. And by cause of virtues and sweet
smell and savor. For by fairness they feed the
sight and pleseth the smell by odour, the
touch be soft handling." A little later, in the
sixteenth century, Richard Banckes stated
that rose water was "good for eyes and in
ointments of the face, for it taketh away
wems [blemishes]." In the Middle Ages, roses
were woven into garlands for feast days, celebrations, and tournaments. The gardening
monk Walahfrid Strabo sums up the medieval
feeling about these flowers.

> It well deserves its name, "the Flower of
> Flowers"
> It colors the oil which bears its name. No
> man can say,
> No man remember, how many uses there
> are
> For Oil of Roses as a cure for mankind's
> ailments.

Rose petals are very easy to dry. Use them
in potpourri, or in preparations as antiseptics
and astringents. Simmer the fresh petals in
honey and water and use this liquid for sore
throats and mouth ulcers.

Rosa 'Ballerina'. Zones 4–10.

'Ballerina' is a hybrid musk shrub rose with
an arching habit that gives the plant the appearance of a ballerina's skirt—hence its attractive name. This 4-foot rose bears pink
flowers with white centers. The blossoms are
single and appear in clusters. 'Ballerina' is
ideal for the perennial border or can be grown
in a pot. This rose is tolerant of some shade.

Rosa banksiae (BANKSIA ROSE, LADY BANK'S
ROSE). Zones 6–10.

This is a lovely thornless climbing rose that
grows to 20 feet and has a spread of 10 feet.
In May and June, pale yellow double blooms
literally smother the plant. These 2-inch
flowers are slightly fragrant. In warmer zones,
the foliage of banksia rose is evergreen. This
is a nice rose for growing on fences or arbors.

Rosa centifolia (CABBAGE ROSE).
Zones 4–10.

Toward the end of the sixteenth century the
Dutch began to excel in rose cultivation. A
major contribution was the development of a
blossom with a hundred petals, aptly named
Rosa centifolia. On account of the multitude
of petals and the globular appearance of the
blossoms, these were referred to as "cabbage
roses." To me, that's hardly a reason to com-
pare one of these beauties to a vegetable! The
true cabbage rose is a little hard to come by,
but many hybrids of *Rosa centifolia* are available. One of the most outstanding is 'Fantin-
Latour'. Many people think that if there is
room for just one rose, this is the one to
choose. Each blossom is made up of dozens
of wonderful pink petals, and its pervading
perfume lingers. In June and July, the bush is
covered with flowers. Grow cabbage roses in
full sun in any reasonable garden soil.

Rosa 'Chrysler Imperial'. Zones 4–10.

I think that this is an very ugly name for one
of the most beautiful of the modern roses.
'Chrysler Imperial' should be the name of an
automobile, not of the queen of flowers! This
is a hybrid tea rose that has wonderful dark
crimson flowers. These blooms are double
and measure 5 inches across. 'Chrysler Im-

perial' reaches 4 to 5 feet. This is a very fragrant rose, with a rich and spicy perfume. Grow 'Chrysler Imperial' in full sun in any reasonable garden soil.

Rosa 'Climbing Cecile Brunner'. Zones 4–10.

This is a vigorous climbing rose that will reach 20 feet or more. And although most blooms occur in the spring, blossoms appear on this rose all summer. The fragrant pink flowers are double and measure 2 inches across—they are formed in clusters. This strong grower is ideal for climbing a fence or cascading over an arbor. 'Climbing Cecile Brunner' can also be used to hide unsightly buildings or can be trained to grow into trees. It needs room to be at its best. 'Climbing Cecile Brunner' is tolerant of light shade, and will grow in most soils.

Rosa 'Climbing Etoile de Hollande'. Zones 4–10.

This is a climbing hybrid tea rose that blooms repeatedly. The double flowers are bright crimson, and when fully open can measure up to 6 inches across. These blossoms are intensely fragrant. At maturity 'Etoile de Hollande' reaches 12 feet and has a spread of 8 feet. Grow this climbing rose in full sun in any reasonable garden soil. 'Climbing Etoile de Hollande' is tolerant of hot garden conditions.

Rosa 'Crimson Glory'. Zones 4–10.

This hybrid tea rose has velvety crimson double flowers. Each bloom is made up of thirty or more petals. The fragrance is strong, a rich damask perfume. 'Crimson Glory' forms neat 2-foot bushes and blooms repeatedly. Grow this rose in full sun in any reasonable garden soil.

Rosa eglanteria (formerly *Rosa rubiginosa*) (EGLANTINE, SWEETBRIER). Zones 4–10.

This is a vigorous climber that has a delightful smell of apples, mainly concentrated in the leaves. This sweet scent is so strong, especially after a rainstorm, that the perfume can permeate the whole garden. In late spring, sweetbrier is covered with single pale pink blooms. This rose is excellent for training along fences or arbors. Grow eglantine in full sun and a well-drained garden soil.

Rosa 'Madame Alfred Carriere'. Zones 5–10.

This is a highly scented and vigorous rose that will reach up to 12 feet with a spread of 10 feet. In the garden, it can be used as a large shrub or can be trained as a climber. 'Madame Alfred Carriere' flowers throughout the season. The very fragrant loosely formed blooms are white with occasional flushes of pink. 'Madame Alfred Carriere' is tolerant of shade—indeed this rose is a good choice for planting on a north wall.

Rosa 'Madame Isaac Pereire'. Zones 4–10.

Some people think that this is the most fragrant rose of all. The perfume is reminiscent of raspberries. A nineteenth-century bourbon rose, it has attractive rose-madder blooms with tightly rolled petals. 'Madame Isaac Pereire' flowers repeatedly and grows between 4 and 6 feet. To get the best from this magnificent rose, plant it in full sun in rich well-dug soil. Use 'Madame Isaac Pereire' as a climber on a fence or grow it as a large bush rose.

Rosa polyantha 'The Fairy'. Zones 4–10.

This charming and delicate rose can be used as a hedge, planted in a flower border, or even grown in a pot. 'The Fairy' blooms repeatedly and grows to between 2 and 3½ feet. This rose has small double pink flowers. 'The Fairy' is tolerant of light shade.

Rosa 'White Lightnin'. Zones 4–10.

This is a grandiflora rose. White blossoms are borne in clusters and have a delicious lemon fragrance. 'White Lightnin' is a bushy rose that grows between 4 and 5 feet. Grow it in full sun in any reasonable garden soil.

ROSMARINUS. Family: Labiatae.

Rosmarinus officinalis (ROSEMARY, INCENSIER, DEW OF THE SEA). Zones 8–10.

Rosemary is a tall evergreen that is native to the Mediterranean region. In late spring and early summer, the whole plant is covered with lovely blue flowers. The word "rosemary" is derived from the Latin *ros*, meaning dew, and *marinus*, which means "of the sea"—a suitable name since this aromatic plant is often found in rocky parts of the coast.

In ancient Rome it was a common practice for scholars to wear crowns of rosemary, which they believed would greatly improve the memory. During religious rites, both the Romans and the Greeks burned the plant as incense. At banquets, the ancients crowned their guest of honor with garlands made from the leaves.

The great Tudor statesman Thomas More described this herb in a most charming manner: "As for rosemary, I lett it runne all over my garden walls, not onlie because bees love it but because it is a herb sacred to remembrance, and, therefore, to friendship: whence a sprig of it has a dumb language that maketh it the chosen emblem of our funeral wakes and in our buriall ground." Until recently, it was customary in various parts of the world to strew the herb on coffins as emblematic of the life to come. This fragrant plant was also a token of the dignity of the marriage sacrament—an old custom was to dip sprigs of rosemary into the bridal cup before the bride and groom drank from it. These sprigs were kept by the couple as a charm to ensure everlasting happiness. Considering the present divorce rate this practice might well be revived!

In Banckes's *Herbal* of 1525, the author advises his readers to make "a box with rosemary wood and smell of it." This optimistic herbalist tells his readers that by constantly sniffing this aromatic casket "it shall, preserve thy youth." He also lists the following uses of rosemary: "Take the flowers and make powder therof and bind it to the right arm in a linen cloth and it shall make thee light and merry. . . . Put the leaves under thy bed head, and thou shall be delivered of all evil dreams. . . . Boil the leaves in white wine and wash thy face therewith, thy beard and thy brows, and there shall no corns grow out, but thou shall have a fair face. . . . Take the timber therof and burn it to coales and make powder therof . . . and rubbe thy teeth therewith and if there be any worms therin, it shall slay them and keep thy teeth from all evils."

Rosemary was believed to grow only in gardens where the mistress was master. To protect his male ego, a husband would often vandalize any rosemary bushes that looked too healthy. "So touchy are the lords of creation upon this point," state the authors of *The Treasury of Botany*, "that we have more than one bad reason to suspect them of privately destroying this evidence of their want of authority." If you have a large enough plant of rosemary, or find a branch that your husband has surreptitiously pulled off, you can make a comb of the wood. This, the medieval books inform us, will cure your daughters of giddiness.

The pungent leaves of rosemary are wonderful with roast lamb, lamb kabobs, fish dishes, and chicken and game dishes. The leaves, boiled in water and strained, make an ideal hair rinse.

RUDBECKIA (CONEFLOWER, BLACK-EYED SUSAN). Family: Compositae.

Rudbeckia fulgida. Zones 3–9.

Black-eyed Susan is one of the handsomest native perennials available. The yellow petals contrast beautifully with the dark central cone. In late summer and fall, this 2- to 3-foot plant is ablaze with color. No wild-flower meadow—indeed no perennial garden—should be without black-eyed Susans. Grow *Rudbeckia* in full sun in average well-drained soil.

Rudbeckia purpurea. See *Echinacea purpurea.*

RUMEX (DOCK, SORREL). Family: Polygonaceae.

Rumex scutatus (FRENCH SORREL). Zones 3–10.

Sorrel is a 2-foot-high perennial with spear-shaped leaves. Reddish green flowers appear in the spring. To keep the foliage tender, it is best to remove the flowers as soon as they form. Plant this herb in rich moist soil in full sun or in partial shade.

This was a popular plant among the ancients. Pliny states, "The wild sorrels heal the stings of scorpions and protects from stings those who carry them on their persons." He adds that this herb "causes belching, is diuretic, and dispels dimness of the eyes: put into the bottom of a bath, or rubbed on the body without oil before taking a bath, it also removes itching of the body."

Today sorrel is cultivated mainly for kitchen use, where its bitter lemony taste can be appreciated in a variety of dishes. These leaves are delicious when added to salad or made into a soup or a green sauce for fish.

RUTA. Family: Rutaceae.

Ruta graveolens (RUE, HERB OF GRACE). Zones 4–10.

Rue is a strong-smelling evergreen woody perennial with attractive metallic-gray leaves. This herb reaches 2½ feet, and from May to July bears clusters of small yellowish flowers. Grow rue in full sun in well-drained soil. This plant can also be cultivated in a lightly shaded position in the garden.

The Roman naturalist Pliny was of the opinion that this aromatic herb would counteract the "bites of serpents." He wrote: "It is said that anyone besmeared with its juice, and even those having it on their persons, were never stung by these poisonous creatures." This author also told his readers that weasels would partake of rue when about to fight with snakes. Pliny considered it good for the vision; he mentions that "engravers and painters use rue as a food, with bread or cress, for the sake of their eyes." Pliny also advised his readers to drink a tea made from rue "to prevent the after-effects of drinking." The great experimenter with poisons in the classical world, the emperor Mithridates Eupator, used rue as a chief ingredient in his antidote to all toxic substances. Banckes's *Herbal* cites rue as a cure for headache: "Take the juice of rue and put it into his nostrils, for he putteth out phlegm and cleaneth the brain."

In the medieval period, this herb was burned in streets during times of plague. To combat jail fever, officials of the law courts wore posies of rue. The *English Leechbook* prescribes this perennial for those pestered with vermin: "Take the juice of rue and anoint the body therewith." And for a "nose that stinketh. Take the black mint and the juice of rue, and take of each equally much; and put it in his nostrils or in a wound that stinketh." According to the Tudor herbalist William Turner, rue is good for preventing lusty thoughts. If you suffer from this condition, you can take his advice and lay the herb "soden in wine" on the kidneys. This, the author assures us, will "consume and remove lechery."

Rue is often called "herb of grace," which probably comes from the fact that holy water both in church services and in exorcism was often sprinkled with rue.

S

SAGITTARIA. Family: Alismataceae.

Sagittaria latifolia (ARROWHEAD). Zones 2–10.

Sagittaria latifolia is an attractive aquatic plant with graceful arrow-shaped leaves. In July and August, showy white flowers with green or yellow centers are borne in loose clusters. Arrowhead grows to 4 feet. It will happily grow in water up to a depth of 18 inches, or can be planted in the muddy soil of a pond or streamside.

SALVIA (SAGE). Family: Labiatae.

Salvia argentia (SILVER SAGE). Zones 5–9.

This is one of my favorite foliage plants. In any landscape silver sage is a showstopper. Its large oval leaves are covered with a beautiful wool which makes them look as if they were made of spun silver. *Salvia argentia* should be grown in dry well-drained soil in full sun. In damper conditions, the leaves tend to turn slightly green. Although this plant is usually a biennial, by removing the flowers as soon as they are formed, you can trick *Salvia argentia* into becoming a short-lived perennial. (The flowers are 4-foot spikes of rather undistinguished blossoms.) Keep it from blooming, and grow this lovely salvia at the front of a border where the silver leaf rosette can be admired. This is a drought-resistant plant.

Salvia officinalis (SAGE). Zones 3–10.

Sage is a 2-foot-high aromatic shrubby herb with silver lance-shaped leaves. From May until July, it produces spikes of violet-blue flowers. Cultivate this plant in full sun or part shade in any well-drained soil. In the spring, cut back old woody stems.

This is a plant that has been used medicinally for thousands of years. The Greek herbalist Dioscorides mentioned sage in his famed herbal, *De Materia Medica*: "It dyes ye hair black, and is a wound herb ... a blood stauncher.... Ye decoction of ye leaves ... assuageth ye itching about ye privities.... Being given to drink, it cure blood-spitters and is available for all cleaning of a woman." Sage was believed to bestow longevity on anybody who took the precaution of adding a little to his or her daily diet. An ancient Arabian proverb says, "How can a man die who has sage in his garden?"

The eleventh-century *Anglo-Saxon Herbal of Apuleius* is a little more prosaic in describing the medicinal properties of this herb. "A bath of sage," counsels the author, "is wonderful for the itching of the seat. It will relieve the itching to a high degree." A little later, Richard Banckes told his readers that it is wonderful for invalids: "Seeth the leaves in water and let the patient sit over it and receive the hot fumes of it, and it shall do him much good. . . . It will make a man's body clean; therefore who that useth to eat of this herb or drink it, it is a marvel that any inconvenience should grieve them that use it." John Gerard had the following to say about sage: "If the woman about the fourth day of her going abroad after her childing, shall drink nine ounces of the juice of sage with a little salt, and then use the company of her husband, she shall without doubt conceive and bring forth a store of children, which are the blessing of God."

Besides being a medicinal herb, sage is wonderful in the kitchen. Add the chopped leaves to stuffings, or add them to coals when cooking pork. Sage is the classic stuffing for goose and roast pork.

Salvia officinalis 'Icterina' is a lovely golden variety of common sage. The leaves are variegated, and although the predominant color is gold, the foliage is suffused with sage green and primrose yellow. Golden sage is cultivated primarily for the color of the leaves. Grow this shrubby perennial in Zones 4–8, in full sun or very light shade in well-drained garden soil. In milder areas of the United States, golden sage is evergreen.

Salvia officinalis 'Purpurea', "purple sage" or "red sage," is an evergreen shrub that makes a striking impact when used in bold clumps in the garden. It is grown for its foliage only. These leaves are a rich dark purple and form a dense foot-high mat. Grow this perennial in Zones 4–8, in full sun in well-drained soil.

Salvia sclarea (CLARY SAGE). Zones 4–9.

Clary sage is a sticky biennial that has a strong spicy odor. This herb grows to 15 inches. The stems bear whorls of whitish flowers that are tinged with purple. Elizabethan herbalist John Gerard wrote that clary "being drunk with wine, stirreth up lust, it clereth the eyes from films and other imperfections." It is still sometimes used for removing foreign bodies from the eye. A modern herbalist, Dr. Malcolm Stewart, writes: "The seed becomes mucilaginous [jelly-like] in water and may then be used to extract foreign bodies from the eye."

Salvia x *superba*. Zones 4–9.

From late May through June, 2-foot spikes of deep violet flowers cover *Salvia superba* 'Blue Queen'. If you remove the dead blooms, this salvia will continue flowering until August. Grow 'Blue Queen' in full sun in well-drained soil.

Salvia x *superba* 'East Friesland' has lovely violet-purple flowers from June until August. These plants mature at about 18 inches. Grow them in full sun in well-drained soil.

SANGUINARIA. Family: Papaveraceae.

Sanguinaria canadensis (BLOODROOT). Zones 3–8.

Bloodroot is a delightful wild flower that blooms in April and May. If planted in masses, the white star-shaped flowers are stunning. When cut, the fleshy roots exude a thick crimson liquid that looks very much like blood—hence the English name. Native Americans employed bloodroot as a body paint. Grow this perennial in light shade in rich moist soil.

Sanguinaria canadensis 'Multiplex' is the double form; the flowers last slightly longer.

SANGUISORBA (BURNET). Family: Rosaceae.

Sanguisorba minor. See *Poterium sanguisorba.*

Sanguisorba officinalis (GREAT BURNET). Zones 4–8.

This is a lovely English perennial wild flower. It has elegant feathery leaves, and from June until September crimson "bottle brush" flowers are held on tall stems. *Sanguisorba officinalis* grows between 3 and 4 feet. Cultivate great burnet in full sun in moist soil.

SANTOLINA. Family: Compositae.

Santolina chamaecyparissus (COTTON LAVENDER). Zones 6–10.

Cotton lavender (sometimes called lavender cotton) is a slightly tender shrubby perennial that grows to 2 feet high. The fernlike foliage is a lovely silver color, and the leaves are aromatic. In summer, yellow button-shaped flowers appear. Cotton lavender makes an ideal low hedge for the herb garden. In milder areas, Zones 6–10, this herb can be used as an evergreen. In colder areas it is best treated as an annual, although specimens covered with sand before really cold weather sets in have survived in my Zone 5 garden. When dried, cotton lavender can be added to potpourri; placed in closets, it is effective as a moth deterrent. Grow cotton lavender in full sun in well-drained soil.

Santolina virens (GREEN SANTOLINA). Zones 6–10.

This is similar to *Santolina chamaecyparissus* but the foliage is dark green. In August and September, yellow button-like flowers cover green santolina. The cultivation requirements are the same as for cotton lavender.

SAPONARIA. Family: Caryophyllaceae.

Saponaria officinalis (SOAPWORT, BOUNCING BET). Zones 4–8.

Soapwort is a sprawling perennial that can grow to 32 inches. In summer, pink flowers cover the plant. This is a very easy herb to grow in any garden soil, in full sun or part shade. In fact, be careful where you plant soapwort: it can become invasive.

Boiled in water, this herb produces a soapy solution that is good for washing delicate fabrics. Infusions of soapwort roots are used today for treating eczema and other skin conditions.

'Roseo-Plena' is an improved variety of soapwort. In midsummer, double rose-pink flowers cover this 2-foot perennial.

SASSAFRAS. Family: Lauraceae.

Sassafras albidum (SASSAFRAS). Zones 5–10.

Sassafras is a hardy deciduous aromatic tree, native to North America. In the South, sassafras grows to 60 feet, but in the North, although fairly common, it matures as only a small shrub. This is a decorative tree with variable double- or triple-lobed leaves and attractive yellowish flowers in spring. It can be grown in poor gravelly soil, in full sun or light shade.

Sassafras was first discovered by settlers in the early seventeenth century. Shortly after, shipments of leaves were being sent to major European cities, making it one of the first commercial products exported from the United States. Sassafras was used to flavor soups, and the leaves were used as a tea. Early settlers used an infusion of this herb for treating venereal diseases. In modern times, sassafras is used for relieving upset stomach and increasing perspiration. Powdered sassafras leaves (filé) are widely used in the South for thickening gumbo.

SATUREJA (SAVORY). Family: Labiatae.

Satureja hortensis (SUMMER SAVORY). Zones 3–10.

Summer savory is an aromatic hardy annual with narrow leaves. This herb grows 2 feet high, and from midsummer on, the whole plant is covered with pale lilac, blue, or white flowers. Sow seed or plant summer savory in full sun in any well-drained soil.

Satureja montana (WINTER SAVORY). Zones 5–10.

Winter savory is a durable hardy evergreen perennial with small lance-shaped leaves. The blossoms appear in June, and are the same color as summer savory. The plant grows up to 16 inches high. Grow *Satureja montana* in full sun in any well-drained soil. Winter savory can be trimmed as a low hedge.

Both types of savory are useful in the kitchen, although gourmets consider winter savory a little coarser in taste than summer savory. If you want to dry the plant for use in the kitchen, collect the herb before the flowers form.

The hot aromatic flavor of both savories enhances stuffings and roast meats. If either summer or winter savory is boiled with cab-

bage or turnips, the unpleasant odor of the vegetable is not as noticeable. Summer savory is used mainly with beans of all kinds. In Germany this plant is known as *Bohnenkraut,* or "bean herb."

The fourteenth-century Italian author Pietro Crescenzi advised savory as a purgative and as a bleach for the complexion: "It purgeth the lungs and looseth the great humors and compelleth and putteth them out by the mouth by spitting." This author did not think too highly of using savory as a seasoning because of its supposed aphrodisiac qualities: It "stirreth him that useth to lechery, therefore it is forbidden to use it much in meats." According to the Elizabethan herbalist John Gerard, summer savory "maketh thin, and doth marvellously prevail against winde; therefore it is with good success boiled and eaten with beanes, peas, and other windie pulses."

SEDUM (STONECROP, ORPINE). Family: Crassulaceae.

Sedum acre (WALL-PEPPER). Zones 3–9.

Who could resist a flower called wall-pepper? It is an apt name, for the fleshy leaves of this plant have a peppery taste. *Sedum acre* is a perennial native to the British Isles, and throughout the English counties, this brightly colored hardy sedum is known by some of the most outrageous and delightful vernacular names. "Welcome-Home-Husband-Though-Never-So-Drunk," "Jack-in-the-Buttery," "Poor Man's Pepper," and "Love Entangled" are just a small sampling! Truly, this was (and still is) a much-beloved plant, and it's easy to see why. *Sedum acre* is a low-growing evergreen that forms dense 2-inch mats of fleshy leaves, which are crowned with lovely bright yellow blossoms in June. Grow wall-pepper in full sun in well-drained soil. *Sedum acre* is very suitable for planting on low walls or for growing in the rock garden. This is a drought-tolerant plant.

Sedum sieboldii. Zones 3–9.

In September and October, bright pink flowers cover this sprawling perennial. The semi-evergreen leaves are round, thick, and fleshy, and are an attractive silvery gray color. *Sedum sieboldii* creeps along the ground and forms 6- to 9-inch mounds. Grow this sedum in full sun in well-drained soil. This perennial is ideal for planting by pathways, in pots, or in the rock garden.

Sedum spectabile 'Autumn Joy'. Zones 3–9.

'Autumn Joy' is a perennial that I tend to include in nearly every garden design. Once you have seen this bold and striking plant, you will covet it. One reason I like it so much is because it is a late bloomer. Lovely pink flowers appear in August and September, and butterflies find these bright blooms irresistible. 'Autumn Joy' is a fleshy perennial that grows up to 24 inches tall. The flowers are wide, and initially are pale pink; as they mature they deepen to salmon pink, then finally turn brick red. Even in the winter, the dead flower heads of 'Autumn Joy' look attractive. By early winter, blooms will have become sun bleached and golden.

SEMPERVIVUM. Family: Crassulaceae.

Sempervivum tectorum (HOUSELEEK, HEN-AND-CHICKENS). Zones 3–10.

Houseleeks are small succulent perennials that produce compact rosettes of fleshy leaves. In July, pinkish-red blossoms appear on the 9-inch flower stems. Grow this herb in full sun in well-drained soil. Houseleeks can also be cultivated on the roof of a house or on stone walls. Many of the old names of this plant, such as the Dutch *Donderbloom* (thunder flower), reflect the common belief that if it was planted on the roof of a building, it could be used as a preventive against lightning. In the eighth century, the great European monarch Charlemagne issued an ordinance that farmers and tenants on the imperial estates should plant this flower on their roofs as a prevention against lightning and fire. In Europe it is still very common to see houseleek growing on the roofs of old houses.

The Roman author Pliny mentions this plant. To combat sleeplessness he suggests houseleeks "wrapped in a black cloth and placed under a pillow without the knowledge of the patient." The medieval herbal *Hortus Sanitatis* recommends "the juice of houseleek" dropped "into the ear" for deafness. The author of this herbal stresses that "the hearing will come back without fail."

On the more practical side, the juice of houseleek is a proven remedy for burns and insect bites.

SHORTIA. Family: Diapensiaceae.

Shortia galacifolia (OCONEE BELLS). Zones 5–8.

The round, glossy, evergreen leaves of this perennial make Oconee bells a plant for all seasons. In June and July, solitary white bell-shaped blossoms appear on 8-inch stems. The dainty flowers are fringed. Grow *Shortia* in shade, in acid moist well-drained soil.

SILENE (CAMPION). Family: Caryophyllaceae. Zones 5–9.

Silene alba (WHITE CAMPION).

White campion is a lovely English wild flower that blooms from May until August. This 32-inch perennial has, at the tips of the stems, clusters of pure white flowers. Blooms are round and flat and have a long corolla. Grow this attractive wild flower in full sun in any reasonable garden soil.

Silene dioica (RED CAMPION).

This is similar to the white campion but has red flowers and blooms for a slightly longer period, from May until October. Red campion prefers light shade, but will grow in full sun. Give this wild flower moist soil.

SILPHIUM (ROSINWEED). Family: Compositae. Zones 4–8.

Silphium laciniatum (COMPASS PLANT).

This plant looks like a sunflower, and because the leaves often orient themselves in a north-south direction, *Silphium laciniatum* is known as compass plant. This perennial takes a little time to establish itself, but it is very easy to grow. Mature plants are a spectacular sight in July and August, when 2- to 5-inch "sunflowers" cover the upper stems. During this period, compass plant can produce over a hundred blooms. This is a large perennial that reaches 4 to 7 feet. Cultivate compass plant in full sun, and grow it in either moderately dry or moist soil.

Silphium perfoliatum (CUP-PLANT ROSINWEED).

Seeds of cup-plant rosinweed sent to me by a gardening friend in Nebraska yielded unexpected results. In their second season, my plants just grew and grew and grew! At the end of the season the cup-plants had reached 11 feet and were at least 5 feet wide—almost the dimensions of a small tree. In a vegetable garden where I planted a row of cup-plants, they formed one of the most attractive floral fences I have ever seen. *Silphium perfoliatum* is called "cup-plant" because opposite pairs of stalkless leaves are fused to the thick stems, forming a natural cup in which rainwater gathers. This little floral reservoir is the delight of hummingbirds and I'm sure provides a mini bird bath for other species as well. In July and August, cup-plant is covered with small "sunflowers." Cultivate this perennial in full sun and moist soil.

SOLIDAGO (GOLDENROD). Family: Compositae.

Goldenrods are lovely plants, but because they are prolific as wild flowers they are really neglected as additions to garden borders. In England these lovely late-blooming perennials are much more appreciated. For many years gardeners thought that *Solidago* species caused hay fever, but recently experts have determined that goldenrod pollen is harmless. Since so many garden varieties are now available, it is a pity that more use is not made of these colorful flowers. The following are some of the best of the new goldenrod cultivars. Grow these perennials in full sun or partial shade, in any type of garden soil.

Solidago speciosa (SHOWY GOLDENROD, NOBLE GOLDENROD). Zones 3–10.

This native goldenrod is quite a spectacular sight when in bloom in late summer and early fall. The 3- to 6-foot bushy plants are topped with foot-long wands of vivid yellow flower clusters.

Solidago virgaurea. Zones 4–10.

Solidago virgaurea 'Golden Dwarf' is a smaller variety of garden goldenrod that matures at around 12 inches. It flowers in August and September.

'Golden Mosa' bears lovely 3-foot golden spikes in August and September. The leaves are an attractive pale yellow. Grow 'Golden Mosa' in sun or partial shade. It will grow in poor soil.

STACHYS. Family: Labiatae.

Stachys byzantina (also listed as *Stachys lanata* and *Stachys olympica*) (LAMB'S EARS). Zones 4–9.

This well-known garden perennial has lovely soft woolly leaves—in shape and texture not unlike the ears of a lamb. The foliage is exceptional in that it is a most lovely silver color. *Stachys byzantina* is grown only for its leaves; the flowers pale in comparison to the foliage. To keep the leaves in top shape, remove flower heads (or grow *Stachys byzantina* 'Silver Carpet', the nonflowering type of lamb's ears). *Stachys byzantina* forms 15-inch mounds which are lovely for edging borders or pathways, or when planted in a garden of silver plants.

Grow lamb's ears in full sun and in well-drained soil. This perennial does not do well in heavy, soggy soils.

STOKESIA (STOKES' ASTER). Family: Compositae. Zones 5–8.

Stokesia laevis

This lovely perennial (sometimes listed as *S. cyanea*) blooms in late summer. From June until frost, the 1- to 2-foot-high plants are covered with lavender-blue aster-like flowers. Blooms are large, up to 4 inches across. Grow this perennial in sun or light shade, in moist well-drained soil.

Stokesia laevis 'Alba' is a white form.

SYMPHYTUM. Family: Boraginaceae.

Symphytum officinale (COMFREY). Zones 3–10.

Comfrey is a hairy perennial with large lance-shaped leaves. This herb flowers in June and grows to 3 feet. The bell-shaped blossoms can be either pink or blue. Grow comfrey in full sun or part shade in any rich soil. It can also be cultivated in damp soil near water.

In his book on natural history, the Roman author Pliny explains the Latin name for this plant: "So excellent is it for healing wounds, that, added even to pieces of meat that are being boiled, it binds them together. Hence the Greek name 'symphyton.'" Pliny further adds that comfrey is "good for broken bones. . . . Moreover, chewed it alleys thirst, and is especially cooling to the lungs. It is also applied to dislocations and bruises and it sooths the intestines." All through the Middle Ages, comfrey was a highly regarded medicinal herb. "If one be busted within," says the *Anglo-Saxon Herbal of Apuleius*, "let him take the roots of this wort, let him roast them in hot ashes, then swallow then in honey . . . he will be healed."

According to the Elizabethan herbalist John Gerard, bodily hurts caused by youthful exuberance are cured by taking comfrey: "The slimie substance of the root made in a posset of ale, and given to drink against the pain in the back, gotton by violent motion, as wrastling, or overmuch use of women, doth in four or five days perfectly cure the same, although: the involuntary flowing of the seed in men is begotton thereby."

Today comfrey is mainly used externally as a poultice for sprains, swellings, and bruises: Crush the fresh leaf or root and apply it to the afflicted part of the body. If no fresh comfrey is available, boil the dried root and apply a bandage soaked in the resulting thick liquid to the swelling or sprain.

Symphytum x *uplandicum* (RUSSIAN COMFREY). Zones 5–10.

This is a very attractive hybrid of comfrey. From June until August, lovely inch-long blue-purple flowers are arranged in clusters on the upper leaves. Russian comfrey grows to 3 feet. Cultivate it in full sun or partial shade, in moist soil.

SYRINGA (LILAC). Family: Oleaceae.

When mature, lilac forms a large shrub that measures between 8 and 15 feet. But if pruned after flowering, specimens can be kept more compact. Lilac is a delight in May and June, when the fat clusters of fragrant blossoms can scent the whole garden. Many varieties of lilac are available. Grow *Syringa* in full sun or light shade, in rich well-drained soil.

Syringa vulgaris 'Lavender Lady'. Zones 4–9.

As 'Lavender Lady' does not need the long cold winters normally required to make *Syringa* flower, it is a good choice for warmer zones of the U.S. The blossoms are lavender colored and highly fragrant.

T

TAMARIX. Family: Tamaricaceae.

Tamarix ramosissima 'Rosea' (TAMARISK). Zones 2–8.

This is a lovely small tree with feathery silver-blue-green foliage. In June and July, the 8-foot trees are covered with spikes of tiny rose-pink flowers. Mature trees have a delightful gnarled appearance. To encourage new growth, prune specimens somewhat each spring, which causes them to bloom heavily. Some gardeners advise cutting the tree to the ground each spring. This can be done, and the ensuing growth will bloom prolifically, but you will not get the attractive knotty shapes associated with mature tamarisk. Grow tamarisk in full sun in well-drained soil. This tree prefers rather poor types of soil, making it one of the best choices for the seaside.

TANACETUM. Family: Compositae.

Tanacetum vulgare (TANSY). Zones 3–9.

Tansy is an erect leafy perennial that grows to about 3 feet. Flat yellow blossoms made up of dozens of individual "buttons" cover the plant in August and September. Grow tansy in full sun or part shade, in rich loamy soil.

Tansy was once widely used in the kitchen. And centuries ago, tansy pudding was traditional on Easter Sunday. The sixteenth-century English herbalist William Turner explained this custom: "It is well devised of physicians of old time that after Easter, men should use tansies to drive away the wynds that they have gotten all the Lent before with eating fish, peas, beans and diverse kynds of wiynde making herbes." Turner also recommended tansy as a face wash for those people "that be sunne burnt and would be fair." Another sixteenth-century English herbalist, John Gerard, considered tansy a valuable herb: "The seed of tansy is a singular and approved medicine against worms ... also being drunk with wine, it is good against the pains of the bladder, and when a man cannot pisse but by drops."

TAXODIUM (CYPRESS). Family: Taxodiaceae.

Taxodium distichum (SWAMP CYPRESS). Zones 4–9.

Anybody who has gone sightseeing in the Florida Everglades or motored past some of the Louisiana bayous will have fond memories of this exotic-looking tree. But northern gardeners take heart–the swamp cypress is one of the most adaptable trees. Specimens will grow in Zone 4 conditions! Swamp cypress has much to offer. And although *Taxodium* can be grown in dry soil, the fact that swamp cypress will grow in water makes it an ideal choice for planting by ponds and streams. It is a very attractive tree, easily recognized by the smooth, swollen trunk that tapers upward. The outer cinnamon-colored bark exfoliates and reveals the lighter shades of the juvenile bark beneath. This mottled effect is very striking. Since *Taxodium* is not an evergreen, it loses its leaves in winter. The foliage casts a light shade, and because of the gossamer quality of the leaves, it is not bothersome when it sheds in autumn. New leaves emerge at the end of spring–sometimes not until late May. This foliage, initially a handsome emerald green, turns beautiful shades of gold. Swamp cypress is a fast-maturing tree; in ideal conditions it will grow 2 feet a year. Mature specimens can reach 50 to 100 feet, and in the warmer conditions of the South,

swamp cypress can reach 150 feet. To get *Taxodium* established in standing water, plant young trees in mounds: pile earth up in shallow water and dig a hole in the middle large enough to accommodate the swamp cypress. As the tree matures, roots will pull it farther into the water. If you are growing *Taxodium* in damp or garden soil, plant it as you would any other tree.

TAXUS (YEW). Family: Taxaceae.

Taxus x *media* 'Hatfieldii' (HATFIELD YEW). Zones 4–7.

Hatfield yew is ideal for clipping into a hedge. It will mature at around 10 to 12 feet but by clipping can be kept much lower. The branches of this yew are held erect. Grow *Taxus media* 'Hatfieldii' in sun or shade, in moist well-drained soil. Do not plant *Taxus* in very windy sites. Many yews are now available; if you want to use this plant as a hedge, check with your local garden center for the best type for your area.

THYMUS (THYME) Family: Labiatae.

All thymes are aromatic perennials that grow less than an inch in height to over 1 foot tall. Nineteen hundred years ago, Pliny gave instructions for gathering this versatile herb. His advice is still useful for the modern gardener: "They blossom about the solstices when the bees sip from it. . . . Thyme ought to be gathered while it is still in blossom, and to be dried in the shade." According to Pliny, the herb could be used for "brightening the vision . . . for a chronic cough . . . and in cases of aberration of mind or of melancholy. Thyme is also administered to epileptics, who when attacked by a fit are revived by its smell. It is said too that epileptics should sleep on soft thyme." In the Middle Ages, Pietro Crescenzi advised his readers to "drink wine in which thyme had been cooked." This, he stated, "would warm the heart, the liver and the spleen."

Today thyme is one of the most widely used kitchen herbs. It is also one of the main ingredients of the herbal blend *bouquet garni*. The dried leaves or fresh sprigs add flavor to all meat dishes. As this herb helps with the digestion of fatty food, it is excellent when included with pork or goose dishes. Thyme can also be made into an antiseptic gargle for sore throats. Grow all thymes in full sun in well-drained soil.

Thymus x *citriodorus* (LEMON THYME). Zones 3–9.

In appearance, lemon thyme resembles common thyme. The intense citrus aroma released when the leaves are bruised identifies the lemon variety. Plants make 6-inch mounds of evergreen blue-green leaves. In June, the whole plant is covered with attractive rosy blooms.

Thymus x *citriodorus* 'Argenteus' (SILVER LEMON THYME) has dark green leaves edged with silver. Silver lemon thyme flowers in June.

Thymus x *citriodorus* 'Aureus' (GOLDEN LEMON THYME) has golden tips on the leaves. I like to use this attractive plant for edging pathways or as a ground cover in sunny well-drained sites. Golden lemon thyme flowers in June.

Thymus herba-barona (CARAWAY THYME). Zones 5–9.

This ground-hugging creeping thyme forms dense mats of tiny dark green leaves. The whole plant has a delicious caraway scent. Plants grow up to 4 inches, and in June *herba-barona* is covered with pink and mauve flowers. Sprinkled on steaks before cooking, it imparts a delicious flavor to the meat.

Thymus serpyllum (WILD THYME). Zones 3–9.

This creeping thyme grows to only 3 inches. In June the evergreen mats are covered with minute lavender flowers. Wild thyme is nice to plant in the cracks of stone or brick pathways. When walked upon, this aromatic herb releases a delightful odor.

Thymus vulgaris (COMMON THYME, ENGLISH THYME). Zones 5–10.

Common thyme is an upright bushy plant that reaches 6 to 12 inches. This herb has small gray-green leaves, and the flowers can be either lilac or white. From early summer to late autumn these blossoms occur in dense terminal spikes.

TIARELLA. Family: Saxifragaceae.

Tiarella cordifolia (FOAMFLOWER). Zones 3–8.

Foamflower is a lovely perennial for shady sites, where it will soon become a weed-smothering ground cover. The maple-like leaves remain green for much of the year. In my Zone 5 Connecticut garden the foliage of foamflower is still attractive in December. In milder areas it will remain verdant until spring, when the emerging new leaves will cause the old foliage to wither. The veining on the leaves of some plants is highlighted by purple markings. Foamflower grows between 6 and 8 inches tall, and from June until August bears spikes of white flowers. Grow this perennial in rich moist acid soil, in partial to full shade.

TRADESCANTIA (SPIDERWORT). Family: Commelinaceae.

Tradescantia virginiana (VIRGINIA SPIDERWORT). Zones 4–9.

Like daylilies, the blossoms of these perennials last only twenty-four hours or less, but also like daylilies, *Tradescantia* is very prolific with its blooms. From spring until summer, the 1- to 2-foot-tall plants of spiderwort are covered with 2- to 3-inch-wide violet-blue flowers. Grow this perennial in full sun or in light shade. *Tradescantia* will grow in dry soil as well as damp soil. In optimum growing conditions spiderwort can sometimes become aggressive. If this happens, restrain plants by digging them up and replanting them in plastic pots. This simple procedure will restrict any overenthusiastic *Tradescantia*.

TRILLIUM. Family: Liliaceae.

Trillium grandiflorum (WHITE TRILLIUM, SNOW TRILLIUM). Zones 4–8.

This lovely spring flower blooms in April and May and is considered by many to be the most beautiful of the native trilliums. The leaves form a natural triangle, and the blooms are held on short stems above this foliage. The pure white flowers consist of three overlapping petals. As they mature, the blossoms turn a delicate shade of pink. White trillium grows between 9 and 18 inches high. Cultivate this wild flower in light to heavy shade, in moist rich well-drained soil. White trillium is not difficult to grow, and once established will form thick colonies.

TRITOMA. See *Kniphofia*.

TROLLIUS (GLOBEFLOWER). Family: Ranunculaceae. Zones 4–9.

Trollius x *cultorum* 'Etna'.

This beautiful garden perennial blooms in April and May. The deep orange flowers are delicate and goblet-like, rather like a much improved buttercup. Each blossom has a wavy appearance which makes the flowers glow in sunlight. The leaves are deeply cut and very attractive. 'Etna' grows to 30 inches. Grow this perennial in shade, in rich moist soil. If it is grown in sun, it will need very moist soil. If dead flowers are removed, 'Etna' will bloom again in the fall. Although globeflowers are used mainly in shady gardens, they are also ideal for planting around the edges of a pond or stream.

Trollius laxus (SPREADING GLOBEFLOWER).

From April until June, this native American plant bears attractive greenish-yellow flowers on foot-long stems. These blossoms measure 1½ inches across and are much more open than other species of *Trollius*. The foliage on mature plants can grow to 2 feet. Cultivate *Trollius laxus* as you would *Trollius* x *cultorum* 'Etna'.

TYPHA. Family: Typhaceae.

Typha angustifolia (NARROW-LEAVED CATTAIL, BULRUSH). Zones 2–10.

Typha are elegant waterside plants with macelike flower heads, a familiar sight around ponds, streams, and rivers throughout the U.S. The more common species of cattail, *Typha latifolia*, is a lovely native plant, but is a little too aggressive for domestic landscapes. For water gardens, the narrow-leaved cattail is more suitable. This bulrush grows between 2 and 5 feet high. At the top of the flowering stems are the familiar brown, rounded, fat flower heads—blossoms that always look to me like a speared hotdog covered with brown fuzz! The cattails appear in summer. The narrow straplike foliage grows up to 2 feet tall. Narrow-leaved cattail is a plant for larger ponds and wet areas, not really suitable for a small artificial pond. Grow this perennial in wet mud, and plant the rhizome about 6 inches deep. *Typha* can be grown under water so long as the water is no more than 6 inches deep. Cattails are wonderful in flower arrangements.

little smaller, reaching 6 to 18 inches. Flowers of wood merrybells are light yellow.

Uvularia sessilifolia (LITTLE MERRYBELLS).

This is the smallest of the merrybells, reaching only 10 inches. The flowers are pale greenish yellow and appear at the same time as other native *Uvularia*. In a shady site, little merrybells can make an attractive ground cover.

U

UVULARIA (MERRYBELLS, BELLWORT). Family: Liliaceae. Zones 4–9.

These lovely woodland plants are native to the northeastern regions of the U.S. They have delicate bell-shaped flowers, and the leaves are fused into the stem in such a manner that the foliage looks as if it has been threaded onto the stalks. These are perennials for shady woodland gardens. *Uvularia* will take dense shade, and so is a wonderful flower for really gloomy gardens. Give merrybells moist humus-rich soil.

Uvularia grandiflora (BIG MERRYBELLS).

This is a very showy plant. The lovely bell-shaped lemon-yellow flowers are 2 inches long and appear from mid-May until mid-June. Big merrybells grows between 1 and 2 feet tall.

Uvularia perfoliata (WOOD MERRYBELLS).

Wood merrybells flowers at about the same time as big merrybells, but the plants are a

V

VALERIANA. Family: Valerianaceae.

Valeriana officinalis (VALERIAN, ALL-HEAL, SET-WELL). Zones 3–10.

This is a tall perennial. From June until September, it produces round clusters (umbels) of pink flowers. This graceful herb is best grown in light shade in moist soil.

Since the days of the Roman author Pliny, valerian has been used for treating nervous spasms. During World War I, an extract of this herb was used for treating shell shock. This was the Valium of the early twentieth century. In fact, even though they are in no way chemically related, the word "Valium" derives from the name of this healing herb.

The roots of the dried plant have an offensive odor. Because of its smell the Greek herbalist Dioscorides called the plant *phu*. Cats, enamored of the odor, will roll in beds of valerian and even try to dig up the plants. Rats also like the scent. Because of the fondness of these rodents for valerian, this herb was formerly used by rat-catchers. During the medieval period, the smell of this herb was

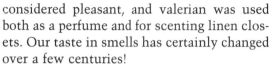

considered pleasant, and valerian was used both as a perfume and for scenting linen closets. Our taste in smells has certainly changed over a few centuries!

A fourteenth-century recipe mentioned in Mrs. Grieve's *A Modern Herbal* gives valerian a most incredible virtue: "Men who begin to fight and when you wish to stop them, give to them the juice of valerian and peace will be made immediately." A tea made from the roots, or a liquid extract (available at health food stores), is used today as a sedative and painkiller. Many people consider a few drops of valerian taken in water excellent as a nighttime sedative.

VERATRUM (FALSE HELLEBORE). Family: Liliaceae.

Veratrum viride (WHITE HELLEBORE, AMERICAN WHITE HELLEBORE). Zones 4–8.

White hellebore is a very handsome native plant that should be included in many more gardens. When I first saw this plant in the wild, it was early spring and the leaves had just started to emerge from the damp soil. On the ground was a rosette of the most beautiful pleated foliage. When I returned a few weeks later, this stately perennial was at least 6 feet tall and was crowned with pretty spikes of greenish-yellow flowers. White hellebore grows between 4 and 7 feet, with neatly arranged pleated leaves held on the statuesque stems. In May and June, the flowers are held high on the upper tips. *Veratrum viride* needs damp rich soil and shade. White hellebore is a wonderful plant for a permanently damp part of the garden, or near water or in a wild garden. The only sad thing about it is that shortly after flowering the whole flower spike withers. But white hellebore provides beauty in the garden from spring until at least midsummer, and it is a long-lived perennial.

VERBASCUM. Family: Scrophulariaceae.

Verbascum should be planted in full sun in well-drained soil.

Verbascum bombyciferum. Zones 4–10.

This is one of the most beautiful of garden flowers. The plants look like candelabra, and the silvery down that covers them gives them an ethereal quality. Mature plants grow 6 feet or more, and 1½-inch-wide yellow flowers stud the branches. *Verbascum bombyciferum* is a biennial, but once established produces seedlings and soon becomes a permanent feature of the garden.

Verbascum chaixii 'Album'. Zones 4–8.

Although not quite as attractive as some of the biennial species, *Verbascum chaixii* 'Album' is a true perennial. From June until September, 3-foot stems appear, each of them studded with white flowers, and at the center of these blooms is a mauve eye. The foliage forms handsome rosettes of gray-green crinkled leaves.

Verbascum thapsus (MULLEIN). Zones 4–10.

Mullein is a common European plant that is thoroughly naturalized throughout the United States and is always noticeable because of its exceptional height. A biennial, *Verbascum thapsus* produces a rosette of whitish-gray woolly leaves the first year, and during the following summer sends up a tall spike, 4 to 5 feet high, covered with lovely yellow blossoms.

The countless ways in which mullein was employed in earlier centuries is recorded in the numerous vernacular names given to this plant: "blanketleaf," "candlewick," "flannel flower," and "high taper" among them. Classical authors Pliny and Dioscorides both mention that figs do not putrefy if wrapped in the leaves of mullein—a practice which continued through the Middle Ages. The seventeenth-century English herbalist John Parkinson noted that mullein was "called of the Latines *candela regis,* and *candelaria,* because the elder age used the stalks dipped in suet to burne." The fine down of the leaves was also used for making wicks for oil lamps and as a natural tinder for kindling with flint. An infusion of the yellow blossoms was used as a hair dye. As a medicinal plant, mullein has been used since the time of Dioscorides and Pliny for diseases of the chest. It is still used today for this purpose. The Romans also used mullein in veterinary medicine. According to the Latin authors this herb was excellent for "healing broken-winded horses."

Verbascum was a magical plant. The *Anglo-Saxon Herbal of Apuleius* notes, "If a man beareth with him one twig of this wort, he will not be terrified with any awe, nor will a wild beast hurt him, or any evil come near." The fifteenth-century *English Leechbook* recommends the following treatment for hemorrhoids: "Take a pan with coals . . . put thereon the leaves of a herb that is called mullein, put it under a commode that the smoke may ascend to thy fundament as hot as thou mayest suffer." The seeds of mullein are slightly narcotic, and because of this, they were employed by the monasteries to stupefy fish. Medieval people used the leaves of the herb as a bathroom tissue, and travelers placed *Verbascum* in their shoes, believing that it would prevent tired feet. Today a tea made from the leaves is used to soothe coughs, and the blanched leaves are effective as an astringent poultice. If you use this herb as a medicinal tea, strain it well to remove the fine leaf hairs.

VERBENA. Family: Verbenaceae.

Verbena officinalis (VERVAIN). Zones 4–10.

Vervain is an erect perennial that grows 1 to 2 feet high. From June until October, spikes of small violet flowers are borne on the square stems. Vervain will grow in any well-drained sunny position.

According to the Roman author Pliny, vervain was a highly revered plant in the ancient world: "With this the table of Jupiter is swept, and homes are cleansed and purified . . . and the people of Gaul [use vervain] in fortune telling and in uttering prophesies, but the Magi especially make the maddest statements about the plant: that people who have been rubbed with it obtain their wishes, banish fevers, win friends and cure all diseases without exception. . . . They say to that if a dining couch is sprinkled with water in which this plant has been soaked, the entertainment becomes merrier." In the Middle Ages other, rather curious properties were ascribed to vervain. Many are recorded in the *Anglo-Saxon Herbal of Apuleius:* "If any one has with him this wort [vervain] . . . he may not be barked at by dogs. . . . Administered in drink; it driveth away all poisons; it is also said that sorcerers use it for their crafts." The reputed magical properties of vervain were numerous: It would drain witches of their will, and it would open all locks and bolts. "They that have vervain about them," says Banckes, "they shall have love and grace of great masters, and they shall grant him his asking, if his asking be good and rightful. . . . Who that useth it will make a good breath and doth away stink of the mouth." The Elizabethan herbalist John Gerard advised his readers to "make a garland of vervain for headache when the cause of the infirmitie proceedeth of heat. . . . The herb stamped with oil of roses and vinegar . . . keepeth the haires from falling, being bathed and anointed therewith."

Vervain is widely used on the continent—especially in France, where both a liquor and a dried tea are made from this herb. These preparations are used both as a tonic and for headaches.

VERNONIA. Family: Compositae. Zones 4–8.

Vernonia noveboracensis (IRONWEED).
This is a lovely native plant that can really brighten a fall garden. In August and September, sometimes even October, the majestic 5- to 6-foot stems are covered with brilliant purple flowers. To keep plants smaller and more compact, William Brumback, native-plant expert at the New England Wild Flower Society, recommends cutting ironweed right back to the ground when they have reached 1½ feet in height. New plants will grow the same season but will flower on shorter stalks. Grow ironweed in full sun in moist or wet soil.

A similar species, *Vernonia fasciculata* ("prairie ironweed" or "western ironweed"), will tolerate drier soil. *Vernonia fasciculata* is available from Prairie Nursery (see Suppliers list).

VERONICA (SPEEDWELL, BROOKLIME). Family: Scrophulariaceae.

Veronica teucrium (also listed as *V. latifolia*). Zones 3–9.
In late spring and summer, this sprawling 18-inch perennial is covered with spikes of long-lasting gentian-blue flowers. In informal settings let veronica tumble along the ground; in more formal gardens, give it some support. Grow this flower in full sun or partial shade in any good garden soil. To encourage a longer flowering period, remove spent blooms.

VINCA. Family: Apocynaceae.

Vinca minor (PERIWINKLE). Zones 4–8.
Periwinkle is a creeping evergreen that grows 3 to 6 inches high and produces star-shaped blue flowers in the spring. It prefers light shade and moist well-drained soil. *Vinca minor* is an ideal ground cover for shady sites.

The *Anglo-Saxon Herbal of Apuleius* advocates the following uses for this herb: "It is of good advantage for many purposes, that is to say against devil sickness and demonical possession and against snakes, and wild beasts and against poisons. . . . And if thou hast the wort with thee, thou shalt be prosperous, and ever acceptable." Bunches of periwinkle were placed over the lintels of medieval dwellings to protect the house from any evil spirits. "Whoever carries this herb with him," advises the fifteenth-century *Hortus Sanitatis*, "the devil has no power over him . . . and if there be any witchery in the house, it will drive it out soon." Another medieval volume, *The Book of Secrets* of Albertus Magnus, claims that if periwinkle is "beaten into a powder with worms of the earth wrapped about it, and with a herb called houseleeke, it induceth love between a man and wife, if it be used in their meats."

VIOLA (VIOLET). Family: Violaceae.

Viola cucullata 'Freckles'. Zones 4–9.
In April and May, 'Freckles' is covered with creamy white flowers dotted with purple

spots. 'Freckles' grows to 5 inches. Grow this violet in sun or shade in moist well-drained soil.

Viola labradorica (LABRADOR VIOLET). Zones 4–8.

This violet forms a lovely dense ground cover in semi-shaded parts of the garden. The small rounded leaves have a delightful purple tinge. In May, mauve flowers are borne on 5-inch stems. This is a good plant to cultivate beneath deciduous trees, where it soon forms a dense weed-smothering carpet. Grow this perennial in moist soil.

Viola odorata (SWEET VIOLET). Zones 5–10.

The sweet violet is a small perennial with heart-shaped leaves and strongly scented blue flowers that appear in mid to late spring. Cultivate this low-growing perennial in moist well-drained soil in part shade. Violets can be planted under trees and act as a good ground cover.

According to mythology, the violet was once a fair nymph. To avoid the amorous pursuits of Apollo, Diana changed the young maid into this tiny flower.

To prevent headaches and giddiness and to cure hangovers, the Romans bound violets to the head. The Roman naturalist Pliny wrote: "Placed on the head in chaplets, or even smelt, [violets] dispense the after-effects of drinking and its headaches." This flower was also the emblem of Athens. The Athenians used violets in a drink to moderate anger and promote sleep. The tenth-century herbal of Macer Floridus states that violets are powerful against "wicked spirits." In medieval Europe the violet was used in soup, sauces, and salads. The leaves were often included in herb omelets. Medieval physicians also considered the violet a strongly medicinal plant. One medical textbook from the Middle Ages tells the doctor: "If the skull of the brainpan be broken or bowed, so the patient may not speak, stamp violet and bind it to the sole of the left foot. . . . And the bone shall rise up, and the patient shall speak again." The following, translated by Sir John Harington, was one of the maxims of the medieval medical school at Salerno:

> To dispel drunkedness and repel migraine
> The violet is sovereign:
> From heavy head it takes the pain,
> And from feverish cold delivers the brain.

Askham's Herbal makes use of violet flowers for insomnia: "For those that may not sleppe for sicknesse seeth this herbe in water and at evening let him soak well his feet in the water to the ankles, when he goes to bed." Today the dried flowers can be used in potpourri or, candied, on confections. Made into a tea, this herb is used for insomnia and headaches. The leaves have been employed in modern times as an antiseptic poultice.

Viola pedata (BIRD'S-FOOT VIOLET). Zones 4–8.

From March until June, the bicolored flowers of this long-blooming violet add beauty to the garden. The upper petals of the flowers are dark violet and the three lower petals are pale lilac. If given some water during the summer, these violets will flower again in the fall. The trifoliate leaves of *Viola pedata* look like bird's feet—hence the English name. *Viola pedata* grows between 4 and 10 inches high. Cultivate bird's-foot violets in sun or part shade, in light sandy soil. They also do well in poor soils.

Viola tricolor (JOHNNY-JUMP-UP, PANSY, HEARTSEASE, LOVE-IN-IDLENESS). Zones 4–8.

This is an annual or short-lived perennial that grows to 10 inches high. The flowers, which appear throughout the summer, are variable — yellow, purple, and cream-colored blossoms being the most common. Cultivate pansies in full sun in any reasonable garden soil.

This flower traditionally belonged to amorous Venus, and the pansy is the flower that Oberon describes in *A Midsummer Night's Dream* — the plant that was hit by a "bolt of Cupid" when the arrow missed its target and fell instead

> . . . upon a little western flower,
> Before milk-white, now purple with love's wound,
> And maidens call it love-in-idleness.
> Fetch me that flower; the herb I showed thee once:
> The juice of it on sleeping eyelids laid
> Will make man or woman madly dote
> Upon the next live creature that it sees.

In modern herbalism the pansy is sometimes employed as a blood-purifying agent, and it is highly regarded for treating rheumatism and chronic skin complaints.

W

WISTERIA. Family: Leguminosae.

Wisteria sinensis (CHINESE WISTERIA). Zones 5–9.

This is one of the most beautiful vines. In April and May, before the leaves emerge, the plants are covered with lovely pendulous blue flower spikes. The abundance of these fragrant blooms gives the impression that the wisteria is hung with blue curtains. The blossoms of wisteria open simultaneously, and these floral tassels can be a foot long. Delicate leaves cover the vines for the rest of the summer. Even in winter, wisteria looks attractive, especially when specimens are mature — the graceful trunks intertwine and create pleasing gnarled sculptural shapes. This is especially apparent when the wisteria is grown on an arbor. Cultivate this vine in full sun, in deep moist well-drained soil. Wisteria can be trained into a tree shape.

WOODWARDIA. Family: Polypodiaceae.

Woodwardia virginica (VIRGINIA CHAIN FERN). Zones 3–10.

Woodwardia virginica is a giant deciduous fern that loves boggy acid soil — permanently damp parts of the garden perfectly suit this plant. This is one of the few native American ferns that tolerate full sunlight. The beautiful leaves are deep green to yellow-green and mature between 3 and 4 feet. In the fall, this foliage turns an attractive bronze color. If grown in full sun, keep this fern moist at all times. In drier soils give it some shade.

Y

YUCCA. Family: Agavaceae.

Most people have a strong reaction to this evergreen, and more than once when I have suggested including yucca in a garden design, a client has declined by saying "Yuck, not yucca!" My own initial encounter with this plant was not very pleasant. While overseeing a garden restoration in Tuscaloosa, Alabama, I made the unfortunate mistake of backing into a mature yucca. I then realized why this plant is sometimes called "Spanish bayonet." My "point" is that not everyone likes yucca. For those averse to them, please, I suggest you take another look—especially at the newer hybrids. Yuccas are desert plants that will thrive in most regions of the U.S. They give tropical elegance to a garden, and look magnificent either as a specimen in a lawn or planted with other drought-resistant perennials in a "desert garden."

Grow yuccas in full sun in a well-drained site. If your soil is heavy, add some sand before planting.

Yucca filamentosa 'Bright Edge'. Zones 4–10.

This is the aristocrat of the yucca family. Its dark green leaves have a delicate gold margin—truly a majestic shrub in any garden, desert or otherwise. 'Bright Edge' forms 3-foot clusters of evergreen leaves. In summer, 5-foot spikes of creamy orchid-like bells of flowers make the plant a spectacular sight. Blossoms are so thickly clustered that it would seem the stems could not bear the weight.

Yucca glauca (SOAPWEED). Zones 3–10.

These are beautiful plants. The narrow stiff evergreen leaves, edged with a thin white stripe, look very exotic. The tight clusters of leaves form 3-foot mounds and in summer, slender spikes of greenish white flowers are borne on 4½-foot spikes. The blossoms are not as showy as *Yucca filamentosa*.

beach plum

SUPPLIERS

GENERAL

Carroll Gardens
444 East Main Street
P.O. Box 310
Westminster, MD 21157
Tel. outside Maryland
(800) 638-6334
Tel. in state (301) 876-7336
Catalogue: $2.00

This nursery offers an excellent informative catalogue of perennials, trees, evergreens, shrubs, ferns, herbs, roses, and bulbs. Many hard-to-find items in all categories are listed.

Forest Farm
990 Tetherow Road
Williams, OR 97544
Tel. (503) 846-6963
Catalogue: $2.00

Nice list of native American plants, perennials, and hard-to-find trees and shrubs. Good source for plant collectors.

Wayside Gardens
Hodges, SC 29695-0001
Tel. (800) 845-1124
Catalogue: $1.00

Wide range of plants in catalogue, including trees, shrubs, perennials, and roses. Catalogue is fully color illustrated.

BULBS

McClure & Zimmerman
1422 West Thorndale
Chicago, IL 60660
Tel. (312) 989-0557
Catalogue: free

This company offers a wide range of both common and rare bulbs.

GRASSES

Kurt Bluemel, Inc.
2740 Greene Lane
Baldwin, MD 21013
Tel. (301) 557-7229
Catalogue: $1.00

Very wide range of ornamental grasses, sedges, and rushes; also ferns and many unusual perennials.

HERBS

Logee's Greenhouses
55 North Street
Danielson, CT 06239
Tel. (203) 774-8038
Catalogue: 50¢

Extensive list of greenhouse and exotic plants, including *Datura chlorantha*. Good herb listing.

Sunnybrook Farms Nursery
9448 Mayfield Road
P.O. Box 6
Chesterland, OH 44026
Tel. (216) 729-7232
Catalogue: $1.00

This catalogue offers a very wide range of herbs, aromatic plants, scented geraniums, and herb seeds.

Well-Sweep Herb Farm
317 Mount Bethel Road
Port Murray, NJ 07865
Tel. (201) 852-5390

Wide range of herbs, herb seeds, silver foliage plants, and scented geraniums. This company also supplies nonflowering chamomile—the type suitable for using as an aromatic lawn.

PERENNIALS

Bluestone Perennials Inc.
7211 Middle Ridge Road
Madison, OH 44057
Tel. (216) 428-7535
Catalogue: free

Economical way of buying plants: this company sells smaller perennials that average out to about $1.00 per plant.

Holbrook Farm & Nursery
Rt. 2, Box 223B
Fletcher, NC 28732
Tel. (704) 891-7790
Catalogue: $2.00

A fine collection of unusual and common perennials, wild flowers, and some trees and shrubs.

Lamb Nurseries
E. 101 Sharp Avenue
Spokane, WA 99202
Tel. (509) 328-7956
Catalogue: free

Wide range of perennials, ferns, rock plants, and some shrubs.

Laurie's Garden
41886 McKenzie Highway
Springfield, OR 97478
Tel. (503) 896-3756
Catalogue: send first-class
    postage

Very wide range of iris. Suppliers of *Iris foetidissima*, *Iris foetidissima* 'Lutea', and *Iris versicolor*. Also lists *Sanguinaria canadensis* 'Multiplex' (double bloodroot).

Nutmeg Flower Farm
Box 281, Rt. 97N
    (Pudding Hill Rd.)
Scotland, CT 06264
Tel. (203) 423-0554
Catalogue: $1.00

Nice selection of perennials; also many biennials like *Verbascum bombyciferum*, *Cynara cardunculus* (cardoon), and *Onopordum acanthium* (Scotch thistle).

Shady Oaks Nursery
700 19th Ave. N.E.
Waseca, MN 56093
Tel. (507) 835-5033
Catalogue: $1.00

Specialist in perennials for shady places.

Siskiyou Rare Plant Nursery
2825 Cummings Road
Medford, OR 97501
Tel. (503) 772-6846
Catalogue: $1.50

Mainly rock garden plants. Many hard-to-find items are listed in this catalogue, including *Lysichitum americanum* (western skunk cabbage).

Springbrook Gardens, Inc.
6776 Heisley Road
P.O. Box 338
Mentor, OH 44061-0388
Tel. (216) 255-3059
Catalogue: $1.00

Good range of both common and unusual perennials.

Andre Viette Farm & Nursery
Rt. 1, Box 16
Fishersville, VA 22939
Tel. (703) 943-2315
Catalogue: $1.50

One of the best suppliers of perennials. List includes shade plants, sun perennials, grasses, plants for the waterside, herbs, daylilies, and hostas.

We-Du Nurseries
Rt. 5, Box 724
Marion, NC 28752
Tel. (704) 738-8300
Catalogue: 50¢

Good collection of rock garden and native American plants.

White Flower Farm
Litchfield, CT 06759-0050
Tel. (203) 496-9600
Catalogue: $5.00

Very informative color catalogue. This company offers unusual perennials and some less common shrubs and bulbs.

Gilbert H. Wild and Son, Inc.
1112 Joplin Street
Sarcoxie, MO 64862
Tel. (417) 548-3514
Catalogue: $2.00

Wide selection of daylilies, iris, and herbaceous peonies. Special collections of daylilies are offered at considerable reductions.

ROSES

Pickering Nurseries Inc.
607 Kingston Road
Pickering, Ontario, Canada L1V
   1A6
Tel. (416) 839-2111
Catalogue: free

An extensive list of both old-fashioned roses and modern varieties.

Roses of Yesterday and Today
Brown's Valley Road
Watsonville, CA 95076
Tel. (408) 724-3537
Catalogue: $2.00

Wide range of roses; many older hard-to-find varieties available.

SEEDS

Thomas Butcher Ltd.
60 Wickham Road
Shirley, Croydon
Surrey CR9 8AG, England
Tel. 01-654-3720 or 4254
Catalogue: free

A wide selection of seeds of perennials, trees, and shrubs is offered. Since they accept Access or Visa credit cards, there is no need to send international money orders.

Chiltern Seeds
Bortree Stile
Ulverston
Cumbria LA12 7PB, England
Catalogue: $2.00 (send U.S. notes)

Seeds of plants from all over the world, described in an excellent catalogue. Also a wide variety of wild flowers of the British Isles. They accept Visa and Access credit cards.

Maver Nursery—Rare Seeds
Rt. 2, Box 265 B
Asheville, NC 28805
Tel. (206) 725-9823
Catalogue: $1.00

Wide selection of seeds, and generous amounts in packets. Also sells perennial plants.

Thompson & Morgan
Farraday and Gramme Avenues
P.O. Box 1308
Jackson, NJ 08527
Tel. (800) 367-7333
Catalogue: free

Excellent color catalogue with hundreds of items. Largest seed list in the world.

WATER PLANTS

Lilypons Water Gardens
6800 Lilypons Road
P.O. Box 10
Lilypons, MD 21717-0010
Tel. (301) 874-5133
Catalogue: $3.50

Wide variety of water lilies and other aquatics. This nursery supplies *Nymphaea odorata* (fragrant white pond lily).

Waterford Gardens
74 East Allendale Road
Saddle River, NJ 07458
Tel. (201) 327-0721
Catalogue: $3.50

Good selection of water lilies and some aquatics, including *Menyanthes trifoliata* (bogbean).

WILD FLOWERS

Gardens of the Blue Ridge
U.S. 221 N
P.O. Box 10
Pineola, NC 28662
Tel. (704) 733-2417
Catalogue: $2.00

Listing includes native plants, ferns, orchids, trees, and shrubs.

Prairie Moon Nursery
Rt. 3, Box 163
Winona, MN 55987
Tel. (507) 452-5231
Catalogue: 2 first-class stamps

Wide collection of economically priced native plants. Seeds and mixes of native grasses are also supplied.

Prairie Nursery
P.O. Box 365
Westfield, WI 53964
Tel. (608) 296-3679
Catalogue: $1.00

Excellent source of plants and seeds of prairie wild flowers. This nursery supplies many types of wild grasses.

BIBLIOGRAPHY

Albertus Magnus. *The Book of Secrets.* Edited by Michael R. Best and Frank H. Brightman. Oxford: Clarendon Press, 1973.

Anderson, Frank. *An Illustrated History of the Herbals.* New York: Columbia University Press, 1977.

Anglo-Saxon Herbal of Apuleius. See: Thomas Oswald Cockayne, ed., *Leechdoms.*

Arango, Luisa Cogliati. *The Medieval Health Handbook.* Translated by Oscar Ratti and Adele Westbrook. New York: George Braziller, 1976.

Arber, Agnus. *Herbals, Their Origin and Evolution.* Cambridge: Cambridge University Press, 1912.

Art, Henry W. *A Garden of Wildflowers: 101 Native Species and How to Grow Them.* Pownal, Vt.: Storey Publishing, 1986.

Askham's Herbal. London: 1550. [This book is based on Banckes's *Herbal.*]

Avicenna. See: Ibn Husain, *Avicennae Liber Canonis.*

Bacon, Francis. *The Essayes or Councils . . .* (including "Essay on Gardens") 1627.

Banckes, Rycharde (Richard). *An Herbal.* Facsimile of the 1525 London edition. Edited by Stanford V. Larkey and Thomas Pyles. New York: New York Botanical Garden, 1941.

Bartholomaeus Anglicus. *De Proprietatibus Rerum* (On the Properties of Things). (1495.) Translated by John Trevista. 2 vols. Oxford: Clarendon Press, 1975.

Barton, Barbara J. *Gardening by Mail—A Source Book.* San Francisco: Tusker Press, 1986.

Benner, David. "The Moss Lawn." *Garden* (March/April 1980).

Boccaccio, Giovanni. *The Decameron.* Translated by G. H. McWilliam. Harmondsworth: Penguin Books, 1973.

Brodin, Gosta, ed. "Agnus Castus: A Middle English Herbal." In *Essays and Studies in English Language and Literature,* Vol. VI. Upsala: English Institute, 1950.

Brooks, John. *A Place in the Country.* London: Thames & Hudson, 1984.

Chatto, Beth. *The Damp Garden.* London: J. M. Dent & Sons Ltd., 1982.

————. *The Dry Garden*. London: J. M. Dent & Sons Ltd., 1978.

Chaucer, Geoffrey. *Complete Works of Geoffrey Chaucer*. 6 vols. Edited by Walter W. Skeat. Oxford: Clarendon Press, 1900.

Clark, David E., ed. *Sunset New Western Garden Book*. Menlo Park, Calif.: Lane Publishing, 1979.

Cockayne, Thomas Oswald, ed. *Leechdoms, Wortcunning and Starcraft of Early England*. London: Longman, Roberts, and Green, 1864–66.

Cosman, Madeleine Pelner. *Fabulous Feasts—Medieval Cookery and Ceremony*. New York: George Braziller, 1976.

Crescenzi, Pietro. *Opus Ruralium Commodorum*. Augsburge: 1471. See modern French translation: *Les Profits Champêtres*. Paris: 1965.

Crisp, Sir Frank. *Medieval Gardens*. 2 vols. London: John Lane, The Bodley Head Limited, 1924.

Culpeper, Nicholas. *The English Physician Enlarged*. London: P. Cole, 1653.

Dawson, Warren R. *A Leechbook, or Collection of Medical Recipes of the 15th Century*. London: Macmillan & Co., 1934.

Dioscorides. *De Materia Medica*. Translated by John Goodyer (1655). Edited by Robert T. Gunther. London: Hafner Publishing Company, 1933.

Douglas W. L., S. R. Frey, N. K. Johnson, S. Littlefield, and M. Van Valkenburgh. *Garden Design*. New York: Simon & Schuster, 1984.

Emerson, Gordon. See: George Schenk, *The Complete Shade Gardener*.

English Leechbook. See: Warren R. Dawson, *A Leechbook*.

Favretti, Rudy, and Joy Favretti. *For Every House a Garden*. Chester, Conn.: The Pequot Press, 1977.

————. *Landscapes and Gardens for Historic Buildings*. Nashville: American Association for State and Local History, 1978.

Febvre, Lucien. *Life in Renaissance France*. Translated by Marian Rothstein. Cambridge, Mass.: Harvard University Press, 1977.

Fish, Margery. *Cottage Garden Flowers*. London: W. H. & L. Collingridge Ltd., 1961.

————. *A Flower for Every Day*. London: Studio Vista Ltd., 1965.

————. *Gardening in the Shade*. London: W. H. & L. Collingridge Ltd., 1964.

————. *We Made a Garden*. London: W. H. Collingridge Ltd., 1956.

Fitzstephen, William. *Vita Sancti Thomae* (Life of St. Thomas). Edited by J. C. Robertson. Rolls Series, 1875–83. Kraus reprint, no. 67, pt. 3.

Folkard, Richard. *Plant Lore, Legends and Lyrics*. London: Sampson Low, Marston, Searle, & Rivington, 1884.

Gardener, Jon. *See* Jon Gardener.

Der Gart der Gesundheit. Mainz: Peter Schoeffer, 1485.

Genders, Roy. *The Cottage Garden*. London: Pelham Books, 1969.

Gerard, John. *The Herball* (1597). 3rd ed., 1633. New York: Dover Books, 1975.

Le Grant Herbier. Paris: Jacques Nyverd, after 1520.

The Grete Herball. London: Peter Treveris,

1526. All entries are from the 1551 edition, retitled *The Greate Herball*.

Grieve, M., Mrs. *A Modern Herbal*. Edited and Introduction by Mrs. C. F. Leyel. London: Jonathan Cape, 1931.

Grigson, Geoffrey. *The Englishman's Flora*. London: Phoenix House, 1958.

Hanmer, Sir Thomas. *The Garden Book* (1659). London: G. Howe, 1933.

Harington, Sir John, trans. *Regimen Sanitatis Salernitanum — The School of Salernum* (1607). New York: A. M. Kelley, 1970.

Herbarius Latinus. Mainz: Peter Schoeffer, 1484.

Hortus Sanitatis. Mainz: Jacob Meydenbach, 1491.

Hyams, Edward. *A History of Gardens and Gardening*. New York: Praeger Publishers, 1971.

Ibn Husain. *Avicennae Liber Canonis, de Medicinis cordialibus et Cantica . . .* Venice: 1544.

Jekyll, Gertrude. *Wall and Water Gardens*. London: Country Life, 1901.

———. *Wood and Garden*. London: Longmans, Green & Co. 1899. (Reprinted by the Antique Collector's Club Ltd., 1981.)

Jon Gardener. "Feate of Gardening." *Archaeologia* LIV (1894).

Lawson, William. *A New Orchard and Garden; The Country House-Wife's Garden*. 1618.

Littlefield, Susan. See: Marina Schinz, *Visions of Paradise*.

Lloyd, Christopher. *The Well-Chosen Garden*. New York: Harper & Row, 1984.

Longland, David. "Lawns, Meadows, or Both?" *Wild Flower Notes*. New England Wild Flower Society, Fall/Winter 1985.

Macer Floridus. *De Virtutibus Herbarum*. Venice: 1506.

Markham, Gervaise. *The English Husbandman*. London: T.S., 1613.

Megenberg, Conrad von. *Buch der Natur*. Edited by Franz Pfeiffer (1861). Hildesheim, West Germany: George Olms, 1962.

Parkinson, John. *Paradisi in Sole: Paradisus Terrestris*. London: Humphrey Lownes and Robert Young, 1629.

———. *Theatrum Botanicum*. London: T. Cotes, 1640.

Petchey, John. *The Complete Herbal of Physical Plants*. London: Henry Bonwicke, 1694.

Pliny (Gaius Plinius Secundus). *Natural History*. 10 vols. Vols. I–V and IX translated by H. Rackham, 1938–52; Vols. VI–VIII translated by W. H. S. Jones, 1951–63; Vol. X translated by D. E. Eichholtz, 1962. Cambridge, Mass.: Harvard University Press, Loeb Classical Library.

Powers, Eileen. Introduction to *The Goodman of Paris*. Translated by Eileen Powers. London: George Routledge and Sons, 1928.

Repton, Humphrey. *Fragments of the Theory and Practice of Landscape Gardening*. New York: Garland Publishing, 1982.

Robinson, William. *The Wild Garden*. London: J. Murray, 1870.

Rohde, Eleanor Sinclair. *The Old English Herbals*. London: Longmans, Green & Co., 1922.

Sabuco, John J. *The Best of the Hardiest.* Flossmoor, Ill.: Good Earth Publishing Ltd., 1985.

Schenk, George. *The Complete Shade Gardener.* Boston: Houghton Mifflin Company, 1984.

Schinz, Marina. *Visions of Paradise.* New York: Stewart, Tabori & Chang, 1985.

Scott-James, Anne, and Osbert Lancaster. *The Pleasure Garden.* Ipswich, Mass.: Gambit, 1977.

Sperka, Marie. *Growing Wildflowers—A Gardener's Guide.* New York: Harper & Row, 1973.

Stevenson, Matilda Coxe. "Ethnobotany of the Zuni Indians." *30th Annual Report Bureau American Ethnology 1908–09.* Washington, D.C., 1915.

Stokstad, Marilyn, and Gerry Stannard. *Gardens of the Middle Ages.* Spencer Museum of Art, Lawrence, Kans.: University of Kansas Press, 1983.

Strabo, Walahfrid. *Hortulus.* Translated by Raef Payne. Pittsburgh: Hunt Botanical Library, 1966.

Stuart, Malcolm. *The Encyclopedia of Herbs and Herbalism.* New York: Grosset & Dunlap, 1979.

Tacuinum Sanitatis. See: Luisa Cogliati Arango, *The Medieval Health Handbook.*

Thomas, Keith. *Man and the Natural World.* New York: Pantheon Books, 1983.

Thompson, William A. R., ed. *Medicines from the Earth—A Guide to Healing Plants.* Rev. ed. San Francisco: Harper & Row, 1983.

Treasury of Botany. 2 vols. John Lindley and T. Moore. London: Longmans, Green & Co., 1864.

Turner, William. *New Herball.* 3rd ed. Collen (Cologne): Arnold Birckmann, 1568.

Ukers, William H. "All About Coffee." *The Tea and Coffee Trade Journal Co.* 1935.

Verey, Rosemary. *Classic Garden Design.* New York: Congdon & Weed, 1984.

Williamson, John. *The Oak King, the Holly King, and the Unicorn—The Myths and Symbolism of the Unicorn Tapestries.* New York: Harper & Row, 1986.

INDEX

Numbers in *italic* indicate illustrations